Praise for *Poets and Dreamers*

"A brave and inventive spirit, Tamara Saviano has cre[ated a] [affec]tionate chronicle of the Americana phenomenon th[at she is uniquely qual]ified to deliver. Hers is a view from the inside—rich, authoritative, and always honest."

—Michael Streissguth, author of *Johnny Cash: The Biography* and *Outlaw: Waylon, Willie, Kris, and the Renegades of Nashville*, among others

"Americana is more than the music, it's the stories and the soulfulness of the people who bring it to life. One of them is Tamara Saviano, a journalist turned industry insider, who, in this memoir, skillfully peels back the layers to show how the genre became the powerhouse it is today. But far from a forensics report, this book is told through her own story of facilitating projects and careers that together helped drive the new century's revival of American roots music. A thrilling behind-the-scenes look that shows both the rewards and the toll of making the music a vocation for life."

—Mark Guarino, author of *Country & Midwestern: Chicago in the History of Country Music and the Folk Revival*

"Tamara Saviano wasn't just there for the infancy of the Americana music scene—she helped birth it. Her deep friendships and professional relationships with Guy Clark and Kris Kristofferson anchor this evocative memoir of a genre's fight for industry recognition. But in recounting her own scrappy and remarkable life—populated by the likes of Johnny Cash, Loretta Lynn, and John Prine—she also shows just why she is such a respected leader in a male-dominated field. Winning a Grammy as a rookie producer is one thing, but when Elvis Costello fetes you in public, you know you've really rung the bell."

—Alanna Nash, author of *The Colonel: The Extraordinary Story of Colonel Tom Parker and Elvis Presley* and *Golden Girl: The Story of Jessica Savitch*, among others

"With her superb biography of Guy Clark, *Without Getting Killed or Caught*, Tamara Saviano established her credentials as an outstanding chronicler of Americana music. *Poets and Dreamers* tells us how she came to be a multimedia popularizer of those roots-based styles and performers that populate Americana. Saviano's own journey into the heart of Americana rivals that of the protagonist in Hank Snow's 'I've Been Everywhere,' a backstory she's skillfully intertwined with that of the songwriters, musicians, promoters, and publicists who continue to invest this music with beauty, variety, and vitality."

—Bobbie and Bill C. Malone, authors of *Traveler: The Musical Odyssey of Tim O'Brien* and *Nashville's Songwriting Sweethearts: The Boudleaux and Felice Bryant Story*

POETS AND DREAMERS

The Gary Hartman Series in Texas Music
Sponsored by the Center for Texas Music History,
Texas State University
Jason Mellard, General Editor

Publication of this book was made possible in part with the support of Gary and Francine Hartman, The Texas Heritage Songwriters Association, and Joe and Alice Specht.

POETS AND DREAMERS

My Life in Americana Music

TAMARA SAVIANO

TEXAS A&M UNIVERSITY PRESS • COLLEGE STATION

COPYRIGHT © 2025 BY TAMARA SAVIANO
All rights reserved

First edition

∞ This paper meets the requirements of ANSI/NISO Z39.48-1992 (Permanence of Paper).
Binding materials have been chosen for durability.

LIBRARY OF CONGRESS CATALOGING-IN-PUBLICATION DATA

Names: Saviano, Tamara, author.
Title: Poets and dreamers: my life in Americana music / by Tamara Saviano.
Description: First edition. | College Station: Texas A&M University Press, 2025. | Series: Gary Hartman Texas music series | Includes bibliographical references and index.
Identifiers: LCCN 2024053896 (print) | LCCN 2024053897 (ebook) | ISBN 9781648433214 (paperback) | ISBN 9781648433221 (ebook)
Subjects: LCSH: Saviano, Tamara. | Sound recording executives and Producers—United States—Biography. | Americana (Music)—History and criticism. | Americana musicians. | LCGFT: Autobiographies.
Classification: LCC ML429.S176 A3 2025 (print) | LCC ML429.S176 (ebook) | DDC 782.42164092 [B]—dc23/eng/20241119
LC record available at https://lccn.loc.gov/2024053896
LC ebook record available at https://lccn.loc.gov/2024053897

Dedicated with love to all of my Americana kindred spirits—friends who remain and those who have departed. And for Daniel and Keast, for whom the magic is just beginning.

Remember, no man is a failure who has friends.

—Clarence Odbody, *It's a Wonderful Life*

CONTENTS

Galleries of images follow pages 82, 114, 178, and 242.

Acknowledgments   xi

PROLOGUE	Are You Sure Hank Done It This Way?	1
ONE	Now That's Americana	8
TWO	The Backstory	20
THREE	Radio, Records, and the Fledgling Americana Music Scene	34
FOUR	Music City, USA	48
FIVE	Finding My Way	58
SIX	The Future of Your Record Collection	67
SEVEN	O Brother	75
EIGHT	American Country, American Roots	82
NINE	Free Speech and The Chicks	90
TEN	Kris Kristofferson	98
ELEVEN	The Sage and the Student	108
TWELVE	Beautiful Dreamers	117
THIRTEEN	Pilgrims	129
FOURTEEN	The Road Goes On Forever and the Party Never Ends	140
FIFTEEN	Choices	152
SIXTEEN	Closer to the Bone	161

SEVENTEEN	A Moment of Forever	170
EIGHTEEN	Heaven	179
NINETEEN	This One's For Him	190
TWENTY	For the Sake of the Song	202
TWENTY-ONE	These Days	214
TWENTY-TWO	Old Friends	225
TWENTY-THREE	Desperado Waiting for a Train	236
TWENTY-FOUR	A Season of Grief	248
TWENTY-FIVE	Serendipity	260
TWENTY-SIX	Darkness and Light	270
EPILOGUE		280

Sources 283

Index 291

About the Author 305

ACKNOWLEDGMENTS

While writing is a solo gig, getting the story requires a mighty village. Each of my past creative projects benefited from a tight-knit group of like-minded souls. The process of writing this book brought all those parties together. It was a blast to revisit people and places from the last thirty years of my life. We reminisced. We laughed. We grieved. We marveled at the wonder of it all—how a tattered group of poets and dreamers like us transformed the legacy of Americana music.

It would take another five hundred pages to name everyone who helped get this story written. You'll hear from many of them in these pages. Just as many ended up on the cutting room floor due to word count restrictions. This book could easily be twice as long, but my wise editors curbed my obsession.

Thank you to all of my friends in the Americana community who spent time with me to recount their stories and place the rise of this music genre in context. Special thanks to Rob Bleetstein, Jon Grimson, and Brad Paul, who started this whole dang thing when they conspired to create the Americana radio format and convinced the *Gavin Report* editors that it was a good idea. And to Jill Block White, who lovingly shared the archives and stories of her late husband, Billy Block, an important Americana pioneer.

Thank you, Thom Lemmons and the team at Texas A&M University Press, for seeing the value in publishing this personal history of Americana music. Working with Texas A&M is a pleasure.

This book would not be in your hands without the kind patronage of my dear friends Gary and Francine Hartman, Joe and Alice Specht, and the Texas Heritage Songwriters' Association—the lionhearted group that deemed me an honorary Texan and presented me the Darrell K. Royal Texas Music Legend Award for my work with Texas songwriters. Thank you, my friends, for believing in me once again. I love all of you.

To my husband and best friend, Paul Whitfield, thank you for always having my back and loving me as I am. I am grateful every day that I get to live with you. I love you forever and ever.

PROLOGUE

Are You Sure Hank Done It This Way?

Country music unearthed extraordinary icons in the 1960s. Sixty years on and they are still recognized worldwide by singular names: Dolly and Loretta, Buck and Merle, Willie and Waylon. And Cash, the Man in Black, a genre-spanning superstar, who made country music cool.

Before, Nashville embraced records produced with smooth pop and jazz instrumentations, including string sections and vocal choirs. When people asked RCA chief Chet Atkins about the "Nashville Sound," he'd rattle the loose change in his pocket and say, "It's the sound of money."

After the deaths of torchbearers Patsy Cline in 1963 and Jim Reeves in 1964, producers Owen Bradley and Billy Sherrill pushed the lush productions even further. The Nashville Sound morphed into slick Countrypolitan. Nashville A-Team studio musicians played on all the records, sweetening the sound with layers of guitars, strings, and pianos. Countrypolitan launched artists Tammy Wynette, Jeannie C. Riley, Glen Campbell, Charley Pride, Eddy Arnold, and Porter Wagoner to the top of the charts.

Not everyone was on board.

Monument Records head Fred Foster signed Dolly Parton to his label and produced her 1967 debut album, *Hello, I'm Dolly*. "I wasn't looking to make money. I wanted to make music as good as I can make it," Foster said. "I was attracted mightily to the individualist artist, one who didn't sound like anybody, one that had her own thing going, and Dolly was 100% on all those points."

Wagoner offered Dolly a regular spot both on his road show and on the syndicated television show *The Porter Wagoner Show*. With the encouragement of Wagoner, Dolly recorded the Jimmie Rodgers heirloom "Mule Skinner Blues (Blue Yodel #8)." But deep down, Dolly was a songwriter, and her 1973 album *Jolene* proved it.

People magazine called Loretta Lynn the poet laureate of blue-collar women. She married at fifteen and had four kids by eighteen. She wrote honest and unapologetic songs about cheating husbands, heartache, alcoholism, and growing up poor in Butcher Hollow, Kentucky. Loretta was banned from country radio many times, once for singing "The Pill." "If they'd had that pill a little earlier, I'd have eaten them like popcorn," she said.

In California, Buck Owens and Merle Haggard pioneered the grittier Bakersfield Sound, a blend of country and rock 'n' roll, rich with twangy Telecaster guitars and a backbeat. Buck wore glitzy rhinestone suits, fronted a band named the Buckaroos, and hosted the popular *Hee Haw* variety show. Haggard spent two years in San Quentin Prison, wrote hundreds of songs about the daily struggles of the common man and his mama, and played all over the world with a band called the Strangers.

Texans Willie Nelson and Waylon Jennings fought the Nashville system and won. Willie fled to Austin, Texas, where KOKE-FM had recently flipped its format to "progressive country," spinning records by Merle Haggard, Bob Dylan, and the Stones. Willie and Waylon shared a manager, Neil Reshen, who helped force the record companies to let them make the albums they wanted to make. Waylon poked fun at Nashville with "Are You Sure Hank Done It This Way?" and Willie recorded the low-budget *Red Headed Stranger* in Texas. Columbia Records hated it, but it produced Willie's first number one hit, "Blue Eyes Crying in the Rain."

Willie and Waylon teamed up with Tompall Glaser and Jessi Colter in 1976 for *Wanted! The Outlaws*, the first platinum record in country music. "Call them outlaws, call them innovators, call them revolutionaries, call them what you will," *Rolling Stone*'s Chet Flippo wrote in the liner notes. "They're just some damned fine people who are also some of the most gifted songwriters and singers anywhere."

Johnny Cash, too, was a revolutionary. As a social justice activist, he embraced folkies, hippies, Native Americans, union workers, and prisoners. Cash recorded live albums at Folsom Prison in 1968 and San Quentin in 1969.

Earlier, in 1964, Cash invited Bob Dylan to join him at the Newport Folk Festival. In turn, Dylan came from New York to record his 1966 album *Blonde on Blonde* and the 1969 *Nashville Skyline* at Columbia Studios in Nashville, inviting Cash to sing with him on "Girl from the North Country." Cash brought Dylan in as a guest on his ABC music variety program, *The Johnny Cash Show*.

A Rhodes Scholar and army captain who loved William Blake, Shakespeare, Bob Dylan, and Willie Nelson showed up in Nashville in 1965. Kris Kristofferson was drawn to Nashville because of Willie, but he stayed because he met Cash.

"The first time I got to Music Row I walked from downtown to 17th Avenue South in my uniform. It was the most exciting creative atmosphere I'd been around," Kristofferson said. "I spent that whole night listening to Cowboy Jack Clement and Bobby Bare and I was head over heels. Then I got to shake Johnny Cash's hand, backstage at the Opry, and that put the nail in the coffin right there."

As a struggling songwriter, Kristofferson worked as a janitor at Columbia Studios when Dylan recorded *Blonde on Blonde*. It was there that he and Cash became friends and Cash encouraged Kris to continue to write songs. The struggle paid off when Monument's Fred Foster heard them.

"The imagery he put out there was unlike anything we had going at the time: 'The Sunday smell of someone fryin' chicken,' or 'Somewhere far away, a lonely bell was ringing.' It was articulate. Sophisticated but still earthy," Foster said.

"William Blake influenced my thinking and my relationship with the creative process," Kristofferson said. "What I was trying to be, more than anything, was a creative person, some kind of an artist. I know feelings about freedom and about the imagination were all things that were important...the freedom to do what you were meant to do, and obliged to do."

Foster signed Kristofferson to a publishing deal and a recording contract. *Kristofferson*, his 1970 debut album, was not a hit, but it sure did shake things up. Four songs from *Kristofferson* soared to the top of the charts that year. Ray Price and Sammi Smith scored number one hits with "For the Good Times" and "Help Me Make It Through the Night." Johnny Cash's version of "Sunday Morning Coming Down" topped the chart and won Country Music Association Song of the Year. To cap off the incredible run, blues singer Janis Joplin recorded "Me and Bobby McGee" just weeks before her death in the fall of 1970. It hit big and stayed big.

Another intellectual, Gram Parsons from Harvard University, joined Roger McGuinn and Chris Hillman in the rock band the Byrds in 1968. Together they made *Sweetheart of the Rodeo*, recorded at Columbia Studios in Nashville. The album includes songs by Bob Dylan, the Louvin Brothers, Cindy Walker, Merle Haggard, and Woody Guthrie. *Sweetheart* insisted country music was hip.

After *Sweetheart*, Parsons and Hillman left the Byrds. In March 1973, Gram Parsons and the Fallen Angels recorded Boudleaux Bryant's song "Love Hurts" in front of a studio audience during a live radio broadcast. Parsons's protégé Emmylou Harris sang with him. Six months later, Parsons was dead.

Sweetheart of the Rodeo was a pivotal record for the Nitty Gritty Dirt Band, a jug band from the Southern California folk-rock scene. The band had a hit in 1970 with Jerry Jeff Walker's "Mr. Bojangles," but it was the Byrds album that made them think about recording with old-time country and bluegrass legends. The first volume of *Will the Circle Be Unbroken*, titled after the song handed down by the Carter Family, was recorded in Nashville in August 1971. Roy Acuff, Earl Scruggs, Mother Maybelle Carter, Jimmy Martin, Doc Watson, Merle Travis, Vassar Clements, Randy Scruggs, and others joined the Nitty Gritty Dirt Band on the lively three-disc album.

"We were bridging a generation gap and a cultural gap," said the Dirt Band's Jeff Hanna. "Once we got in the studio and started speaking the universal language of music, we were off and running. It didn't matter that we were hippies from California. Vietnam was raging and people glanced across the cultural aisle with distrust of the hippies and the rednecks. I think the record had an impact partly because of the time in which it was recorded. That was a big deal. And I think it was the first time some rock fans were exposed to acoustic American mountain music."

"Nashville in the 1970s is what I imagine Paris in the '20s to be," Kristofferson said. Other songwriters agreed with him. One of them was Texan Guy Clark. Clark chose to live in Nashville over New York or Los Angeles because of Kristofferson. The press often compared Clark to Kristofferson, and *Playboy* called Clark "Larry McMurtry set to music."

"Kristofferson was the first songwriter I knew about that made me think Nashville would be a good place for me," Clark said. "All those songs on his first album, he was writing like Dylan."

Clark's best friend from Houston, Townes Van Zandt, came to Nashville in January 1972 to be the best man in Clark's wedding to Susanna Talley. Van Zandt stayed for eight months. While living with Guy and Susanna, Van Zandt dreamed up "If I Needed You" in his sleep and wrote the melody and lyrics down after he awoke. Along with his signature song "Pancho and Lefty," "If I Needed You" is on *The Late Great Townes Van Zandt*, an album he recorded during the time he lived with Guy and Susanna.

Rodney Crowell and Steve Earle came to Nashville from Texas in the early 1970s. Guy and Susanna Clark folded Crowell and Earle into their songwriter salon. Crowell spun off to join Emmylou Harris's Hot Band after Harris recorded Crowell's "Bluebird Wine" on her 1975 album *Pieces of the Sky*. The album included songs by the Louvin Brothers, Boudleaux and Felice Bryant (Felice, a Milwaukee native like me!), Dolly Parton, and Merle Haggard, as well as a song Harris wrote about her friend Gram Parsons, "Boulder to Birmingham." The same year, Harris released *Elite Hotel*, featuring songs by Parsons, Hillman, Hank Williams, Buck Owens, and Don Gibson and Crowell's tender "'Til I Gain Control Again."

In the mid-1970s the son of Hank Williams and the daughter of Johnny Cash forged their own trails in country music. Hank Williams Jr. wrote and performed rowdy southern rock anthems. Rosanne Cash turned to serious songwriters for inspiration.

"I had just written 'Seven Year Ache' and we were sitting at the table in our house and I started playing it," Cash says. "I really wanted Guy to hear it, but I was too afraid to actually turn to Guy and say, 'Do you want to hear my new song?' I just couldn't do it. So, I started playing it, and Guy whipped his head around and said, 'What's that?' I said, 'It's a new song I wrote called 'Seven Year Ache.' Guy gave me his approval. I was just a puddle of joy. It meant so much to me. It's good to know people who think songwriting is truly an honorable profession. I swear it has been the mandate of my life, the things I learned from Guy and Rodney and Townes. People can be mentors without even realizing they're mentors. I want people to know those kinds of songwriters exist and how important real, true songwriting is."

On September 17, 1985, the *New York Times* announced the death of country music. "The audience for the Nashville Sound—lovesick laments, tales of marital strife and other plain-spoken lyrics, sung with a rural twang, and often accompanied by arrangements more redolent of Las Vegas than of Southern cotton fields—is dwindling, growing old along with its favorite stars."

Country music *was* changing again. The circle expanded to include neo-traditionalists Keith Whitley, George Strait, Randy Travis, Reba McEntire, mother-daughter duo the Judds, and Ricky Skaggs from Emmylou Harris's Hot Band. Dwight Yoakam brought back the Bakersfield Sound and even teamed up with Buck Owens to record "Streets of Bakersfield."

In 1989, Keith Whitley died in Nashville and a baby girl named Taylor Swift was born in Pennsylvania. Country's storied "Class of 1989" signaled a new era in Nashville. Major record labels signed a suburban breed of cowboy-hat-wearing dudes, Clint Black, Alan Jackson, and Garth Brooks; southern rocker Travis Tritt; and songwriter Mary Chapin Carpenter, who followed in Rosanne Cash's footsteps. All of them were heirs to the expanding country music dynasty.

The year 1989 also unveiled Vince Gill, a masterful songwriter and guitar player with an angelic voice and a deep connection to country music. In his high school band, Gill sang Guy Clark's "Rita Ballou." A few years later, after Gill sang Rodney Crowell's "'Til I Gain Control Again" on the stage at the Troubadour in Los Angeles, Clark and Crowell burst into Gill's backstage dressing room to ask him why he was singing the song better than Crowell could.

After the Class of 1989, country music exploded, amped up with guitars, drums, fiddles, and steel, twangy vocals, and nightclubs built for country line dancing. Garth Brooks was a phenomenon, a commercial powerhouse who earned earth-shattering record sales and scored big with his sold-out honky-tonk arena rock shows.

Yet traditions continued.

The Nitty Gritty Dirt Band revisited *Will the Circle Be Unbroken* two more times. Volumes 2 and 3 mixed contemporary original material with traditional songs and brought more family members into the studio together.

In the last decade of his life, when no one in Nashville seemed interested anymore, Johnny Cash teamed up with rock producer Rick Rubin. Together they explored a wide spectrum of musical styles, expanding the infinite circle of country music as they worked. At first, Cash recorded his own compositions along with traditional country and folk songs. Rubin encouraged Cash to stretch his boundaries, to record songs written by rock artists including Beck, Nick Lowe, Tom Waits, Chris Cornell, Jude Johnstone, Sting, John Lennon and Paul McCartney, and Glenn Frey and Don Henley. Tom Petty and the Heartbreakers worked as the studio band for two albums.

Cash's groundbreaking farewell is "Hurt," a dark paean written by Nine Inch Nails front man Trent Reznor. The powerful, heart-wrenching video, now a historical document, is rife with religious imagery, haunting clips from Cash's life, photos from the crumbling House of Cash, and profound anguish. June Carter Cash died three months after the filming. Cash only lived four months longer. "That song isn't mine anymore," Reznor said.

At Cash's memorial service, daughter Rosanne sang her father's hit song "I Still Miss Someone," adding another chapter to country music's family story. It is a legend that continues to grow and bridge generations, folding more and more poets and dreamers into the unbroken circle of country music. Or is it Americana music?

CHAPTER ONE

NOW THAT'S AMERICANA

Friday, September 13, 2002

I place my hand over my heart and vow to remember this moment for the rest of my life. I know there will never be another like it. As the night unfolds, tears flow down my cheeks. I remind myself to breathe. I know to my core that this is the start of something monumental. And I am fortunate to bear witness.

I am in the Hilton Hotel ballroom in downtown Nashville, Tennessee. Five hundred of us stand on our chairs at the first Americana Honors and Awards show as the legendary Johnny Cash walks to the stage. Johnny Cash. Here, with us, a fledgling music trade organization founded a couple of years ago by a bunch of music business misfits. J. D. May, the executive director of the Americana Music Association, managed to keep the Cash appearance a secret, aided and abetted by Dualtone Music Group staffers Scott Robinson and Kissy Black. Despite his weathered face, thin hair, and stooped stature, Cash retains the presence of a giant. He stands teary-eyed before us as a standing ovation waves across the ballroom. It is two days past the first anniversary of the September 11, 2001, terrorist attacks. Emotions are high all around.

Cash is here to accept the inaugural Spirit of Americana Free Speech Award, presented in partnership with the First Amendment Center. Looking out at a crowd of idealists clad in jeans and T-shirts, Ken Paulson, executive director of the First Amendment Center, jokes, "We're the only guys here in ties." Paulson continues:

"Recognizing the good work of people who have made the best possible use of freedom of speech, the Spirit of Americana Free Speech Award is to be given each year to an artist for his or her work as a singer, as a songwriter, as a citizen. The award honors those who use their music to make a difference, lending a voice to those who would otherwise go unheard, shining a light on issues that would otherwise go unseen. At a time when so much of the music industry is preoccupied with making a buck, the Spirit of Americana Award honors those who use their music to make a point."

Paulson introduces the founder of the First Amendment Center, John Seigenthaler. Seigenthaler motions for us to sit. We stop screaming, but no one moves to take a seat as Seigenthaler turns to speak to Cash:

"I speak for every person in this room and so many people so far removed from this place when I say these words come from the depth of a universal heart that beats with sincere appreciation and admiration for your talent, your courage, your candor, your passion...all an inseparable part of your character and an intrinsic part of your music. We live in a time when crass commercialism dominates much of what our ethos is about. It affects our corporations, our politics—both parties—it affects our government, our religion, our culture, our art, our music. At such a time, it's important for us to honor and remember a man who has identified himself and music as an advocate for the poor and the powerless, the beaten down, the hungry, the dispossessed, the forgotten outcasts, those in prison, those addicted and rejected, those innocents who die in unholy war. A man who stood against war and took his music to the front to sing for soldiers caught in the trap of war. A man who admonished an industry not to ignore, because it was controversial, music that reminded us of what we'd rather forget, that we had taken from them—a noble, heroic, native people—their land. A man who stands against racism and made an enemy of the Klan. In a time of tragic and terrible evil, strife and danger, he knows we must reach beyond the bombs and bans to embrace Christians, Jews and Muslims as one. This man in black once spoke of his dress as a symbol of rebellion against those whose minds are closed to other ideas. Because his music resonates, because his music has indeed opened eyes, opened minds, opened hearts to other ideas, it is with great pride that I present the first Freedom of Americana Free Speech Award to the great Johnny Cash."

Cash is emotional and a bit shaky. He had fallen earlier that day and it was questionable that he'd make it to the event at all.

"Thank you very much, folks," Cash says. "This is kind of you. Your words are wonderful. I'd like to offer my thanks by reciting a poem I wrote in 1974. After all the flag waving the last few days, I'm glad to see that on September 13, 2002, we're still down here waving the flag tonight."

His body weak, his voice strong, Cash recites his iconic spoken-word piece "The Ragged Old Flag" to a silent and reverent audience.

Four years earlier, Cash worked with rock producer Rick Rubin on Cash's American Recordings albums. It was Rubin who brought Cash back into the light, inspiring Cash to explore different genres of music and introducing the Man in Black to new generations of music fans. Cash's second American Recordings album, *Unchained*, won the 1998 Grammy for Best Country Album. But the truth is that the mainstream country music business and country radio had turned its back on Cash long ago. Columbia Records, Cash's musical home for twenty-six years, dropped Cash from the label in 1986. After *Unchained* won the Grammy, Rubin took out a full-page ad in *Billboard* magazine. The ad featured a famous photo of Cash flipping the bird, taken by Jim Marshall in 1969 at California's San Quentin Prison. Next to the photo of Cash's sneer and extended middle finger, Rubin had written the caption, "American Recordings and Johnny Cash would like to acknowledge the Nashville music establishment and country radio for your support."

It is not a stretch to say that mainstream country music's disdain of its legendary artists had a big hand in the founding of the *Gavin Report*'s Americana Music Chart in 1995 and the Americana Music Association in 1999. Johnny Cash is with us tonight at the same time that George Strait is entertaining twenty thousand people at the arena across the street. A show of hands would likely find a good number of Strait fans in our audience, me included, but there is nowhere else I'd rather be tonight. We have Johnny Cash at our family reunion.

It does feel like a family reunion. The Americana Music Association sports nine hundred members in 2002. We work as artist managers, booking agents, publicists, record label employees, and executives at performing rights organizations, music nonprofits, radio stations that report to *Gavin's* Americana Music Chart, music magazines, and other media outlets that embrace Americana music. In my case, I am the operations manager at Great American Country cable television channel. We are here covering the first Americana Honors and Awards.

Jason Ringenberg, looking dapper in his long red western-cut coat and cowboy hat, is the host tonight. In 1981, Jason moved from an Illinois hog farm to Nashville to pursue his dream of "making a band that could kick American roots music into the modern age." He met the visionary Jack Emerson at punk rock night at Springwater, an infamous Nashville dive bar. Emerson had started Praxis International out of his garage. Jason and the Nashville Scorchers was born that night at Springwater.

Andy McLenon and my dear friend Kay Clary joined Emerson at Praxis, using the tagline "Out of the cradle endlessly rocking." Praxis expanded and became the management team for several rock and Americana artists of the 1980s. The Georgia Satellites sold two million records and scored a massive hit with "Keep Your Hands to Yourself." Praxis worked with iconic Texas songwriter Billy Joe Shaver. They managed songwriter John Hiatt when he released his classic album *Bring the Family*. Webb Wilder, Steve Forbert, and Sonny Landreth were all part of the Praxis family.

"During those critical early days, Jack stayed consistently proactive," Jason wrote in *No Depression* magazine on the occasion of Emerson's death in 2003. "He never allowed events to shape him. He shaped events. When no major labels would sign us, Jack, again using only his words and good intentions, orchestrated the recording of our finest work: *Fervor*, the mini-LP that permanently put us on the Americana music map."

By 1995, the Praxis owners had moved on to other projects. Emerson started E-Squared Records with Texas troubadour Steve Earle, recording Earle's album *I Feel Alright* on "Jack's credit card," Earle says. In the 1980s, Earle coined the phrase "the great credibility scare" when it looked for a moment like the major record labels might embrace the left-of-center country music we now call Americana when they signed artists including Lyle Lovett, Guy Clark, Nanci Griffith, Rodney Crowell, Bela Fleck and the Flecktones, Rosanne Cash, Rosie Flores, and countless other prolific singers, songwriters, and musicians. It didn't work, though, and the outsider artists unknowingly started a new genre to bypass mainstream country music.

Ringenberg is a charming host. At one point during the show, he puts on a somber face and says, "I'm sad to announce some bad news I heard backstage. A major A&R [artists and repertoire] man from one of the big country labels has just been hit by a train. What a tragedy. He just didn't hear it." The crowd roars.

Bobby Bare Jr., son of singer-songwriter Bobby Bare and collaborator on the hit father-son tune "Daddy, What If," recorded when Bare Jr. was eight years old, presents the first Instrumentalist of the Year award to dobro master Jerry Douglas. During his thanks Jerry says, "This is a room full of the bravest people in the country." I assume he is referring to the balls it takes to start a radio format, trade organization, and award show for a music genre that is largely ignored by the mainstream music business.

Jim Lauderdale, who consistently earns critical praise for his eclectic albums spanning country, folk, blues, bluegrass, and rock, wins Song of the Year for "She's Looking at Me," his duet with bluegrass great Ralph Stanley on Lauderdale's *Lost in the Lonesome Pines* album.

We don't know it on this night, but Lauderdale will go on to host many years of Americana Honors and Awards shows and coin the phrase, "Now, that's Americana!"

Chris Hillman, a pioneer of Americana who defined the genre along with frequent collaborator Gram Parsons as part of the Byrds and Flying Burrito Brothers, is here to present the Album of the Year award. Hillman reads the nominees for Americana Album of the Year: Gillian Welch for *Time (the Revelator)*, the Flatlanders for *Now Again*, a various-artists tribute to Webb Pierce, and *Buddy and Julie Miller*, the roots-rock-country self-titled album from the extraordinary couple. Buddy and Julie take home the honor.

There is a direct line from Chris Hillman, to Gram Parsons, to Americana queen Emmylou Harris.

Buddy and Julie Miller present the Lifetime Achievement Award for Performer to Emmylou. Emmylou's exquisite voice and creative spirit carry forth the cosmic American music passed down by her mentor Gram Parsons. "Singing is praying twice and right now we need all the prayers we can get," she says to the crowd. "I like all of you people who like weird music."

After Gram Parsons died, Emmylou signed a solo deal with Warner Brothers Records. Warner told her to form a "hot band" to back her. She did. The Hot Band included guitarist James Burton, who had played with Elvis Presley and Jerry Lee Lewis, along with Elvis's pianist Glen D. Hardin. Steel guitar player Hank DeVito, drummer John Ware, and bass guitar player Emory Gordy Jr. rounded out the Hot Band. Then Emmylou's producer Brian Ahern brought Texas songwriter Rodney Crowell into the fold. "Rodney was the only thing Brian played for me that I liked," Emmylou says. "I loved his harmony singing. We recorded 'Bluebird Wine' and 'Til I Gain Control Again.' He was entrenched."

In 1972, Rodney and his pal Donovan Cowart moved from Houston to Nashville under false pretenses.

"Donovan and I made a record with producer Jim Duff. He went to Nashville and told us he had sold it to Columbia Records, that we had a ten-year recording contract and we were going on the road with Kenny Rogers and the First Edition for a full year," Rodney says. "The only problem is, none of it was true. He sold the publishing and the tape for $100 to the Wilburn Brothers publishing company, Sure Fire Music. We went in there one day at lunchtime, Donovan distracted the receptionist and I went in and stole the tapes. I started hanging out in Centennial Park looking for a girl that would take me in. Then we learned that we could play and pass the hat and make a few dollars at Bishop's Pub down on West End. You might make four or five dollars passing the hat. You could get into Bishop's Pub about four nights a week and play. Tim Bishop's girlfriend took a liking to me. She would give me a hamburger and a beer, so I had dinner."

Crowell met Skinny Dennis Sanchez at Bishop's. Skinny Dennis lived with songwriter Richard Dobson, and Rodney moved into their rental house on Acklen Avenue in Hillsboro Village. From midnight to dawn, the house was the meeting place for underground songwriters and musicians. Guy and Susanna Clark, Townes Van Zandt, Dave Loggins, Steve Earle, Robin and Linda Williams, and Johnny Rodriguez were regulars.

In 1973, Crowell landed his first music publishing deal with country star Jerry Reed thanks to Townes Van Zandt sleeping with Rodney's girlfriend.

"Susanna hipped me that Townes was having a go with my girlfriend," Crowell says. "I got all pissed off and wrote this song, 'You Can't Keep Me Here in Tennessee,' and played it at a happy hour gig in Green Hills at the Jolly Ox. Jerry Reed and his manager were there and they just came up and said, 'We want to record that tomorrow.' Right away, Jerry did that song and 'Home Sweet Home Revisited,' and 'Everybody Has Those Kinda Days,' back to back to back. Marginal songs, not yet fully formed, but filler for his albums."

The publishing deal saved Crowell from an acting gig at the Opryland theme park.

"Opryland opened that year and they needed somebody to play the lead role in their day-to-day production of Jimmie Rodgers," Crowell says. "I auditioned and sang 'Lovesick Blues.' I yodeled like Hank Williams and got the gig. I was really depressed about it because I did not want to do this schmutz thing. I got the songwriting gig with Jerry Reed right before I was supposed to start work at Opryland, so I bailed on that. Reed paid me $100 a week, which was a goldmine at that time. Soon after I got that job, I wrote 'Bluebird Wine,' "Til I Gain Control Again,' and 'Song for the Life.'"

Skip Beckwith, who played bass with Anne Murray's band in Canada, came through Nashville looking for songs for Anne. Guitar player Bob Cardwell introduced Rodney to Skip. Skip took Rodney's tape back to Canada and it ended up in the hands of Brian Ahern, Emmylou's producer.

"Emmy tells the story that my tape was the last one they listened to when they were looking for songs. When she heard it, Emmy said 'This is my guy' and asked to meet me," Rodney says. "They sent me a plane ticket to DC to see Emmy play at the Childe Harold, kind of a famous music saloon near Dupont Circle. We stayed up all night and played songs after the gig and Emmy said, 'Alright, we're friends now.' Then, after I met Emmylou and knew she was interested in my songs, I went to Harry Warner, who ran Reed's publishing company, said I want to start working with this singer, and I wonder if you'll give me the songs back. They said, 'Well, we'll give you some of the songs back,' but they didn't pick "Til I Gain Control Again.' They didn't pick 'Bluebird Wine.' They didn't pick 'An American Dream,' which was a big hit. They gave them to me. Those were the ones I wanted and they gave them back to me."

After living in Nashville for two years, Crowell decamped for Austin, Texas, at the end of 1974. But he wasn't there long.

"I got an apartment on Enfield Road in December 1974," Rodney says. "Emmy came through and played Armadillo World Headquarters in early January. I went and sat in with her at the Armadillo. She was going to LA the next day and invited me to go with her. I went to LA with Emmy and stayed seven years."

Not only is Rodney a peer of Emmylou Harris and Steve Earle, he is a direct descendant of Texas singer-songwriters Willie Nelson, Waylon Jennings, Kris Kristofferson, Guy Clark, Townes Van Zandt, and Billy Joe Shaver. Another group of great Texas songwriter offspring is the Flatlanders, talented guys from Lubbock, Texas. The Flatlanders (Joe Ely, Jimmie Dale Gilmore, and Butch Hancock) are at the Americana Awards tonight to present the Lifetime Achievement Award for Songwriting to Billy Joe Shaver. "I've never received any award and I don't know what to say," Shaver says. "All of us Texans stick together. If we didn't, we'd get beat up."

Billy Joe Shaver presents the Artist of the Year award. The nominees are Gillian Welch and Dave Rawlings, the Flatlanders, Buddy and Julie Miller, and Jim Lauderdale. Lauderdale takes home the big prize...if you can call it that, coming from this bizarre new organization that embraces what the mainstream has cast aside.

Gillian Welch, who is nominated for four awards tonight with her partner Dave Rawlings thanks to their lovely folk-meets-rock album *Time (the Revelator)*, presents the Lifetime Achievement Award for Executive to producer, composer, and musician T-Bone Burnett. "The notion of an Americana Award for an executive is peculiar," Gillian says. This whole affair is peculiar. Burnett doesn't bother to show up to accept the award. No one can blame him for choosing not to fly from Los Angeles to Nashville for an "Americana Award." He's probably shaking his head and wondering what the hell this is, just like the rest of the music industry.

Doug Sahm is the recipient of the first Americana President's Award, dedicated to a deserving artist posthumously and at the sole discretion of the Americana board president. Sahm, a child prodigy who got his start on the *Louisiana Hayride* radio program at age five, later started the band the Sir Douglas Quintet. The quintet scored a hit with "She's about a Mover" in 1965. After several acclaimed albums, Sahm signed with Atlantic Records producer Jerry Wexler in 1973 when Wexler believed progressive country was becoming a thing. They made the album *Doug Sahm and Band* with Bob Dylan, Dr. John, and accordion player Flaco Jimenez, which included Sahm's seminal "(Is Anybody Going to) San Antone?" Until his untimely death from a heart attack in 1999, Sahm recorded and performed Americana music around the world as part of the Sir Douglas Quintet, Texas Tornados, and the Last Real Texas Blues Band. Tonight, the preeminent music journalist and author Chet Flippo accepts the award for the Sahm family.

Johnny Cash comes back to close the show with his wife, June Carter Cash, and the remaining Carter Family. We don't know it at the time, but we are witnessing history—the last performances of June and Johnny. Despite failing health, Johnny and June lead their family band through a nostalgic set of songs as the audience sings along. "We have a big family," Johnny says. "I'm the first Carter brother."

"John's always been so good to me," June says. "I've followed him around for years everywhere he went. I feel really good about this because, honest to goodness, I've always been privileged to be married to John. He's always encouraged me to go ahead and do what I do. And he's always wanted to be a Carter brother. This is our family up here—a little bit of everybody that's part of our family that can sing. Some of them couldn't sing worth anything so we left them at home."

One hour later, I interview Johnny and June backstage. The couple leans on each other as they stand awkwardly in front of our film crew. "I'm sorry that we aren't feeling our best, sweetheart," Johnny says. I cut the interview short and dismiss the film crew. As I say goodbye to Johnny and June, Johnny takes my hand in his and says, "Thank you for your time and patience. God bless you." June leans in for a hug. I watch them slowly make their way out. It is the last time I see them alive.

But Cash had one last groundbreaking farewell in him. He recorded "Hurt," written by Nine Inch Nails front man Trent Reznor. In the video, filmed at the House of Cash museum in Hendersonville, Tennessee, June looks on as Johnny sings, "What have I become? My sweetest friend. Everyone I know goes away in the end." June Carter Cash died on May 15, 2003, three months after the filming, from complications from heart surgery. Johnny lived four months longer. He followed his wife to the other side on September 12, 2003, almost a year to the date after tonight's event. It seems fitting that they were with us, the Americana freaks, for their final show.

This Americana conference is a pivotal moment. It is the weekend I meet Tom Frouge at a barbecue and beer party at the Slow Bar in East Nashville. Al Bunetta, John Prine's partner in Oh Boy Records, introduces us. Tom runs Triloka, a world music record label in Los Angeles. Al says Tom is the leading authority on nontraditional marketing and suggests we talk about American Roots Publishing, the new nonprofit I've dreamed up to publish Joe Ely's novel and road journals.

Joe Ely ran away from his home in Lubbock, Texas, and joined the circus in the 1960s. He returned to his hometown in 1971 and teamed up with Butch Hancock and Jimmie Dale Gilmore to form the Flatlanders band. As a solo artist, he signed to MCA Records and issued *Joe Ely* in 1977, followed by *Honky Tonk Masquerade* in 1978. Not country enough for country radio, or rock enough for rock radio, Joe's music fell into the Americana category before there was a name for it.

"There's no mistaking a Joe Ely album," Mario Tarradell wrote in the *Dallas Morning News*. "His stinging, road-hued voice commands lyrics about life, life and the wandering spirit. When you listen to his music, you're enjoying the essence of Joe Ely. That's the essence of Texas music."

An early adopter of technology, Joe experimented with recording using an Apple II computer. He made his albums B484 and *Hi-Res* on an Apple II many years before home recording was in vogue.

Over lunch several months earlier, Joe confided to me that publishers in New York had rejected his books because they don't know what to do with Joe. What? He is Joe Ely, I know exactly what to do with him. I'm determined to start the nonprofit to publish Joe's books and other niche music projects. I envision quality over quantity. Ventures not attractive to big corporations because they are not slam dunks to sell millions. Attractive enough to me because they will quite possibly sell tens of thousands, enough to finance the next project.

Tom is a Joe Ely fan, a marketing genius, and works in the nonprofit and fundraising space. We stand on the sidewalk outside the Slow Bar talking for more than two hours before moving the conversation across the street to the bar at Margot. By the time the Margot staff nudges us out the door after midnight, we feel like old friends.

The same weekend, Guy Clark and I undergo a subtle shift from colleagues to friends. It starts at dinner with the Sugar Hill Records staff. Sugar Hill invited me to the intimate dinner because I wrote the liner notes for Guy's new record, *The Dark*, released this week. I first met Guy at an American Society of Composers, Authors, and Publishers (ASCAP) party in 1998 when I was the managing editor at *Country Music* magazine. We became friendly after Lee Roy Parnell took me to Guy's house on April 1, 2000. That day we sat in Guy's workshop for nine hours while the tape recorder ran and I asked questions. Guy started drinking Marilyn Merlot wine at noon. He chain-smoked—first a joint, then a cigarette, then a joint and another cigarette. By late afternoon, he was into the whiskey. I didn't join him in any of the smoking or drinking. "You know, Tamara, I'm not sure I trust anyone who doesn't partake," Guy said at the time. "That line won't work on me," I said. Guy laughed and we became fast friends.

Since then, Guy and I have had lunch together several times, I've visited Guy and Susanna at their home off White Bridge Road. Guy suggested that Sugar Hill hire me to write the liner notes for the new album.

I sit next to Guy at dinner and we have a great time. Unlike the first day at his house, tonight I drink too much wine and Bailey's Irish Cream and smoke cigarettes and weed with Guy. I never smoke and I rarely drink.

Guy is a bad influence on me and we have a blast. This sixty-year-old man is the coolest cat in any room. We cut up with Guy during dinner and at the Sunset Grill bar and then our group heads to 12th and Porter to see Jim Lauderdale. Guy likes to get loose and party—talk to people, listen to music, watch the scene. It is heady to be with him, and to be here as part of this Americana family. We are just getting started.

CHAPTER TWO

THE BACKSTORY

How do I end up hanging with Guy Clark and other Americana dreamers? It all starts in the 1960s in my great-grandparents' upper flat in Cudahy, Wisconsin. That's where I first fell in love with folk music. The object of my affection is my great-grandfather Oliver's Regina music box, an 1898 model that plays hole-punched metal discs. The plucking of teeth on a steel comb is inspired by the carillon bell towers used in Europe, so beautiful and magical it makes me cry. Stephen Foster's "My Old Kentucky Home" and "Beautiful Dreamer" are my favorites.

The Regina sits at the end of a wide, carpeted hallway. The flat smells like Grandma Gert's rosewater perfume and the chocolate chip cookies she bakes daily. My mom's parents, Ellis and Jeanne, live on the first floor, where there is more of a molasses cookie scent because they are Grandpa's favorite. My cousins and I climb the steep curved stairway many times a day to visit our great-grandparents Oliver and Gert. That's where the music lives. Gert plays piano and accordion while Oliver accompanies her on a marimbaphone as they run through pop standards from the 1930s and 1940s made famous by Kay Kyser, Glenn Miller, Benny Goodman, Dinah Shore, and the Mills Brothers. We are mesmerized by our great-grandparents' enthusiastic live performances and the obvious joy it brings them. Before returning to the first floor, we sit in a semicircle around Oliver as he spins his favorite discs on the Regina.

In the third grade at Willow Glen Elementary School, a quarter mile across the tracks in my hometown of St. Francis, our music class sings folk songs, too. Stephen Foster's "Old Folks at Home (Swanee River),"

Woody Guthrie's "This Land Is Your Land," Thomas Allen's "Erie Canal," and "John Henry," which the teacher says is so old no one remembers who wrote it. In 1969, my third-grade year, our music teacher is a young hippie—although I could not peg her as such. Her passion for folk songs captivates me and I practice singing them in and out of school.

Our entire family loves music. On Sunday drives through the country, Dad leads us in singing the Carter Family's "Church in the Wildwood" with his own version of the lyrics: "Oh come, come, come to the church in the wildwood, no lovelier church in the dale, no love is so dear to my childhood as the little brown church in the dale." We sing that chorus over and over again, four kids shoulder to shoulder in the back seat of the Ford, as Dad drives us through the same Wisconsin country roads Sunday after Sunday—blue skies and nothing but farm fields dotted with barns and old houses.

My grandparents and great-grandparents, all musicians, love popular music of the 1920s, 1930s, and 1940s. My mother is into Johnny Mathis, the Platters, Elvis Presley, and hits from the 1950s. My stepfather is a soul man. He gravitates to Memphis soul artists of the Stax and Sun record labels. Dad is a fanatical Johnny Cash follower.

At ten, my bedroom walls are filled with posters of David Cassidy and Donny Osmond. By junior high, Elton John and Bernie Taupin are my jam. My love for Elton dominates every waking thought and all of my conversations...so much so that Mom worries out loud whether I'll ever care about anything else. Elton seems otherworldly to me, although I can't tell you why. Years later, my mom admitted that she couldn't understand how thirteen-year-old me could be so obsessed with a flamboyant gay man. It's the music, Mom. Who cares that he's gay? I still love Elton with the same passion I had at thirteen.

Summerfest is Milwaukee's multigenre music festival based next to Lake Michigan at a former fifteen-acre airport. Summerfest blows my thirteen-year-old mind the first time I experience it in 1974. The Schlitz Country Stage, the Pabst International Folk Festival Stage, the Miller Jazz Oasis, and the Rock Stage anchor the festival in those early years. Seals and Crofts, Charlie Pride, Ronnie Milsap, the O'Jays, Harry Chapin, Gladys Knight and the Pipps, Sha Na Na, and Helen Reddy are part of my first Summerfest. In the following years, Waylon Jennings, Mac Davis, the Little River Band, Kiki Dee, the BoDeans, Chick Corea, Emmylou Harris, Marshall Tucker Band, Kris Kristofferson, Rita Coolidge, Steve Miller Band, Stray Cats, Muddy Waters, Cheap Trick.... It's a burning ring of fire that inflames my passion for music. Summerfest bills itself as "the Big Gig" and "the World's Largest Music Festival." Prepandemic, it was a ten-day festival. Now Summerfest happens three weekends in a row in June and July with more than six hundred artists performing on twelve stages. Working in the music business, I've been to many festivals around the world. None of them come close to the seductive Summerfest. I cannot abide being in a farm field with porta potties after living with the luxury of permanent, clean bathroom buildings at Summerfest. In 2023, I went back to Summerfest to see Sheryl Crow, James Taylor, and Lyle Lovett. I get high just walking in the place.

As a high school freshman, at the roller-skating rink, my skate name is Dr. Love, from the Kiss song "Calling Dr. Love."

You need my love baby, oh so bad
You're not the only one I've ever had
And if I say I want to set you free
Don't you know you'll be in misery.

Pretty racy for a naïve fifteen-year-old. Sophomore year, my Taco Bell coworker Cheryl turns me on to Barbra Streisand. My friends and I pile into two cars and spend several nights at the local drive-in theater obsessing over Barbra in *A Star Is Born*. And that cute Kris Kristofferson, too. The following year, we are infected with disco mania, John Travolta, and *Saturday Night Fever*. It starts my lifelong love for the Bee Gees, my favorite band to this day. Have you seen Dave Grohl and the Foo Fighters as the Dee Gees? Look it up. Yes, even the Foos are Bee Gees fans.

Senior year, my boyfriend Bob and I make out to the Rolling Stones album *Some Girls* in his classic T-Bird. And at a party at Jeff Anderson's house, a group of us stand around the turntable and marvel as "Running with the Devil" blares from the first *Van Halen* album. It is monumental.

People like to knock 1970s music, but for me it is revolutionary and forever shapes me as a music lover.

I am in love with songwriters, too. Acoustic guitars and story songs move me. I find my way to the popular California folkie-sounding records of the 1970s—the music coming from Laurel Canyon and the Troubadour club in Los Angeles (the Byrds, Carole King, the Eagles, Linda Ronstadt, Jackson Browne). Bread and Lobo are also favorites.

Songwriter Jessi Colter thrills me. Jessi's single "I'm Not Lisa," from her 1975 album *I'm Jessi Colter*, is all over pop radio and I love it. I save my allowance to buy a copy of the album. I'm hooked by the mesmerizing album art before I even get to the music. Jessi is cast in shadows, her arms draped across an antique piano keyboard. Her dark hair flows around her shoulders and she wears a long white hippie dress slit above the knee. Even her name, etched in a swoopy logo, exudes cool.

Then, the music, oh, the music. The album is a masterpiece, all ten songs written solely by Jessi. It's impossible to categorize. Jessi shows off her singular voice and piano prowess as she moves easily between the sensual funk of "Come on In" and "Love's the Only Chain," and the southern rock "Is There Anyway (You'd Stay Forever)." "You Ain't Never Been Loved (Like I'm Gonna Love You)" is a rollicking roadhouse blues number, while "For the First Time" and "Who Walks thru Your Memory (Billy Jo)" veer to classic country. Jessie leans on cosmic western soul in "What's Happened to Blue Eyes," the aching "I Hear a Song," and the heartbreak of "I'm Not Lisa." I try to imitate Jessi's beautiful phrasing as I sing along to my favorite song on the album, the incomparable "Storms Never Last." I play the hell out of *I'm Jessi Colter*, not only in high school but throughout my life.

In 1973, Hazel Smith, a secretary at the Music Row office of Glaser Studios, also known as "Hillbilly Central," searched for a word to describe Waylon Jennings and Willie Nelson's renegade music. Smith grabbed a dictionary, landed on the word *outlaw*, and the tag stuck. By the time *Wanted! The Outlaws* lands in 1976, Jessi Colter is not just the token chick on the cover of the *Outlaws* album with Waylon, Willie, and Tompall Glaser. Jessi is a star. *The Outlaws* is the first country record to sell more than a million copies.

"Jerry Bradley [RCA Records executive] likes to take credit for that album but Waylon put together the whole thing," Jessi says. "We were in the RCA vault looking for tapes and Waylon found all this great stuff. They didn't do a lot of compilations in those days and I think the label resisted it. The old guard at the record companies back in those days had an attitude that they had to babysit artists and that artists didn't know anything even though we were the ones out in the world selling the albums and the songs."

After high school, my musical education continues as I tend bar at the punk rock club the Lost Dutchman Mine. My uniform is torn jeans, rock 'n' roll T-shirts, big frizzy hair, and thick black eyeliner. Bands including the Prosecutors, Die Kreuzen, and the Misfits play as I tap draft beers and pour tequila shots for the slam dancers and punk rockers. I have a torrid affair with a bad-boy regular customer. He whisper-sings, "Love is kinda crazy with a spooky little girl like you …," to me each morning in the bedsheets under his mirrored ceiling.

I'm also a cocktail waitress at El Robbo's Disco, dodging Electric Slide dancers in my polyester miniskirt as I carry drink trays full of Long Island iced tea and Manhattans to tables of traveling businessmen wearing cheap leisure suits. One of those guys in a cheap suit pinches my ass while singing along to the Vanity 6 song "Nasty Girl." I throw my tray of drinks at him and lose my gig.

On nights off, I frequent the Brick House Disco and Dance and Beverage Company. My friends and I love to dance. We still love disco music in 1980. The previous year, WLUP Chicago racist shock jock Steve Dahl did his best to ethnically cleanse music he didn't like with his horrifying Disco Demolition Night riot at Comiskey Park. Like many knobs before and after him, he succeeded in ruining life for others. Yet Prince and Michael Jackson picked up the mantle to keep dance clubs alive in the early 1980s.

I start college late, at twenty-six, and attend Alverno College weekend program. As part of my journalism and communications studies, I apply for an internship at Sundance Broadcasting, a small, local radio company that owns WOKY-AM and WMIL-FM in Milwaukee.

THE MOST FUN WINS. The words are carved into a wooden sign that hangs in the secret space beyond the private reception lobby at Sundance Broadcasting. I spot the sign on my first visit to the station as promotions director Jesse Garcia gives me a behind-the-scenes tour. We loop around the building and Jesse points out the studios, the traffic department, the copywriting office, and the "bullpen" in the center of the building where the sales reps holler over cubicle walls and laugh louder than any group of people I'd ever met.

"Any questions?" Jesse asks as we return to his office.

"Yes, tell me about the sign that says 'the most fun wins.'"

"It's the Sundance Broadcasting mission statement," Jesse says.

Sure as hell, I want to work here.

Jesse signs me on as an intern for the fall semester. I'm years older than most college interns. I choose radio rather than print or television because I am a music junkie. I choose Sundance because WOKY is the top forty station of my youth. I fell in love with the songs of the 1960s and 1970s on WOKY and that spiritual connection is what brings me in the door today. WOKY is now an MOR (middle of the road) station that plays the likes of Frank Sinatra, Rosemary Clooney, and the stars of *Lawrence Welk*. It is now my grandmother's station. But that's okay, too. WMIL is a country station. I know Jessi Colter, Willie and Waylon, Kris Kristofferson, and Johnny Cash, but modern country music is a mystery to me.

I suppose my internship is like most. I hang banners, stuff envelopes, haul coolers, and clean the FM106 Rolling Radio RV. That is just fine with me. I'm here to absorb as much as I can about the radio business and am happy to do whatever is asked of me. On one of my first weekends, WOKY hosts a listener appreciation picnic in Washington Park. As I work the hot dog line, senior citizens dance on the green to Louis Prima and Keely Smith. They sprawl out on picnic tables sharing stories and reminiscing about the good old days. My grandpa and two great-grandmothers had died within the last eighteen months, and I love every minute with these old people.

A guy about my age comes through the line for a hot dog. He is decades younger and more smartly dressed than anyone else in the park. The wind blows my curls across my face and straight up in the air but his flaming-red hair, styled in a perfect ducktail, remains pristine. He is clearly out of place in a park full of gray hair. I smile as I throw a hot dog on a bun and hand it to him.

"Do you work at the station?" I ask.

He sticks his hand out to shake mine and says, "Yes, I'm Brian Ongaro."

"Hi, I'm Tamara, rhymes with camera. Do you work in the sales department?"

"No," Brian says. "I'm the general manager." The smile never leaves Brian's face as we talk. I don't know it that day, but Brian Ongaro will become the most important mentor in my life. The rest of the chapters in this book would not exist without Brian. It is Brian who sets me on this path, teaches me to be confident, and shows me how to make my dreams come true.

Brian and my other teachers—promotions director Jesse Garcia, program director Kerry Wolfe, music director Mitch Morgan, news director Debbie Young, marketing director Jerry Arndt, and sales associate extraordinaire Lavonne Beecher—spend the next few months answering my every question about radio. At the conclusion of the semester in December, Jerry calls me into his office. "I want to show you something exciting," he says. Two magazine cover mock-ups are pinned to his wall. One is titled WMIL *Wisconsin Country*. The other is called WOKY *The Best of Times*. Jerry says that Sundance plans to publish quarterly magazines for each station. The company is creating a database marketing department to publish the magazines, create special promotions, install an interactive phone system, and build a database of listeners with the intent to form a more intimate relationship with them. This is the early 1990s. It is years before the internet is widely used and almost two decades before social media becomes a thing.

It *is* exciting, original and imaginative. I can barely breathe as Jerry asks me if I want to run the new department. The word *yes* is on my lips but I'm terrified. Opportunity is knocking and my oversize imposter syndrome blocks the door. *I'm not that good*, I think. *There are people more qualified. What if I fail? Why me?*

I voice my doubt.

"Jerry, are you sure I can do this?"

"You can do anything you put your mind to," Jerry says. "You'll have to interview with Brian, but he knows I want you for the job."

Brian does hire me. And he expects a lot. Brian is committed, energetic, and unwavering in his passion about the company and he wants that from everyone around him. Three lessons (among many) I learn from Brian that continue to serve me: First, don't be afraid to make decisions. If you make the wrong decision, you can make another to correct it. Second, always be willing to walk away from a negotiation. If you are not getting what you want and need, you won't be happy with the deal. And third, surround yourself with people smarter than you and hire people who want your job. They will force you to up your game and make you look good.

The job at Sundance comes to me at an ideal time. I am grieving the loss of my grandpa and great-grandparents. I'm vulnerable, lost, and searching for connection to something. I find a safe haven and kindred spirits at Sundance and this new world of country music.

Artists with large crossover appeal ruled at mainstream country radio in the 1980s. Kenny Rogers, Alabama, Exile, and Hank Williams Jr. led the pack. The new traditionalists, Texan George Strait and Kentucky boys Ricky Skaggs and Dwight Yoakam, won the attention of a younger demographic of listeners. Kids who had grown up on rock 'n' roll invented new rules now that they had jobs as disc jockeys, music journalists, and entertainment executives. The old guard was dying, and it was anyone's guess how things would shake out on Music Row.

Pop country, new traditionalists, and hip outliers like Guy Clark, Emmylou Harris, Iris Dement, Uncle Tupelo, Steve Earle, Lyle Lovett, Nanci Griffith, the O'Kanes, Bela Fleck and the Flecktones, Kelly Willis, the Jayhawks, and Foster and Lloyd jockeyed for position. Some left-of-center record executives hoped that country radio might see the light and play more progressive music.

The explosion of the Class of 1989 pushed radio in one direction. Garth Brooks, Clint Black, Alan Jackson, Mary Chapin Carpenter, Travis Tritt, and Vince Gill broke out in 1989 and by the early 1990s set the course for the next decade in country radio. The Class of 1989 were the new trailblazers for country radio. And from the perspective of radio and the major record labels, it was a good thing. Everyone made money. Everyone except the artists of the genre we now call Americana.

Vince Gill and Garth Brooks championed Americana right from the beginning. Garth is a fan of the progressive bluegrass band New Grass Revival. Sam Bush, John Cowan, Bela Fleck, and Pat Flynn recorded Dennis Linde's song "Callin' Baton Rouge" on their 1989 album *Friday Night in America*.

"We met Garth when he was still going to college in Stillwater," John Cowan says. "We played a little club there and Garth and his bluegrass band opened for us. He loved us. He was a fan. Then we did a festival in this place somewhere between Stillwater and Tulsa. I have a poster of this festival called Horse Thief Canyon. It was Garth Brooks and New Grass Revival. When Garth got to Nashville, he got a deal on Capitol and we were with Capitol. Garth opens a show for us in Johnson City, Tennessee, and our crowd was so rude to him. They talked through his whole show. He was just crushed. He went back to his booking agent and said, 'I love these guys, but I can't open for them anymore.' We put 'Callin' Baton Rouge' on our album and I think it went to number thirty-four, our highest-charting song ever. The video did great. It went to number one on CMT. But Bela had already told us he was leaving the band. The minute we told Capitol that Bela was leaving and we were probably going to break up, they dropped the record like a hot potato. A few years after that, we get a call from Garth. Garth is like, 'I'm really pissed. I thought 'Callin' Baton Rouge' was a number one song. You guys should have had a number one song on it. By God, now I have the power to make it a number one song. I want to re-record it, and you guys come and sing and play with me on it.'" Garth's version of "Callin' Baton Rouge" made it to number two on the *Billboard* Hot Country Singles chart.

Although he is known more for his soaring success in mainstream country music, Vince Gill's eminence in Americana is undeniable. A multi-instrumentalist, Vince plays guitar, banjo, fiddle, dobro, mandolin, and bass guitar. In high school, he played in the bluegrass band Mountain Smoke. After graduation, he moved to Kentucky and joined Bluegrass Alliance for a short stint, followed by Ricky Skaggs's Boone Creek, and then lit out for Los Angeles, where he joined fiddler Byron Berline's band

Sundance. In 1979, Vince joined the country rock band Pure Prairie League and scored a top-ten pop hit with "Let Me Love You Tonight." Rodney Crowell invited Vince to join his backing band the Cherry Bombs in 1981, with Richard Bennett, Tony Brown, Larrie London, and Emmylou Harris's Hot Band alumni Hank DeVito and Emory Gordy. The Cherry Bombs toured with Rodney and his wife, Rosanne Cash. In the 1980s, Emmylou tapped Vince to be in her band for three albums, *The Ballad of Sally Rose*, *Angel Band*, and *Thirteen*. As a producer, Rodney Crowell brought Vince in to be part of Guy Clark's band on *The South Coast of Texas* in 1981 and *Better Days* in 1983.

Digging into Rodney Crowell, Emmylou Harris, and Vince is the moment my education in and love of Americana music begins. At Sundance, I share office space with music director Mitch Morgan. Because Mitch sits right behind me, I listen in on his phone calls as label promotion guys pitch singles and artists to be played on the station. I'm also privy to Mitch's running commentary as he opens the gazillions of compact discs that land on his desk each week. He sorts them into piles, and sometimes he takes a CD from its padded envelope and with a loud "Ugh!" tosses it into a corner on the floor.

Some of the albums I retrieve from Mitch's corner or the WMIL prize closet (where good music goes to die): Uncle Tupelo's *Anodyne*, Johnny Cash's *American Recordings*, Iris Dement's *Infamous Angel*, John Prine's *The Missing Years*, Emmylou Harris and the Nash Ramblers' *At the Ryman*, Todd Snider's *Songs for the Daily Planet*, Kevin Welch's *Western Beat*, New Grass Revival's *Friday Night in America*, Rosie Flores's *Once More with Feeling*, Delevantes's *Long About That Time*, Alison Krauss and Union Station's *Every Time You Say Goodbye*, the Mavericks' *From Hell to Paradise*, and Kim Richey's eponymous album.

My job is fun—showbiz. It is hard work with a lighthearted attitude. The culture is a far cry from anything else I've encountered professionally. My colleagues are my dearest friends. Our car phones are lifelines to each other as we drive around Milwaukee doing business. There are field trips to Brewers baseball games, Cubs baseball games, White Sox baseball games, Packers football games, Bucks basketball games, Admirals hockey games, casinos, restaurants, and too many concerts to count. WMIL and

WOKY host remote broadcasts and listener parties at taverns, parks, car dealerships, fairs, and festivals. We gather for potluck dinners, karaoke, and trivia nights in the conference room and bullpen. We raise a boatload of money for the Child Abuse Prevention Fund hosting annual concerts, events, and fundraisers all over southeastern Wisconsin. And we meet every Friday night at Wendt's, a corner bar not far from the station.

The early 1990s are a magical time in Milwaukee radio. WMIL is number one in the market. According to Arbitron research data, WOKY, our AM station, is regularly top ten in the market. Radio advertising prices are calculated at a cost per ratings point. Those great ratings for each station mean that we charge more money for advertising. Plus, my magazines earn nonspot revenue from advertising that does not take up air time on the radio. It makes me somewhat of a rock star, bringing in a million bucks a year without taking up on-air space. Sundance is profitable. We are having a great time. THE MOST FUN WINS.

At the same time, country music is the dominant radio format across the nation. There are nearly two thousand radio stations in the United States playing country music full time. Those in larger markets, including WMIL, are "reporting stations," meaning they report airplay lists to trade magazines. *Billboard* and *Radio and Records* are the big ones. *Cash Box* and the *Gavin Report* are smaller trades.

Country music is so hot that the major record labels in Nashville sign a slew of artists and add subsidiary labels to sign even more. Contact information for record label staff at MCA, Mercury, Polygram, Capitol, Liberty, Patriot, Atlantic, Giant, RCA, BNA, Arista, Epic, and Columbia is pinned to the bulletin board above my desk. Artists are selling hundreds of thousands of CDs. Gold (five hundred thousand) and platinum (one million) records are common, and a record is not considered a success unless it achieves gold status.

In my unique position as publisher of WMIL's *Wisconsin Country* (later renamed *Country Today*) and WOKY's *The Best of Times*, I absorb as much as I can about the radio, records, and magazine businesses. Reporting radio stations get special privileges from the major record labels in Nashville. WMIL is an important radio station, and I forge friendships with the label radio promotion people—Jean Cashman at Warner Brothers, John

Ettinger at Mercury, Rob Ellis at MCA, Joe Devine at BNA, Mark Westcott at Epic, and Gussie Thomason at Asylum.

Before her Warner Brothers gig, Jean (radio name Cashman, actual last name Batcha) worked as the music director for WKIS, Miami's only country radio station in the early 1990s. At the time, the Mavericks were a hot local band in Miami, and even their hometown radio station ignored them.

"It wasn't for lack of trying on Bob's [program director Bob McKay] part," Jean says. "At the time, radio stations used consultants for everything. A consultant could save a program director's ass if the ratings were down, someone to blame, but the other side of it is that the program directors had to listen to the consultants. Bob did a workaround for the Mavericks by starting a New Music Show so he could play them. They did a lot of shows in Miami, but they weren't signed by a label and radio ignored artists without major labels at that time. Then Bruce Hinton [from MCA Records] came to Miami and he and Bob went together to see a Mavericks show and that's when they got their MCA deal.

"It was frustrating to hear all this great music that we wouldn't play," Jean says. "Our owners, it was two guys, if they didn't like something it wasn't getting played. Bob and I were having a music meeting one day and listening to Dwight Yoakam. I don't remember the song, but to us it was clearly a hit. The owners walked by and said, 'That will never be played on this radio station.'"

Jean left WKIS because it wasn't fun anymore, and in 1993 she started as a promotion rep for Warner Brothers, where she immediately began working with Dwight Yoakam. "Dwight is one of the best artists I ever worked with," Jean says. "He was a character and so brilliant and talented. I was the first woman promotion rep at Warner Brothers and he was always so respectful of me. I loved working with him."

Jean and her promotion counterparts at the other major labels introduce me to artist managers and agents. Because part of my job is as magazine publisher and editor, the label's public relations departments are also in the loop. Because our magazine sells print advertising, the record label sales departments buy advertising from me. On any given day I am on the phone with promotion, publicity, sales, artist managers, agents, and artists based in Nashville. My education in the music business dovetails into my lessons about the radio business and launching and managing a magazine with a quarter million subscribers. It is music business boot camp.

My department focuses on generating alternative revenue sources for the stations—promotions we can create that don't take up advertising space on the air. We run print ads in the magazine and I brainstorm with record labels in Nashville to design nontraditional campaigns. Hank Tovar, a sales rep for Capitol Records Nashville, is one of my more creative partners. Capitol's new artist George Ducas reminds me of Dwight Yoakam. George has a cool Bakersfield-meets-Texas sound and his song "Lipstick Promises" is making its way up the chart. Because George is scheduled to perform at the Pabst Theater in Milwaukee on Valentine's Day, Hank and I pull in L'Oréal Cosmetics and set up end-cap displays in Walgreen's drugstores with George's CD and L'Oréal lipstick. We build in a contest where customers can sign up to win a Valentine's package that includes dinner from a restaurant advertiser, a dozen roses from a florist client, and two tickets and backstage passes to George's show, courtesy of Capitol Nashville. It's a win all around for Walgreens, L'Oréal, George, Capitol Records, and our radio station.

The labels often bring artists in to play an acoustic set in the conference room. They treat the program director, music director, and other key staff to restaurant dinners with the artist. There is a revolving door of country stars and upstarts coming and going through the station.

The incomparable Hal Ketchum is my first artist interview. We meet backstage in his dressing room at the Bradley Center. I admit to Hal that he is my first interview and I'm nervous. "I'll be gentle with you," Hal says. He is and we have a great interview. For the rest of his life, every time I see Hal, he says, "Remember, Tamara, I was your first."

David Ball sings "Thinkin' Problem" in our conference room. Suzy Bogguss comes over when she plays West Allis Western Days. I interview George Strait on his bus backstage at the Wisconsin State Fair, Alan Jackson in his dressing room at the Bradley Center arena, Tanya Tucker at Summerfest, and Vince Gill at the Riverside Theater. David Lee Murphy accompanies us to the Brewers Opening Day, and songwriter Marc Beeson shows up to go to the state fair with us. Reba McEntire allows us to photograph her, with our music director, Mitch Morgan, for the cover of my magazine. James House plays a free listener appreciation concert. Billy Dean headlines our annual Country Fest, also a free concert. Many artists come to play our Child Abuse Prevention Fund benefit shows. Artists call the station constantly to thank us for supporting them.

Country radio dominates the mainstream country music business.

CHAPTER THREE

RADIO, RECORDS, AND THE FLEDGLING AMERICANA MUSIC SCENE

Radio and record labels make interesting bedfellows. From the radio side, the *music* is programming but the *advertising dollars* drive everything. Radio is in the advertising business more than the music business. Everything hinges on ratings. Good ratings mean more money for advertising and more profits. The goal of the station is not to break new artists or to sell recorded music; it is to keep listeners listening longer so the station can sell advertising.

On the other hand, the record label promotion people are hired to get radio airplay to sell records. If it works out that singles are hits and the radio station has good ratings and the label sells records, then everybody wins. Nothing sells records like radio play, especially before the dawn of digital music, YouTube, and social media. Therefore, record company promotion departments spend a lot of time and money courting reporting radio stations.

Rodney Crowell enjoyed enormous success on country radio in the late 1970s and 1980s. His 1978 debut, *Ain't Living Long Like This*, produced by Brian Ahern, showcases Rodney's extraordinary songwriting chops and his singular voice—the man knows how to vocally deliver a song with honesty and emotion. The album includes the now-classic Crowell songs "Leaving Louisiana in the Broad Daylight," "Voila, an American Dream," and "I Ain't Living Long Like This." The last song was written largely from a jail cell in California after Rodney was picked up for forty-seven leash law violations.

"I lived in Hermosa Beach, about three blocks from the ocean," Rodney says. "I had a dog named Banjo. Everybody knew Banjo. This was no ordinary dog. I was actually his pet. I mean at Bishop's Pub in Nashville, I had a car and when I would get distracted—I would meet a girl and go off with a girl for a night or two and leave my car. Banjo would get up on the roof of the car and cross his legs and wait patiently for me to come back. When I came back, I'd go, 'Banjo, I'm so sorry.' I'd get him water and food. He indulged me that way, so I owed him a lot. When we moved to California, I refused to put Banjo on a leash. I expected the law enforcement people there to understand. First time I got a leash law violation, they came around and I said, 'You don't understand. This dog does not belong on a leash.' He ran free in Hillsboro Village in Nashville and in Austin, Texas. I didn't neuter him or anything like that. I wasn't going to do it. So one day I was sitting at this old desk I had in the living room in Hermosa Beach working on a song. I had this riff going and some kind of Texas boogie thing that I was going on about, 'Ain't that a gone Texas boogie that's going on with me,' or something like this. When I was in high school playing in a football team, we would go drink beer after practice. Out of boredom, we would go around and pull up stop signs; get drunk and just pull up stop signs. The cops caught us doing it and he pulled his gun and he says, 'If you make one move, you're a dead man,' to all of us. I remember that line, which is in the song. I was tinkering with it and lo and behold, the police came with a warrant to arrest me for forty-seven leash law violations. I had the first two verses nailed when they arrested me. I told my wife at the time, Muffin, to take her time coming to get me out because I wanted to work on this song. I wrote the last verse literally in jail."

The rock band Foghat, country singers Gary Stewart and Waylon Jennings, Jerry Jeff Walker, and Rodney's good friend Emmylou Harris all cut "I Ain't Living Long Like This."

Rodney's following albums were filled with radio hits, sometimes with Rodney singing them and sometimes with other artists recording them. In 1982, Bob Segar and the Silver Bullet Band recorded Rodney's

"Shame on the Moon" for their album *The Distance*. "I haven't played 'Shame on the Moon' live since Bob cut it," Rodney says. "My version of it is anemic compared to his. That's his song now. I'll collect the songwriting royalties but it's his song and he's earned it."

Country singer Crystal Gayle took "'Til I Gain Control Again" to number one in 1982. Lee Ann Womack clocked in at number four on the radio chart with "Ashes by Now" in 2000.

Rodney's 1988 album *Diamonds and Dirt* yielded five chart-topping hits and put Rodney on the country music map. "It's Such a Small World" is a duet with Rodney's then-wife Rosanne Cash. His song cowritten with Guy Clark, "She's Crazy for Leaving," also shot to number one along with "Crazy Baby," "After All This Time," and "I Couldn't Leave You If I Tried."

By the 1990s Rodney is considered too left of center, what we now call Americana. I learn this because Mitch throws Rodney's CD *Jewel of the South* directly into the pile on the floor the moment it arrives on his desk. "You didn't even listen to it," I say. "I don't have to," Mitch says. "It's Rodney Crowell. We won't play this." I pick up the CD and put it on. I love it. *Love* it. Immediately. I know to my bones that "Please Remember Me" is a hit song. I take the song to our program director Kerry and play it for anyone who is willing to listen. Everyone at the station likes the song but there is no way Rodney's recording of "Please Remember Me" is getting airplay on WMIL. I spend weeks trying to convince Mitch and Kerry to play the song. It's an inside joke at the station that if I like something, it is *not* a hit record. My left-of-center tastes are not compatible with country radio. (Later, in 1999, Tim McGraw records the song and takes it to number one on the *Billboard* chart for five straight weeks. I knew it was a hit.)

During the Sundance years, two key artists foreshadow my future life in Nashville: Shawn Camp, a new artist on Warner Brothers Records, and Raul Malo of the Mavericks, a band signed to MCA Records. Country radio gives scant attention to Shawn Camp's "Fallin' Never Felt So Good" and "Confessin' My Love" from his 1993 debut self-titled album. Both songs peak at number thirty-nine on the *Billboard* chart. The Mavericks have better luck with "What a Crying Shame," "There Goes My Heart," and "O What a Thrill" from the 1994 album *What a Crying Shame*, although none of the singles crack the top ten.

Shawn and I meet at the Wisconsin State Fair in August 1994. It is day ten and the final day of the fair. WMIL broadcasts remotely at every summer festival and fair in the Milwaukee area. Pure exhaustion sets in by the time the state fair closes in mid-August. We draw straws to decide who gets stuck at the final night of the fair with the young artist. I draw the short straw. It's the best contest I ever lost because it leads me to Shawn. More than thirty years later, we remain dear friends and have collaborated on many beautiful music projects.

I meet Raul Malo earlier in 1994 at Whiskey River nightclub in Chicago. Raul is the lead singer and songwriter with the Mavericks. Rob Ellis, promotion man for MCA Records, invites me to the show and introduces me to the band. Raul and I hit it off and from that moment on, I show up every time the Mavs played in Milwaukee or Chicago. One late night after a show in Milwaukee, after the bar closes and we have nowhere else to drink, Raul and I end up at Ma Fisher's diner on Milwaukee's east side. At 3:00 a.m., over toast and eggs and a lingering wine buzz, Raul says, "Tamara, you need to move to Nashville."

"Why?" I ask. "I've got a great gig here."

Raul responds, "Because you are too creative to work in radio and I think you'd dig Nashville."

"What would I do?"

"Anything you want," he says.

As I am considering my next move in Milwaukee, a hardy group of music lovers in Nashville, Austin, San Francisco, Los Angeles, Boston, Chicago, and Seattle band together, perhaps unknowingly, to create a new business model, one that puts the art before commerce. A paradigm emerges that eventually helps thousands of artists build businesses outside the major label system. The focus is to connect artists with music lovers without the burden of spending millions of promotion dollars at mainstream radio. Americana, alt-country, cosmic American music, cosmic cowboy, country rock, new grass, singer-songwriter, outlaw country, progressive country—whatever people call it, artists and executives come together to build a new community and support system.

The unquestioned leaders of the movement to start an Americana radio chart are California radio programmer and music enthusiast Rob Bleetstein and record label promotion men Jon Grimson and Brad Paul.

Many years before this trio launches the current Americana movement, there is talk in the business about starting a name for this music genre. In the 1970s the term *progressive country* was in vogue in some regions. Austin's KOKE-FM took up the mantle for progressive country. Texan Michael Martin Murphey called it "cosmic cowboy music." After Willie Nelson, Waylon Jennings, Jessi Colter, and Tompall Glaser sold more than a million copies of the compilation album Wanted! The Outlaws, the music was tagged "outlaw music," and country artists including Johnny Cash, Kris Kristofferson, Hank Williams Jr., David Allen Coe, and Billy Joe Shaver were folded into the outlaw mix. Progressive country, outlaw, cosmic cowboy...none of them had the support of a radio format, a record store category, a publicity angle, or a group of industry professionals working on behalf of the genre.

Kevin Welch started his career signed to the country division of Warner Brothers Records in Nashville. Warner tried to break Welch at mainstream country, but it just did not work.

"As artists, we all ran into this thing where if you said you played country music and lived in Nashville, people pegged you with whatever they were hearing on the radio, like Kenny Rogers and all that stuff," Welch says. "I was having a conversation about this with Mark Germino in the late seventies. Mark said, 'You know what we need? We need another name for what we do. We need something to separate us from country radio.' I thought his logic was spot on. Years later, I was heading to Montreux, Switzerland, with Bob Saporiti. Bob was an exec at Warner Brothers and a really interesting guy. Anyway, we're on the flight to Montreux to play the Montreux Jazz Festival with Joe [Ely], Butch [Hancock], Jimmie Dale [Gilmore], and [Jim] Lauderdale, and the Texas Tornados. On the flight, I told Saporiti the story about the conversation I'd had so long ago with Germino. He sat there for a minute and he said, 'Why don't you call it Western Beat?' We get to Montreux and Claude Nobs, the promoter of the festival, came to us and he said, 'Is there anything else

I can call you? If I say country music, they're going to be throwing tomatoes.' He'd had a really rough experience a couple of years prior to this where he had decided that he wanted to try having country music at the Montreux Jazz Festival. The booking agents sent the Oakridge Boys and Barbara Mandrell, and it did not work with that crowd at all. Claude took a ton of shit for this."

Welch called a meeting with the other artists to discuss Claude's dilemma.

"We met in this little sidewalk café on the main street there in Montreux to discuss it. I said, 'Coincidentally, Saporiti suggested Western Beat the other day when we were talking about this.'"

The artists agreed to use the Western Beat moniker at Montreux. "We told the European music press that back home in the United States, everybody called our kind of music Western Beat," Kevin says. "Montreux is a beloved institution of a festival so word got around."

The Western Beat label didn't stick as a genre name, but after asking permission from the other artists who played Montreux, Welch named his 1991 album *Western Beat*.

Jon Grimson works with Welch at Warner Brothers Nashville as the promotion manager for progressive music. From his view inside the label, he also sees a need for a new brand of country outside of the conventional.

"Warner signed Take 6, and right out of the box had a gold record," Grimson recalls. "They're one of those groups that didn't fit anybody's format. They're a black gospel, jazz, vocal group. We also signed outliers like Beth Nielsen Chapman, Maura O'Connell, Bela Fleck and the Flecktones, Tish Hinojosa, Kevin Welch, Shawn Camp, Jim Lauderdale, and Dwight Yoakam. Dwight was played on country radio but he was hip and cool and it was my mission to get him played on Triple A [Adult Album Alternative]. We were promoting Kevin Welch and Shawn Camp to country radio, but it wasn't working."

Iris Dement and Uncle Tupelo sign to the rock division in Warner's Burbank office. The Burbank staff enlists Grimson for help at Triple A radio. Grimson gets traction with those artists, and with Native American artist Bill Miller, who is chosen by pop star Tori Amos to open her concerts.

"Every time something like that would happen, we seized the moment and jumped on it with both feet to take advantage," Grimson says. "We'd take Bill into radio stations while he's out on the road with Tori to open that door."

Out in Boston, Brad Paul moves from working at the Emerson College radio station to a job with independent Rounder Records fresh after graduation.

"I was very active with my college radio station, WERS, right out of the gate when I was a freshman," Paul says. "We started a morning show called *The Coffeehouse* in 1980. We played a mix of roots music and cast a pretty broad net. It's ostensibly a folk channel, but from the very beginning, we played country blues, Delta blues, Cajun and Zydeco and Appalachian old-time music. It was a heady time for new acoustic music. Jerry Douglas, Bela Fleck, Mark O'Connor, David Grisman, and Tony Rice are all exploring new themes and ideas with what was traditionally bluegrass instruments, taking it to a whole new range of sounds and ideas and arrangements. I was the first person in the Boston market to play Nanci Griffith, to play Shawn Colvin and Suzanne Vega and John Gorka and Patty Larkin, and the list goes on of all those great songwriters that were just coming up at the time in the early eighties."

By the time Paul graduated from Emerson, the show was intertwined with the vibrant folk scene in Boston that had given birth to Joan Baez, Bob Dylan, and Tom Rush in the 1960s. The 1980s rebirth, in part thanks to WERS, got attention from the folks at Rounder Records. They hired Paul in radio promotion, where he worked with Alison Krauss, Tony Rice, Del McCoury, the Johnson Mountain Boys, the Cajun band BeauSoleil, and a host of other roots music artists.

"My time at Rounder coincided with the rise of roots music around the country," Paul says. "In addition to its own artists, Rounder was a distributor for more than three hundred roots music labels. Artists made great records, and radio stations played them—WERS in Boston, KPIG in Santa Cruz, WCBE in Columbus, Ohio, along with WFPK, WXPN, WFUV, KDNK, KBCS, KUTX, KEXP—but the stations were not being surveyed. There was no chart for this music. Triple A started in the late 1980s, but it was not covering all of this great roots stuff."

Grimson and Paul groused to each other about country and Triple A stations not playing enough roots music. Grimson had the same conversations with Rob Bleetstein, a radio friend in San Francisco.

In the mid-1980s, Bleetstein started his career as music director at KHIP radio in Hollister, California.

"When I first moved to California, I knew about this station KFAT in Gilroy, California, near Santa Cruz, south of San Jose, but they had a signal that you could get in Mill Valley near San Francisco and you could get it past Salinas," Bleetstein says. "It was these renegade disc jockeys smoking dope and playing George Jones, Bob Wills, Eric Clapton, and the Grateful Dead all at the same time. It wasn't just a radio station, it was a lifestyle. It was popular with artists, too. Rodney [Crowell] and Rosanne [Cash]. Emmylou stopped in when Tony Brown was in her band, they'd be on their knees pulling out records and DJ-ing. It was a real thing. When I was in college doing radio at San Jose State, KFAT was my thing. Just when I moved to Santa Cruz, living the KFAT lifestyle after I finished college, KFAT goes off the air. In 1985 these DJs reemerged at KHIP in Hollister, which is the next town over from Gilroy. If you can't be FAT you can be HIP. I drove down there the first day and said, 'I am FAT and I'm not leaving here until I have job. I just got a degree in radio and I live this music.' I started doing overnights and working in the office, which was basically rolling people's joints. Within a month of that I saw Dwight Yoakam open for Los Lobos in Santa Cruz and I walk up to him after his set and say, 'You are fuckin' it, man. We've got this radio station down the road and you've got to come by.' Dwight wasn't even signed to Warner Bros yet. I became a music director within weeks and helped educate all these KFAT DJs on what was new and hip out there."

KHIP didn't last, but Bleetstein was not about to give up his musical lifestyle. In the summer of 1994, after spending time working on the road with Texas honky-tonker Robert Earl Keen, Bleetstein attended a party with a group from the radio trade magazine the *Gavin Report*. Naturally, they discussed the current state of radio and lack of airplay for roots music artists.

"I went home after that party and I sat down at my computer and thought about what needed to happen," Bleetstein says. "I made a list of all these people who couldn't break at Triple A or country. There was no room for Junior Brown, there was no room for Emmylou Harris. Johnny Cash was dropped from country. They wouldn't play Waylon and Willie anymore. I thought we should bring in the legends, bluegrass, folk, hardcore country, alternative country, we just had to know how to make it work together. Here's this list of artists, they tour successfully, the press loves them, they sell records, and they have fan bases. Radio is the black sheep in this family. We have two formats [country and Triple A] that won't give an inch and we need a new format."

At the same time, on July 4, 1994, in Los Angeles, Billy Block started the *Western Beat Radio Hour* at KIEV 870 AM. His playlist included Joe Ely, Emmylou Harris, Jim Lauderdale, Jimmie Dale Gilmore, Iris Dement, Kevin Welch, Guy Clark, Duane Jarvis, Lucinda Williams, Los Lobos, the Mavericks, and other artists that are now considered Americana pioneers. In a press release at the time, Block said, "It is very important that the people of Los Angeles realize there is an incredible wealth of talent here that is not being heard. The music scene in the coffeehouses and honky-tonks from Hollywood to the Inland Empire are bringing us an exciting new breed of troubadour. *Western Beat Radio* is providing a musical home for the artists who are creating wonderful musical hybrids combining elements of country, rock, folk and blues that don't fit on tightly formatted radio stations. We are creating a music family and building a musical community, on the radio."

While Block used the Western Beat moniker, Jon Grimson coined the term Americana for the new format at *Gavin*.

"I wanted it to be a name that wouldn't suck in some way that artists would hate it, that would cover a broader spectrum," Grimson says. "Most artists don't like labels. They don't want to be pigeonholed. Yet, I felt like they were suffering because they had no radio home, no record space on the shelves, no one advocating for them. The *Gavin* Americana chart was a place to start."

"My initial pitch in my first meeting with the *Gavin* brass was the 'Crucial Country' chart, words I borrowed with permission from Peter Rowan," Bleetstein says. "But that got shot down immediately as it pretty much deems commercial country not crucial and *Gavin* was dependent on mainstream's ad dollars. In September of '94 when this was going down, we were hell bent on not using the term *alternative country*, mainly due to the proliferation of the alternative format and the overuse of the word *alternative*. When Jon first pitched Americana I had mixed feelings, but KHIP used the Blasters song 'American Music' as a key promo, and when I thought about what Americana meant in terms of music, it basically meant nothing, so that was our window to grab it and make it our own."

"*Gavin* was always about music discovery, breaking new music and being on top of new trends in radio," Brad Paul says. "We had a meeting with *Gavin* and I told them Rounder would support them with advertising dollars if there is a national platform, some kind of a chart, that shows that these artists have a home and are getting airplay."

Thanks to the cooperation, innovation, and creative effort of Rob Bleetstein, Jon Grimson, Brad Paul, and leaders at the *Gavin Report*, the new Americana music radio chart debuts in 1995, with Bleetstein on board as editor.

The *Gavin Report* publishes the first Americana Music Chart on January 20, 1995. Nanci Griffith, Mary Chapin Carpenter, Nick Lowe, Robert Earl Keen, Lyle Lovett, the Mavericks, and Jim Lauderdale are in the top ten. The number one album on the chart is *Tulare Dust: A Songwriters' Tribute to Merle Haggard*, which includes tracks by Iris Dement, Rosie Flores, Dwight Yoakam, Robert Earl Keen, Joe Ely, Lucinda Williams, Billy Joe Shaver, Dave Alvin, John Doe, and others. From WGBH in Boston and World Café in Philadelphia, to KPFK in Los Angeles and KNEW in San Francisco, to KPFT in Houston, Texas, to KTOO in Juneau, Alaska, more than forty-five scrappy radio stations and *Gavin* head into a new frontier to kick-start the new Americana genre.

What is Americana? That question is like asking, What is rock and roll? You know it when you hear it. Americana is American roots music. Singer-songwriter, alternative country, progressive country, folk, cosmic cowboy, cowpunk, bluegrass, new grass, blues, jazz. It's a big tent. Americana music is artist driven—music made by songwriters and musicians who write, sing, and perform their own songs. It is separate from the major label hit-making machine (not that there is anything wrong with that).

In the mid-1990s, hopes are high for the new Americana genre. In Nashville, artists Kevin Welch, Kieran Kane, Mike Henderson, Tammy Rogers, and Harry Stinson launch Dead Reckoning Records, an indie label, to release their own records so they will not be at the mercy of upheavals at a major label. Around the same time, musicians Alison Brown and Garry West start the roots label Compass Records, specializing in bluegrass and new grass. Bloodshot Records opens in Chicago, championing what they call "the good stuff nestled in the dark, nebulous cracks where punk, country, soul, pop, bluegrass, blues and rock mix and mingle and mutate." In North Carolina, Barry Poss's Sugar Hill Records continues to sign interesting folk musicians, bluegrass artists, and singer-songwriters including Guy Clark, Townes Van Zandt, Peter Rowan, Terry Allen, New Grass Revival, and Jesse Winchester. In Austin, partners Robert Earl Keen, Waterloo Record Store owner John Kunz, and Heinz Geissler own Watermelon Records (named after Guy Clark's song "Watermelon Dream"), and release critically acclaimed work by Alejandro Escovedo, the Austin Lounge Lizards, the Derailers, Tish Hinojosa, and more. The philosophy of Redhouse Records in St. Paul, Minnesota, is to provide a home for singer-songwriters and folk, blues, and instrumental artists to make records in total freedom, without interference from "mogul types" looking for the next hit single.

Americana music maven Shilah Morrow's roots go back to Gram Parsons. "Mom was an actress and a singer and knew Gram Parsons," Shilah says. "Polly, Gram's daughter, and I used to twirl around the floor at the Troubadour, and the Coral in Topanga Canyon, and the Palomino, when we were three years old. Gram died when we were five. My mom was in Dickey Betts's wedding when I was seven. I would spend time on the road with the Allman Brothers. I was around a lot and so I was raised by artists and musicians. But I didn't want to be a performer. I wanted to be on the other side. I worked at record stores. Then I got my job at WEA [Warner Elektra Atlanta Records' distribution arm] when I was eighteen, packing and shipping records from the warehouse in LA. I went to sound engineering school at the same time."

Shilah moved up the ranks at WEA and started working closely with artists. "I started working with Jim Lauderdale on his *Pretty Close to the*

Truth record. Dusty Wakeman produced it and Buddy Miller plays guitar on it. They made it out in Joshua Tree. I was absolutely smitten. Then I was working with a band called the Screamin' Cheetah Wheelies, which Mike Ferris fronted. I lost my mind over this band. Lucinda Williams's record was coming out on Chameleon, I remember her coming in and playing in the office. That was the music that was speaking to me."

In 1995, Shilah went to New York as the head of marketing for a division of Atlantic Records called TAG (the Atlantic Group) and worked with the Bottle Rockets. "All roads lead back to Lauderdale," Shilah says. "It's Lauderdale and the Bottle Rockets. I was absolutely in love. I did not like living in New York and I would spend as much time on the road with the Bottle Rockets as humanly possible. They were touring with Wilco back then. We wanted the Bottle Rockets to have a jukebox hit, there was one trade magazine that had a jukebox chart, so I made a phone call to *Coin Op* magazine, which covered jukeboxes, pinball machines, and anything that was coin operated. Jeremy Tepper was the editor and he was DJ Rig Rocker. We met up on the Lower East Side, and I said, 'I want to make a seven-inch single for this band the Bottle Rockets.' Jeremy had a label called Diesel Only Records and he said, 'I'll license the Bottle Rockets.' We made a single with the Bottle Rockets' 'Radar Gun' on one side and Junior Brown's 'Highway Patrol' on the other." The fabulous and irreplaceable Jeremy Tepper, my dear friend, would move on to a program director job at Sirius Satellite Radio, running the Outlaw Country and Willie Nelson channels from the early 2000s until his untimely death in 2024.

Back in Milwaukee, I consider Raul Malo's advice about moving to Nashville. In some ways I have outgrown my radio gig. I feel restless to create something new, but am I willing to give up the great thing I've got going at Sundance? I love the work and the people, who are like family to me. It is an honor to be a Sundancer. What waits on the other side of this?

I ask Brian for his advice. Here's another thing about Brian Ongaro. I run a successful department at his radio station that helps the bottom line. I've been promoted and promoted again. I know I am valued. Many people may not feel comfortable telling their boss they are thinking about leaving. But I trust Brian with all my heart. I know he will always have my back. Brian is supportive and offers to introduce me to Nashville executives, to help me find a job if I want to move on. He says that he'll miss me but does not want to hold me back.

Rising country artist Terri Clark and her manager Woody Bowles come to Milwaukee for a station visit in July 1995. Terri is promoting her first single, "Better Things to Do." Visiting WMIL and other reporting stations is part of the job. Terri's manager wines and dines us. After several hours of hanging out, I give Terri and Woody a ride to their hotel. I mention that I was in Nashville the previous week looking for a job. "Oh yeah? What do you want to do in Nashville?" Woody asks. "I want to work in the music business," I say. By the time we get to the hotel, Woody has offered me a job at his management company. See the kind of doors working for a reporting radio station opens? I am terrified to move to Nashville. I'm thirty-four years old and have been around the same people my entire life until my radio job. I do not travel much outside Wisconsin. I am not worldly. I'm a single mom. My family and friends are all here in Wisconsin. There are many reasons not to leave. But I choose to leave anyhow.

On July 7, 1995, Brian writes a memo to Team Sundance: "After pursuing her dream to work in Nashville, Tamara has made the decision to go for it. She has decided to move to Nashville next month. Tamara has done a fabulous job as the editor of our magazines and heading up our databases and we're going to miss her dearly. I know you'll join me in wishing her all the best in Music City."

Over the next couple of weeks, I train my replacement at WMIL and WOKY, pack up my apartment, and say goodbye to friends and family. On my last day at the station, my friend LaVonne takes me out to her car and plays Michael W. Smith's song "Friends."

Packing up the dreams God planted
In the fertile soil of you
I can't believe the hopes He's granted
Means a chapter of your life is through
But we'll keep you close as always

*It won't even seem you've gone
'Cause our hearts in big and small ways
Will keep the love that keeps as strong
And friends are friends forever.*

We hug each other and bawl our eyes out. LaVonne slips me a hundred-dollar bill. I resist her generosity but she insists I will need the pocket money. In this moment, holding on to LaVonne, I wonder if I am making the biggest mistake of my life.

CHAPTER FOUR

MUSIC CITY, USA

I pull into Nashville on August 1, 1995. I'm terrified and excited. I can't get into my apartment for several weeks, so I move in temporarily with my friend Joya Caryl, a Wisconsin native who works for Mavericks manager Frank Callari. John Leal, who first introduced me to the Mavericks, works for Callari now, too. Joya introduces me to Lisa Jenkins, another manager in Callari's office. To this day, Lisa remains one of my best friends.

Nashville is extraordinary. Country music is the hottest thing going and the Americana underground is infiltrating many country institutions. It is impossible to overstate what a pivotal year 1995 is for the Americana music community.

Young people stream into Music City from all over the country, hanging their hopes and dreams on a career as an artist or to work in the music business. It is an exhilarating time. Record sales thrive and the labels are rolling in dough. So are publishers, booking agents, managers, radio, magazines, and all the ancillary businesses surrounding music. Parties on Music Row pop up several times a week—album release parties, gold and platinum record celebrations, new artist luncheons, and showcases. Business is done over leisurely lunches and at the music clubs every night. My first friends are publicists. Sandy Neese, Kim Fowler, and Lisa Wahnish at Mercury Records, which is Terri Clark's label. Jules Wortman at MCA. Susan Niles at Warner Brothers, Wendy Pearl at Epic, and indie publicists Ronna Rubin, Ellen Pryor, Liz Thiels, Alison Auerbach, Erin Morris, Lisa Shively, and Kay Clary.

One of the first people I meet in Nashville is Billy Block. Billy and his wife, Jill, moved to Nashville from Los Angeles. They had been a big part of the Palomino Club scene in LA and brought that vibe to Nashville in the form of Billy Block's Western Beat at the Sutler every Tuesday night. It is ground zero for Americana music lovers. I see some of my favorite songwriters and musicians on those Tuesday nights. Kevin Welch, Kieran Kane, Rosie Flores, Jim Lauderdale, Buddy Miller, Duane Jarvis. Billy Block's Western Beat artists are the core of the roots music scene in Nashville.

Billy's widow, Jill Block White, remembers falling in love with Billy in 1991 at the Ronnie Mack Barn Dance scene at the Palomino night club in Los Angeles.

"I walked into the Palomino and Billy was playing drums and Ronnie Mack was up there, too. All these great artists played the Palomino—Jeffrey Steele, Marty Stuart, Jim Lauderdale, James Intveld, Rosie Flores, Duane Jarvis, Delbert McClinton…the whole gang," Jill says. "The whole Palomino thing was such a blast. I got to know Billy there and it was a really amazing time. Being part of the whole Ronnie Mack Barn Dance scene was really fun. Billy was playing drums for all these people at the Palomino and that's when he started Western Beat at Highland Grounds in 1991. Billy was playing drums for Jeffrey Steele and Jim Lauderdale and Lucinda Williams, and nobody was paying attention to them as songwriters. They would have their great crowds at the Palomino but there wasn't this crossover to commercial success and that was always Billy's goal.

"The Palomino and Western Beat were very synergetic. Artists were touring through the Palomino and Billy was a house drummer there, and he started developing really nice relationships with people in Nashville. The California country scene was so strong then, but there was this weird pull from Nashville. We'd go to Nashville for business because Billy was the LA writer for *Music Row* magazine. We'd see Lucinda Williams driving around in a Range Rover and we're still back in LA in our beat-up old trucks just trying to survive every day. We're like, *Look at that, Lucinda's doing really well here, isn't that great?* People had houses and they'd go to their kids' baseball games. We thought, *That looks like fun; maybe we should move to Nashville.*"

The Blocks moved to Nashville in January 1995. Right from the start, Billy was playing with Walter Hyatt, of the famous Uncle Walt's Band, at the Sutler on Eighth Avenue South on Monday nights. Hyatt had formed Uncle Walt's Band with his friends David Ball and Champ Hood in Spartanburg, South Carolina, in the 1970s. The band broke up for a time and Hyatt played and recorded with his band the Contenders, with Champ Hood and Nashville musicians Steve Runkle, Tommy Goldsmith, and Jimbeau Walsh. In 1978, Uncle Walt's Band reunited and released three albums on the Austin, Texas, independent label Lespedeza Record Company. In 1990, Hyatt became the first vocalist for MCA's Master Series label. Lyle Lovett produced Hyatt's first solo MCA album, *King Tears*. Lovett was a fan of Uncle Walt's Band. Hyatt opened some shows for Lovett for a time and then released his second solo album, *Music Town*, on Sugar Hill Records in 1993. There is no doubt Walter Hyatt was already an Americana star when Billy Block started playing drums with him on Monday nights at the Sutler in 1995.

"It was this groovy little scene at the Sutler with Allison Moorer and all that gang," Jill says. "Billy wanted to create something here so he could stay home, play the drums, and use his personality—he loved to do radio and TV and stuff. That's when he got Ronnie Mack's blessing to start the Western Beat Barn Dance, and we started it at the Sutler on Tuesday nights."

Billy's sister Nancy Block helped get Western Beat on the air at Nashville's Triple A station Lightning 100. Nancy helped Billy put together a proposal and they pitched it to Lightning 100. Nancy had music business experience working with Bill Young Productions in the Blocks' hometown of Houston, Texas.

"The Sutler was packed every week," Jill says. "John Cowan, Sam Bush, all those amazing talented guys that couldn't get on the radio, this was a way to get some radio play.

"People were sitting on the floor it was so crowded. We got one band offstage, and the next band would jump on. Nobody ever had a sound check. It was just back to back, live on the radio. It was exciting and fun. Billy's motto at the time was anything but mainstream country was welcome on his show. The roots people like BR549, Duane Jarvis, Dale

Watson, Kevin Gordon, the Delevantes, Jim Lauderdale, Buddy Miller, Rosie Flores, Joy Lynn White. We couldn't afford to pay anybody anything. We would charge five dollars at the door for eighteen years. The only way we made money was off of getting sponsors for us to try to pay our bills and to hire people and to produce the shows."

I spend every Tuesday night at Western Beat at the Sutler. Other nights I see Keith Urban and the Ranch at Pub of Love, Jim Lauderdale at 12th and Porter, the Mavericks at Ace of Clubs, the Delevantes at Exit In, Joe Ely at 328 Performance Hall, BR549 at Robert's Western World, and every good songwriter in town at the Bluebird Café. Just like I was in my radio job, I am captivated by the artists we now call Americana. I'm out almost every night to see live music. My friends and I are young, on fire, and in love with Americana music.

Everyone, including me, goes to Robert's on Lower Broadway for BR549 shows. It is the hottest ticket in town. People are lined up around the block to get into the joint, including band members from the Mavericks, songwriter Steve Earle, music executive Barry Coburn (who became BR549's manager), and producer Paul Kennerly. By the time I get to town, BR549 has signed with Arista Records and is about to release the EP *Live at Robert's*.

BR549 cofounder Chuck Mead moved from Lawrence, Kansas, to Nashville in 1993 because he wanted a gig at Tootsie's Orchid Lounge. Tootsie Bess opened the bar across the alley from the Ryman Auditorium in 1960. Willie Nelson, Kris Kristofferson, Waylon Jennings, Roger Miller, and Patsy Cline drank there. Dolly Parton and Loretta Lynn sang for the Tootsie's crowd, and the bar was also a filming location for *Coal Miner's Daughter*, the story of Loretta's journey from her early teen years to her rise as a country artist.

"There wasn't anything going on downtown then," Mead says. "I was in a band, sort of a roots-rock-slash-country band, which would have been totally Americana in the eighties, called Homestead Grays. Every time we came through Nashville, we'd go down Lower Broadway, because that's where Faron Young and Willie Nelson and Roger Miller and all those guys from the Opry hung out at Tootsie's Orchid Lounge. And there's nothing going on there and it should be a happenin' strip. So, it was my goal to get a job at Tootsie's Orchid Lounge singing in the window. And I did."

As Chuck Mead takes over Tootsie's, musician Gary Bennett fronts a band that plays a couple of doors down at Robert's Western Wear.

"Robert Moore put a bar in there in that Western wear store to compete with Tootsie's. It wasn't wall-to-wall bars down on Broadway like it is now," Mead says. "I was playing several nights down at Tootsie's, which was really the best job on the street then. Gary was playing in the front window of Robert's."

Gary is down a guitar player one day and asks Mead to play and sing with him at Robert's.

"It was great. I mean, like right off the bat, we were singing harmony like we'd been singing forever together," Mead says. "BR549 happened real organically. I was still in a band with my buddy Shaw Wilson from Lawrence, we were doing kind of hillbilly rockabilly shit. I called Shaw, because he was still back up in Lawrence, and said come down for the summer and check it out. Because every freak in the world comes through the doors of this place and you're going to love it."

"Hawk'" Shaw Wilson, "Smilin'" Jay McDowell, and Don Herron join Chuck Mead and Gary Bennett in the band. They take the name BR549 from a Junior Samples comedy sketch on the television show *Hee Haw*.

"We got signed because Timothy White put us on the cover of *Billboard* in the summer of 1995," Mead says. "A few labels came calling but we ended up at the right place with Arista. Tim DuBois [label head] understood what we were trying to do. We played a tour with the Black Crowes, we played a line of shows with Tim McGraw and Faith Hill, and then played with George Jones. We were accepted in more than just the country mainstream, although Arista was definitely going for country radio play."

BMI's Jody Williams saw New Jersey natives the Delevantes play at the New Music Seminar in New York and invited the brothers to Nashville. Bob and Mike Delevante show up in Nashville for the first time in 1988 or 1989; they don't remember the exact date. What they do remember is seeing U2's Bono play at Tootsie's Orchid Lounge their first night in Nashville.

"We pulled into town at ten o'clock at night," Bob says. "We thought we should say hello to the Ryman [Auditorium] so we pulled off the highway. It's a Sunday night and we drive all the way down Broadway. There's nothing. Sunday in Nashville. I made a U-turn and parked in front of the Tootsie's."

"Bob looked in the Tootsie's window and says, 'That looks like Bono from U2.' The stage is right by the window so we could see in," Mike says. "We went inside and sat at the bar and Bono's singing. Adam Clayton's playing bass and this older guy is playing pedal steel and they're singing 'I Still Haven't Found What I'm Looking For.' There were about ten people in Tootsie's."

"Nobody in Tootsie's seemed to know who they were," Bob says. "We are at the bar and the bartender asked if we were pickers. That was a new one. We play guitar but no one ever called us pickers."

"Then the bartender said: 'You guys are pickers; you're next,'" Mike says. "We got up and played. Our first night in Nashville, we are playing at Tootsie's and Bono is in front of us dancing with a girl to one of our songs. We played four songs and the steel player played with us."

The Delevantes moved to Music City permanently in 1993.

"We played a lot in New York and New Jersey on a club level," Bob says. "We played a lot of different shows but the business end of it was hard for us. We started finding records, like Steve Earle and Foster and Lloyd records, and seeing they were produced in Nashville. When Jody invited us to Nashville, we showed up pretty quickly. We had cassettes and played songs for a lot of people. We met Mike Porter, who coproduced the first record."

"On the first trip to Nashville, we also met Garry Tallent at a Steve Earle show," Mike says. "He came up to us because we were wearing leather jackets. He says, 'You must be from New Jersey.' That's a true story and we got to know each other. We went back to New York, kept in touch."

Although known best for his work with Bruce Springsteen, Garry Tallent produced Americana albums for Steve Forbert, including his 1988 album *Streets of This Town*, and Greg Trooper's 1992 album *Everywhere*. Tallent played bass on Robert Earl Keen's *A Bigger Piece of the Sky* in 1993 and

Gringo Honeymoon in 1994. Tallent also worked with Steve Earle on his *Copperhead Road* album.

"It was like this awakening and finding a home in Nashville," Mike Delevante says. "We felt understood musically, but also emotionally—in the way people here are so creative and collaborative. New York was great for certain things, but as far as trying to find a community of people that understood us, it just wasn't there. It was too big."

The Delevantes signed a publishing deal with Warner Chapell and a record deal with Boston's Rounder Records. They released the Garry Tallent–produced *Long About That Time* in 1995, just in time to have a hit record on the new Americana radio chart. The single "Pocketful of Diamonds" became the number one music video in Europe and Steve Earle took the Delevantes on a three-month tour of Europe to open for him.

As the Americana underground heats up in Nashville, Peter Blackstock and Grant Alden start *No Depression* magazine in Seattle. The debut issue, in the fall of 1995, adopts the tagline "The alternative country quarterly." Son Volt is on the cover. The magazine includes live concert reviews of Merle Haggard in Nashville, Steve Earle in Chicago, Shane McGowan in Minneapolis, and Johnny Cash with Mark Lanegan in Portland, Oregon. The first issue also covers the Bottle Rockets, Whiskeytown, and the Waco Brothers. The album review section, titled "Waxed," includes Emmylou Harris, Pete Anderson, Stephen Bruton, Joe Ely, Jesse Dayton, Kim Richey, Jim Lauderdale, Stacy Dean Campbell, Joan Osborne, and Southern Culture on the Skids. The first editor's note reads in part,

"By now you've heard some of the buzz words, the catch phrases everyone has tried to come up with for this 'alternative country' thing that's been picking up steam for the past couple years. Americana. Western Beat. Twangcore. Countrypolitan. Insurgent Country. Outlaw Country. Cowpunk. Grange Rock. Country Wok.

"We prefer *No Depression*. Why? Because it captures a sense of both the storied American history this music is deeply rooted in—'No Depression' is an old Carter Family song from the 1930s—and the innovative spark being applied to the form by contemporary artists—*No Depression* was the title of Uncle Tupelo's groundbreaking debut album in 1990."

"The magazine largely grew out of discussions that I was having on America Online, in what they called folders back then," Blackstock says. "I had come across a bunch of other people who were in this discussion board that was called Uncle Tupelo. When the folks who were posting there started talking about other bands besides Uncle Tupelo, the members took a vote and settled on No Depression-Alternative Country as a new name for the folder. *No Depression*, of course, is the name of Uncle Tupelo's first album. Those people were talking about all these other bands like the Jayhawks and Blue Mountain and the Bad Livers or other associated groups. I stumbled into it in September of '94, so I started posting regularly there.

"A bunch of us came down to Austin for South by Southwest in 1995. I was working one month out of the year for South by Southwest at that time, and so I was leaking out information from the inside saying, 'Hey, Wilco is going to be here. Jay Farrar's new band is going to play here.' People started getting really excited about it, and so they came to Austin. I started underhandedly trying to push No Depression along as a description for the genre. If I wrote a review of the Jayhawks record, I might mention that there was this community of people who were on this message board. I know I mentioned No Depression in the South by Southwest program guide in 1995, and this is six months before the magazine started. It was some sort of showcase that had a lot of alternative country bands on it, and so I alluded to this No Depression folder in there. I was trying to surreptitiously push the term No Depression into the lexicon in these little bits and pieces of places where I could do so."

Blackstock grew up in Austin and went to college at the University of Texas in Austin, where he discovered the singer-songwriter scene at the campus listening room the Cactus Café.

"Butch Hancock played there," Blackstock says. "Whenever Townes Van Zandt was in town, he'd play the Cactus. I don't remember how I first got so into those artists. I think probably because I had flipped over Bob Dylan at that time and then just discovered these people locally who were very renowned country and folk singer-songwriters, and I just loved what they were doing. Butch and Townes, Darden Smith, Jimmie Dale Gilmore, Joe Ely, Alejandro Escovedo. Lyle Lovett and Nanci Griffith would do surprise pop-up shows. Peter Case and Maura O'Connell crossed over in that realm. There was a show I vividly remember in 1989 when Shawn Colvin played just as her first record had come out, and she was just so happy to be back in Austin because she hadn't been back here in more than ten years. She said from the stage that it was absolutely the best show of the tour. Sure enough, three or four years later, she moved back to Austin. When I look back at how alternative country and how *No Depression* started in my head, it was very obviously the collision of two things for me personally: the Texas country and folk singer-songwriters with the college alternative-rock bands I was seeing at places like the Continental Club and Liberty Lunch. I wrote a column for the *Austin American Statesman* at that time that was a country folk column. I didn't use the term *alternative country* at the time. It certainly was well before anybody was saying Americana."

Blackstock left Austin in 1991 because he couldn't get full-time work at the *Statesman*. He moved to Seattle and within a month landed a gig at the *Seattle Post-Intelligencer* covering nightclub music just as the grunge scene in Seattle was exploding nationally. Blackstock also freelanced for a music magazine called the *Rocket*.

"Grant Alden was managing editor at the *Rocket* and that's how I got to know him," Blackstock says. "I wanted an outlet for writing that I might not be able to do for the daily, and the *Rocket* was a great place to do it. I think Grant took me on partly because most of the writers there were crazy about all of the punk indie underground stuff and I wanted to write about Jimmie Dale Gilmore and Don Walser. I was the guy to do that. Grant was the leading journalistic voice for the punk scene at that time, and he was intrigued about the stuff that I was into. Most of the things I wrote about for the *Rocket* while Grant was the managing editor were people he was only tangentially familiar with or maybe didn't know at all—a lot of this country crossover stuff and the stuff that became known as Americana. I definitely knew that stuff better than Grant in the days before we started *No Depression*. He caught up pretty quickly on that, but I think he leaned on me for the breadth of that knowledge early on. That said, Grant had incredible instincts. He was writing a seven-inch singles column for the *Rocket* and pulled a Whiskeytown record off the shelf and said, 'Hey, we ought to write about this in our new magazine,' so he knew about them before I did.

"In April, after South by Southwest 1995, Grant and I were at a Bad Livers show and he offhandedly said we should start a magazine. I went over to his house a couple days later. We started talking about it, and he said, 'Well, what should we call it?' I said, 'We should call it *No Depression*.' Over the course of that spring and summer, we lined up everything that we needed to do to actually make it happen."

In Nashville, I'm out five or six nights a week seeing Americana shows and my personal music collection is filled with Americana CDs. Yet I still work in mainstream country music.

My gig with Woody Bowles and Terri Clark is not what I expect. Although we work out of his house, Woody is unavailable most days and I cannot deal with the day-to-day management of a new artist without help. I'm as green as green can be, yet I learn on the job to decipher booking contracts; answer all inquiries from Mercury Records about Terri's schedule, preferences, and availability; and deal with the director at a music video shoot. I accompany Terri when she opens for George Strait in Indianapolis. It's a big show and, as Terri's manager, Woody should be there. I hate to disappoint Terri, but this job is not for me. In September 1995, Bill Catino hires me to work in the promotion department at Capitol Records Nashville. I am thrilled and excited to work at Capitol. It is the home of the Beatles and Frank Sinatra and a rich musical history.

The year 1995 ends on an Americana high note. *No Depression* prepares to release its second issue.

The *Gavin* Americana chart is coming up on its one-year anniversary. In his *Gavin* column, Bleetstein lists his top albums for 1995: Emmylou Harris, *Wrecking Ball*; Joe Ely, *Letter to Laredo*; Bruce Springsteen, *The Ghost of Tom Joad*; the Jayhawks, *Tomorrow the Green Grass*; Joan Osborne, *Relish*; A. J. Croce, *That's Me in the Bar*; Bob Dylan, *Unplugged*; Buddy Miller, *Your Love and Other Lies*; Mark Germino, *Rank and File*; Toni Price, *Hey*; Steve Earle, *Train a Comin'*; Greg Brown, *The Poet Game*; Son Volt, *Trace*; and various artists, *Tulare Dust*. The future of Americana music is in good hands.

CHAPTER FIVE

FINDING MY WAY

Bill Catino is the senior vice president of the promotion department at Capitol Nashville and I am his executive assistant. In addition to me, the staff includes the regional promotion directors in charge of getting Capitol artists airplay on country radio. Bill has a quick temper and a heart of gold. Sometimes I adore him, but other times he is extremely difficult. Bill is a screamer. I don't think he intends to instill fear in his staff, but he does. I'm not afraid of Bill, but I am thirty-four years old, coming from the top-notch and professional Sundance Broadcasting, and I am not a fan of his harsh management style. Working for Bill is exhausting. He rules the roost and expects everyone to fall in line and put up with him. I'm not cut out for it.

In early 1996, I spend a considerable amount of time planning showcase junkets for Capitol artist Billy Dean. We host one at the Four Seasons on Amelia Island near Jacksonville, Florida; another in Reno at Harrah's Casino; one in Washington, DC; and the final showcase at home in Nashville. I fly into each city to do a site visit before the event, work with the venue to book hotel rooms for our radio guests, and plan golf outings in Florida, gambling time in Reno, and sightseeing in DC, as well as meals, meet-and-greet time with Billy, and the musical showcases. All of the radio programmers and music directors we invite work for reporting stations, which, like my alma mater WMIL, report to *Billboard* and *Radio and Records* charts. I learn the hard way at my Capitol gig that not all radio people have the work ethic and morals of my old compadres at Sundance Broadcasting.

There is a rare snowstorm in Nashville during Billy Dean's final radio junket at the Hermitage Hotel. Flights are canceled and a handful of radio guys can't get out of town. Catino orders me to stay at the hotel and take care of them—to make sure they have room service food and drink and that everyone is comfortable. The ruthless display of boorish and disgusting behavior is appalling to me. It's still shocking to write about nearly three decades later. These blockheads stockpile liquor bottles to smuggle home in their suitcases, order enough room service food to feed half of Nashville, and act like frat boys on a bender—all on Capitol Records' expense account. And I don't know this for sure, but I bet a lot of that expense is recoupable to Billy Dean. That means that those costs are passed off to the artist and taken out of record royalties. At the same event, a pompous and extremely gross Capitol staffer tries to put his hand up my skirt. It takes me a week to wash off the ick from this one.

Another time, as part of Country Radio Seminar, Capitol hosts a M*A*S*H-themed party at the Hard Rock Café in Nashville. Catino gives me a big budget for this party, somewhere in the neighborhood of $75,000–$80,000. We blow it up big time with food and an open bar. The 440th Airborne unit from Clarksville brings in jeeps and military gear as party props. We all wear M*A*S*H costumes. Capitol artists, radio staff from all over the country, and much of Nashville's music industry show up for the party. It is the party of the week during Country Radio Seminar. A few days later, two people in our department are laid off due to budget cuts. The party budget could have covered both salaries for another year. Catino says the party money comes from a different budget. It's pretty simple to move money from one budget to another but the party took precedence over the people.

And the toughest reality to swallow? Garth Brooks (nothing against Garth personally or musically; I'm a fan) is such a big kahuna at Capitol that the other artists are penalized for it. Regularly, Catino tells his promo team to negotiate with radio and ask them to drop Suzy Bogguss or Billy Dean or Deana Carter or Lisa Brokop or George Ducas for more spins on Garth. Honestly, this is just the way the radio game is played and it is not Garth's fault. He probably has no idea this happens. And I doubt the other artists are told they will be collateral damage when they sign to Capitol.

The final straw for me and Catino comes during the early days of Trace Adkins's tenure on the label. Trace's first wife shoots him and word leaks out about it. She claims she shot Trace in self-defense because he beat her. Sitting in on conferences listening to people talk about how to spin the Trace Adkins narrative makes me sick. I work with a lot of smart and kind people at Capitol, but somewhere along the line it has become clear that having a hit artist and making money are paramount. I realize that I am not cut out to work at a major record label. Catino knows it, too. One day Bill is out of the office and calls to talk to me about invitations arriving from the printer. He is pissed that he did not have one more chance to see the proof. I hang up on him in the middle of his screaming tirade. Bill calls back immediately and I tell our promotion coordinator that I will not take the call, that Bill can come to the office and fire me. Which is exactly what happens. I walk out relieved that I never have to come back. I know in my bones that I will never work for a major record label again. I am finished with the record business.

Two jobs in one year. My confidence is shaken. Maybe Nashville is not for me. Maybe those years of working for outstanding leaders at the impeccable Sundance Broadcasting has made it impossible for me to accept anything less. Going back to Sundance is not an option. Thanks to the Telecommunications Act of 1996, which President Bill Clinton signs into law on February 8, Sundance Broadcasting is no more. The primary goal of the Telecommunications Act is to deregulate broadcasting and telecommunications markets to allow fewer but larger corporations to own and operate more media outlets. The result is a massive consolidation of media. The changes amount to a complete rollback of New Deal market regulation. And it allows Clear Channel Communications (now known as iHeart Radio) to dominate as they buy up thousands of radio companies around the country, including Sundance Broadcasting.

My only option is to move forward. After my stint at Capitol I am ready for a big change. Right or wrong, as a music lover, I care about the art and the artist, not the number of units shipped. I want to go back to covering artists and introducing them to the world. I hear through the grapevine about a senior writer position at *Country Weekly* magazine, a weekly rag available at the front checkout stand in every grocery store in America. *Country Weekly* emerges in 1994, owned by American Media, the same company that publishes the *National Enquirer*, the *Star*, and *Weekly World News*. I admit this gives me pause. But I am a single parent to a teenager and need to pay rent and buy groceries. I interview with Cliff Barr, a very British Englishman running the show for all of American Media's publications headquartered in Lantana, Florida.

In the fall of 1996, I land the gig and move into the *Country Weekly* office at 1225 Seventeenth Avenue South on Music Row in Nashville. At the time, there are only three staff writers. Joining me on the second floor are Wendy Newcomer (also new at *Country Weekly*) and veteran writer Gerry Wood. Gerry had done a long stint at *Billboard* before *Country Weekly*. The writing part of the job is easy. Formulaic writing without too much thought. We are churning out a hell of a lot of copy. It is a weekly magazine, but we run production schedules much like a daily newspaper, interviewing nonstop and getting stories in the can so we are always ahead of the game. How does one stay in the music business without being responsible for selling records or managing egos? We work in the media. Covering artists as a journalist at a national publication gives me the chance to work with artists in fun, short stints.

My photographer partner for many of my features is the late great Tim Campbell. We call ourselves the Tim and Tamara Show until Tanya Tucker renames us T-Bone and T-Bird. Tanya is our favorite artist to cover. Tanya is fun. Always. For a cover story titled "Watch Out! Tanya's Making a Fresh Start," we spend a memorable week with her at the Canyon Ranch in Tucson. At her insistence, I break Tanya out of the joint and we joyride through the Arizona desert. Tanya rides shotgun while I drive fast through the Arizona darkness until we spot a neon Circle K sign. Tanya saunters into the Circle K like she owns the place. It is empty except for two young men working there. Tanya walks to the cooler, pulls out a six pack, takes it to the cash register, and asks for a pack of Marlboros. Then she pops open a beer, lights a cig, hops up on the counter, blows a perfect smoke ring, and says, "How are you boys doing tonight?" One of them looks at her in awe and asks, "Are you Tanya Tucker?" "In the flesh," Tanya replies as she passes the beer around.

George Strait sells more magazines than any other country artist. Seriously, George on the cover sells four times as many magazines as Garth, Shania Twain, Alan Jackson, or any of the other hot country artists of the day. Which means we do everything we can to pull together cover stories on George once a month. This is tough to do considering George rarely gives interviews. Yet *Country Weekly* continues to recycle George Strait copy. Every once in a while, George's manager Erv Woolsey throws us a bone. Such is the case when Tim Campbell and I have the chance to interview and photograph George in St. Louis on February 14, 1997, at the Kiel Center. We drive five hours from Nashville and arrive at noon. The road manager tells us George will see us later. We wait around the hotel until showtime. Still no George. We go to the show. After the show, we go backstage and wait for George by his bus. George shows up about an hour after the show ends. Erv tells me I have five minutes for the interview and Tim is allowed to shoot three frames. Okay. Total of eight minutes with George. That interview gives us at least three more cover stories on George.

For one story, Hal Ketchum suggests we go fly fishing with him. Tim and I haul fishing and photo gear to Hal's house early one morning. We knock. We ring the bell. No answer. Hal eventually shows up at the door barefoot, wearing nothing but blue jeans and messy hair. A beautiful woman walks down the stairs behind him in an oversize men's shirt. Hal says, "Not today, guys, something has come up," as he smiles back at Gina (whom he later married).

On August 7, 1997, Garth Brooks headlines a show in New York's Central Park. Labeled "Garthstock" by fans, the concert is free and the biggest concert ever held in the park. More than one million fans gather in the park for the show and HBO films it for a special. Radio and the media talk incessantly about Garth being the first country artist to play Central Park. The truth is, songwriter Victoria Shaw is the first country artist to play Central Park. She opens for Garth on this hot August night. I'm there to cover it for *Country Weekly*. Victoria cowrote Garth's number one hits "The River" and "She's Every Woman," and he invited her to open the show. Victoria sings five songs from her new album, plus a medley of hits she has written for other artists. It is heady to watch her play in front of a million people, and I can't even imagine how it feels on the stage. Garth comes to see Victoria after her set. "How is it out there?" he asks. "You're going to have a ball," Victoria answers as she gives Garth a kiss.

One of my favorite parts of working at *Country Weekly* is working with the iconic Loretta Lynn. Loretta is part of my beat and I spend many weekends with her at the Grand Ole Opry. I was a teenager in the 1970s when I first laid eyes on Loretta in the flesh. Loretta's daughter Betty Sue owned the Sundown Tavern in Conover, Wisconsin, just down the road from my family's vacation home on Pioneer Lake. Loretta's tour bus pulled in next to Sundown and word got around the neighborhood before the engine had time to cool. Our parents caravanned over to have a drink and see Loretta. We teenagers played pool and observed. We had no idea how cool it was to be in the presence of the great Loretta Lynn. Fast-forward twenty years and now I'm hanging in Loretta's dressing room at the Opry listening to her tell fabulous stories. Other artists come to pay respects to Loretta and she brags that I'm one of the kids from Conover that she's known since the 1970s. Not exactly true, but I love hearing Loretta tell it her way.

Often it is fun to work for *Country Weekly*, but there is no room for anything original or thought provoking. The goal is to sell magazines to the lowest common denominator. Cliff Barr often uses "Hazel in Iowa" as our audience and gets mad at me when I suggest "Hazel in Iowa" is smarter than he thinks. I pitch a story on Emmylou Harris with the title "Emmylou Still Breaking the Rules—One Song at a Time." *Country Weekly* reluctantly lets me write it. Emmylou uses the word *serendipitous* during our interview. During a phone call, Cliff insists that I change the quote because our readers will not know what *serendipitous* means. I say, "They have dictionaries in Iowa, Cliff." He orders me to fly to Florida to meet with him about my attitude. I am summoned to Florida often for mouthing off. It always goes the same way. I sit in front of Cliff's desk while he pontificates about the ignorance of Americans in general and country music fans more specifically. I disagree and attempt to change his mind. After a few hours of that, Cliff takes me out to a nice steak dinner where we talk about the weather and our families. I stay in a beautiful hotel on the beach and fall asleep to the sound of waves crashing. The next morning I fly home. In the end, Cliff lets the Emmylou quote stand.

While I am wrangling stories at *Country Weekly*, those Americana guys Brad Paul, Jon Grimson, and Rob Bleetstein host the first Americana conference in the fall of 1997. Dubbed "In the Pines," a nod to the song of the same name on the Louvin Brothers' *Tragic Songs of Life* album, the gathering takes place at a hundred-year-old camp on Squam Lake in New Hampshire.

"I had this idea to hold it at the camp where they filmed *On Golden Pond*," Brad says. "Jon flew in from Nashville, Rob flew in from San Francisco, I took them to the camp and we all agreed it was the perfect venue. There is an old barn that had been converted into a stage that they used for talent shows during the summer camp season. There is a beautiful lodge with a big dining hall, and then individual cabins, every one of them on the water with a dock and canoe. It was the perfect environment to get everybody away from distractions. We had this vision that we needed to grow this thing so it wasn't just about radio. We looked at the International Bluegrass Music Association and the Folk Alliance model where promoters, retailers, booking agents, managers, artists, and people from all aspects of the business gathered."

Artists Emmylou Harris, Doug Sahm, Buddy and Julie Miller, the Blazers, Ricky Skaggs, and Rosie Flores fly to New Hampshire to be part of "In the Pines."

Seymour Stein, cofounder of Sire Records and vice president of Warner Brothers, also shows up at "In the Pines." It is a mark of distinction for Americana that the music business innovator is there. In the 1980s, Stein signed groundbreaking artists the Ramones, Talking Heads, the Pretenders, Madonna, the Replacements, Depeche Mode, the Smiths, the Cure, Echo and the Bunnymen, and other seminal artists in punk and rock. The Seymour Stein stamp of approval on Americana is huge.

Stein isn't the only major label record man who digs Americana music. Because the music business makes a ton of money in these days, there is room at the majors in Nashville for artists outside mainstream country.

In 1996, Nashville attorney and artist manager Ken Levitan opens Rising Tide Records, a subsidiary of Universal Music. Rising Tide signs

Americana artists Matraca Berg, Delbert McClinton, and Jack Ingram. Kathi Whitley handles business administration and creative for the new label. "That was a fun, yet short, run," Whitley says. "We had a great team. Lyndsay McDonald was Ken's personal assistant and Steve Fishell and Emory Gordy handled A&R." Rising Tide's publicist Ellen Caldwell introduces me to Kathi, the beginning of a decades-long friendship that endures to this day. For *Country Weekly*, I interview Ingram, Berg, and McClinton, continuing to push the boundaries of what defines country music with my boss, Cliff Barr.

Before his time at Rising Tide, Fishell had produced Americana records including the Mavericks' *From Hell to Paradise*, Radney Foster's *Del Rio, TX 1959* and *Labor of Love*, Bob Woodruff's *Dreams and Saturday Nights*, Rosie Flores's *Honky Tonk Reprise*, and *Mama's Hungry Eyes: A Tribute to Merle Haggard*. Fishell played steel guitar in Emmylou Harris's touring band, on many of her recordings, and on records by John Prine, Jimmie Dale Gilmore, Flaco Jimenez, Steve Goodman, and more. Emory Gordy played in Emmylou's Hot Band, on recordings with Emmylou, Guy Clark, and others. Gordy produced Patty Loveless and, in his role at Rising Tide, records by Matraca Berg, Delbert McClinton, and the Nitty Gritty Dirt Band. Fishell and Gordy's Americana cred is solid.

Mercury Records releases Lucinda Williams's seminal 1998 album *Car Wheels on a Gravel Road*. Gurf Morlix produced early recordings of *Car Wheels* in Austin. Lucinda later scrapped those sessions and worked with producers Steve Earle and Ray Kennedy in Nashville to finish the album. To date, *Car Wheels* has sold nearly nine hundred thousand copies. It won a Grammy for Best Contemporary Folk Album in 1999, was voted the Best Album of the Year in the 1998 *Village Voice*'s annual pop and jazz critics poll, and was eventually ranked number ninety-eight of the top five hundred albums of all time by *Rolling Stone*.

Tony Brown, formerly of Emmylou Harris's Hot Band and Rodney Crowell's Cherry Bombs, is now head of A&R at MCA Nashville. He produces records by Rodney Crowell, Rosanne Cash, Vince Gill, Marty Stuart, Todd Snider, Nanci Griffith, and Allison Moorer.

In the spring of 1998, MCA Nashville releases the soundtrack to the Robert Redford film *The Horse Whisperer*, tagged as "songs from and inspired by" the film. Produced by Brian Ahern (Emmylou Harris, Billy Joe Shaver, Bela Fleck, and more), *The Horse Whisperer* soundtrack is pure Americana. It features tracks by Lucinda Williams, the Flatlanders, Allison Moorer, the Mavericks, Emmylou Harris, Don Walser, Gillian Welch, Steve Earle, Dwight Yoakam, and Iris Dement.

Joe Ely hosts a party to celebrate *The Horse Whisperer* release during the South by Southwest music conference in Austin. I drive from Tennessee to Texas for the party. As the Flatlanders sing "The South Wind of Summer" in Joe's studio, my eyes open to the extraordinary Texas branch of Americana music. While in Austin, I also catch a Jack Ingram show at the fabled Stubbs Bar-B-Q outdoor stage and hear the Mavericks perform at the Austin Rodeo. Texas had intrigued me since the days when I first heard Guy Clark's mythical songs about the Lone Star State. Now I am in Austin feeling that mythology come to life. Texas seeps into my bones—and my heart. I can't even begin to imagine what will come.

CHAPTER SIX

THE FUTURE OF YOUR RECORD COLLECTION

In the January 7, 1998, issue of the *Wall Street Journal*, Craig Havighurst writes, "Under the radar guns of the Soundscan record sales counting system, a new breed of country music is emerging that's less about star-making machinery than about banjos, trains, dust, love and life. It reflects a contemporary folk music revival that's less self-conscious or politicized than that of the 1960s but pervasive nonetheless.... Today's folk and underground country scene is every bit as musically rich, historically evocative and lyrically intelligent as the best popular music of the 1960s, or the 1940s for that matter. Baby boomers, estranged rockers, grieving Grateful Dead fans, I have seen the future of your record collection, and it is called 'Americana.'"

Over at *Gavin*, veteran radio programmer Jessie Scott takes charge of the Americana chart in 1998. Scott started spinning Americana records at her first radio job as evening disc jockey at New York's WHN in 1975.

"Ed Salamon was my first boss," Jessie says. "He came over to my house for a photo shoot one day, and he pulls out Gram Parsons, the Flying Burrito Brothers, and the Byrds out of my vinyl library. We put them on my radio show. At that time, they called it progressive country in New York. I'd weave those artists in between Glen Campbell and Tanya Tucker and the Eagles and the Everly Brothers. This sonic difference was already paving the way for what was to come later. It was pretty radical, the country infusion, especially for those of us who lived in markets where country music wasn't a big thing."

Jessie and her team broadcasted live from the Lone Star Café, a townhouse turned club at Thirteenth and Fifth Avenue. The Café was the place to be. Chet Flippo from *Rolling Stone* was a regular. The crew from *Saturday Night Live*, the New York Jets, the Yankees, and bands that came down from Woodstock. "It was an Americana hang and an unbelievable scene," Jessie says. "A haze of smoke and a gaggle of bodies."

Eddie Rabbitt and the Bellamy Brothers played at the Café, but so did Texans Rusty Wier, Kinky Friedman, Delbert McClinton, Joe Ely, and Roy Orbison. "There was a very Texas mindset to it," Jessie says. "They served Texas chili. Texas was Americana early on. There are places in this country where there's a really deep, rich reverence for music. It's part of your birthright. Texas is one of those places. Texas is fertile soil for it. The dance hall tradition was a family event. You danced on your dad's shoes. The whole family shared a Sunday afternoon with music. It was part of the normal thing to do. That spawns the next generation that follows in the footsteps of all that have come before. I think that's why Texas still has such a great amount of people that make live music and a great amount of people that go out to support live music. There are very few places in the country left like that."

"Texas music is like a big old boot stomping on everything else," Craig Havighurst says. "It's so important. It's such an amazing set of influences. Texans tell tall stories. There's a mythology to being a Texan, and that lends itself to the storytelling ethos. Those older songwriters, Willie, Waylon, Kris, Guy, Townes...they found each other when they were young and cajoled each other and mentored the next generations. As soon as you had that little core of idols—now Robert Earl Keen can build a shrine to guys who were just ten to twenty years older than him. It turns a smoldering thing into a fire. It's one of the most genuine folk arts that I've ever seen. That is an extraordinary thing."

One day while sitting at my desk at *Country Weekly*, a recruiter calls to ask if I am interested in an editor position at a new magazine. My office mate and coworker Deb Barnes gets the same call. Intrigued, Deb and I both agree to interview with the new company. By the end of 1998, Deb and I work at Sussex Publishing, the new owners of Country Music magazine. Sussex also owns Spy, Mother Earth News, and Psychology Today.

Our new bosses, Jo Colman and Lawrence Rose, move us into second-floor office space in a charming brick bungalow at 7 Music Square West, the Hummingbird building, at the base of Music Row across the street from the American Society of Composers, Authors, and Publishers (ASCAP). The first editor they hire, Neil Pond, defects for Country Weekly. Deb is promoted to editor in chief, I am managing editor, Michael McCall is senior editor, and Wendy Stamberger is art director. The gig at Country Music brings me more joy than I've felt since Sundance Broadcasting. I am again surrounded by creative people who love what they do. We are enthusiastic about bringing our new magazine into the world.

Sussex leaves us alone to build the magazine we want to build. As long as we cover mainstream country music, we are free to cover anything else under the "country" umbrella. To us, that means Americana, the emerging genre we all love. Truthfully, we slip in a little bit of mainstream country but we give more real estate in the magazine to the artists we love, many that rarely or never get played on country radio.

Our first cover story is "Dixie Chicks: Why They Rule the Roost." In that first issue, we also feature Hal Ketchum, Deana Carter, and Mandy Barnett—blazing a trail away from mainstream country. We allow space for big features on Americana artists Kelly Willis, June Carter Cash, Dwight Yoakam, Mary Chapin Carpenter, Marty Stuart, Emmylou Harris, Merle Haggard, Dolly Parton, Steve Earle, and Lee Ann Womack. There simply isn't room for anyone we don't feel is worthy of our pages.

As the editor of the Country Music album review section, I put the word out to freelancers that I am looking for writers to review the best music, whether it is played on country radio or not. Some of my favorite scribes write for us during that time. Grant Alden, cofounder of No Depression magazine; Craig Havighurst, who now works for Americana radio station WMOT; Michael Streissguth, who has written books about outlaw country, Johnny Cash, Rosanne Cash, Marty Stuart, and Ricky Skaggs; Elvis expert and author Alanna Nash; Cyndi Hoelzle, one of the instigators of the Americana chart at Gavin; and country music historian Bob Oermann, who edits the Journal of Country Music insert in our magazine.

Our first issue of *Country Music* includes mostly Americana album reviews: Steve Earle and the Del McCoury Band, Jon Randall, J. D. Crowe, and Emmylou Harris, Dolly Parton, and Linda Ronstadt's *Trio II* album.

Another section of the magazine under my domain is a feature called Horizons, where I interview up-and-coming artists, often their first feature in a national magazine. Again, I focus as much as possible on Americana artists. Some titles from Horizons features include "Sibling Revelry: Bruce and Charlie Robison Delight in Their Differences"; "Soul Survivor: Label Deals May Come and Go, but Jack Ingram Keeps Making His Own Kind of Music"; "Playing a New Game: Radney Foster Reinvents Himself on a Rocking New Album"; "Free Wheelin': Musical Renegade Kevin Welch Hits the Highway for Inspiration"; "A Little Bit Moorer: Sultry Southern Songbird Allison Moorer on Shyness, Sisterhood, and Other Odds and Ends"; and "Buck with a Bang: With a Little Help from Buck Owens, Twangy Hipsters the Derailers Add Sauce to the Bakersfield Sound"; "Wit Happens: Surprise! Tart-Tongued Robbie Fulks Doesn't *Really* Hate Nashville"; and "Lynne through the Out Door: Leaving Music City Pays Off for Shelby Lynne."

Keith Urban, who had been playing around town with his Americana band the Ranch, releases his first solo album on Capitol Nashville. Keith and I meet at the Flying Saucer tap room to talk about his solo debut for the Horizons feature. The first hour is official interview about the album. But over the next several hours, as drink loosens us up, we share intimate details about our struggles and relationships, and compare notes on how men and women approach or avoid conflicts within romantic entanglements. "Guys are strange creatures," Keith says. "We are so macho sometimes. We'll be out together and one guy will say, 'Oh, I've got to call my girlfriend,' and act like it's a real hassle. The truth is, we really want to be home with our wives or girlfriends. Once you're willing to open yourself up to that kind of intimacy with someone, I think it becomes more apparent how silly it is to play those kind of games." Neither one of us knows at the time that Keith will become a big star, and marry actor Nicole Kidman, but I think he has an inkling of what is to come. "I don't feel like I'm chasing a dream as much as pursuing my destiny," Keith says.

One of the early events we cover in Nashville is the groundbreaking ceremony for the new Country Music Hall of Fame and Museum. The small museum on Music Row at 4 Music Square East is closing, and a giant will take its place. On June 17, 1999, the entire music community marches downtown to Demonbreun Street to witness history. We also take home commemorative Hatch Show Prints that read, "We busted rock for country."

In the spring of 1999, a group of Americana music lovers gather at the South by Southwest music conference to talk about forming a trade organization to support the Americana genre. The *Gavin* Americana radio chart is four years old and there is a groundswell of support for a more organized approach to marketing and promoting the brand. The motley crew of music people meet again in the fall of 1999, this time with strategic planner Liz Allen Fey on hand to moderate a two-day meeting about getting the new association off the ground.

"That first meeting was a bunch of people who kind of knew each other just feeling each other out," says J. D. May, later named first executive director of the Americana Music Association. "We had to figure out if there was authentic interest to start an organization or if there were too many personal agendas that would keep us from working together. We spent the first half of the first day debating all of the different names that were out there: Americana, roots, alt-country, No Depression, Western Beat.... There are thirty people in the room and opinions on what it should be called. Because of *Gavin*'s Americana radio chart, it made perfect sense that we should carry that title over to the organization.

"The radio chart led us into believing we need Americana sections in record stores, we need a Grammy category, we need television, we need festivals and clubs and promoters and agents and the industry all calling this thing Americana," May says. "Our goal from the beginning was to make it authentic, something that could grow and something for everyone in the industry making this style of music to rally around, a conference where we could bring everyone together to network, do educational things, and be together for the long haul."

Before joining Americana as its first executive director, May spent five years at the independent Dead Reckoning record label, a Nashville-based artist-owned-and-operated label. The artist partners included Kieran Kane, Kevin Welch, Mike Henderson, Tammy Rogers, and Harry Stinson.

"Several of those artists had been on major labels with varying degrees of commercial success but high degrees of critical success," May says. "As all of their deals expired simultaneously, they thought, *We kind of already play together; we're friends. Let's start a label, make our records, do something.* They thought it would be a really interesting way to make the records they wanted to make, think about it more from a direct-to-consumer standpoint, but also take advantage of traditional marketing, distribution, publicity, radio, touring."

Kevin Welch recalls Kieran Kane pitching him the idea of Dead Reckoning. "He called and pitched the idea and I was in—the first three seconds, I was in," Welch says. "Kieran kept stridently pitching me this. I said, 'You're preaching to the choir, man. I got it, I'm in!' The premise was that major labels hire independent promotion and independent publicists to augment their staff so why don't we just do that and have our own label. We didn't have any money, but we just figured we'll come up with some somehow or we'll talk people into working for free. That's really what happened the most. There was something called the Dead Reckoning deal, which meant no money.

"We didn't have anything to model it after," Welch says. "There might have been something out there but we weren't aware of it. Kieran made that first record, which is called *Dead Rekoning*. Then I came in right over the top of that with *Life Down Here on Earth*. We recorded just live, straight to two-track, the same way we recorded the major label records— the same engineer, the same studio, the same musicians. They spent $200,000 for the last Warner Brothers record and we spent $15,000 for the first Dead Reckoning record. Go figure!"

"I was twenty-five when I joined Dead Reckoning," May says. "I thought I knew everything. I was really arrogant and brash when, in fact, I knew nothing and had no experience, but I think my naïveté is what made me willing to just jump in," May says. "I love these artists' music; I really believe in it, so I'm going to go out and help them go sell it. At Dead Reckoning, I witnessed on a day-to-day basis the challenge that anybody who didn't fit into the mainstream had with being accepted. I saw from the vantage point of artists who used to be part of the mainstream now having most of those outlets—radio, press, television, touring, agencies, and so forth—turn their back, not in a mean way but in a very practical way saying, 'You're not Garth Brooks; you're not on a major anymore. There's really nothing that we can do to help you out.'

"Over the next five years, what we did was systematically go country by country, distributor by distributor, publicist by publicist, radio format and so forth, to find an outlet for this music, whether it's shipping a hundred records a month into Italy, to doing deals in Canada and Australia and England and probably twelve or thirteen different countries while I was there. In some cases, it was a full label deal where we got advances and made videos. In other cases, we just printed the CDs ourselves and shipped them over.

"What I took away from my experience at Dead Reckoning, and into the group that ultimately founded the Americana Music Association, is that I'd been having doors slammed in my faces for three, four, and ultimately five years," May says. "I realized we had the opportunity to create an organization that will work together to shine a light on some of the challenges and opportunities that exist in the market if we start speaking and working as one voice as opposed to many different voices under ten different brands with competing interests. I'd traveled the world over many times at that point and just thought we could do it."

The founders of the Americana Music Association include Jon Grimson and Brad Paul, who had worked with Rob Bleetstein five years earlier to start the Americana Music Chart at *Gavin*. Also in the room at the storied 1999 meeting in the chapel at RCA Records' Nashville campus were Grant Alden from *No Depression*; Jack Emerson from Praxis and E-Squared; Bev Paul from Sugar Hill Records; Scott Robinson and Dan Herrington from Dualtone Records; Dan Einstein from Oh Boy Records; Steve Wilkison from Eminent Records; Western Beat's Billy Block; radio promoters Al Moss, Bill Wence, and Leslie Rouffe; radio jock Jessie Scott; and other stakeholders in the Americana music space.

Dennis Lord is the first president of the Americana Music Association. At the time, Lord is senior vice president at the performing rights organization SESAC.

"The way we saw it at SESAC is that this is sustainable music," Lord says. "If we support it, some of these copyrights will be evergreen copyrights. They will be ours to license. Americana is true art. When you have art, you have success. You have passion. You have beauty and great music. The beginning of the Americana Music Association was like the Country Music Association in 1960, very small, very organic, not much going on. When you organize, you develop and you know things are going to happen. If you build organically like that, things happen. It's going to continue to grow. When SESAC invested money in Americana we were feeding a giant in its infancy.

"In Americana, the artist is the artist because the artist has no choice because that's who they are," Lord says. "We have writer-artists at SESAC that have been making records for five, ten, twenty years. They put out a record a year, get in their cars and drive around the country playing festivals and clubs and make a great living. They are the troubadours."

As the Americana music radio chart and association ascend, mainstream cynics criticize Americana as being the place where old country artists go to die. Cash, Willie, Waylon, Kristofferson, Rodney Crowell, Rosanne Cash, and the like are not wanted at country radio anymore. Yet these artists continue to innovate and create. They are artists.

"Maybe country radio doesn't want them anymore, but that's no dark place to be," Lord says. "They were naturally Americana artists from the start. The country labels, if they can't break an artist at country, sometimes they'll try to put them in Americana or Triple A or rock. One thing that is very clear to all of us in Americana, and I think we have communicated, is that just because country radio doesn't take you it doesn't mean you're Americana. To me, and contrary to what the Country Music Association will say, country is a subgenre of Americana. Not the other way around."

CHAPTER SEVEN

O BROTHER

The biggest thing that happens in Americana music in 2000 is the soundtrack for O *Brother, Where Art Thou?* Written, produced, and directed by the Coen brothers, the film is a comedy-drama set in rural Mississippi during the 1930s and follows three bungling escaped prisoners. O *Brother* is loosely based on Homer's *The Odyssey* and stars George Clooney, John Turturro, and Tim Blake Nelson as the convicts on the lam.

The Coen brothers hire T Bone Burnett to produce the soundtrack. Burnett, from Fort Worth, Texas, made his name producing Counting Crows, Elvis Costello, Los Lobos, the BoDeans, the Wallflowers, Jimmie Dale Gilmore, and Bruce Cockburn in the 1990s. Working on the soundtrack in Nashville, Burnett calls Alison Krauss's manager Denise Stiff and asks for her help booking musicians and setting up auditions.

"T Bone wanted somebody that knew the acoustic music and the bluegrass world and the kinds of artists that would be a good fit for O *Brother*," Stiff says. "The timing was good for me because Alison was off the road for a little while. T Bone hired me as kind of a consultant. He was finding the songs and such, but he needed help getting people to audition. The Coens came to town for a few days and we had meetings with them. They were really nice people, down to earth and funny. I enjoyed working with them. I was involved in everything from helping to find musicians and then helping to find labels when it came time to set up those meetings."

Burnett set up shop in an old church converted into a studio on Music Row now known as Ocean Way. The album is a gorgeous mix of traditional, bluegrass, and old-timey country songs. It includes Ralph Stanley singing the traditional "O Death," the Stanley Brothers on "Angel Band," Alison Krauss and Gillian Welch on "I'll Fly Away," Norman Blake on "You Are My Sunshine," the Peasall Sisters singing Mother Mabelle Carter's "In the Highways," Harry McClintock on "Big Rock Candy Mountain," the Whites singing the Carter Family's "Keep on the Sunny Side," and more.

The fictional Soggy Bottom Boys from the film, George Clooney, Tim Blake Nelson, and John Turturro, also appear on the soundtrack. Tim Blake Nelson sings the Jimmie Rodgers song "In the Jailhouse Now." In one scene from the film, Clooney's character, Ulysses Everett McGill, sings "Man of Constant Sorrow." In real life, the voice on the soundtrack is that of Dan Tyminski, a bluegrass vocalist and instrumentalist from Alison Krauss's band Union Station.

"When it came time for the 'Man of Constant Sorrow' audition, Dan just nailed it. I mean, there was no question," Stiff says.

Finding a record label to release a soundtrack featuring old-time country, bluegrass, and gospel music in the year 2000 is no easy feat. But the Coen brothers' authenticity is a big draw, and there are major label honchos who understand an audience outside mainstream country.

"Joel and Ethan were going to be in town for a few days and they wanted to have meetings with record labels so I just started calling the majors," Stiff says. "They were really casual meetings in the studio. It was more of a vibe thing. Who is going to be the best fit for the Coen brothers' vibe."

Luke Lewis is the head of Mercury Records in 2000. Mercury made a ton of money on Shania Twain under his leadership. On the other end of the spectrum, Lewis had gone to high school with Americana trailblazer Gram Parsons, and that fact alone gave Luke enormous credibility in the Americana world.

"We went to this sort of a bad boys' school in Jacksonville, Florida," Lewis says. "Gram and I spent holidays together and all that kind of stuff. We were tight. Now this was before 1970. It was early sixties. We were like anybody else who was into music at the time. We were into folk music: Celtic ballads, and 'Barbara Allen,' and all that kind of stuff. I guess we were just starting to spread our wings. That first Bob Dylan record came out while we were there. The Ray Charles *Modern Sounds* record came out then. Those things had a pretty big impact on both of us in terms of our taste. My friendship with Gram led me to all that good stuff—the Byrds' *Sweetheart of the Rodeo* and all those things. I followed Gram's tastes for sure."

Lewis went to work for *Record World* magazine as the southeastern editor in the mid-1970s. "It was during that whole outlaw thing, which I was pretty much taken with, and I wanted to run a record label in Nashville," Lewis says. "I went off to learn how. I came back in 1992 after working for CBS and MCA for a long time to run Mercury Records in Nashville. The first record I worked was Billy Ray Cyrus's 'Achy Breaky Heart,' which was a nice way to start financially. It didn't quite fit my taste, but I was working for a living."

Denise Stiff invites Lewis to the studio to talk with the Coen brothers about releasing O *Brother, Where Are Thou?* on Mercury Records.

"We started talking about a deal pretty quickly," Lewis says. "The only other person chasing it at the time that I remember was Bruce Hinton at MCA. It kind of was a little bit of a bidding war, and I wanted it really badly. For sort of comparable projects, it was fairly expensive, but not really. One of my business affairs guys in LA was telling me I was crazy and I was going to lose all kinds of money. I thought, *Well shit, I think I can break even with this.* It reminded me of the Nitty Gritty Dirt Band's *Will the Circle Be Unbroken,* a record that had a big impact on me when I was young. A lot of people are not aware of this, but all those songs had been hits in their time. The songs were seventy years old but they had all been big giant hits. And all the artists on this soundtrack are people that are at the top of their game in that niche. There is no slouch shit on that album at all."

The soundtrack to O *Brother, Where Art Thou?* was released on December 5, 2000. Earlier in the year, on May 24, 2000, Joel and Ethan Coen present "Down from the Mountain," the first in a live concert series featuring music from the Americana artists who participated in the O *Brother* soundtrack. Alison Krauss, Emmylou Harris, Dan Tyminski, Gillian Welch, John Hartford, Ralph Stanley, and others. The Ryman Auditorium in Nashville hosted the first concert in the series. Documentary directors Nick Doob, Chris Hegedus, and D. A. Pennebaker captured the action for an accompanying film.

"I remember that John Hartford was really, really sick then," Denise Stiff says. "He was sitting on the side of the stage in an easy chair, which is where he sat in between sets. A nurse and I were sitting in the balcony saying, 'Okay, what's plan B?' Nobody knew if John was going to be able to do it. We'd already started planning a tour, but Nashville was the test to see if it was viable. Then we did the show in New York at Carnegie Hall. We were doing all these things promoting a show of a movie that no one has ever heard of, that hasn't been released yet with the title *O Brother, Where Art Thou?* It was tough for a while to fill the seats, but once the music started to leak, and the buzz about it started to build, it was fantastic."

The "Down from the Mountain" concert is one of those cool Nashville moments that can't possibly be scripted. Soft lighting, vintage costumes, sets and microphones, beautiful acoustic music. As a violent thunderstorm rages outside, the Ryman is warm and cozy and filled with music business friends and colleagues. All of us lucky enough to be in the room are in Americana heaven. The after-show party is just as much fun as the concert. I interview Joel and Ethan Coen, and get a chance to talk with my favorite actor, Frances McDormand, who is married to Joel Coen. At this point, none of us know if the film or soundtrack will be successful. The Coen brothers are critical darlings but not big mainstream filmmakers.

"We didn't think of it as a hit record at the time," Luke Lewis says. "It seemed like it could be a coffee table book, I hate to use that term, but we packaged it and spent more money than normal on the packaging and all that business. The sigh of relief came when they released the movie in France before they released it in the US. It blew up. The guy that ran our company in France called me and says, 'Hey, we just sold eighty thousand of this in a month, watch out.' We loaded up on inventory. We spent more money launching it. We jammed it out there, if you will. Thank goodness because it blew through the damn roofs."

John Grady is the head of marketing, sales, and promotion at Mercury Records during the *O Brother* era. He believed *O Brother* could have the same kind of success that *Buena Vista Social Club* had in 1999.

"I believed right from the beginning that *O Brother* would be successful," Grady says. "We were with PolyGram worldwide for distribution, and they were really strong in Europe. You could watch the figures every day. How did we sell eighty thousand gospel records in France? People were calling it a bluegrass record, but it wasn't really a bluegrass record. That's okay. I didn't care what they called it at that point. *Buena Vista Social Club* was my roadmap. When I saw that movie it was one of the only times in my life I cried in public. I thought it was such a beautiful film. The music was so good, but let's face it; it was a bunch of seventy- and eighty-year-old Cuban guys. That's even more obscure than O *Brother* if you think about it. It became a sensation in the United States. That's why I kept telling myself that this could be done with O *Brother*, because they did it with *Buena Vista Social Club*. O *Brother* opened in twelve theaters. Every one of those markets where the movie opened immediately sold out on the soundtrack. We could trace that and had a pretty good idea what was going on. All the malls had record stores then. All the movie theaters were usually attached to a mall. When the film came to Nashville I went to see it thirteen times so I could watch the people leave and listen to what they said. They were all talking about the music. We also had the secret weapon. George Clooney was singing in it. It was Dan Tyminski's voice but fans thought it was Clooney. We had George fucking Clooney."

"That was pretty helpful," Lewis says. "CMT and VH1 played the hell out of the George Clooney music video. Then the film had several lives. It would go on cable and then it would go on regular TV. Every time it hit a new platform, the soundtrack exploded all over again. It was really profitable, probably the most profitable thing in my entire career, and I worked on Michael Jackson records. It was frustrating not getting it on the radio. 'Man of Constant Sorrow' would have been a huge radio smash. It just scared radio. It scared them worse than Chris Stapleton scares them now. They didn't know what to make of it."

O Brother, Where Art Thou? sold a million copies within four months of its release. Three months later, it was double platinum. It shot to number one on the *Billboard* 200 and remained on the chart for twenty weeks in a row. It won Album of the Year at the Country Music Association Awards and the Academy of Country Music Awards and took home two International Bluegrass Association Awards. All of these sales and accolades poured in without support from mainstream country radio.

"This record was blowing up but country radio wouldn't touch it," Denise Stiff says. "With 'Man of Constant Sorrow,' T Bone knew that he had something really special."

Mainstream country radio ignores O Brother. Some program directors are angry at the attention it takes from hit radio songs. In a Country Radio Seminar panel titled "Nashville Incorrect," Dean James, the operations manager at Dallas country station KSCS, complains bitterly about the O Brother soundtrack and its place in country music.

"I think we have too much split focus and things like the O Brother soundtrack take us off the game plan," James says. "Of course, no one would argue the success that Michael and his team, and John Grady and Luke Lewis had with O Brother. Great, incredible sales story, and so on and so forth, but is it mass appeal? One could argue that it is because the millions of records they sold. When we go back and look at 'Dueling Banjos' it was a massive pop hit and didn't start a resurgence of country music. The Grammys are out of touch. Don't be thrown off focus thinking that Ralph Stanley is the male vocalist of the year in country music and Dolly Parton's the female vocalist of the year. It's no slight on those individuals or on O Brother the movie or the soundtrack, but who is buying those records? Who can we attract to country radio realistically?"

"I ended up getting fired because Luke thought I was being too hard on the radio promotion staff about 'Man of Constant Sorrow,'" John Grady says. "I was pushing them. I said radio could play that record once every morning in the middle of their morning show, any radio station on earth at that point. When this music is going that deep into the American psyche and it's coming out of Nashville, why wouldn't you play it?"

Radio refuses to engage with O Brother, Where Art Thou?, but it becomes the first soundtrack since *The Bodyguard* of 1994 to win a Grammy for Album of the Year. It also wins for Best Compilation Soundtrack, Best Male Country Performance (Ralph Stanley's goose-bump-raising recitation of "O Death"), and Best Country Collaboration with Vocals for "I Am a Man of Constant Sorrow." Its sister record, *Down from the Mountain*, wins Best Traditional Folk Album.

"I think it won five Grammys. It was pretty damn gratifying," Lewis says. "People often ask me, 'What's the highlight of your career?' I'd say the Grammy Awards. After a lot of fighting, they agreed to put Ralph Stanley on the Grammys, standing in the middle of the audience to sing 'O Death' acapella. It was unbelievable. I was sitting in the middle of a bunch of hip-hop folks and they are saying, 'Who's that guy? What planet did that come from?' It was magical."

CHAPTER EIGHT

AMERICAN COUNTRY, AMERICAN ROOTS

I witness the success of O Brother from my front-row seat at Country Music magazine. Life at Country Music is beautiful. Our charming and warm office is a laid-back place where Deb brings her baby and dog to work.

I fall more deeply in love with Texas when Country Music takes Lee Roy Parnell to Fredericksburg for a photo shoot on his ranch and at Luckenbach. It is my first taste of the Texas Hill Country, a place that still has my heart decades later. The story begins, "Lee Roy Parnell is content. As the sun dips below the horizon on his ranch—nestled deep in Texas hill country—it casts a warm glow across the green fields and carefully tended oak trees." During the three days in Texas, Lee Roy and I bond over our love of Americana music and the place Texas holds in it.

When we return to Nashville, Lee Roy invites me to go over to Guy Clark's house. Guy's famous workshop is in the basement of his home on Stoneway Close, a narrow, tree-lined, dead-end street tucked between Knob Road and White Bridge Road on the west side of Nashville. The house itself is unremarkable, but Guy's workshop is a cozy refuge. On this day, the sweet scent of wet grass and spring rain wafts through open windows to mix with the heady aroma of coffee, cigarettes, marijuana, whiskey, and fresh wood shavings. The floor is covered with sheets of thick particleboard. Two workbenches—one for writing songs and one for building guitars—flank the small room.

Praxis International founders Andy McLenon (left) and Jack Emerson (right) with bluegrass great Bill Monroe. Jack and Andy signed early Americana bands Jason and the Scorchers and the Georgia Satellites to Praxis in the 1980s, long before Americana had a name. Photo courtesy of Kay Clary and Praxis archives.

In the late 1980s, Radney Foster, Steve Earle, Bill Lloyd, and Joe Ely (left to right) didn't fit into the mainstream country radio format. The Gavin Report's new Americana chart, founded in 1995, was built for them. Photo courtesy of Cyndi Hoelzle.

Kay Clary from Praxis International on the cover of the *Nashville Scene* in 1989, more than five years before the Americana radio chart launched. Photo courtesy of Kay Clary and Praxis archives.

Left to right: Dusty Wakefield, Juke Logan, Lucinda Williams, Jim Lauderdale, Donald Lindley, Duane Jarvis, and Rosie Flores at the Palomino Club in Los Angeles, early 1990s. Photo courtesy of Block Family archives.

Billy Block started the *Western Beat Radio Hour* on July 4, 1994, at KIEV 870 AM in Los Angeles. His first playlist included Joe Ely, Emmylou Harris, Jim Lauderdale, Jimmie Dale Gilmore, Iris Dement, Kevin Welch, Guy Clark, Duane Jarvis, Lucinda Williams, Los Lobos, the Mavericks, and other artists that are now considered Americana pioneers. Photo courtesy of Block Family archives.

Brian Ongaro, my first boss at Sundance Broadcasting, with Tanya Tucker in 1994. Tanya instigated several great adventures when I covered her as a reporter for *Country Weekly* magazine in 1996 and 1997. Photo courtesy of Tamara Saviano archives.

My coworkers at Sundance Broadcasting, music director Mitch Morgan (*left*) and program director Kerry Wolfe (*right*), flank my first Nashville boss, Terri Clark in 1995. This is the day that Terri invited me to move to Nashville to work for her. Photo courtesy of Tamara Saviano archives.

Shawn Camp on his tour bus backstage at the Wisconsin State Fair, 1994. This is the first day I met Shawn. Little did I know he'd be a strong common thread through my thirty-plus years in the music business. Photo courtesy of Tamara Saviano archives.

Raul Malo of the Mavericks performs at Chicago's Whiskey River nightclub in 1994. This is the night Raul and I first met. He talked me into moving to Nashville in 1995. Photo courtesy of Tamara Saviano archives.

The *Gavin Report* solicits Americana radio reporters with this ad in the *Gavin Report* in 1994. Image courtesy of Cyndi Hoelzle.

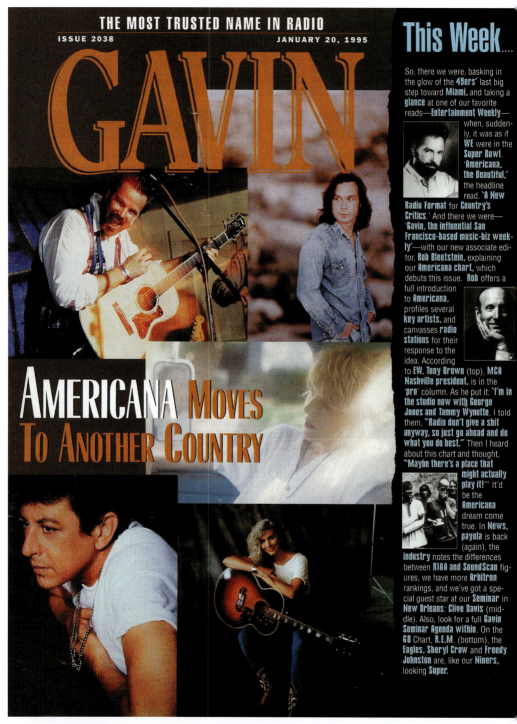

The debut Americana issue of the *Gavin Report*, January 20, 1995. Image courtesy of Rob Bleetstein.

An eerie Townes Van Zandt stares from a portrait above the band saw next to the scarred songwriting workbench. A rack of cassette tapes fills the entire wall behind Guy's rolling desk chair. There are hundreds of cassettes. Many of the labels are too faded to read but I make out a few: "Townes, Cactus Club 1991," "Better Days sessions," "Demos March 4," are noted in Guy's careful printing on the spines.

On the opposite wall, Guy's antique woodcarving tools hang on a pegboard next to the second workbench, the one where he builds acoustic guitars made of rosewood—an art he's practiced since he lived in Houston in the early 1960s. A blueprint for a Flamenco guitar is taped next to an open window, which faces the lush, green backyard.

The songwriting workbench is littered with graph paper and pencils, Guy's preferred writing materials. The centerpiece is a cluster of rolling papers, a canister of Peter Stokkebye 1882 Danish import tobacco, a Ziploc bag of pot, and a heavy round pottery ashtray ringed with ceramic skulls and roses, a gift from his friend Emmylou Harris.

Watching Guy hand-roll tobacco cigarettes and marijuana joints becomes old hat, but that first day I am hypnotized at the way his slender fingers—topped with acrylic nails to aid his guitar picking—methodically dip into his tobacco can, remove just the right amount of the dried leaves, and roll a perfect cigarette. Guy rarely looks down at what his hands are doing and holds up his end of the conversation with ease. I don't think I ever look up at Guy because I can't take my eyes off the movement of his hands and the extraordinary turquoise ring. I don't know it on this day, but it is the first of hundreds of days I will spend in that workshop with Guy.

Later that week, I return to Texas to interview Willie Nelson after his concert at the Cypress Creek Café outdoor theater in Wimberley. Lee Roy opens for Willie and joins him on a few songs. Willie plays for more than three hours and then spends a few more hours signing autographs and taking pictures. By the time we gather on his bus, it is long after midnight. I'm exhausted and getting a contact high from the weed smoke, but Willie is energized and we talk for nearly two hours as he and Lee Roy pass some fat Cheech and Chong–level joints between them.

Our most ambitious piece at *Country Music* is a year in the making. The cover story "Who's Gonna Fill Their Shoes?" is a one-of-a-kind portrait gallery featuring living legends with the artists who hope to carry on their tradition in the coming century. I gasp as I look at these photographs twenty-three years later. Chet Atkins with Vince Gill. George Jones with Alan Jackson. Willie Nelson with Lyle Lovett. Ralph Stanley with Ricky Skaggs. Dolly Parton with Lee Ann Womack. Bill Anderson with Brad Paisley. Tom T. Hall with Billy Ray Cyrus. Merle Haggard with Clint Black. Emmylou Harris with Trisha Yearwood. Kitty Wells with Pam Tillis. Waylon Jennings with Travis Tritt. Loretta Lynn with Patty Loveless. Earl Scruggs with Marty Stuart. Perhaps some miscalculations on the younger artists, but man, what a thrill to look back and think about the history we made with that photo shoot. Most of the trailblazers we photographed are gone now. How lucky am I to have been there in that moment?

The magazine is profitable. Everyone is happy. Then, with little warning, Sussex Publishers sells *Country Music* to American Media. The news is soul-crushing. I had already worked at American Media's *Country Weekly* and am not going back there. The once-joyful tone of our office turns mournful. I put the word out to the industry that I am looking for a new gig. The sale is official in August. I cry in my office as the new regime walks up to the door with plans to take us to lunch to celebrate, followed by a champagne toast at the *Country Weekly* office. They celebrate as Deb, Michael, Wendy, and I grieve our extraordinary time at *Country Music*. It is a heartbreaking day. Michael stays on with the new magazine; he's got a family to feed. Wendy stays with Sussex to design *Mother Earth News*. Deb moves on to freelancing for *Disney* magazine.

Still numb, I accept a gig as a talent booker at Jones Radio Network and Great American Country cable network. Headquartered in Denver, they had just opened a Nashville office at 33 Music Square West to produce shows from Music City.

Our landlord is Oh Boy Records, the indie record label founded in 1981 by Grammy-winning folk artist John Prine and his manager and business partner Al Bunetta. Al and I take a shine to each other immediately. Bunetta. Saviano. It's an Italian thing. Prine and Bunetta are a riot together and I spend more time in their office than mine. It's a different vibe. It's a chance to dig more deeply into Prine's catalog. After office hours, we drink wine and Al and John turn me on to their favorite Americana artists. Prine is from Chicago and we spend a lot of time comparing notes on our favorite clubs, restaurants, and hidden gems on Lake Michigan in Chicago and Milwaukee.

The Jones Radio Network and Great American Country production home base is across the street at 40 Music Square West in Reba McEntire's Starstruck broadcast studio. My new gig does include talent booking but, a surprise to me, I am thrust into producing the radio show *Nashville Nights* with Dallas Turner, plus two cable television shows, *Country Request Live* and *GAC Classic*. Yikes. I have zero production experience. My boss is Scott Durand, a fellow Wisconsinite and great guy. Scott says he has faith in my ability. I spend a lot of time crying in the ladies' room. I'm grieving the loss of *Country Music* magazine and, at the same time, everything at Jones and GAC is intimidating and chaotic. This is not a company that has its act together, not by a long shot. But the money is good and I get a raise after the first few months when it becomes clear that I am managing the entire operation in Nashville. Talk about being thrown in the deep end.

Country Request Live (CRL) is, as the name suggests, a live show. Every afternoon, Monday through Friday, we are on satellite uplink with Denver as our host, Dallas Turner, takes live calls from people all over America requesting music videos. Dallas chats with the caller and sets up the video, and while the three-minute video plays we have a couple of minutes to prepare the next caller.

As producer, I write and prepare the show content, go over everything with Dallas, and make sure the show runs smoothly. I sit in the control room with engineer Lonnie Napier and an intern who runs the teleprompter and takes calls from viewers. Starstruck studio engineer Jim Jordan is always around in case we have technical difficulties. Jim teaches me television production on the fly. Paul Whitfield, the audio-video engineer who built the broadcast studio, copies pages from his college textbooks on television production and gives them to Jim to give to me.

Things are more laid back with GAC *Classic*. Hosted by legendary WSM disc jockey Bill Cody, the show is taped, so there isn't the pressure of the live experience. I write the scripts from my home office and we film a week's worth of shows in one day. Bill and I have a blast together. As I get more comfortable in the job, this is where I feel most connected. We are covering classic country and we stretch the definition in any direction we want to stretch it, which includes Americana. We have George Jones on the show one day, followed by a Foster and Lloyd reunion, Delbert McClinton, and the Flatlanders. I even book famous music photographer Jim McGuire, who took iconic photos of Johnny Cash, Kris Kristofferson, Guy Clark, Townes Van Zandt, and many others.

With CRL, too, the more comfortable I get, the more I push the envelope. It is a mainstream show, but I throw in a couple of videos each day by Americana artists. When Dallas goes on maternity leave, we decide to have artists as guest hosts. I take that opportunity to book the Flatlanders, Charlie Robison, and Jack Ingram. Lucky Dog Records, an Americana offshoot of Columbia Records, is home to Jack and Charlie, along with Charlie's brother Bruce Robison, BR549, the DeRailers, Deryl Dodd, Joy Lynn White, and other artists who don't fit on country radio.

In addition to my gig at GAC, I still write about country and Americana music as a freelancer. *Playgirl* magazine covers country music and I land a few stories there, including a couple of covers, which are big pay days. In late 2000, my editor at *Playgirl* is looking for a hot country guy to be on the April 2001 cover. "Who is up and coming and really cute?" Charlene asks. I tell her about Keith Urban, who had recently scored his first number one hit with "But for the Grace of God." *Playgirl* pays $6,000 for cover stories, and they are typically written in a question-and-answer format and not a long narrative. I had written a Q&A with newcomer David Kersh the previous year and found it an easy way to make six grand. Instead of going through proper channels and calling the label publicist to set up an interview with Keith, I call him directly. The label will likely turn down a *Playgirl* story, and I want to give Keith the chance to decide for himself. Much to my surprise, Keith is game. He meets me for lunch in the conference room at Starstruck for the interview. I assure Keith that although the photo shoot will be sexy, he will not be naked. Likely shirtless, but not all-the-way naked. Keith is not the least bit concerned and says he thinks it will be fun. Of course, I can't keep a photo shoot secret from the label. Capitol's head of publicity, Fletcher Foster, insists we do the shoot at his home so he can keep an eye on things. Fletcher's beautiful home is an ideal place for the shoot. *Playgirl* sends photographer Greg Weiner from New York to photograph Keith. I walk into Fletcher's kitchen the morning of the shoot and find Keith standing at the counter eating a muffin and wearing nothing but silk boxer shorts. Oh boy. As Keith and I chat, Fletcher races through the kitchen and says, "I've got an emergency at the office." He points and me and adds, "Don't let anything bad happen here!" Keith and I laugh. Of course nothing bad is going to happen. Well, in the end, the shoot *does* get out of hand. Keith is more willing to be provocative than I ever dreamed he'd be. In some of the shots Keith wears nothing but a strategically placed guitar. Twenty plus years later, I regret that *Playgirl* story. I bet Keith does, too. He has had to endure late-night talk show hosts ribbing him about it. Keith Urban is a rock star now, a far cry from the young upstart standing in silk boxer shorts in Fletcher's kitchen in 2001. As a keepsake, I do have a signed copy of *Playgirl* with Keith Urban on the cover. Keith wrote, "To Tamara, thank you so much for getting me like no one else has!! Love, Keith."

The best part of my job at Great American Country is Paul Whitfield. Paul built the broadcast studio at Starstruck and often comes in to repair and upgrade the equipment. One day, Paul stands on a ladder as I hand him gels for the set lights. We talk about music and art, and Paul says, "I hate to see society decompose into abject mediocrity." Smarts and heart in one statement. He has my attention from that moment forward.

After all my years of looking for love, Paul is my big score. His deep thinking is just one of the reasons I fall for him. Paul is a grown-up with the playfulness of a child. He doesn't try to fit in or impress anyone. Paul is open, affectionate, a good listener with a wry sense of humor and the most soulful eyes I've ever looked into. And his lips. I can stare at them all day and never get tired of looking at Paul's lips.

Our first date for late-morning coffee lasts more than four hours. I excuse myself twice and huddle in the hallway next to the restroom to whisper into my cell phone and cancel my other meetings for the day. My attraction to Paul is so strong I cannot pull myself away from him.

Again, we talk about music. I tell Paul about my love for Joe Ely and the Flatlanders. It reminds Paul of the 1884 satirical novella *Flatland*, a story about a fictional two-dimensional world, which observes the hierarchy of Victorian culture.

This leads us to a discussion about collective consciousness and how after 9/11, the entire world believed we were all in this together. Now the public debate is more focused on destroying the enemy than any real problem-solving. Paul and I agree that instead of social justice, our society is now driven by pervasive self-interest with no regard for the greater good, and people clutch their beliefs like pearls, with an urgency that ignores nuance or middle ground.

Heavy stuff for a first date, yet I am impressed that I am dealing with an intelligent, thoughtful man who treats me as an intellectual equal. Our relationship unfolds slowly (yet oh so sweetly) because Paul works on the touring side of the business and is on the road with Kenny Chesney as a video engineer.

On November 12, 2002, I take Paul to "Concert for a Landmine Free World" at the Birchmere in Alexandria, Virginia. Emmylou Harris receives the Leahy Humanitarian Award from the Vietnam Veterans of America Foundation for her work with the anti-landmine movement. Vermont senator Patrick Leahy, for whom the award is named, presents Emmylou with the award. She performs along with her friends Steve Earle, Nanci Griffith, John Prine, Guy Clark, Rodney Crowell, Buddy and Julie Miller, Jamie O'Hara, and Patty Griffin. It's an incredible night of Americana music and it is my way of introducing Paul to this community I love.

Things are chaotic at Great American Country. The network hires daytime drama star Bobbie Eakes to replace Dallas Turner on our live show CRL when Dallas leaves after having a baby. Bobbie is fantastic. A total pro and a joy. In addition to CRL, she is hosting a countdown show and other specials for the network. We've got her on the red carpet at the Country Music Awards interviewing the artists before the big show. We fly to Tampa and Bobbie cohosts an event with Billy Ray Cyrus.

On the other hand, we are understaffed and the staff we do have is underpaid. Our production quality is like *Wayne's World* compared with our competitor CMT. The bosses don't pay much attention to GAC. It feels like we are an afterthought in their universe. They especially take

Bobbie for granted. Daytime drama *The Bold and the Beautiful* asks Bobbie to return to the show. Her character, Macy Alexander, was killed in a car crash two years ago but her body was never found. Since then, fans of the show have relentlessly lobbied for Macy's return. The show is planning to bring the character back on location in Italy. I think it is a fantastic opportunity for GAC to leverage Bobbie's celebrity. The suits disagree. *The Bold and the Beautiful* has 450 million viewers, but the GAC brass ignores that potential and opportunity for cross-promotion. They'd rather lose Bobbie than share her with the soap opera. What the hell can I do when I have a network of short-sighted executives who just don't get it? Suzanne Alexander takes over for Bobbie as host of CRL. Suzanne is great, a wonderful host and human, but we are starting from scratch with someone new who does not have any audience awareness.

On the side, I'm working to get American Roots Publishing off the ground. We are granted 501(c)3 tax status. I've got a badass board of directors: Bobbie Eakes, Emmylou Harris, noted author and music critic Dave Marsh, Tom Frouge from Triloka, New West Records president Cameron Strang, Kathi Whitley from Vector Management, producer and musician Steve Fishell, publishing and music executive Stephen Bond Garvan, and, most incredibly, Steve Wozniak, inventor of the Apple computer. Every one of them is passionate about our mission to preserve and celebrate American culture through music, literature, and art. My goal is to raise funds as soon as possible so I can move on from GAC, publish Joe Ely's novel, and work full time doing what I love.

As part of my research for American Roots Publishing, I read the book *Cultural Creatives: How 50 Million People Are Changing the World*. Those of us in the Americana community fit into this psychographic of the population. The cultural creatives are my audience for American Roots Publishing. Things are aligning the way they are meant to align.

CHAPTER NINE

FREE SPEECH AND THE CHICKS

In 2003, the drumbeat for war in Iraq surrounds us. I get myself into a jam at work for arguing about democracy with Charlie Daniels. Yes, that Charlie Daniels—the long-haired country boy, devil-went-down-to-Georgia, 1970s pot-smoking hippie turned right-wing conservative Christian. After the September 11 terrorist attacks, American emotions are up and down like teenage hormones. Right, left, Republican, Democrat, Christian, non-Christian—suddenly everyone's opinions take on a new fury. We're on the verge of war, damn it, and there is no room for civil discourse. You're either with us or against us. You're a good American or a traitor. There is nothing in between.

I never thought of myself as particularly political. I have my opinions on democracy, and I've voted in every election since I came of age in 1979. But I'm neither a chest-thumping, Fox-watching conservative nor (in the words of Todd Snider) "a pot-smoking, porn-watching, lazy-ass hippie." I am a middle-of-the-road, average, reasonable human.

My trouble at work begins when I get an email from Charlie Daniels forwarded by a publicist. The email is Daniels's "Open Letter to the Hollywood Bunch," and in it he takes the actor Sean Penn to task for traveling to Iraq: "Sean Penn, you're a traitor to the United States of America. You gave aid and comfort to the enemy. How many American lives will your little 'fact-finding trip' to Iraq cost?"

Free Speech and The Chicks • 91

The first time I receive the email, I delete it. The second time I get the same email, I write back and ask to be taken off the mailing list. The third time, I respond and write that civil discourse is the cornerstone of democracy. Americans' freedom of speech is protected by the First Amendment. Just like Charlie Daniels is free to say whatever he wants, so is the Hollywood Bunch.

GAC is not happy that I responded and they fire me on March 7, 2003. My termination is debated publicly and there is a brief firestorm in Nashville. I receive hateful emails from several people on Music Row who are more than happy to tell me my career in country music is over. The viciousness is stunning and includes death threats from cowards hiding behind anonymous monikers.

Americana songwriters, artists, and music industry colleagues advocate on my behalf. John McEuen from the Nitty Gritty Dirt Band calls me from Los Angeles to tell me that he asked GAC to pull all the Dirt Band videos from their library. I run into Rodney Crowell, who grabs me in a bear hug and says, "We've got your back." Radney Foster calls and says, "I have my checkbook out, how much do you need?" Beth Nielsen Chapman calls the First Amendment Center to ask if they can do anything to help me. Phone calls and emails pour in from all over the country. I am deeply moved by the support of my music community.

The attack on me is short lived as the haters turn their attention elsewhere. On March 10, just three days after my termination and on the brink of war, the Dixie Chicks (now known as The Chicks) perform at the Shepherd's Bush Empire theater in London as part of the Top of the World tour to support their sixth studio album, *Home*. Introducing the song "Travelin' Soldier," singer Natalie Maines says to the audience, "Just so you know, we're on the good side with y'all. We do not want this war, this violence, and we're ashamed that the President of the United States is from Texas."

Journalist Betty Clarke from the *Guardian* reports that the audience cheered at Natalie's comment. Clarke wrote, "At a time when country stars are rushing to release pro-war anthems, this is practically punk rock."

Until this moment, The Chicks are country music darlings. Natalie Maines's voice, sisters Emily Strayer and Martie Maguire's masterful musicianship, and their collective songwriting skills prove over and over again that The Chicks are ferociously talented. Long before they arrive to record in Nashville for a major label, The Chicks performed for years in Texas and released several independent records. Natalie is new to the band but The Chicks are not, by a long shot, a Nashville-manufactured corporate country act.

The Chicks are a rare band with mainstream country success and support from the Americana community. True artists, The Chicks care about creative vision. They do not care about insider politics in country music or pleasing the good ol' boy network. The Chicks refuse to be pushed around by their label or the industry. They insist on playing their own instruments on their albums. They push back when the label asks for a remix without banjo and fiddle. The Chicks are adamant about having equal say on the songs, the production, the artwork, and everything about the band's image. That is standard in Americana music but not a given in the mainstream country, major record label world.

The Chicks' debut album, the 1998 *Wide Open Spaces*, sells more than thirteen million records and appeals to a generation of new listeners. The single "Wide Open Spaces" becomes an anthem for women of all ages. In 1999, their album *Fly* hits the eleven million mark. Both *Wide Open Spaces* and *Fly* win Best Country Album at the Grammys, and both are nominated for Album of the Year. The Chicks' first headlining tour takes in more than $47 million in tickets over eighty-eight dates.

The hip, colorful, and gifted trio soar to stardom outside country music's hemmed-in lines. They perform along with Sheryl Crow and Sarah McLachlan on the Lilith Fair tour, are handpicked as spokeswomen for Candie's footwear, and are profiled in nonmusic magazines *Harper's Bazaar*, *People*, *Seventeen*, and more. They appear on MTV's *Loveline*, a talk show where hosts and celebrity guests take questions from and offer advice to teenagers and young adults on subjects including sex, relationships, and drug use.

Texas Monthly reports that when The Chicks are introduced as new artists at a Sony conference in 1997, Natalie says from the stage, "We get confused with the Spice Girls so we've come up with names for each other." One of those names is Slutty Spice. Natalie also nonchalantly remarks that the band has been referred to as "Dixie Cunts." It leaves a bad taste in the mouths of the traditional values country folk in the room. The freewheeling, here-to-have-a-good-time personality coming from three young feminists does not sit well with ingrained country music industry sexism. Any woman who speaks openly about sex is considered "wild" or "sassy." The code is different for men, of course.

When Natalie and Emily write "Sin Wagon" for the *Fly* album, the uptight Sony brass freak out about the sexual reference "mattress dancing." In response to the complaint, Natalie adds the coda, "That's right, I said 'mattress dancing.'" "Goodbye Earl," also on *Fly*, is a darkly humorous tune about a serious subject—spousal abuse—written by Dennis Linde. In the song, two best friends, Wanda and Mary Ann, kill Wanda's violent husband. The comedic music video stars actors Dennis Franz as Earl, Jane Krakowski as Wanda, and Lauren Holly as Mary Ann. Sony is reluctant to release "Goodbye Earl" as a single but give in when The Chicks decide to sing it at their 2000 Grammy Awards debut. Some radio stations refuse to play "Goodbye Earl." "We always figured whoever was complaining must be beating their wife," Natalie said in several interviews.

The Chicks are from Texas, and Texans are known for doing things their way. Instead of playing by Nashville's unwritten rules of coordinating with other artists' camps to stagger show dates and ticket sales so that they do not overlap, The Chicks choose not to route their tour around other artists' dates. They schedule a national on-sale date for tickets to their shows. Some of the Nashville suits are livid at the audacity of The Chicks making plans without consulting them first.

There is a joke in Nashville about "creative accounting" practices in the music business. The Chicks refuse to play the game. In 2001 they accuse their label, Sony Music, of engaging in fraudulent accounting practices and stealing at least $4 million in unpaid royalties. The Chicks consider it a contract breach and try to walk away from Sony. In turn, Sony sues them for breaking the contract. The Chicks countersue for unpaid royalties. The fight is front-page news at the *Tennessean*.

During the conflict, with no Sony producers or executives to get in their way, The Chicks retreat to Cedar Creek Studios in Austin, Texas, to make an acoustic album with Natalie's father, Lloyd Maines, at the helm. Lloyd was an Americana music giant as a multi-instrumentalist, legendary steel guitar player, and producer long before The Chicks existed. He is a member of the Maines Brothers Band with his siblings Kenny, Donny, and Steve, formed in the late 1970s in Lubbock, Texas. Lloyd plays pedal steel on albums by artists including Joe Ely, Terry Allen, Uncle Tupelo, and Wilco. He produced the Terry Allen classic album *Lubbock (on Everything)* and also produced Americana masterpieces for Robert Earl Keen, Ray Wylie Hubbard, Butch Hancock, Jimmie Dale Gilmore, Jerry Jeff Walker, and more.

"Before we went in to the studio, we had a few arrangement sessions at Martie's house and I recorded everything on cassette tapes as we hashed things out," Lloyd says. "I wouldn't say it was a bluegrass record, but right from the start it was acoustic oriented. The whole thing was well thought out in advance by The Chicks. They knew what they wanted. In the studio, everyone was totally upbeat and the Sony lawsuit was never mentioned. Sheryl Crow was in town and came to the studio just to hang out for a couple of days. We had a great time making that record."

The resulting album, *Home*, is revelatory. It is pure Americana, loaded with acoustic guitars, mandolin, banjo, fiddle, and dobro; guest appearances by Emmylou Harris and Chris Thile; songs by Darrell Scott, Patty Griffin, Bruce Robison, and Radney Foster; and cowrites with Marty Stuart and Terri Hendrix.

The opening track, Darrell Scott's "Long Time Gone," sets the tone about modern country radio with the lyric, "We listen to the radio to see what's cookin', but the music ain't got no soul, now they sound tired but they don't sound Haggard, they've got money but they don't have Cash, they got Junior but they don't have Hank."

The rollicking tunes "White Trash Wedding" (written by The Chicks), "Tortured, Tangled Heart" (The Chicks and Marty Stuart), and "Lil' Jack Slade" (The Chicks and Terri Hendrix) are fun interludes between the heartfelt "A Home" (Maia and Randy Sharp), "More Love" (Gary Nicholson and Tim O'Brien), "Travelin' Soldier" (Bruce Robison), "Godspeed" (Radney Foster), "Top of the World" (Patty Griffin), and "I Believe In Love" (Martie, Natalie, and Marty Stuart). *Home* is rounded out with Griffin's "Truth No. 2" and Natalie's gorgeous voice on the Stevie Nicks classic "Landslide."

AllMusic hails *Home* as not only The Chicks' best album but the best album released in 2002. *Entertainment Weekly* calls it "deeply exhilarating and timeless." *Pop Matters* says *Home* "kicked country music in its ass once again when it needed it the most."

The Chicks' single "Travelin' Soldier" sits at number one on the *Billboard* Hot Country Songs chart as Natalie offhandedly comments from the London stage that The Chicks are embarrassed the president of the United States is from Texas. Written by Bruce Robison, the song is about a teenage girl waiting for her love to come home from war, and it was released by The Chicks just as the United States was gearing up to send thousands of young soldiers to fight in Afghanistan.

At the time, Emily Strayer is married to Bruce's brother Charlie Robison. The brothers sign to the Sony Americana imprint Lucky Dog Records around the same time The Chicks join mainstream Sony Music. The brothers have busy solo careers, and Bruce takes off as a songwriter, too, with cuts by country artists. George Strait records Bruce's song "Wrapped." Tim McGraw and Faith Hill cut "Angry All the Time."

The Robison brothers and the members of The Chicks, all Texans, run in the same circles, playing gigs together and seeing each other at events. They consider themselves old friends. Charlie and Emily marry, and the brothers and the band are family.

"The Chicks were in the stratosphere when they made *Home*," Bruce Robison says.

"They were the biggest band in the world when they made that record. When I heard the finished record, even beyond being part of it as a writer, I thought it was going to be [Willie Nelson's] *Redheaded Stranger*. At that moment, The Chicks were number one on the charts with 'Travelin' Soldier,' a song with no freaking drums on it. Unheard of. Completely unheard of at that time. And then, after that incident, country music took a hard-right tilt. I wrote 'Travelin' Soldier' in a really, really open-hearted place during the buildup of the previous war in the same region. Then everybody quit talking about the song because the song didn't fit the politics. After The Chicks thing happened, then the flag waving started, and since then it has been full on. To me, it seems like that is when the polarization started."

Country star Toby Keith delivers "Courtesy of the Red, White and Blue (The Angry American)," with lyrics, "You'll be sorry that you messed with the U.S. of A, 'cause we'll put a boot in your ass, it's the American way." Darrell Worley writes the pro-war anthem "Have You Forgotten?" The lyrics include, "Some say this country's just looking for a fight, after 9/11 man I'd have to say that's right."

Word spreads quickly about Natalie's comment in London. I am in Austin for the South by Southwest music festival when I hear the news. Raw from my own traumatic experience with the cruelty and death threats over my dustup with the Charlie Daniels camp, my heart breaks for Natalie, Emily, and Martie. I've been in the business long enough to know that there is a major blacklisting campaign coming for them. There will be a heavy price to pay for any woman in country music who dares to express an opinion.

The backlash is swift. Thousands of phone calls flood into country radio stations demanding that the Chicks be removed from station playlists. Country radio not only capitulates, they add to the madness by setting up dumpsters for people to drop off The Chicks' music. They host parties to destroy The Chicks' CDs. One station hires a steamroller to crush them. In *Texas Monthly*, John Spong reports that CDs are being mailed back to the Sony Music office in Nashville, one with feces smeared on it. People mentioned in the album liner notes are tracked down and threatened. Toby Keith starts performing in front of a backdrop of Natalie Maines beside Saddam Hussein and adds an image of a dog pissing on The Chicks. Conservative media outlets feed the frenzy and encourage their followers into total insanity. And this is years before social media is a thing.

I'd like to point out that Toby Keith and Darrell Worley did just fine on country radio with their songs. Men in country music are allowed to have opinions.

The retaliation against The Chicks is beyond reason. In 2006, filmmakers Barbara Kopple and Cecilia Peck made *Dixie Chicks: Shut Up and Sing*, a documentary about the controversy.

"It was a pretty tumultuous time," says Lloyd Maines. "But I'll tell you, those women circled up and bound to each other and totally weathered through it."

The Chicks may weather it, but it permanently changes them. And me. I'm still not over the nastiness I witness against The Chicks. Just as mainstream country turns its back on The Chicks, this is the moment I turn my back on mainstream country. Country music has provided for me for more than a decade. Now I am ashamed to be associated with it.

CHAPTER TEN

KRIS KRISTOFFERSON

I'm forty-two years old in the spring of 2003. I have zero job prospects and a questionable reputation thanks to the squabble with my former employer and the Charlie Daniels camp. One of the bigwigs at GAC actively campaigns against me in Nashville, going so far as to vilify me publicly at a Leadership Music event.

As I try to figure out my next move, Paul lands a new gig as the video engineer-in-charge on Bruce Springsteen's *The Rising* tour. I join Paul for a romantic week in Italy. While Paul and I are falling in love in Florence, my friend Al Bunetta at Oh Boy Records secretly cooks something up for me back home.

I touch down in Nashville after an idyllic holiday to find several frantic messages from Al on my voicemail.

"Saviano, it's Bunetta. Where are you? Call me the minute you get this."

"Hey, Saviano, where the hell are you? Call me."

"Tamara, seriously, you need to call me the minute you get this message. It's important!"

I'm jetlagged and just want to go to bed. But Al calls again and I answer.

"Saviano, you need to come over to my office today."

"Al, I just got back from Italy. Can I come see you on Monday?"

"No, Tamara. You need to get over here."

If it were anyone other than Al, I would tell him to go to hell ... but it's impossible to say no to Al Bunetta. I walk into Al's office as he yells into his speakerphone, a scene I have witnessed many times. Once it was

Studs Terkel. Another time Leon Russell. It's always amusing to hear Al in conversation on his speakerphone. Today Al yells to the black box, "She's here! Tamara's here! She just walked in." A gravelly, deep, and somewhat familiar voice booms from Al's speaker box: "Tamara, this is Kris Kristofferson. Al told me about what happened with you and GAC. I like people who stand up for themselves and others. I want you to come work for me."

My jetlagged brain is trying to process this as Al yells, "Say something!" I manage to squeak out a weak "okay." I'm in shock so it's the best I can muster at the moment. They both laugh. Kris says, "Let's talk on Monday, okay?" I say "okay" again. Geez, Tamara. A legendary songwriter has just asked me to work for him and I can't string together one coherent sentence.

Few songwriters transform an entire American musical art form. In a single line, Kris turned modern music into literature: "Freedom's just another word," he wrote, "for nothing left to lose." Today, songwriters all over the world replay the classic to seek inspiration. Kristofferson's first recording of the song as a demo, made while working as a janitor at Columbia Records in 1968, only hinted at the gems yet to come.

As his most famous lyric suggests, Kris has lived a Renaissance man's life. He was born in Brownsville, Texas, on June 22, 1936, to Mary Ann (Ashbrook) and Lars Henry Kristofferson. Kris loved country music from the start.

"My parents told me that I loved Gene Autry," Kris says. "They recounted a story about listening to the radio in the car, and my father said, 'Good God, that's awful,' about an Autry song and my mother agreed with him. They said that I spoke up—I was only five at the time—I said, 'I think he sounds real good.' My parents said it was the first time I showed independent thinking. My first real, real love of music was the first time I heard Hank Williams sing 'Love Sick Blues.' I'd never heard anything like him. I bought every 78 record that came out before I even heard it. I still feel the same way about Hank Williams today. Years later, I was on the Merv Griffin show, and Hank Jr. was also on it. That was back in the days when Junior was wearing his daddy's clothes—the nudie suits with the little music notes on it. Junior sang 'Your Cheatin' Heart.' Merv Griffin was trying to be nice to me and he said, 'Your songs are so much more personal than the one that Hank Jr. just sang.' I said, 'How can they be more personal than "Your Cheating Heart?" If you can talk about my songs this many years after I'm gone, in the same breath with Hank Williams, then maybe we can have some discussion about that.' Hank Jr. came up to me afterwards and thanked me for sticking up for his dad."

Always drawn to words and music, Kris studied creative writing in a liberal arts program at Pomona College in Claremont, California. He won an *Atlantic Monthly* short story competition, and his philosophy professor talked Kris into applying for a Rhodes Scholarship.

"I almost didn't go to Oxford," Kris says. "When I was a senior, I figured that I'd been in school all my life and I wanted to get out and do something in the real world. My professor, Dr. Frederick Sontag, talked to me for an hour after I told him that I was not going to try for the Rhodes Scholarship. He said, 'Listen, if you try for it and fail that won't be too bad, but if you don't even try, you're going to regret it for the rest of your life.'"

Kris landed the scholarship and headed to England. His biggest influence at Oxford was long-dead writer William Blake, who speculated that anyone who "refuses spiritual acts in favor of worldly desires and the need for natural bread will be pursued by sorrow and desperation through life and by shame and confusion for eternity." Kris says Blake made him a believer, that writing and creativity are indeed spiritual acts.

"The time at Oxford was my opportunity to go deeper into literature," Kris says. "Over there, I was able to really get into Shakespeare and William Blake. It was a very exciting time for me. I was lucky to be there. It was so interesting. Blake influenced my thinking and my relationship with the creative process. His feeling, the most important thing, was the creative imagination. I was just trying to be a creative artist. So many things that Blake referred to were the creative process. I think what I was trying to be, more than anything else at the time, was a creative person, some kind of an artist. I know feelings about freedom and about the imagination were all things that were important to Blake and became important to me."

Kris's paternal grandparents are Swedish, and his father was a major general who served in World War II and worked as a commercial airline manager and pilot after he retired from duty. After Oxford, Kris fought as a Golden Glove boxer, joined the US Army, and earned the rank of captain.

"I came from a military background," Kris says. "My father and both my grandfathers were officers in the army. My grandfather Kristofferson was in the Swedish Army. My father was in the Second World War and ended up major general when he retired. The military was part of everybody's life in those days because there was a draft. It was just assumed in my family that I would take ROTC when I was in college. It was just a fact of life, like going to school. But I was not at all suited for the military; emotionally, intellectually, or otherwise. I did make a lot of good friends there and spent three years in Germany flying helicopters all over Europe. I've never regretted being in the army. I think it happened at a time, after I had graduated from Oxford, when I didn't really know what I was going to do, being a would-be writer. I already had a wife and a child to support, and it gave me time to figure out what I wanted to do and what I did not want to do. I was in the army for almost five years."

Kris was assigned to a teacher position at the United States Military Academy West Point when fate stepped in. A trip to Nashville awakened a hunger in Kris, a longing he could not pinpoint until then.

"I went to West Point and got briefed about what might be expected of me, which looked pretty frightening," Kris says. "They told me cadets would come into class and sit in a semirectangle around me. They'd be at attention, I'd say, 'Seat,' and they'd sit down. And then I'd have had to turn in a lesson plan twenty-four hours before that, about what I'd be doing that day in class. It sounded like hell to me."

So when Kris visited Nashville for the first time in 1965, he was looking for a way out of hell.

"I'd always liked country music, and Nashville was the home of it. I was writing country songs when I was in Germany. I had a platoon leader who had a relative in Nashville, Marijohn Wilkin. Marijohn cowrote 'The Long Black Veil' and several big standard country songs. I sent her some of my songs and she sent word back through my friend that if I was ever in the area to come by and she'd show me around. I know now that she was just being polite to Donny's friend, but I showed up in Nashville to take her up on her offer. The first time I got to Nashville, I walked from downtown to Seventeenth Avenue South in my uniform. By the time I got to Music Row, I was soaking wet…and exhilarated."

Kris spent the first night in Nashville at a bar called the Professional Club with Cowboy Jack Clement. Jack was a songwriter, a dreamer, and a carefree soul. Jack's motto about the music industry was simple: "We are in the fun business. If we are not having fun, we are not doing our jobs." The faithful travelers who followed Cowboy Jack to Music City believed in his philosophy. Kristofferson was an early faithful traveler.

"It was the most exciting creative atmosphere I'd been around," Kris says. "Granted, I'd been in the military for four and a half years, and that's less than exciting creatively. I spent the whole first night listening to Cowboy Jack and Bobby Bare and I was just head over heels."

The next morning, Cowboy and the still-in-uniform soldier headed down to the Gulch beside Eleventh Avenue, where trains moved in and out of Music City. "Cowboy had a thing about trains," Kris says. "He talked about how he'd get onto a train and ride from Nashville to New Orleans and back. Just ride down, come back."

Kris knew on that first trip that Nashville was where he wanted to be. William Blake's riff about "refusing spiritual acts in favor of worldly desires and the need for natural bread" bounced around Kris's head. He was drawn to the spiritual acts—worldly desires and natural bread be damned.

"I knew right away I was coming back here," Kris says. "Then, I got to shake Johnny Cash's hand, backstage at the Opry, and that put the nail in the coffin right there. I felt that these people I met in Nashville were so fun and fascinating that if I didn't make it as a writer of songs I could write about the people. Backstage at the Opry, breathing the same air that Hank Williams breathed, it all felt enchanted. I said to Marijohn when she drove me back to the hotel my last night in Nashville, 'I'm coming back to Nashville, and I'm going to write for you.'"

Marijohn spent two weeks being hospitable to her cousin's military friend. She did not encourage him as a songwriter or offer him a job. Nonetheless, the visit emboldened Kris to abandon his solid military career for what appeared to be a dreadful life decision.

"When I said I was coming back to be a songwriter, Marijohn's head went right to the steering wheel," Kris says. "She said, 'Oh, my God.' That's exactly what she said, 'Oh, my God.' And it didn't look like a smart choice for several years. My family thought I'd lost my mind."

His family did think Kris had lost his mind. They immediately disowned him, and that hurt. Kris had spent the first twenty-nine years of his life trying to make his family proud. Now he had found his calling and his family spurned him for it.

"My mother sent me a letter saying nobody over the age of fourteen listens to country music, and if they did, it wouldn't be anybody we'd want to know," Kris says. "Jack Clement liked that letter so much. I was reading it in his office when I got it. Jack said, 'You've got to give me that letter. I'm going to show it to Johnny Cash.' And he did. The first time I met John after that, when I was a janitor over at the Columbia Recording Studios, John said, 'It's always nice to get a letter from home, ain't it, Kris?' It was funny because the letter was pretty disparaging of him, too. She wrote, 'Nobody knows anything about Johnny Cash except that he's a dope addict, and you seem to think he's something special, and Hank Williams was the same.' It was a very liberating reaction because I didn't have to live up to anybody's expectations anymore. They thought I was already past help. It was very depressing, too, that, even to Dr. Sontag, the guy that had talked me into trying for the Rhodes Scholarship, he thought I'd lost touch with reality. But I'm glad I followed my heart."

Kris, his wife Fran, and his daughter Tracy lived in the West End of Nashville in a small house. Kris Jr. was born in 1968. By then, Fran had had enough. She took the kids and left Kris. He moved into a condemned flat on Music Row between the RCA studios and the Tally Ho Tavern, his inspiration for the song "To Beat the Devil."

"My rent was twenty-five dollars a month and I had holes in the wall bigger than I was," Kris says. "It was a place to live, and not someplace you wanted to take people. I spent a lot of time sleeping in a lot of other beds. I couldn't provide adequately for my children working as a bartender and janitor."

Something had to change. Although Dave Dudley had a top twenty hit in 1966 with Kris's "Vietnam Blues" and famed producer Billy Sherrill produced a single on Kris in 1967, his songs were not catching fire. To earn some cash, Kris finally took a job flying helicopters around oil rigs in the Gulf of Mexico.

"I took my daughter Tracy into the Tally Ho to say goodbye to the people in there that knew her," Kris says. "Somebody saw us and said, 'Look, here comes Critter and the kid.' Some people called me Critter back in those days. Not long after that I wrote a song called 'Jody and the Kid.' When I was working in the Gulf, I wrote songs all the time. I was flying for hours without anything to think about except for the songs. I'm surprised they didn't all come out with the same rhythm of the blades."

Publisher and record label owner Fred Foster signed Kris on the basis of four songs: "Jody and the Kid," "To Beat the Devil," "Duvalier's Dream," and "Best of All Possible Worlds." Foster told Kris that he'd sign him on the condition that Kris would record an album for Foster's Monument Records.

Kris thought Foster was nuts. "I sing like a frog," Kris told Foster. Foster shot back, "Yeah, but a frog that can communicate." Scared about mounting bills and feeling stuck, Kris admitted to Foster that he had run out of songs. Foster offered money to tide Kris over. And he threw out a song idea.

"I was about to fly back down to the Gulf of Mexico and Fred said he had a song title," Kris says. "Boudleaux Bryant worked in the same building and Boudleaux's secretary was named Bobby McKee. I thought Fred said McGee, not McKee. Fred said, 'The hook is that Bobby McKee is a she.' I'm thinking to myself, *I can't write this shit*. I've never written on assignment, anyway. I wanted to do well because I had just gone to work for Fred and I hadn't had any hits or good songs. I was flying around Baton Rouge at the time, and lower Louisiana, so that's kind of where it set itself. It finally came together with the lines, 'With the windshield wipers slapping time and Bobby clapping hands we finally sang up every song that driver knew.' Billy Swan and I went into the studio at the publishing office and spent all night overdubbing it and cutting it. We were pretty knocked out by it. I took it to Fred and he loved it. So I split the writing credit with Fred, like Hank Williams and Fred Rose did."

In hindsight, these little victories were signposts of his imminent culture-shaking successes, but Kris couldn't see it. He walked up and down Music Row on quiet Sunday mornings, waiting for the bars to open at noon, and mourned the estrangement from his family. In his sorrow, Kris wrote the powerful lines that shaped one of his most meaningful songs:

> On the Sunday morning sidewalk
> Wishing, Lord, that I was stoned
> 'Cause there's something in a Sunday
> Makes a body feel alone
> And there's nothing short of dyin'
> Half as lonesome as the sound
> On the sleepin' city sidewalks
> Sunday mornin' comin' down

Kris had been giving tapes of his songs to Johnny Cash for a couple of years, but Cash just threw them in a pile with all the other unsolicited tapes. Convinced that Cash would like his stuff if he would take the time to listen, Kris took a tape with him in a National Guard helicopter and landed the chopper on Cash's lawn.

"I thought I might impress John if I landed there. I'd known him before that. I was not coming in as a stranger." Legend has it that Kris got out of the helicopter with a beer in one hand and a cassette with "Sunday Morning Comin' Down" in the other. Many of us know that it is Johnny Cash himself who started that rumor.

"That is 100 percent not true," Kris says. "First, there is no way to fly a helicopter with a beer in one hand, and I would never do that. Second, John wasn't even home. I did leave a tape for him but it had some shitty songs on it that I don't even remember. I could have damaged the house or the helicopter, and I could have gotten into trouble with the law, or John could have shot me out of the sky. It could have gone real wrong."

It did not go wrong. In 1969, Roger Miller recorded "Me and Bobby McGee," "Best of All Possible Worlds," and "Darby's Castle." Cash cut a stunning version of "Sunday Morning Comin' Down" the same year and invited Kris to sing with him at the Newport Folk Festival.

"I started performing, I think it was in June of 1970," Kris says. "John put me on his show at the Newport Folk Festival. I did 'Bobby McGee' and 'Sunday Morning Comin' Down.' After that, they put me on one of the workshops in the afternoon with all these great songwriters, like Joni Mitchell and James Taylor. James was great. He was living in an old school bus at the time. I got invitations to sing at the Berkley Folk Fest. Then, my first real gig was at the Troubadour in Los Angeles."

In the spring of 1970, Kris released his first album, the self-titled *Kristofferson*. In terms of units sold and dollars earned, it is likely considered a flop. But the songs on that album are beloved Kristofferson classics.

"For the Good Times" hit number one for Ray Price, and Johnny Cash took "Sunday Morning Comin' Down" to the top of the chart, too. Both songs cleaned up at the country music award shows. Kris went from zilch to superstar in what seemed like a nanosecond. In reality, it had been five years of struggle and heartache.

"A lot of the hits happened around the same time. It was real fortunate," Kris says. "Sammy Smith cut 'Help Me Make It through the Night.' I remember when Ray Price cut 'For the Good Times.' He had a whole orchestra behind him, with strings all over the place. I knew immediately, if Ray Price cut it with all that music behind it, that that would become his song. It won the record of the year. Cash made 'Sunday Morning Comin' Down' his song, too. I can remember the country music awards like it was yesterday. I was so tickled to be in the same category as Merle Haggard and Marty Robbins. We were all sitting kind of close together at the Ryman, and I had no idea that I would win. Merle's 'Okie from Muskogee' was a big hit and 'Sunday Morning Comin' Down' was not a big hit at the time. When they announced it as Song of the Year, I almost knocked myself out on the bench behind me. Finally, Merle said, 'Get on up there!' I think he and Marty were as tickled that I got it as they would've been if they got it. It seemed that way to me. I'd never seen such happy losers. I never had to work again."

Kris Kristofferson's songs changed country music in the same way that Bob Dylan transformed folk music. An entire generation of literary songwriters came to Nashville to follow in Kris's footsteps. And singers outside Nashville cut his songs, too. Kris's friend and companion Janis Joplin transformed "Me and Bobby McGee." Then Janis died and the song became a monster hit.

"I bawled like a baby when I first heard it," Kris says. "And, if I'm being honest, I still feel sad every time I hear Janis sing 'Bobby McGee.'"

The 1970s should have been fun for Kris, but he lived with a lot of guilt and regret. A broken marriage, his parents' disappointment, love affairs gone wrong, the lingering notion that maybe the payoff was not worth the struggle. His success was made possible by what others might call selfishness. People whispered about Kris as if he were a myth, with the drunken nights and helicopter piloting and hit songs. Kris wrote the lines, "He's a pilgrim and a preacher and a problem when he's stoned, he's a walkin' contradiction, partly truth and partly fiction, takin' every wrong direction on his lonely way back home."

"Of course I was writing about myself," Kris says. "I was tickled because Johnny Cash always thought I wrote that song about him. I guess if the shoe fits you can wear it. But what me and Ramblin' Jack Elliott and Cash and Waylon and Willie had in common is that our lives are partly truth and partly fiction."

Kris's songwriting led to a performing career that found him playing major venues throughout the 1970s. He was a revered writer, a sex symbol, and a movie star.

"From there, the films were just offered to me," Kris says. "I never thought I could get up and perform my songs in front of people, but I did it, and thought films would be worth the shot."

In film, Kris hit big with his costar Barbra Streisand in *A Star Is Born*. In real life, Kris's stardom also skyrocketed.

"I enjoy the filmmaking process," Kris says. "The more I did it, the more I came to appreciate the creative part of acting, just as I've come to appreciate performing my songs. The same creative process works in both of them. It is about being as honest as you can, being convincing and authentic to the audience that you're telling the truth. That works for me anyway."

CHAPTER ELEVEN

THE SAGE AND THE STUDENT

I know diddly-squat about being a music publicist and my first client is an icon. Maybe I should be terrified, but Kris is lovely and welcoming and I don't have time to think about it. I do have experience being on the other side of the desk. Publicists have been pitching me stories for many years in my editor and producer roles. Now the tables are turned, and it is up to me to sell Kris's story to the media. I open my business, Tamara Saviano Media, with Kristofferson and Oh Boy Records as my first clients. My job is to direct and manage the public relations campaign for Kris's 2003 album *Broken Freedom Song: Live from San Francisco*, recorded at the Gershwin Theater at San Francisco State. Stephen Bruton accompanies Kris on guitar and mandolin, and Keith Carper plays bass.

My first real conversation with Kris is on Monday, June 16, 2003. Kris and I spend more than an hour on the phone getting to know each other. At least half of that time we talk about social justice, journalism, and the First Amendment. Kris says, "I like that you stood up for your beliefs even though it cost you your job." It's not a stretch to say that Kris and I hit it off immediately. "We're old friends already," Kris says as he signs off.

A few weeks later, I meet Kris and his wife, Lisa, at the WTTW television studio in Chicago for a taping of the music show *Soundstage*. Actor Russell Crowe and his band Thirty Odd Foot of Grunts open the show. On Kris's closing set, Russell and his band join Kris on "Sunday Morning Comin' Down" and "Me and Bobby McGee."

During the downtime, Kris, Lisa, and I compare notes on the music business and laugh about every little absurdity. We have a similar sense of humor. Philosophically, we are on the same page. Kris and Lisa are refreshingly kind and down to earth. It feels like we've been friends forever.

It is astounding to watch Russell Crowe worship Kris. We sit together at lunch and Russell peppers me with questions about Kris. I tell him that Kris and I have only been working together a short time and this is all new to me. "Wow, great gig," Russell says. I agree.

The stripped-down instrumentation on Broken Freedom Song gives the lyrics plenty of room to shine. Kris says he likes to write and record political songs, and there are several on this album: "Sandinista," originally written and recorded for Kris's Third World Warrior album; "Broken Freedom Song," from the 1974 album Spooky Lady's Sideshow; and a new song, "The Circle (Song for Layla Al-Attar and Los Olvidados)." "The Circle" is a devastating account of the disappeared ones in Argentina and the beloved Iraqi artist Layla Al-Attar, who was killed when a missile hit her home during the Clinton administration's bombing of Baghdad. "The American press never even mentioned Layla or her family," Kris says.

Back in 1991, the New Zealand journalist Paul Holmes asked Kris (and the other Highwaymen, Johnny Cash, Willie Nelson, and Waylon Jennings) to give his opinion on what is wrong with the United States.

Kris said, "Well other than the fact that it reminds me a lot of the flag-waving and choreographed patriotism that we had back in Nazi Germany half a century ago, the fact that we've got a one-party system which is in control of all three branches of our government, and lap dog media that's cranking out propaganda for the administration that'd make a Nazi blush. Other than that we're doing pretty good."

There is no American outcry about Kris Kristofferson criticizing the United States while in another country. If there is backlash from the music industry, it is quiet. Country radio does not host parties to destroy Kristofferson CDs. Kris is not condemned. One could argue that his career suffered because he didn't sell as many albums, but that was never Kris's biggest goal anyhow.

"The entire country music business should be ashamed of themselves for the way they treated the Dixie Chicks," Kris says. "The fact that they didn't step up and protect their own, I just can't get over that."

While I'm having a ball with the Kristoffersons, I also have the time and space to think about American Roots Publishing. I'm determined to start a nonprofit organization that puts out records and books celebrating American artists who may not have mainstream appeal. A colleague introduces me to David Macias, who owns Emergent Music, a record label and marketing company (now known as Thirty Tigers). Over lunch, I tell David about Joe Ely's book and other projects that are percolating in my brain. David instantaneously grasps the concept and says he always wanted to produce an Americana tribute album to Stephen Foster, America's first professional songwriter. We decide to explore it together.

Throughout the summer of 2003, I'm immersed in my work with Kris and dreaming up ideas for American Roots Publishing. Creatively, I am finally free to do whatever I want to do. It suits me.

A reporter from Associated Press wakes me at 6:00 a.m. on September 12, 2003, and breaks the news that Johnny Cash is dead. June had died four months earlier. The AP reporter wants a comment from Kris, and so does everyone else. I spend all day and night fielding media calls, juggling between my office line and cell phone. Everyone wants to talk with Kris about his friendship with Cash. Producers from ABC, NBC, CBS, and CNN's *Larry King Live*; editors and writers at the *New York Times*, the *Washington Post*, *Rolling Stone*, *Time*, *People*, *Billboard*, the *Tennessean*, and the *Austin American Statesman*; and dailies and weeklies and radio shows all over the country. It is an insane day and I am numb. It is surreal to be in the middle of the media circus around Johnny Cash's death. My relationship with Kris is new, yet we are living through unimaginable moments together.

I attend Cash's funeral with the Kristoffersons and Al Bunetta. The pianist plays "I Walk the Line" as a haunting gospel hymn while the congregation settles into cushioned pews. The lifeless body of the icon lies still in an open casket, dressed, of course, in black. The opening to Cash's 1970s television show flashes on an oversize video screen at the front of the church. Johnny, larger than life, proclaims, "Hello, I'm Johnny Cash," and I half expect to see him walk out onstage with the Tennessee Three and kick things off with "Folsom Prison Blues."

I make myself small in the corner of the church pew. Lisa and their five children sit to my right. Kris paces the aisle on my left. He moves like a panther, slunk low, his shoulders hunched as he wears a path on the sea-green carpet. I focus on Kris's black trench coat as he walks back and forth. The sun pouring through the stained-glass windows tinges his coat with shades of green and blue.

Al Gore stands at the altar behind a podium. The former vice president describes Johnny Cash as a man of contradiction—like in Kristofferson's song "The Pilgrim (Chapter 33)," "a walking contradiction, partly truth and partly fiction"—and recalls how Cash faced those contradictions: he didn't deny or run from them but embraced them as part of being human.

Tears sting my eyes as I sit here in the First Baptist Church of Hendersonville, Tennessee, wrapped in the tenderness and kinship of our music community. I feel Kris's hand on my shoulder. I smile and nod to let him know I'm okay. Kris leans over me to kiss Lisa. Then he walks to the front of the church and talks about his long friendship with the Cash family and how Johnny was like a father and grandfather to his children—to all the children Cash knew. "I will miss his generosity, his spirit, his kindness," Kris says, and then he sings "Moment of Forever," a song he wrote when Lisa's father was dying. I hang my head and weep with the rest of the congregation. Emmylou Harris and Sheryl Crow follow him to harmonize on "The Old Rugged Cross."

Rodney Crowell takes his turn at the podium and speaks of his early relationship with Johnny. Upon visiting Johnny and June at their home in Jamaica while he and Rosanne were dating, Rodney expected to share a bed with Rosanne. Johnny said, "Son, I don't know you well enough to miss you when you're gone."

Rodney also recalls a conversation between Rosanne and Carrie Cash, Johnny's mother, when Rosanne asked her grandmother how she bore the pain of childbirth without medicine. Carrie replied, "Why, child, we just endured it." Rodney says Carrie's words can be used to describe how we will live in a world without Johnny Cash: "Child, we'll just endure it."

Now Rosanne is at the front of the congregation, remembering her father. "I can almost live with the idea of a world without Johnny Cash because in truth there will never be a world without him. His voice, his songs, the image of him with his guitar slung over his back, all that he said and sang and strummed changed us and moved us and is in our collective memory and is documented for future generations." Rosanne pauses before she continues. "I cannot, however, even begin to imagine a world without Daddy."

A week later, we are all together again for the Americana music conference and award show. This year, Kris receives the Spirit of Americana Free Speech Award from the First Amendment Center. It was just a year ago that Cash was honored with the same award and he and June performed for the final time. Last year I covered the awards for GAC. This year, I am here to shepherd Kris Kristofferson.

Johnny Cash wins Album of the Year for *American IV: The Man Comes Around*, Song of the Year for "Hurt," and Artist of the Year. The coolest thing is that the awards were voted on before Johnny's death. These are not meant to be posthumous honors.

Kris accepts the Spirit of Americana Free Speech Award. The standing ovation is loud and long and touching. I am proud to be here representing Kris as he performs "Don't Let the Bastards Get You Down," "To Beat the Devil," and "In the News," a new song he has yet to record. Kris also presents the Lifetime Achievement in Songwriting award to John Prine.

Rodney Crowell says that seeing Kris Kristofferson and John Prine onstage together makes him realize that we still have a few of our musical icons. Oh Boy Records pretty much owns the night with Kris and John. Bunetta is grinning from ear to ear.

I spend a considerable amount of time alone with Kristofferson this week. I've been around many celebrities in my career. Kris is the least "celebrity" of all of them. He's just a regular guy who has made some extraordinary contributions to the world of music, film, and the social justice movement. Kris is also a tender soul. We talk about his friendship with Cash and the funeral. Kris tears up. "I guess I am having a delayed reaction," he says. I reply, "Kris, John only died a week ago." Kris wears his grief and vulnerability openly, and that makes him all the more likable.

During Americana week, Kris is a guest on *Speaking Freely*, a show hosted by the First Amendment Center and broadcast on Nashville Public Television. He is articulate and knowledgeable about the issues. Not your average country singer.

Kris interviews at Country Music Television (CMT) on a show titled *Controversy*. The topic is "Sunday Morning Comin' Down" and the controversy about the line, "Wishing Lord that I was stoned." Well, it was a controversy back then, but Kris didn't intentionally write controversial songs. The reporter wants Kris to say that it was purposeful, that Kris wanted to be a rebel.

Kris is frustrated by the line of questioning. "No, man, I was not trying to stir things up or be a rebel," Kris says. "I just wanted to fit in and write good songs."

"That guy does not get it," Kris says after we leave the building.

"If I were the reporter, instead of pushing an agenda for the show, I would have questioned you more deeply on the different lyrics in your songs," I say. "'Wishing Lord that I was stoned,' 'hold your warm and tender body close to mine,' 'where two bodies lay entangled,' and made the story about how you were writing honestly from your heart but society at the time wasn't ready for that honesty. You were not *trying* to be a rebel but may have been considered a rebel because you were breaking new ground."

"I love you, Tamara," Kris says. "You get me."

The man is so much better than the myth. And I don't take the privilege of knowing him for granted.

Kris performs at the Grand Ole Opry. Although the performance is great, the rest of the evening is a nightmare. For some reason, they allow fans backstage at the Opry. It is a mob scene around Kris and is not pretty. People are rude and pushy, and there are a few times I feel like we are really in danger. These people are nuts, or at least inappropriate. I have a hard time getting Kris from the stage to his dressing room. A woman tries to push me out of the way to get to Kris before he is safe in his room. I stumble into Kris, he hits his head on the door frame, and I jam my elbow into the door. We manage to get in the room and close the door, but we are both bruised and shaken. Kris is scheduled to do some interviews, but it is out of the question because there is no way we can walk around the backstage area to get him to the interview room safely. I am truly surprised by how persistent and rude people are, even when Kris pleads with them to allow him to go to the restroom unscathed. It is a chilling scene. One that makes me realize that I am lucky not to be a public figure.

The 2003 Americana music conference is wildly fun and successful. It is a beautiful thing to be around people who cherish the same beliefs and live their lives honestly. It's the music that brings us together once a year, but it's the way we choose to live that truly bonds us. I see the Mavericks play the Uptown Mix with Tom Frouge and Al Moss. A group of us have dinner before the show and it seems like half of Nashville is there for the Mavs show.

Jack Ingram and Joe Ely perform at the Belcourt Theater. We go to the Mercy Lounge to see the Bottle Rockets. I hang out for a little while with the Compadre Records guys—Logan Rogers and Brad Turcotte—twenty-six-year-old guys who started a record label to sign Billy Joe Shaver. Not bad for a couple of young Belmont music business graduates. They also put out Suzy Bogguss's *Swing* record and hire me to write the bio. I love that independent labels are doing well. That's really what we celebrate at Americana—the independent spirit.

We close out the conference at an Albert Lee show at the Belcourt. Several of my favorite Americana friends are there: Al Moss, Rob Bleetstein, Melissa Farina, John Lomax, Steve Fishell, Steve Garvan, Rosie Flores. It is interesting how many people come up to me during the conference just to say hi and thank me for standing up for my rights during the entire GAC fiasco. Dennis Lord from SESAC tells me he was in the Leadership Music class when a GAC executive tried to publicly shame me. Dennis says that a number of people stopped him from smearing me, as I wasn't there to defend myself. The support of the Americana community means the world to me. One night Jeremy Tepper, program director of Sirius Satellite Radio's outlaw country channel, says, "Here's our poster child for the First Amendment." I did not do anything special. I just want to be able to look at myself in the mirror every day. Landing Kristofferson as a client because of the controversy is a bonus.

Left to right: Lucinda Williams, Rob Bleetstein, Cyndi Hoelzle, Jim Lauderdale, and Emmylou Harris celebrate *Gavin*'s new Americana chart at the launch party in Nashville, 1994. Photo courtesy of Cyndi Hoelzle.

Mike (*left*) and Bob (*right*) Delevante (the Delevantes) with Tamara Saviano at the Capitol Records M*A*S*H party, 1996. Photo courtesy of Tamara Saviano archives.

Billy Block creates the groove at his groundbreaking Western Beat Show at the Sutler in Nashville, 1996. Photo courtesy of Block Family archives.

Gavin's "In the Pines" gathering at Squam Lake in New Hampshire, September 1997. Surprise guest Doug Sahm entertains friends. *Top row, left to right:* Rob Bleetstein, Mattson Rainer, Jon Grimson, Jeremy Tepper, Al Moss, Fred Eaglesmith, and Robbie Fulks. *Bottom row, left to right:* Tom Frouge, Chris Marino, Doug Sahm, Doug Neal, and Tiffany Suiters. Photo courtesy of Rob Bleetstein.

Left to right: Young Americana artists Jack Ingram, Bruce Robison, Kelly Willis, Radney Foster, and Allison Moorer backstage at Symphony on the Range in McKinney, Texas, in the late 1990s. Photo courtesy of Cyndi Hoelzle.

Country Weekly staff writers Rick Taylor, Tamara Saviano, Wendy Newcomer, and Gerry Wood (*far right*) with country superstar Loretta Lynn in 1997. Loretta was part of my reporter beat for *Country Weekly* and I spent many weekends at the Opry with her. We had a connection because of our shared experience in Conover, Wisconsin. Loretta's daughter Betty Sue owned a bar down the road from where my family lived. Photo courtesy of Tamara Saviano archives.

Left to right: Rodney Crowell, Guy Clark, Austin City Limits producer Terry Lickona, Lee Roy Parnell, and Hal Ketchum at Davis-Kidd Booksellers in Nashville celebrating the release of the Austin City Limits twenty-fifth anniversary book in 1999. Photo courtesy of Tamara Saviano archives.

Jim Lauderdale (*left*) and Ralph Stanley (*right*) in 2002. Jim recruited Stanley and the Clinch Mountain Boys for his album *Lost in the Lonesome Pines*. Photo courtesy of Cyndi Hoelzle.

John Seigenthaler (*left*) and Ken Paulson from the First Amendment Center give Johnny Cash the first Spirit of Americana Free Speech Award at the inaugural Americana Honors and Awards at the Nashville Hilton Hotel, September 13, 2002. Photo by Barry Mazor.

Left to right: Julie Miller, Buddy Miller, Jim Lauderdale, Emmylou Harris, Jason Ringenberg, Gillian Welch, and Dave Rawlings perform at the inaugural Americana Honors and Awards at the Nashville Hilton Hotel, September 13, 2002. Photo by Barry Mazor.

Kris Kristofferson and Russell Crowe perform on PBS's *Soundstage* in Chicago in summer 2003. This was the first day I met Kris in person. We spent the next twenty years working together. Photo courtesy of Tamara Saviano archives.

Tom Frouge, Kris Kristofferson, and Tamara Saviano backstage at the Grand Ole Opry in September 2003. Tom and I started the nonprofit American Roots Publishing and produced *The Pilgrim: A Celebration of Kris Kristofferson* together. Photo courtesy of Tamara Saviano archives.

Emmylou Harris and Mavis Staples at Sound Emporium Studio in March 2004. Mavis recorded "Hard Times Come Again No More" for *Beautiful Dreamer: The Songs of Stephen Foster*. American Roots Publishing board member Emmylou stopped in to say hello. Photo courtesy of Tamara Saviano archives.

Left to right: Vince Gill, Billy Joe Shaver, Guy Clark, and Todd Snider pay tribute to Kris Kristofferson at the 2004 Country Music Hall of Fame Medallion Ceremony, where Kris was formally inducted into the Hall of Fame. Photo courtesy of Tamara Saviano archives.

During Americana week, I host our first official American Roots Publishing board meeting. Everyone is excited about the Stephen Foster tribute album, and I get the thumbs-up to move forward with David Macias and Emergent Music to partner on the project. We meet with OmniSound Studios to barter for studio time to start recording in 2004.

Kris returns to Nashville in November for a concert at the Belcourt Theater and to honor Cash at the Country Music Association Awards. Kris shares a dressing room with Willie Nelson, Travis Tritt, Hank Williams Jr., and Joe Nichols. During rehearsals, Willie walks over to me and says, "Hi, I'm Willie. If you're taking care of Kris, we're going to get to know each other real well."

It is fascinating to watch the artists interact with each other. And I am delighted by the reverence for Kris. At one point Kris and Travis jam together singing Johnny Cash songs—just pulling them out of the air and trading off. Another time Kris and Willie tell stories from their youth.

The Chicks come up more than once. Kris and I look at each other and laugh every time someone speaks their name. Kris says, "Hey, it's the Andrew Sisters." After Kris's concert Monday night, Peter Cooper wrote a great review in the *Tennessean*. Our favorite line is "Kris Kristofferson makes the Dixie Chicks sound like the Andrew Sisters." Peter is referring to Kris's statements from the stage. He proudly wears his political convictions in words and song selection. One audience member at the Belcourt yelled out, "Shut up and sing." Kris replied, "Shut up and listen."

I've covered the CMA Awards for many years as a journalist. And it was always a blast to be on the red carpet and in the media room with my cohorts. On this night, I don't have to think about filing copy or producing sound bites or getting the right quotes. All I have to do is escort Kris through the media jungle on the red carpet and then relax and watch the show on the monitor in the dressing room. I see things from a different perspective.

All night long the artists who share the dressing room wander in and out, tuning guitars, practicing vocals, joking about what is happening onstage. I'm an observer and it is extraordinarily fun. I really like Travis Tritt. He plays the hell out of his guitar, sings great, is polite to everyone, is tender with his wife, and puts off a really good vibe. We are probably not on the same page on a lot of things, but I enjoy him. Travis's wife, Teresa, is nine months pregnant and sweet and cute. Joe Nichols, who wins the Horizon Award, breaks into song and everyone in the room immediately stops to give their attention to Joe. That boy's got a country voice on him and carries a flask of whiskey in his jacket. Old school.

Everyone loves Kris. It is fun for me to watch, especially now that I've gotten to know him and I see what's happening behind those intense blue eyes. He is nervous before he performs. That's one of the reasons Kris was such a hard partier back in the day—liquid courage. I swear, it shows all over him. He's shaky, he says his stomach is upset, he can't eat, he can't talk—he has the worst case of stage fright of any performer I've known. Kris is also very emotional. In the six months that I've known him, I've witnessed him cry more times than I can count. He cares so much about many people and many issues. His sixty-seven years shows in every line in his face. People are surprised by Kris's age because they carry the vision of the feisty, sexy man in *A Star Is Born*. In truth, Kris is a wise old sage, and I adore him.

The Johnny Cash tribute at the CMA Awards is cool. Willie sings "I Walk the Line." Kris sings "Folsom Prison Blues." Travis Tritt and Sheryl Crow duet on "Jackson." The Nitty Gritty Dirt Band sings "Will the Circle Be Unbroken."

Later in the week, we spend an entire day at the Bunetta farm shooting the CMT show *Inside Fame* and Kris does a photo shoot for *Cowboys and Indians* magazine. The CMT interview is tough on Kris. They ask about his parents, his friends, and Johnny Cash. Kris whispers to me, "I'm beginning to feel like I'm at my own funeral."

CHAPTER TWELVE

BEAUTIFUL DREAMERS

The year 2003 melts into 2004 and my business is bustling. To be more in the thick of things, I sell my house in Bellevue and buy a townhouse on Music Row. Songwriter Larry Henley lives on one side of me. Larry is most well known for writing "Wind Beneath My Wings," which Bette Midler took to the top of the charts in 1988. Larry was also in the 1960s pop group the Newbeats. He sings the lead falsetto on the 1964 hit song "Bread and Butter." Larry is sixty-seven when I move in next door to him. His live-in girlfriend, Laurie Norton, is a flight attendant. Because Laurie travels so much, Larry gives me a key to his house in case he locks himself out. The cases of Larry locking himself out are too numerous to count. Some of my fondest memories of Larry involve him sheepishly standing on my front step in his blue bathrobe with his little white fluff ball of a dog in his arms. Larry comes up with cute stories each time I answer the door. "You know, Waylon Jennings always locked himself out, too. I'm in good company."

Songwriter John Wiggins lives on the other side of me. John and his sister Audrey had a short stint at Mercury Records as the duo John and Audrey Wiggins, but John now makes his living as a songwriter. George Jones cut John's "The Man He Was" in 2001. A couple of years after I move in next door, John sells his townhouse and buys a house in the country after Joe Nichols hits big with John's song "Tequila Makes Her Clothes Fall Off."

A few doors down from Wiggins is producer and songwriter Jeff Stevens. Jeff produces country music singer Luke Bryan. Before he got involved with Luke, Jeff wrote Alabama's number one hit "Reckless," along with hits for George Strait ("Carrying Your Love with Me" and "Carried Away"), as well as Tim McGraw's number one song "Back When."

Rounding out the creative residents at Peabody Square townhouses are music business attorney Charlie Andrews and film producer and composer John Biord. There is plenty of artistic mojo here, and I intend to call upon it.

Artist Stacy Dean Campbell hires me to help with his *Cottonwood* book and CD project. Oh Boy Records keeps me on to handle public relations for Janis Ian's *Billie's Bones*, Todd Snider's *East Nashville Skyline*, and Shawn Camp's *Live at the Station Inn*.

Shawn recorded *Live at the Station Inn* during his weekly residence at the beloved bluegrass club in Nashville's Gulch neighborhood. Shawn and I go back to my days in radio and I'm elated to be working with him. Shawn's manager, Kerry O'Neil, invites me to comanage Shawn with him and I jump at the chance to be part of Shawn's day-to-day team.

I am elected to serve on the Americana Music Association board of directors. We spend two days at a board retreat, facilitated by Liz Allen Fey. Liz is a master at helping us pinpoint our vision. The Americana board is an ambitious and thoughtful group. We follow the "rising tide lifts all boats" principle and the greater good is paramount in our intentions.

I'm especially busy with Kris. We spend a week in Austin for the South by Southwest Music Festival. Getting around the festival with an artist as popular as Kris is a wholly new and uncomfortable experience. Fans follow Kris everywhere. They crowd around the car as he tries to open the door and get in, loiter in the hotel lobby hoping to get a glimpse, and tell outlandish stories to backstage security in an attempt to get to Kris. They now know my name and that it is my job to take care of Kris. "Tamara, where is Kris? What is Kris doing today? When can we see Kris?" As an introvert who values my privacy, it's too much. Kris is gracious. Except for that one time when a car follows us all over town, racing through stoplights and putting everyone in danger. The driver almost runs over a woman in a crosswalk, and that is the last straw for Kris. We stop the car, the idiot driver pulls in behind us, and Kris gets out of the car and yells at him, "What the fuck is wrong with you? Don't you have any common sense?" Before the stunned fan can answer, we are in the car and down the road.

    Kris participates in a reception for the MoveOn folks and delegates from the Texas Democratic Party. He plays a secret show at the tiny Continental Club on South Congress. Although the show is unannounced, word leaks out and the place is packed. I'm sure there are more people here than the fire code allows. The owner, Steve Wertheimer, says he's never had this many people in the club before. The audience loves Kris, and they cheer loudly to let him know it. "My heart is soaring like an eagle looking out at all of you," Kris says from the stage.

    The fifteen thousand people who show up at Kris's show at the Town Lake outdoor stage are perfectly silent—hanging on every note as Kris plays and sings. When Kris finishes a song, the entire crowd erupts into cheers and loud applause. Then they quiet again for the next song. Kris and I have our preshow routine down. We are alone together after Lisa and the kids leave to take their seats. His 1970s-era boots smack the concrete as Kris paces and runs his hands through his silky shock of gray hair. He blows his nose incessantly. The boots are a work of art. The cracked and peeling leather is worn to the barest tan fibers and molded perfectly to Kris's feet. He replaces the soles now and again but the rest of the boots are more than three decades old. Oh, the stories those boots can tell. The audience revs up as the announcer preps them for Kris. I say, "Have a great show." Kris grins at me with that sparkle in his eye and says, "Don't tell me what to do." We laugh and he grabs me for a hug before he walks out onstage.

    I'm excited when Kris plays Ravinia, an outdoor amphitheater just north of Chicago. It's a venue close to my heart and not far from my hometown. A midlevel country singer opens for Kris. We are in the wings as the singer tries to inflame the audience with talk of "American soldiers kicking Arab ass" over in the Middle East. The audience does not respond but Kris leans down and whispers in my ear, "Someone should beat him up just for wearing his pants like that. Ten years ago I could have taken him. What do you think now?" Kris winks and smiles at me and then grabs my hand to pull me away. "Let's get out of here before he gets an idea about bringing me out for a song."

Kris doesn't know it yet, but he is going to be inducted into the Country Music Hall of Fame this year. It's a secret I am happy to keep. We cook up a plan to have Kris appear on the CBS *Early Show* in New York to announce the nominees for the CMA Awards. Hosts Harry Smith and Julie Chen surprise Kris on the show with the Hall of Fame news.

The political satire film *Silver City*, written and directed by John Sayles, opens in theaters in September. Chris Cooper plays a bumbling heir of a powerful political family who is running for governor of California. Kristofferson plays a billionaire tycoon who is funding the campaign. Kris is happy with the buzz from the film and our agent Steve Levine is fielding calls for more Kristofferson concert bookings. Kris's career is having a revival moment, and it's cool to be on this journey with him.

Shawn Camp and I spend several weeks on the road in the fall of 2004 to promote *Live at the Station Inn*. In Knoxville, Shawn plays a lunchtime show, the *Blue Plate Special*, for WDVX at their studio in a cute little café. He interviews with Wayne Bledsoe of the *Knoxville News Sentinel* before we leave for Asheville, North Carolina. We have a fabulous dinner at the beautiful Grove Park Inn. Spending time with Shawn is comfortable. We met so many years ago Shawn is like a little brother to me.

Collaborators and friends Guy Clark, John Prine, and Cowboy Jack Clement refer to Shawn as the Boy Wonder. A musical prodigy on fiddle and guitar, Shawn moved from Arkansas to Nashville in 1987. He played fiddle with the Osborne Brothers and in bands backing Alan Jackson, Trisha Yearwood, Suzy Bogguss, and Shelby Lynne. Warner Reprise Records signed Shawn to a record deal. "Fallin' Never Felt So Good," Shawn's first single on the eponymous *Shawn Camp*, edged onto the top forty country singles chart in 1993. His second single, "Confessin' My Love," barely made the top forty in early 1994, but critics and music people praised Shawn. I fell in love with the album *Shawn Camp* back in my radio days, and witnessing Shawn perform live at the Wisconsin State Fair cemented me as a fan.

Shawn recorded a second album for Warner Reprise, scheduled to be released in 1994.

"I cut that second album with Emory Gordy Jr. as producer," Shawn says. "It had Bill Monroe and the Bluegrass Quartet on it, Patty Loveless,

James Burton on guitars, and Bobby Hicks, my fiddle hero, on the fiddle, and so many of my instrumental heroes. A few songs I wasn't so knocked out with, and if I had done it on my own, I wouldn't have had those songs on the album. But Jim Ed Norman [label head] wanted me to have some singles for radio. Jim Ed calls me and says he is getting word from the radio promotions staff that there are no singles on the album. He said it didn't sound like the current John Michael Montgomery album. Well, that's kind of the point, you know? I didn't want to sound like John Michael Montgomery. That's not me. Jim Ed said, 'Well, whatever you decide, we're behind you 100 percent.' I should have realized that he meant behind me in my rearview mirror, in my past."

Warner Reprise asked Shawn to erase the fiddles and dobros and add electric guitars to the album. Unwilling to compromise his artistic integrity, Shawn asked the label to release the album as is, or let him out of his recording contract. Warner let Shawn go. The creatives in Nashville knew Shawn as a hotshot songwriter and musician. He did not need a label deal for success. Shawn scored his first number one radio hit with Garth Brooks' recording of "Two Pina Coladas." Brooks and Dunn landed Shawn another top-of-the-chart hit with "How Long Gone." Loretta Lynn, Willie Nelson, John Anderson, Josh Turner, Guy Clark, George Strait, Jimmy Buffett, and many more artists jumped to write with Shawn and record his songs. A gifted musician, Shawn was in demand as a studio session player.

After an eight-year break from recording, Shawn released *Lucky Silver Dollar*, on his own Skeeterbit label, in 2001. Oh Boy Records picked up *Live at the Station Inn*, and here we are, on the road together to promote it. We listen to the Elvis channel on Sirius Satellite radio. Shawn conjures the king of rock 'n' roll with his eerie impersonation of Elvis. He does a badass imitation of Johnny Cash, too.

After radio and media in North Carolina, Shawn and I spend a few days in Louisville and Lexington, Kentucky. Shawn plays an in-store show at Ear X-tacy in Louisville. We meet up with our journalist friend Alanna Nash, who has written several books about Elvis Presley. After all the talk about Elvis, Shawn and I drive over to Louisville Memorial Gardens to find the grave of Elvis's grandfather. After traipsing around the cemetery for an hour, Shawn stumbles upon the grave of Jesse D. Presley—grandfather of the king of rock 'n' roll.

In Lexington, we spend a day doing television and radio interviews before Shawn performs at the *WoodSongs* television taping. Shawn is relaxed during interviews and can sing and play anything on demand. His talent never ceases to amaze me. Jessi Alexander and Jon Randall are playing *WoodSongs*, too. Shawn plays with them, and they with him, and it is one big Americana jam.

Another Americana conference rolls around. Mavis Staples sings "Will the Circle Be Unbroken" at the 2004 Americana Honors and Awards. She brings the audience to its knees. Raul Malo and I watch the performances on a monitor in the backstage area. We've come a long way from the late night at Ma Fischer's when Raul talked me into moving to Nashville.

"So what's going on after this? Where's the party?" Raul asks.

"Are you kidding me?" I answer. "I'm going home to bed."

"What happened to that party girl that I knew in Milwaukee?" Raul laughs.

What an adventure it's been. Next year we will move the Americana Honors and Awards to the storied Ryman Auditorium and I will produce the show. Moving from a hotel ballroom to the Ryman is a big step. For the first time, we will have a television partner. I will produce the live show. My sweetie Paul will direct the television part. I'm determined to make the inaugural show at the Ryman a smash.

A few weeks later, Kris and I are back together for CMA week, the busiest week in the Nashville music industry. Country star Tim McGraw interviews Kris at MJI's annual radio broadcast, where fifty of the top country radio stations gather in one place to broadcast live during CMA week. Everything feels rehearsed, forced, and unnatural. It's obvious that Tim is a fan, but the radio people do not seem to know or care what is going on in Kris's life. No one asks him about the new album, and they are certainly not spinning any songs from it. While Americana radio plays Kris's records and embraces him as a vital and contributing artist, these country radio guys treat him like an old country star put out to pasture. At the same time, they clamor to take pictures with Kris. We nickname the event "Radio Disneyland." The joke between us is that every time Kris comes to Nashville he feels like "Mickey Mouse in fucking Disneyland." On top of the Radio Disneyland absurdity, a country singer who reeks of cologne hugs Kris and Kris smells so bad that none of us can stand close to him. Kris stunk to high heaven the rest of the night. Lisa and I made him ride in the back seat with the windows down. He complained about the cold and rolled up the windows. We all gagged and laughed so hard I had to pull over at a McDonald's. Kris took his shirt off, threw it in a trashcan and put on my raincoat that was in the backseat. Kris said, "Tamara, you're going to have to sell this car, it stinks!"

It is an iconic moment at the CMA Awards when they welcome Kris into the Country Music Hall of Fame. I watch from the wings as Kris's dear friend Willie Nelson talks about Kris's career while they show clips from his life. Faith Hill sings "Help Me Make It through the Night." Randy Travis sings "Sunday Morning Comin' Down." Kris joins Willie, Faith, and Randy to sing "Me and Bobby McGee." Channeling his hero William Blake, Kris says in his acceptance speech that the creative freedom to write songs and not worry about where they end up is what matters most to him. The standing ovation is ironic coming from a crowd that seems to worry a lot about where songs end up.

To round out the week, the Nashville Songwriters Hall of Fame welcomes Billy Joe Shaver and Guy Clark to the ranks. Kris is on hand to sing "Good Christian Soldier" and "Day by Day" for Billy Joe. Billy Joe wrote "Day by Day" after his wife died of a heart attack and then his son died of a heroin overdose in 1999. Kris is emotional as he sings, and Billy Joe sits at the next table and cries. It is powerful. I am lucky to work with these great poets with guitars. During dinner, many artists and executives come over to the table to pay their respects to Kris. Someone at the table asks Kris who his favorite new country singer is. Kris replies, "Todd Snider." I hide my chuckle in my wine glass.

I am surrounded by creative dreamers and doers, and for the first time I feel like one of them. The poet Mary Oliver said, "The most regretful people on earth are those who felt the call to creative work, who felt their own creative power restive and uprising, and gave to it neither power nor time."

David Macias, Steve Fishell, and I produce a Stephen Foster tribute album for American Roots Publishing's first project. Raul Malo, the guy who talked me into moving to Nashville nearly a decade earlier, sings "Beautiful Dreamer." Chuck Mead and BR549, the band who enticed all of us down to Robert's Western World for their lively shows in the 1990s, haul a gong into the studio when they record "Don't Bet Money on the Shanghai." John Prine, the iconic songwriter who gave me a job with Kristofferson after I was fired from GAC, sings "My Old Kentucky Home." David Ball, an artist I met back in my radio days when he sang in our conference room, records "Old Folks at Home (Swanee River)." Roger McGuinn, a Rock and Roll Hall of Famer and Americana pioneer who fronted the Byrds, records "I Dream of Jeannie with the Light Brown Hair."

The most fun for me is having Mavis Staples in the studio to sing "Hard Times Come Again No More." I pick Mavis and her sister Yvonne up at the airport and we hit it off immediately. They are so warm and open, and we talk and laugh like we've known each other for years. Everyone at the studio is excited to be with Mavis. Buddy Miller plays guitar on the track and brings Mavis board tapes from a Filmore East gig Mavis played in the 1960s. Matt Rollings plays piano and says, "This is it—if I never do anything else in my career, this one day has been enough." We all smile so much our cheeks ache. Mavis nails the song in one take, although we record several safeties just to listen to her sing. We grin and say to each other, "Pinch me so I know I'm not dreaming." Emmylou Harris drops in to say hello. At one point, Mavis is singing, Emmylou is watching from the control room, I am on the phone coordinating other studio sessions, and Al Bunetta is handing me a CD master of John Prine's "My Old Kentucky Home." All of this is happening for American Roots Publishing. I am touched by the generosity and kindness of our Americana community.

Our album is titled *Beautiful Dreamer: The Songs of Stephen Foster*. Born on the Fourth of July in 1826 near Pittsburgh, Stephen Collins Foster wrote songs that are forever woven into the fabric of our collective psyches: "Oh! Susanna," "Camptown Races," "Hard Times Come Again No More," "Old Folks at Home," "Jeannie with the Light Brown Hair." Contemporary songwriters stand on the bones of Stephen Foster.

In the days preceding the Civil War, Foster, his brother, and some friends had a garage band—playing their music in the horse barn adjacent to their home. He wrote some of his earliest songs, including "Oh! Susanna," for the group.

In 1846 at age twenty—more than a decade before sound recordings and more than sixty years before the first known radio broadcast—Foster had his first big hit with "Oh! Susanna" when the sheet music was distributed by a Cincinnati publisher and the song was picked up by minstrel troupes. No sound recordings. No radio. Yet a hit song passed around from person to person, making connections across time and space.

By the end of 1848, gold miners were singing "Oh! Susanna" with small changes to the lyrics. Instead of Alabama and a banjo, they sang of going to California with a "washpan on my knee." Pittsburgh's Stephen Foster became a kindred spirit of the California Gold Rush.

A sad aspect of Foster's legacy is that, although he was trying to write what was popular, some of his songs are racially biased. Ken Emerson writes in his introduction to *Doo Dah! Stephen Foster and the Rise of American Popular Culture*, "Stephen Foster is at the heart of the tangled, tortuous interchange between whites and blacks that both dishonors America and yet distinguishes its culture worldwide."

Foster was a product of a society in which degrading images of Black Americans were common—and the images of Black people in some of Foster's earlier songs are alarming. While fewer than twenty of his nearly two hundred songs fall in the "blackface" category, most of these were extremely popular at the time. Foster eventually eliminated dialect from his songs and never allowed cartoons of slaves on his sheet music, but such imagery did show up on pirated editions beyond his control. Some of Foster's songs, in later versions after his death, sadly became a medium for the racist lynch-law era. The truth, however, is that Foster had no sympathy for the institution of slavery or the culture that supported it. Foster strove to make up for his earlier works by giving a measure of dignity to Black subjects, like in the tender depiction in "Nelly Was a Lady."

While Foster was still an amateur songwriter, he realized that the minstrel stage was the key to finding an audience for his songs. When the Christy Minstrels performed "Oh! Susanna," the song was widely pirated by more than twenty publishing companies, which earned tens of thousands of dollars from sheet music sales. Foster received a mere one hundred dollars from his publisher. In that regard, "Oh! Susanna" was a financial failure, but Stephen learned a couple of lessons: one, his potential to earn money from songwriting, and two, the need to protect his artistic property.

Stephen's contracts were written in his own hand, the earliest agreements we know of between a music publisher and an individual songwriter. He kept his own account books, documenting how much his publishers paid him for each song and calculating his probable future earnings on each piece. He made a five-to-ten-cent royalty on sheet music sales or sold his songs outright. In today's music business, Foster would be worth millions of dollars a year.

Stephen Foster died on January 13, 1864, in the Bowery in New York City. Drunk and unsteady, America's first songwriter fell and gashed his head on a sink. He was thirty-seven years old. Stephen's pocket held thirty-eight cents and a scrap of paper that read "dear friends and gentle hearts."

During the making of *Beautiful Dreamer: The Songs of Stephen Foster*, I visit the Foster archives at the University of Pittsburgh. I hold that scrap of paper in my hand. The time between Foster's life, my great-grandparents' lives, and my generation melts away as the electricity from his fragile note binds me to Stephen. His work inspires me, a girl born almost one hundred years after his death, as much as he affected anyone in his own time.

We host a party to celebrate the release of *Beautiful Dreamer*. Roger McGuinn, Raul Malo, Beth Nielsen Chapman, and David Ball perform. I weep tears of joy as Fishell announces from the stage, "I'm Steve Fishell from American Roots Publishing." It had taken two years to will our little nonprofit into being.

I adore my brilliant comrades who have helped make it happen. The artists and musicians. Coproducers Steve Fishell and David Macias. Engineer Dave Sinko. Macias's team at Emergent Music distribute the music in the United States. Cameron Strang and his team at New West Records manage international distribution. Tom Frouge, my cofounder and accomplice at American Roots, leads the marketing campaign. Al Moss and his team promote it to radio. My colleagues in media write glowing reviews. It takes a village.

Beautiful Dreamer is a success. *No Depression* writes, "*Beautiful Dreamer* represents a contemporary anomaly, a tribute album that's not only good but essential." *USA Today* calls it "phenomenal." We sell fifteen thousand CDs out of the gate. There is enough profit to pay our expenses and fund two more projects. We finish 2004 on many critics' lists, as well as with space on Barnes and Noble's "Best of the Year" displays nationwide.

Beautiful Dreamer is nominated for a Grammy award in the Best Traditional Folk Album category. The other nominees are Cajun band BeauSoleil's *Gitane Cajun*; folk darlings Norman and Nancy Blake's *The Morning Glory Ramblers*; Rosalie Sorrels and Friends' *My Last Go Round*; and *… And the Tin Pan Bended, and the Story Ended …*, Dave Van Ronk's last live album before his death from colon cancer.

On February 13, 2005, we win the Grammy in front of thousands of music people during the pre-telecast of the Forty-Seventh Annual Grammy Awards. David Macias and Steve Fishell hold my hands as the three of us make our way to the stage. Steve goes to the microphone first to thank everyone involved with making the record. David talks about the importance of American roots music and arts education. When it is my turn to speak, I say, "Stephen Foster has been dead for 141 years and it's about time he gets this award."

It is a surreal day. David's date for the Grammys is Janet Reno. Yes, that Janet Reno, former attorney general from the Clinton administration. David brings Ms. Reno because she is involved in his next project, *Songs of America*. Also joining our party is Steve's wife, Tracy Gershon, who works in music publishing. Tom Frouge, who is instrumental in getting American Roots Publishing off the ground, flies in from New Mexico to celebrate.

Going in, I thought we were a longshot to win. Dave Van Ronk had recently died, and he deserved the award. Norman and Nancy Blake had been nominated many times; this should be their year. We are newbies. Our album is a compilation. The Grammy award is the biggest honor in the music industry, voted on by our peers. Few people win it in their lifetime. Here I am wearing a hundred-dollar vintage dress I bought on eBay, with my great-grandmother's rhinestone jewelry from the 1960s.

Steve Earle wins his first Grammy right after us. We all have an emotional moment together backstage before being escorted back to the main floor. As we walk back to our seats, we pass the Capitol Records Nashville staff and they scream and hug us. My cell phone rings nonstop. My dad calls from the Bahamas and Paul's brother calls from Seoul, South Korea. Friends from high school and college and former coworkers call, and other music business friends even call from their seats in the audience.

It is surreal being at the Grammys as a nominee and a winner. On top of the bizarreness, we are here with Janet Reno. All during the weekend, artists and dignitaries come over to meet her. She is the biggest star of the weekend. At the nominee party, people stand in line to get a photo with her. The nominees wear Tiffany medallions, and people come up to me constantly to ask about my nomination and congratulate me for the win. I've never spoken to so many strangers in such a short period of time. I get a taste of what it's like to be the center of attention and I do not like it. My claustrophobia is in full force.

The Grammy after-party is a circus-themed event with trapeze artists and strippers. The Black Eyed Peas and Chic perform. Our little group sits in a corner toasting with champagne. "What are we going to do to top this?" I wonder aloud to my friends.

We can't see into the future, but the effects of our *Beautiful Dreamer* album are long-lasting. On top of our winning a Grammy for Best Folk Album, Bruce Springsteen plays *Beautiful Dreamer* as walk-in music on his 2005 tour. Ken Burns uses our Mavis Staples track "Hard Times Come Again No More" and John Prine's "My Old Kentucky Home" for his 2019 PBS documentary series *Country Music*. In 2022, Bob Dylan writes about Alvin Youngblood Hart's recording of "Nelly Was a Lady" in his book *Philosophy of Modern Song*.

Beautiful Dreamer: The Songs of Stephen Foster gives us many gifts. Sometimes we put things into the world and we can never imagine the corners they will reach.

CHAPTER THIRTEEN

PILGRIMS

Winning a Grammy for *Beautiful Dreamer* does leave us with a conundrum. What will we do as a follow-up? Tom Frouge points out the obvious: I work with one of the greatest American songwriters on the planet. Kris's seventieth birthday is next year. It's a perfect opportunity to produce a tribute in honor of Kris and his contributions to the great American songbook. Tom and I pull music journalist extraordinaire Dave Marsh into our circle to get the party started.

Dave's wife, Barbara Carr, is Bruce Springsteen's day-to-day manager. Paul is the video engineer in charge on Springsteen's tour. We often joke that Dave's wife is on the road with my husband. Dave and I meet at South by Southwest every year. Dinner, drinks, shows, breakfast, parties. He is my favorite SXSW companion. Many people call Dave a curmudgeon, but he is actually quite tenderhearted and I love him.

Dave is a huge fan of *Beautiful Dreamer*. He passes it on to Rock and Roll Hall of Famer Jerry Wexler. Wexler is the producer who coined the term *rhythm and blues*. He produced records for icons Ray Charles, Aretha Franklin, Dusty Springfield, Little Richard, Bob Dylan, Dr. John, and more. One morning I answer my phone and the voice on the other end says, "Tamara, this is Jerry Wexler." I don't say anything as my mind flips through a list of my joker friends who might be messing with me. "Hello," the voice on the other end says. "I know what you're thinking but I really am Jerry Wexler. I'm calling to tell you that I love the music and the artists you chose to bring *Beautiful Dreamer* to life. It's beautiful work, and you should be proud." Honestly, this call from Wexler is better than winning a Grammy. We spend two hours on the phone as I scribble notes to my assistant canceling my other calls. United in our love for this music, Jerry and I begin a correspondence and friendship that lasts until his death in 2008.

Tom, Dave, and I ponder artists for the tribute album, *The Pilgrim: A Celebration of Kris Kristofferson*. I insist, and the guys agree, that we invite the Highwaymen family first. Rosanne Cash, Jessi Colter, Shooter Jennings, and Willie Nelson jump at the chance to honor Kris. Now that the core artists are secure, I meet with Randy Scruggs about using his recording studio as home base. Randy lends his studio, his time, and his savvy production skills to the project.

Although *Beautiful Dreamer* is close to my heart, now I am in charge of a tribute to Kris, a man I have come to know and love beyond measure. It is tempting to fill the album with my favorite singers performing covers true to Kris's versions of the songs. Tom and Dave urge me to consider unconventional artists.

The result is astonishing. The essential Americana artists are here, and I cherish each track. Emmylou Harris makes "The Pilgrim (Chapter 33)" her own. Rodney Crowell slays "Come Sundown." Rosanne Cash sings a beautiful "Loving Him Was Easier (Than Anything I'll Ever Do Again)." Todd Snider and Jessi Colter each choose deep cuts: "Maybe You Heard" and "The Captive." Shooter Jennings is perfect on "The Silver Tongued Devil and I." Rounding it out are Shawn Camp's dreamy "Why Me," Bruce Robison and Kelly Willis's uniquely Texas take on "Help Me Make It through the Night," Marshall Chapman's bluesy "Jesus Was a Capricorn," and Willie Nelson's superb and haunting "The Legend."

The outliers are good surprises. Patty Griffin and Charanga Cakewalk sprinkle Latin and electronica sounds into "Sandinista." Brian McKnight transforms "Me and Bobby McGee" into a moody R&B piece. Lloyd Cole and Jill Sobule imbue a soft, tender longing into "For the Good Times." Actor Russell Crowe is endearing on "Darby's Castle." Colombian singer Marta Gomez's poignant interpretation of "The Circle" is breathtaking.

I brush up my negotiation skills to land mainstream country singer Gretchen Wilson for "Sunday Morning Comin' Down." First, I haggle with my own team to even invite Gretchen. Sometimes there is an "us against them" thing going on between mainstream country and Americana. It's silly. I know to my bones that Gretchen will sing the hell out of "Sunday Morning," and my heart is set on her.

Sony Music insists that Gretchen's producer Mark Wright produce the track. That is a deal breaker for me. I counter that Mark is welcome to be in the studio but we will produce the track. After some back-and-forth with Gretchen's label, a date is set. Randy Scruggs's mother, Louise, dies, so Steve Fishell subs in for Randy and puts together a session at Buddy Miller's studio.

Two things surprise Gretchen when she shows at Buddy's. First, she says she has never recorded with a band in the studio before. She is accustomed to singing to musical tracks instead of live. Second, Gretchen says she is afraid we will nix the lyric "wishing Lord that I was stoned." Boy, she doesn't know our Americana world at all. We encourage Gretchen to take charge and have fun. Jon Randall is on hand to play acoustic guitar, and Gretchen enlists him to sing backup vocals. With Fishell egging her on, Gretchen directs the band: Jon, Phil Madeira on keyboard, Larry Atamanuik on drums, and Byron House on stand-up bass. It is fantastic to witness Gretchen indulge her creative vision.

In addition to producing *The Pilgrim*, I'm engrossed in oodles of interesting adventures, including projects with Shawn Camp, Beth Nielsen Chapman, Stacy Dean Campbell, Marty Stuart, and Sweet Honey in the Rock. I am in preproduction for the Americana Honors and Awards. My day-to-day work with Kristofferson is still the foundation of my business. All of it is too much to handle on my own. I hire Annie Mosher as an assistant and junior publicist. Annie is a gifted singer-songwriter. Like many others, she needs a day job to support her folk singer habit. I'm lucky to have her.

As fate has it, Kris is shooting a film based on the novel *Disappearances*, written by Annie's father, Howard Frank Mosher. Although he has written nine novels by now, *Disappearances* was Howard's first in 1977. Howard says that he had Kristofferson in mind for the character of Quebec Bill all along. All of Howard's novels are set in the Northeast Kingdom area of Vermont, where Howard and his wife, Phillis, raised Annie and her brother. Jay Craven, the film's director, hosts a fundraising concert in

Saint Johnsbury in the spring of 2005. Kris headlines and Annie opens for him. Paul and I travel with Annie and her husband, John Williamson, to Vermont. It's cold and raining icicles. Great weather for penguins, not humans. Shooting is canceled for the day and Kris is holed up in his hotel room. Paul and I check into a room across the hall from Kris. I change into warm flannel pajamas and call Kris to tell him we are here. A few minutes later he knocks on the door. It's the middle of the afternoon but Kris wears pajama pants and a T-shirt. Paul says, "The two of you are quite the pair." We all crack up. Kris says, "I'm really glad you're here, Tamara." Lisa is home with the kids, so Kris is flying solo for this week, and I know he is happy to see us.

The day after the concert, we visit the film set to watch Kris work. It is April, and cold and damp in the Vermont woods. I can't even stand an hour of being outdoors in this bitter weather. Kris is working in these conditions for twelve-hour days. Moviemaking—not so glamorous after all.

Kris is honored at the Country Music Hall of Fame Medallion Ceremony on May 1, 2005. The Medallion Ceremony is my favorite event of the year in Nashville, where the Hall of Fame honorees are formally inducted. The Kristoffersons and I arrive to the red carpet in a limo hired by the Hall of Fame. Lisa says, "Here we go again." By now we have walked many red carpets together. Kris hates red carpets because he does not like everyone making a fuss about him. The biggest bummer on this particular red carpet is Jimmy Carter, a local television entertainment reporter. Carter ignores all rules of courtesy and graciousness, jumps in front of other reporters when it is not his turn, and then asks obnoxious questions.

Carter asks Kris, "Do you think it's odd that you're being honored with an induction into the Country Music Hall of Fame when you haven't written a good song in more than thirty years?"

What the holy hell is wrong with this guy?

"I don't think that's true," Kris says. "I'm proud of the songs I've written since then."

Instead of moving on, Carter continues. "Really? You don't think it's odd that you haven't written a hit in so many years yet…"

I grab Kris's hand and pull him away. If all Carter cares about is hit songs, he has no business at a celebration at the Hall of Fame.

Kris, Lisa, and I cry from the front row as Ray Price and the Cherokee Cowboys sing "For the Good Times." We weep harder as John Prine takes the stage to perform "Sunday Morning Comin' Down." We are puddles by the time Vince Gill, Guy Clark, Billy Joe Shaver, and Todd Snider join together on "Me and Bobby McGee." Kris closes the set with "Why Me." There isn't a dry eye in the house. Unimpressed, Kris's youngest son, Blake, sleeps through all of it.

Kris wrote "Why Me" after attending church with Connie Smith back in the early days. Kris says he didn't understand it, but he felt extremely emotional during the service. The minister invited people to come down to the front if they wanted to be saved and show their love for Jesus. Kris says he didn't intend to do it, but something made him get out of his chair. The next thing he knew, he was down on his knees, bawling like a baby. He got a great song out of it.

The Fourth Annual Americana Honors and Awards show is September 9, 2005. It is our first show at Nashville's historic Ryman Auditorium, former home of the Grand Ole Opry. Great American Country is our television partner. For the first time, I produce the live show, and Paul directs the television show for GAC.

It wasn't easy to get here, but the lineup is exceptional. The First Amendment Center is on hand to give the Spirit of Americana Free Speech Award to Judy Collins. Guy Clark is honored for lifetime achievement as a songwriter. Marty Stuart takes home the Lifetime Achievement Award for Performer. In his acceptance speech, Marty sums up what Americana music means to all of us: "There's the chart, and there's the heart. It's great when they both line up but given the choice you'd better follow your heart."

Following our collective hearts gets us extraordinary talent for this show. Todd Snider opens the show with a rousing "Nashville." Steve Earle rocks his protest song "The Revolution Starts Now." Solomon Burke gets down with old-school soul music. Canadian foursome the Duhks play bluegrass. Although I wanted Robert Earl Keen to open the show with "The Road Goes on Forever," his record label bursts my bubble and coerces him into singing "The Great Hank," a song from his new album. Marty Stuart and His Fabulous Superlatives show off their gospel chops.

Guy Clark brings down the house with "Dublin Blues," accompanied by Verlon Thompson on guitar, Shawn Camp on fiddle, and Emmylou Harris singing background vocals.

Billy Bob Thornton gives John Prine the Artist of the Year award. The late John Hartford is honored with the President's Award. The founders of Rounder Records receive the Jack Emerson Lifetime Achievement Award for Executives in Americana music. Sonny Landreth wins Instrumentalist of the Year.

Buddy Miller takes home two awards, Song of the Year for "Worry Too Much" and Album of the Year for *Universal United House of Prayer*. "With two acceptance speeches tonight I think Buddy Miller has said more tonight onstage than in the ten years we've worked together," Emmylou jokes.

Mary Gauthier, a Louisiana native, joins the artists, crew, and audience wearing Mardi Gras beads with love and respect for the victims of Hurricane Katrina. Hurricane Katrina hit New Orleans two weeks ago, unleashing staggering destruction that we can't yet comprehend. Mary wins the Emerging Artist award as her mom weeps in the audience. A recovering alcoholic, Mary says, "I made my momma cry for a long time. I hope that's a different kind of tears now."

I stand at the side of the stage and weep as Arlo Guthrie leads the cast and audience in a breathtaking finale, "City of New Orleans."

It is an emotional and gratifying night. My team meets in the production office for a champagne toast after the show. Our first outing at the Ryman is a triumph. The show needs to be shortened, and we need to rethink the television partnership, as it disrupts the spontaneity of the live show. I'm already thinking about how to make next year better.

As a publicist, I represent Marty Stuart and His Fabulous Superlatives (Kenny Vaughn, Harry Stinson, and Brian Glenn) on the release of their exquisite *Souls' Chapel* album. Some categorize the album as gospel, but it transcends genres. Thom Jurek's review on AllMusic says it best: "Here, blues, soul, R&B, hard country, and early country-rockabilly—along with gorgeous four-part harmony—wend and wind around one another to create a tapestry so rich, so utterly full of honest emotion and joy, that it transcends the intended genre; not by subverting or bastardizing it, but by showing how gospel music is inherent in all of the other traditions that Stuart employs."

We travel to Washington, DC, and Marty and the band perform on an Americana radio show in the XM Satellite studios. NPR's All *Things Considered* welcomes Marty into their studio for a performance and interview with Melissa Block. All good fun, but my favorite Marty memory is our trip to dedicate the Commerce Street Baptist Church Sanctuary in a tiny town in the Mississippi Delta. Marty and his wife, Connie Smith, found the church one New Year's Eve after they played at a nearby casino. Marty and Connie loved the church and became friends with the clergy and parishioners. The church invited Marty and Connie to join them for the celebration of the new sanctuary. We leave Nashville at midnight on Marty's tour bus, stop at the casino in the early morning hours to clean up, and then go to church.

It is my first and only experience at a Black church, a momentous affair that stays with me until this day. Everyone greets us with big smiles. I am hugged like long-lost kin. The minister, who sings like Aretha Franklin, escorts us to seats in the front pew. The testimony is pure and loving. As the minister belts out religious songs and the hallelujah chorus sings along, the B3 organ player's fingers fly across the keys like Jerry Lee Lewis's. The whole place is rocking like Elvis with an aura of unbridled joy and jubilation. The first service starts at noon and ends with a lunch break at 2:00 p.m. The congregation socializes until the service begins again at 3:00 p.m. There is a dinner break at 5:00 p.m. We leave after dinner, so for all I know, they worshiped and sang and prayed through the night.

Kris's new film *Dreamer* is released in October 2005. The film, inspired by the true story of an injured racehorse, stars Kurt Russell, Elisabeth Shue, Dakota Fanning, Luis Guzman, Freddy Rodriguez, and David Morse. Kris's character is Pop Crane, father of Kurt Russell's character Ben and grandfather to Dakota Fanning's Cale Crane. Kris comes in for the Nashville premiere and to do a round of press. We spend a day in a hotel ballroom with media folks coming in one at a time to interview Kris. The questions and answers are largely the same. It would be easier and more efficient to handle this as a press conference with everyone in one big room asking questions and taking notes on Kris's answers. But every individual wants and expects alone time with Kris, so this is how it's done.

In November, we fly to New York for the CMA Awards and premiere of James Mangold's *Walk the Line* film.

Walk the Line is based on the life of Johnny and June, and it stars Nashville native Reese Witherspoon as June and Joaquin Phoenix as John. Gretchen Wilson asks Kris to walk the red carpet with her at the premiere. It is my first New York film red carpet and it is insanity. The crowd is six feet deep around the barricades. The flash bulbs blind us as the paparazzi yell, "Kris! Gretchen! Kris, over here!" I can't imagine being in that crush of people beyond the safety of the barricades. Even with security, it is difficult to navigate Kris and Gretchen through the screaming, chanting, and flashing, and people pull at Kris when he accidentally moves within reach of their outstretched arms. Even inside the theater, the photographers are relentless. Kris sits between Lisa and me and cries and blows his nose throughout the movie. I can imagine how emotional it is for Kris to watch a film based on the lives of his dear friends.

My late beautiful friend Peter Cooper and I meet Kris and Lisa in their hotel room at the Waldorf Astoria so Peter can interview Kris for the liner notes for *The Pilgrim: A Celebration of Kris Kristofferson*. Peter is my first and only choice to write the notes, and he has to get special permission from his day job editors at the *Tennessean*. Peter and I met in 1998 when he visited Nashville to promote his Spartanburg music history book *Hub City Music Makers*. Our mutual friend, publicist Ellen Pryor, threw a party for Peter. Peter and I bonded immediately over our shared love for Kris Kristofferson and Guy Clark. At the time, neither of us knew Kris and Guy. Seven years later, the story has changed significantly. Now Kris and Guy are part of both of our lives. Funny where this love of Americana music has taken us.

Kris is an open book, answers every question thoughtfully, and spends more than an hour drinking coffee with Peter and talking about his history. As we stand to leave, Kris, with tears in his eyes, says, "Tamara, I know I don't express myself well sometimes, but I want you to know how much it means to me that you're doing this album. I'm thankful for everything you do for me. You're the best thing that's happened to my career in more than a decade." Kris admits to being sentimental in his old age, but his kind and soft heart is one of the many things I adore about him.

The Thirty-Ninth Country Music Association Awards are at Madison Square Garden on November 15, 2005. We are at the Garden all day for rehearsal, the red-carpet arrivals, and the show. Kris shares a dressing room with Willie Nelson. The first thing Kris says to Willie is, "Man, thank you for singing 'Living Legend' for the album Tamara is doing. I've never heard anyone do such a great job with that song." "I'm glad to do it," Willie replies. "After singing your songs, I don't want to sing anyone else's."

I stand back and listen to the two old friends talk, and feel proud of the work we are doing at American Roots Publishing. I started out wanting to give Kris this gift for his seventieth birthday next year. Turns out, making this record is a bigger gift for me. Paul Simon and Billy Joel come into the dressing room to say hello to Kris and Willie. My phone rings. It's Marty Stuart, so I move to the corner to take the call. "What are you doing? Am I interrupting you?" Marty asks. "I'm in Kris and Willie's dressing room at the CMA Awards. Paul Simon and Billy Joel just walked in." There is a long pause before Marty squeals, "Name dropper!" Then we laugh so hard that Kris, Willie, Paul, and Billy turn to stare at me.

While we are in New York, Dave Marsh sets aside tickets for the Kristofferson family to see a Bruce Springsteen concert in New Jersey. My Kristofferson world collides with Paul's Springsteen world. The car takes me, Kris, Lisa, and their kids Kelly and Blake directly backstage. Dave escorts all of us to a wine tasting party. Kris greets the actor Tim Robbins and introduces us. Before they have a chance to talk, Dave grabs Kris to take him to Bruce's dressing room for a private meeting. Kris emerges just before showtime. He tells me he gave his United Farm Workers pin to Bruce. That pin means a lot to Kris, so they must have had quite the conversation. We take our seats in the audience. Blake sleeps through the entire show.

Our final New York adventure is an interview with the esteemed CBS *Sunday Morning* television show. It's a blustery morning and the valet at the Waldorf Astoria hails us a cab. Lisa and the kids are upstairs sleeping. Kris rubs his eye with one hand as he holds the door open for me with the other. We crawl into the back seat and hunch together in our thin coats.

Neither one of us is dressed for the winter bite of New York. "Why are we in New York in November?" Kris looks at me, incredulous. "You could have said no," I joke. "This is all your fault." Kris laughs. We are on our way to the Bitter End, the famed music venue in Greenwich Village, where Kris has played many shows.

A trace of last night's whiskey hangs in the air at the Bitter End. The club is dark and dank. We stand just inside the door for a moment to let our eyes adjust to the low light. Tracy Smith, the bubbly, cheerful *Sunday Morning* correspondent, waltzes over to the door to greet us. We make small talk as the crew finishes the setup. Two cameras, one on Tracy and the other on Kris. I stand behind Tracy, next to the camera man who is shooting Kris, right in Kris's sightline in case he needs anything. Kris blows on a cup of coffee as they adjust the lights. The crew talks about Kris's threadbare cowboy boots and how the layers of brown leather have peeled away to a rough sandstone texture. Kris wears them just as he is, cool and casual.

There is plenty to talk about with Kris during the interview. Next June, he will be seventy. New West Records is releasing his album *This Old Road*, Kris's first recording of all-new songs in eleven years. Our tribute album will be released at the same time. It seems appropriate for the press to revisit Kris's long career, and they have been clamoring to get time with him.

Tracy lobs questions at Kris about his early days as a songwriter in Nashville, his time with Janis Joplin, his friendships with Willie, Waylon, and Cash. Then she starts talking about Kris's role in *A Star Is Born*. She mentions the steamy hot tub scene with Kris and his costar Barbra Streisand. Tracy asks Kris how it feels to be a sex symbol. I'm listening to all of this while thinking, "Ewwww!" and just then Kris laughs and says out loud, "Wait, wait, I need a minute. Tamara has her 'ewww' face on." The entire crew erupts in laughter. I apologize and promise to keep a poker face for the rest of the interview. It goes smoothly. We say our goodbyes and step out onto the sidewalk, and Kris hails a cab.

Kris waits until we are settled in the back seat of the taxi before he turns to me and says, "You know, women *did* find me attractive." Without missing a beat, I deadpan, "Well, you're no Jimmy Smits." Kris laughs so loud that he startles the cab driver. We howl together. I laugh so hard my stomach hurts and tears run down my cheeks. "No Jimmy Smits," Kris says. "That's a good one." In my defense, Jimmy Smits *is* pretty dang cute and this is when he played Matthew Santos on the *West Wing* and who didn't love that? For many months and years to come, Kris pulls that gem out when he greets me. "Well, I'm no Jimmy Smits but here I am."

CHAPTER FOURTEEN

THE ROAD GOES ON FOREVER AND THE PARTY NEVER ENDS

The years blur together in one sweet tradition after another. The Americana music community is a giant sequoia, a foundation of deep roots with new branches forming year by year into unbreakable bonds of friendship. We are on a dazzling and colossal adventure together, and it is heady.

We gather for Folk Alliance in February and meet in Austin each March for music business spring break at South by Southwest. Spring and summer are filled with album releases, concert tours, and music festivals. Fall brings the Americana music convention; the Country Music Hall of Fame Medallion Ceremony; the BMI, ASCAP, and SESAC awards; the Nashville Songwriter Hall of Fame dinner; and many other events.

In 2006, music discovery is changing. The major record labels are suing peer-to-peer file-sharing companies like Napster that allow customers to upload music from CDs to share on a worldwide network. Social networks MySpace, YouTube, and Pandora are on the rise. Daniel Ek starts a streaming company called Spotify, although we can't begin to assess the damage it will do to songwriters at this early date. XM Satellite Radio and Sirius Satellite Radio compete for subscribers. Terrestrial radio has competition.

I am the first woman elected president of the Americana Music Association, and I continue to produce the award show at the Ryman. Dualtone Music Group hires me as the public relations director for Guy Clark's album *Workbench Songs*. I'm still managing Shawn Camp, and he releases his *Fireball* album. I also oversee publicity campaigns for Radney Foster's *This World We Live In*, Pinmonkey's *Big Shiny Cars*, and Marshall Chapman's *Mellowicious!* Our nonprofit, American Roots Publishing, is set to release *The Pilgrim: A Celebration of Kris Kristofferson* for Kris's seventieth birthday in June, and Kris releases *This Old Road* on New West Records.

Annie Mosher and I share a rented office over at the Big Yellow Dog Publishing building. The phone rings constantly. Annie is flawless at organizing our schedule, fielding media calls, and helping me stay on track as we pitch media outlets and book artists for interviews. I'm out on the road a good chunk of the year and learn how to work efficiently from planes, trains, and automobiles.

This Old Road, Kris's first album of new songs in eleven years, arrives in March 2006. Paul and I are in Los Angeles this week, staying at the Malibu Beach Inn with the Kristoffersons.

A driver picks Kris, Lisa, and me up at five o'clock in the morning to take us to the Mojave Desert for the video shoot for the single "This Old Road." It's a three-hour drive and we fall asleep minutes after getting in the van. I wake up first, check my watch, and look around. We should be getting close. I ask the driver how much longer until we get to the set. He is lost, and there is no cell phone service out here. I realize too late that I should have asked the New West Records staff for directions instead of counting on the driver. It's clear that we are not just going to stumble upon a film crew in miles and miles and miles of open desert.

Kris and Lisa wake up as we drive into Trona, a ghost town situated halfway between Los Angeles and Death Valley. We stop at Sandy's Desert Café to use the restroom and find out if anyone here might help us. It's a sleepy little café with only five customers. Kris walks toward the men's room as all five heads turn to stare at him.

"Hello," I say. "We are lost. Does anyone know anything about a film crew working around here?"

A pretty woman with a gray bouffant and cat-eye glasses looks at me. "Is that Kris Kristofferson?"

"Yes. We are shooting a music video somewhere out here but we're lost. Have any of you seen a film crew?"

Kris returns from the restroom and signs autographs while I try to get a cell phone signal on my flip phone.

A gentleman wearing a blue ball cap over a long gray ponytail taps his cane to get my attention. "Sometimes film crews work out near the abandoned railyard."

We head out toward the railyard and a crew member intercepts us. Finally at the set, we are greeted by New West Records president Cameron Strang, his wife Tori, and a small production crew standing on the tracks next to an old train tunnel. A deep shaft, dug into an overgrown hill, looks like it has been there hundreds of years. There is barely room for a train to fit through the dark, narrow channel. The director, a camera guy, and Kris walk into the tunnel.

"This doesn't seem like a good idea," Lisa says. I agree.

"Oh, no, this tunnel is not in use," a crew member says. "Trains don't run through here anymore."

A few minutes later, a whistle blows and a train barrels down the track toward the tunnel where Kris and the crew are shooting. The engineer is startled to see a bunch of idiots standing next to the tracks. He blows the whistle again and brakes squeal as he tries to slow the train. Can he see Kris and the crew trapped inside the tunnel? There is not enough room for them and the train. My heart pounds as we all scream, "Train! Train! Get out of the tunnel!" A crew guy with a radio is screaming into the radio, "This is no joke, dude, get the fuck out of the tunnel!"

Lucky for all of us, the engineer manages to slow the train way down as Kris and the crew run out of the tunnel with seconds to spare.

"We got the shot," someone says.

Next, Kris walks back and forth, back and forth, along the tracks with his guitar case on his back, mouthing words to the song. The director calls for a break so they can check the footage and decide if it's time to move to the next location.

We wrap up the "This Old Road" shoot out at the Trona Pinnacles, the tufa spires rising from the bed of the Searles Dry Lake basin. Parts of the films *The Planet of the Apes* and *Lost in Space* were shot at the pinnacles.

As we wait for a new setup, Kris and I get into an SUV and I show him the finished artwork for *The Pilgrim: A Celebration of Kris Kristofferson*.

The cover is an old Jim Marshall photo from the early 1970s of Kris in profile, a shock of curls over his forehead, eyes cast down. "You look deep in thought in this picture," I say. "I was drawn to it the minute I saw it."

"I remember this," Kris says. "I was worried about my son. He was having a lot of health problems at the time." A few tears roll down Kris's cheek.

"You haven't heard Rosanne's 'Lovin' Him Was Easier' yet," I say. "Do you want to hear it while we wait?"

"Hell yes," Kris says.

I have no idea whose SUV we are in, but I turn the key, pop the CD in the player, and find Rosanne's track. Kris and I listen in silence as Rosanne's exquisite voice waltzes around us.

Kris weeps openly now. "Oh, Tamara. This is so beautiful. I'll give Rosanne a call later."

He takes my hand in his. "How can I ever thank you enough? I can't believe you took the time to do this for me. What a lovely, loving gift."

Emotion swells up in me. Love. Joy. Maybe some grief in knowing that this can't last forever.

Someone knocks on the window. I pop the CD out. Kris and I smile at each other. "Ready for whatever is next?" he says.

Yeah, I am ready for whatever comes next.

What's next is *The Tonight Show with Jay Leno*. Don Was, producer of *This Old Road*, joins Kris and Stephen Bruton to perform the title track. Bruton has been in Kris's band for nearly forty years and Kris is more comfortable with him around. We cool our heels in the dressing room between rehearsal and the show. Jay comes in to say hello. He and Kris have known each other since the 1970s. A woman pokes her head into the room to tell Kris that a producer from Kris's film *Wooly Boys* is in the house and wants to say hello. Coincidentally, I recently watched *Wooly Boys*. It's a movie about North Dakota sheep ranchers, played by Kris and Peter Fonda. After I watch it, I ask Kris about it. "You and Peter Fonda sorta subtle *Brokeback Mountain* friends, right?" "Tamara, don't do this to me," Kris says. We laugh nonstop for twenty minutes. Backstage at Leno, Kris looks at me and we both crack up. Then Kris says, "You better let him in so Tamara can tell him she thinks Peter Fonda and I are lovers in that film."

"I'm sticking around for this one," Leno says.

The producer comes in and Kris introduces him around. Kris puts me on the spot and makes me defend my position. But at this point I can barely remember the film and I'm standing there in front of Jay Leno for Christ's sake. I choke. Big time. I stammer out some nonsense while Kris grins at me and watches me hang myself. It is definitely not *Tonight Show* worthy. "That'll teach you to make fun of my movies," Kris says. Just another day on the job.

Our last night in LA, Kris plays an intimate show at the Troubadour, the club where he debuted his first concert, opening for Linda Ronstadt, in 1970. The club is packed with fans and the VIP room is crammed with celebrities, most of whom I do not recognize because I don't keep up with that scene. I spend a few minutes with the actor Luke Wilson but I'm not familiar enough with his work to hold a conversation about it. Kris is nervous. "I can't believe all these people are here," he says, as he does before almost every show. Kris's set is pristine and the room is quiet and reverent as he performs. After the show, Kris, Lisa, Paul, and I sit out on the patio at the Malibu Beach Inn and drink champagne. The Pacific Ocean waves crash around the boulders below us as we celebrate the end of a busy week in LA, the kickoff to the *This Old Road* promotional campaign.

The next stop is Austin, Texas, and SXSW. The festival is our annual attempt to squeeze myriad artist interviews, appearances, events, films, and music into one zany week.

We hit the ground running and Kris shoots a guest cameo for Kacey Jones's music video "San Francisco Mabel Joy" from her *Kacey Jones Sings Mickey Newbury* album. The layers of friendship and connection draw Kris to the project. The music video stars Waylon Payne and Mickey's daughter Laura and is directed by Stacy Dean Campbell. Kris is friends with Waylon and was good friends with Mickey before his death. I had worked with Stacy a couple of years before on the release of his exquisite album *Cottonwood*, the soundtrack to his first novel. I'm handling public relations on Kacey's album. It's a family affair.

Stephen Bruton is part of the Texas Heritage Songwriters' Association. Joe Ables, who owns the legendary Saxon Pub in Austin, is one of the founders of the association. They invite Kris to the inaugural Texas Songwriters Hall of Fame Awards. The event is held at Hill's Café on South Congress Avenue. Joe and I meet for the first time at this event, the beginning of our decades-long friendship. We still laugh about that day, when Joe gets a taste of how audacious Kris's fans can be, rushing at him, pushing and shoving and hollering, just to touch him, with zero respect for Kris's safety or security. As we attempt to leave the venue, I try to protect Kris's teenage daughter Kelly and young son Blake from being trampled by the crowd as Kris climbs into the limo. Stephen Bruton pulls a drunk dude out by his belt loop as he crawls into the car after Kris. The last thing I remember before the limo door closes is Paul leaping in at the last minute. Once we are all settled in the car, Kris asks if everyone is okay. We have a few bumps and bruises, but thankfully no one is seriously injured.

The Texas Film Awards put Kris in their Hall of Fame on March 10. Founded by Evan Smith and Louis Black as part of director Richard Linklater's Austin Film Society, the Texas Film Hall of Fame honors those who have made a significant contribution to the advancement of the Texas film industry. We gather at the Austin Studios for the annual gala. Kris, Lisa, Paul, and I stand on the periphery of the cocktail party before the show. Bill Snider, who played football with Kris in college, and his wife, Sandra, join us. Although everyone is kind and welcoming, the gala is awkward, as the six of us feel like outsiders here, not knowing the Austin crowd. We make it through the cocktail party, and then the fundraising auction, and then dinner and the awards ceremony begin.

Kris and actors Matthew McConaughey and JoBeth Williams are the honorees tonight. Cybill Shepherd is on hand to accept the Frontier Award for *The Last Picture Show*. Screenwriter and script supervisor Anne Rapp gives the AMD Live! Soundtrack Award to Lyle Lovett. John Sayles, who directed Kris in his 1996 film *Lone Star*, presents Kris with his award. Kris's acceptance speech is short and sweet, especially next to McConaughey, who warns us in advance that he is going to be long-winded.

"It's particularly sweet to be honored in your home state," Kris says from the podium. "I've always been proud to be a Texan. I want to thank the Austin Film Society for bringing this Brownsville boy back home again for this honor."

As part of SXSW, Kris is here to support the release of his film *Disappearances*. In addition to the *Disappearances* screening, Dave Marsh interviews Kris in front of five hundred people at the convention center. Kris participates in a radio interview along with Willie Nelson in the lobby of the Four Seasons hotel. We run around to other radio, television, and print journalists to talk about Kris's new album *This Old Road*. It is a busy and successful SXSW and we are all exhausted by the end of it.

The next stop is Nashville, and Kris's concert at the Ryman Auditorium plus a gazillion more media interviews. On March 26, Kris plays Convocation Hall in Toronto, then on to DC for a March 31 show at the Kennedy Center's "Country: A Celebration of America's Music: The Country Salutes Country Festival" with the Judds, Vince Gill, and Lee Ann Womack. We land at the Calvin Theater in Northampton, Massachusetts, for a show on April 5. We are road weary by the time we check in to NBC's *Late Night with Conan O'Brien* in New York, plus more radio and print interviews. After New York, the tour bus takes us to Vermont for the official hometown premiere of *Disappearances*.

This is no rock 'n' roll tour. Kris's bus is a quiet, family place. It's just Kris, Lisa, and their two youngest kids, Kelly and Blake. After shows, Kris may drink a glass of wine or two and then work on a puzzle with Kelly. It takes him some time to wind down after a show, so he stays up until the wee hours of the morning and then sleeps late.

In June, we release *The Pilgrim: A Celebration of Kris Kristofferson*. I meet with television producer RAC Clark, son of Dick Clark, to discuss producing a big seventieth birthday show for Kris. RAC and I are excited, but Kris isn't interested. He just wants to spend his birthday quietly with his family.

I spend the summer pitching *The Pilgrim*, *This Old Road*, and Guy Clark's upcoming album *Workbench Songs*, which is released on September 19. I spend many days running reporters in and out of Guy's workshop as Guy does interview after interview, chain-smoking hand-rolled cigarettes and joints the whole time.

To celebrate *Workbench Songs* and Guy's long career, the Country Music Hall of Fame invites Guy to be the fourth artist in residence following the previous years' artists Cowboy Jack Clement, Earl Scruggs, and Tom T. Hall. Guy curates special performances in the Hall of Fame's Ford

Theater on September 6, 13, and 27. Each performance sells out, with fans traveling to Nashville from all over the world for the special occasion. The reverence for Guy is breathtaking as the theater remains silent during every song and then bursts into applause and big smiles. The kinship between Guy Clark fans is astounding. The sacredness of Guy's poetry and presence vibrates throughout the room.

On September 22, I produce the Americana Honors and Awards for the second year in a row. I write a welcome note on the first page of the program book:

> Greetings Americana Family,
> Welcome to the seventh annual Americana conference and fifth Americana Honors & Awards. Seven years. Wow. The years have slipped by quickly since we held our first conference. The Americana Music Association began with a small, passionate group of people who came together to celebrate our collective love of roots music. We are now more than 1300 members strong—and growing.
> Our constant challenge to focus on the music—allowing the art to drive the commerce—remains, although we continue to make great strides. You'll notice there are no television cameras in the Ryman this year. While last year's experiment was a resounding success, we believe the live show—this music and these artists—are the lifeblood of our organization. Rather than compromise the integrity of the live show with television protocol, we are returning to our roots this year.
> Those roots began in 2002 when Johnny Cash and June Carter Cash performed together for the last time at our little conference. Since then we have been fortunate to experience amazing concerts by a breadth of artists including legends John Prine, Mavis Staples, Kris Kristofferson, Guy Clark, Judy Collins, Solomon Burke, Arlo Guthrie, the Carter Family, and The Flatlanders. We've also been treated to incredible musical performances from emerging artists including Mindy Smith, Mary Gauthier, Hayes Carll, The Duhks, Kathleen Edwards and Allison Moorer. And let's not forget our mainstay artists

including Rodney Crowell, Steve Earle, Slaid Cleaves, Radney Foster, Jim Lauderdale, Raul Malo, Buddy Miller, Todd Snider and the many other artists who embrace the Americana community. Without them, this organization would not exist. It is my sincere pleasure to acknowledge their gifts.

This year, as in the past, the Americana Honors & Awards is all about the music and celebrating our extraordinary artists. I encourage you to buy yourself a beverage, get comfortable in your pew, and sit back and enjoy what promises to be another wonderful night of Americana music at the Ryman Auditorium.

Yours in music,
Tamara Saviano
President, Americana
Music Association

In an attempt to answer the age-old question, What is Americana? *Tennessean* reporter Peter Cooper gives it another whack in his profile of the awards show.

"What is Americana?" Peter writes. "Well, it's modern music that's based on American roots forms, and there are more tendencies than hard-and-fast rules. In a lot of instances, it sounds a whole lot like country. In fact, platinum country act turned platinum non-country act the Dixie Chicks will compete in the Best Song category at the awards show. While country radio booted the Chicks from playlists, Americana stations continue to embrace the band. Americana is a rather amorphous genre, though, and many artists also delve beyond country into rock, folk blues and jazz."

Peter quotes Emmylou Harris as saying, "It's music that is coloring outside the lines, but somehow is connected to that big pool that is folk and country and storytelling and doesn't fit any particular mold."

As the producer of the awards show, I try my best to color outside the lines. I want it to be musically diverse and to showcase artists of excellence. I want to bring the audience along for the ride—to reveal the power and beauty of these artists, to persuade listeners to turn off the radio and discover new and unfamiliar music. The members of the Americana Music Association vote on the nominees and award winners.

Our performers this year include British rock icon Elvis Costello, New Orleans soul man Allen Toussaint, funk band the Dynamites, and Australian band the Greencards. Indomitable Americana artists Kim Richey, Delbert McClinton, Marty Stuart, James McMurtry, and Rosanne Cash round out the night. Country superstar Vince Gill, also an Americana artist in my book, is on hand to present the Lifetime Achievement Award for songwriting to his longtime friend Rodney Crowell. Alejandro Escovedo gets the Lifetime Achievement Award for performer and Kenny Vaughn for musician. I'm thrilled that Barry Poss, founder of Sugar Hill Records, is honored with the Jack Emerson Lifetime Achievement Award for Executive. As the president of the Americana board, it is my distinct privilege to present the posthumous President's Award to Mickey Newbury. During his lifetime, Newbury was friends with my clients Guy Clark and Kris Kristofferson. That endorsement alone is good enough for me, although I'd put Mickey's songwriting chops up against anyone.

During soundcheck, Elvis Costello spends twenty minutes talking with me about how much he loves *Beautiful Dreamer: The Songs of Stephen Foster*. He goes into great detail about each track, and it's obvious he has spent a lot of time listening to our album. During our postshow champagne toast, after I thank everyone for being part of the night, Elvis raises his glass in cheers to *Beautiful Dreamer*. I feel the redness creep up on my cheeks. It's hard for me to accept that kind of praise. But more than that, it makes me happy that he likes the album. During this same time period, Bruce Springsteen plays our *Beautiful Dreamer* album before his concerts as the audience walks in. Knowing that Costello and Springsteen appreciate our work is gratifying.

In October, I go out on a run of concert dates with Kristofferson. One of those shows is in Milwaukee, where Kris plays the Pabst Theater, my favorite venue in town. I ask Kris if he is willing to visit my old radio station alma mater, WMIL. WMIL has not invited Kris, but I know my old colleague Kerry Wolfe would love to have Kris there. Kris agrees and

Kerry agrees, and it is an exciting day for me to drive Kris around my hometown and then take him to the place that started it all for me. A lot has changed at the station in eleven years, but I'm happy to be back at my old stomping grounds with Kris in tow. Kris does a short on-air interview, where he spends most of the time turning the conversation back to me and how happy he is to have this Milwaukee girl taking care of him. That's just Kris.

We end up back in Nashville in November. We spend a painful day at the Ryman Auditorium for a DVD shoot for *The Best of the Johnny Cash Show*. Kris is the host. The producers are not prepared and not professional, and it is one of the worst days Kris and I have together. He sends me out to find a bottle of wine for us to share. "At least let's get drunk so we can get through this," Kris jokes.

We attend the annual BMI Awards, where Merle Haggard is honored with the BMI Icon Award. "I had to get back here to pay my respects to Merle," Kris says. "I think so much of him as an artist and a human being. Merle was one of my heroes when I came to Nashville. The fact that we are friends, the fact that I get to work on the same stage with him, I have to pinch myself. When I met him, I was a janitor at Columbia studios." I understand how Kris feels. I pinch myself a lot these days.

After Kris's shows in Birmingham and Memphis, I return to Nashville for my final work show of the year. Guy Clark plays Nashville's tiny bluegrass venue the Station Inn on November 21.

There is a line around the block to get in. Guy usually performs with Verlon Thompson accompanying him on guitar, but tonight, in addition to Verlon, he rounds out the band with multi-instrumentalists Jamie Hartford and Shawn Camp, and Brynn Davies on bass. We are here to celebrate *Workbench Songs*, but Guy calls out songs spanning his three decades of recording. Guy has had a rough year and it shows. His hair is finally growing back (curly!) after falling out from chemotherapy for his lymphoma. The emotion onstage and in the audience is palpable as Guy sings his masterpieces "L.A. Freeway," "Desperados Waiting for a Train," and "Randall Knife." Shawn Camp sings his Guy cowrites "Sis Draper" and "Magnolia Wind." Rodney Crowell jumps onstage to duet with Guy on "The Partner Nobody Chose" and to sing his own version of "She Ain't Goin' Nowhere." Guy ends the set with "Let Him Roll." After three hours, Guy walks slowly and carefully off the stage at 12:15 a.m. He lights a cigarette in the greenroom as we gather around him with hugs and gratitude, happy to breathe in Guy's second-hand smoke. Did I mention I get paid for this?

CHAPTER FIFTEEN

CHOICES

By 2007, I am frazzled. Exhausted. Bone weary. Something has to change. I've been running around the country as a public relations spokesperson nonstop for four years. In addition to Kris Kristofferson and Guy Clark, this year I'm working on album projects for Gretchen Peters, Beth Nielsen Chapman, Dan Colehour, David Macias's various-artists *Song of America* project, and the Country Music Hall of Fame's *Flatt and Scruggs* television show DVD release. American Roots Publishing will release Shawn Camp and Billy Burnette's *The Bluegrass Elvises* album this summer for the thirtieth anniversary of Elvis Presley's death.

Annie Mosher has a baby boy, Frank James, and will stay home with him. I need to hire a new publicist, maybe two, and find a bigger office. But my heart is not in it. What is it I want to do?

My perspective evolves as I engage more in my community as part of the Leadership Music class of 2007. Founded in 1989, the nine-month program brings together established leaders in the music business to explore how all elements of the industry operate, individually and collectively. It promotes teamwork, camaraderie, and dialogue, exposing participants to varying points of view and philosophies. My classmates work in music publishing, entertainment law banking, government, and the media. They are artist managers, publicists, agents, concert promoters, venue owners, and artists. The individuals in my class (the best class ever) become dear friends and confidants. We are bonded forever by the unique journey we are on together.

At the same time, I'm offered a scholarship at the prestigious Center for Creative Leadership, a top-ranked global leadership education campus in Greensboro, North Carolina. The Leadership Development Program is the longest-running leadership program in the world, with more than one hundred thousand graduates. The center's tagline is, "We don't just change. We transform." I check into an Embassy Suites in Greensboro for a week. We are shuttled from there to the campus. Forty of us have come from all over the world to improve our leadership skills. My classmates work for high-profile corporations in familiar industries like technology, hospitality, and manufacturing. I am the sole entrepreneur and the only one who works in the entertainment business. The week is demanding and enlightening, indeed an awakening for me. I learn just as much from sharing meals and time with my classmates. Oh, how different our lives are. I'm sure all of them make more money than me. No doubt they have employer-provided health insurance, 401(k) plans, year-end bonuses, and other benefits. Being tied to an office forty-plus hours a week, with no time or space to create, getting only two or three weeks of vacation each year, dealing with the bureaucracy, climbing a corporate ladder...just the thought of it freaks me out.

At the end of the week, our instructor shares the parable of the Mexican fisherman. The story is about an American investment banker vacationing in a small, coastal Mexican village. The American spots the fisherman with the morning catch and asks how long it takes to catch the fish. "Only a little while," the fisherman replies. The American asks why the fisherman doesn't stay out longer to catch more fish. When the fisherman replies that he catches enough to support his family's needs, the American asks what he does with the rest of his time. "I sleep late, fish a little, play with my children, take a siesta with my wife, stroll into the village each night and play guitar with my amigos. I have a full and busy life." The American suggests the fisherman spend more time fishing and with the proceeds buy a bigger boat, then a fleet of boats, eventually opening a cannery where the fisherman controls the product, process, and distribution. He'd have to move to a big city to run the corporation, and after twenty years or so the fisherman could announce an IPO and sell his company stock and become a multimillionaire. "And then what?"

the fisherman asks. The American says, "Then you would retire, move to a small coastal village where you can sleep late, fish a little, play with your kids, take a siesta with your wife, and play guitar with your amigos."

The Mexican fisherman parable changes everything for me. *I am the fisherman*, I think. I'm not going to expand my office, expand my business, hire more employees. I will move out of my office, work from home, and only take on as much work as I can handle alone. Instead of only representing the work of others, I will leave space in my life to create my own art. I will try to make enough money to take care of my basic needs and to enjoy extraordinary experiences.

With the decision made, I pare down my business. After the *Bluegrass Elvises* release, I close down American Roots Publishing. Running a nonprofit requires way too much administration and paperwork. I retain Kris as my core client. He is busy enough to keep me busy. I start to work on my first book, a memoir about my relationship with my stepdad and how it shaped my love of music. Kris graciously writes the foreword to my book, and I share chapters with him as I write. It leads us into many intimate discussions about family dynamics and each of our relationships with our mothers and fathers. Although Kris is my client, we are the best of friends. I love Kris and Lisa like family, and it is a joy to spend this time with them.

I clear my calendar to keep mornings for myself so I can sleep in, exercise, write, whatever strikes me. I refuse to answer my phone or emails before noon. Kris lives in Hawaii and likes to sleep late as much as I do, so I know this is not going to be a problem. Any other client I choose to take will have to live with that hard-and-fast rule, or they can find someone else who is willing to work mornings.

On April 16, Rosanne Cash presents Kris with the Johnny Cash Visionary Award at the CMT Music Awards at Nashville's Belmont University. According to CMT, the award recognizes an artist's extraordinary musical vision, innovative and groundbreaking music, and pioneering initiatives in entertainment.

Rosanne's manager is unable to be here, so he asks me to take care of Rosanne. Of course, I'm happy to be around Rosanne Cash anytime. She is a brilliant, talented, fun, insightful woman and I am inspired anytime she is in the room. The CMT Music Awards are clearly not our jam. The word Rosanne uses to describe the night is "bombastic," and it fits. This is the opposite of the Americana awards. Glitzy, over-the-top, egocentric, uncomfortable for all of us, especially Kris. He is mortified when we arrive and all of the staff and volunteers are wearing identical black T-shirts with KRISTOFFERSON silkscreened in white across the chest. "Oh my God," he whispers to me. "Did anyone warn you about this?" "Nope," I reply. Some artists may be flattered by this, but not Kris. The red carpet is a spectacle, although we get to bypass most of it because the press is not interested in talking with Kris Kristofferson and Rosanne Cash. They are clamoring for comedian host Jeff Foxworthy and country stars Toby Keith, Sugarland, Carrie Underwood, Rascal Flatts, and Martina McBride.

Backstage, a video guy follows us everywhere. There is no privacy for Kris at all. And everything they film backstage is broadcast to the big screens in the house. Friends in the audience leave laughing voicemail messages on my phone because I am prominent in my pink coat on the twenty-foot video screen trying to shoo the camera guy away from Kris and Rosanne.

The best part of the night is the authenticity of Rosanne and Kris shining on the stage. As Rosanne presents the award she says, "When I first began to collect my thoughts about presenting this award to Kris and about what I would say I kept thinking nothing I say will be good enough. Nothing I say could convey the respect I hold in my heart, the love, the admiration, and the plain awe of the humanity and talent contained in that one gorgeous man. When I played some shows with Kris last year, I realized and knew that he is an artist with nothing to lose. He can risk everything because he never compromises his integrity. He is his art, and his art is him. They are inseparable. He has the power and the fearlessness of one who acts purely from the truth of his own heart, unsullied by concerns about image or marketing or popularity. He is not a 'walking contradiction, partly truth and partly fiction' as he once aptly described my father. He has whittled away his own contradictions to the essence of his humanity—a man who believes in love, honor, peace, compassion, and who acts accordingly and who writes like an oracle."

As Kris accepts the award, he says to Rosanne, "Don't cry or I'll start crying, too."

"I got to go around the world making music with him [Johnny] and seeing that spiritual communion that went down between John and his audience," Kris says. "I wrote a song for him called 'Good Morning, John.' It was for one of his birthdays or his sobriety celebration or something like that. In it, I said, 'I love you, John. In the cold and holy darkness, you were always shining brighter than a star.' God bless you, John, for the love and joy you've given and the living inspiration that you are. Bob Dylan said it the best. He said that John was like the North Star: You could guide your ship by him."

Kris is my creative North Star. I want to follow his example. Thanks to William Blake, Kris believes, and now so do I, that the work is the gift. The creative process is what matters most. A lifetime of societal brainwashing has taught many of us that *results* are the only thing that matter, that failure is bad, and that we'd better be able to prove ourselves before we even begin. We listen to those outside voices who say, "What makes you think you can do that?" instead of believing our inner voice that screams, "What makes you think I can't?" Kris teaches me another way: to detach myself from outcome and hold true to the belief that the work is the gift. All of us, every last person on this planet, have what it takes to be true to our authentic selves, to create, thrive, and live in our good work. How blessed am I to learn from Kris as a mentor?

I am with Kris in interesting times. He is at the zenith of his long career and is celebrated for it again and again. Kris follows in the footsteps of Guy Clark as the artist in residence at the Country Music Hall of Fame this year. Kris chooses to perform intimate solo shows for two sold-out nights. The Ford Theater is packed with artists and dignitaries. Kris's first Nashville tour guide, Cowboy Jack Clement, is there cutting up with Kris backstage before the show.

Lisa and I sit next to each other in the first row and giggle at the wonder of all of it, the way people respond to Kris's show, the way Kris reacts to a crowd, and how incredibly shy he remains after forty years of entertaining. He sings all of his hits, "Sunday Morning Comin' Down," "For the Good Times," "Help Me Make It through the Night," "Me and Bobby

McGee." He accompanies himself on guitar and harmonica. His shows are sprinkled with humor and social justice commentary. "Did you know that here in the land of the free we've got more people behind bars than anywhere else on the planet?" he ad-libs during "Best of All Possible Worlds." After blowing a note and forgetting a lyric, Kris says, "If I was Roger Miller, I'd think of a clever scat to go out on, but I'm not so I'll just quit right here." At the end of the show, after many standing ovations, Kris places his hand over his heart. "I'll carry this with me. Thank you for your spirit. I'll never forget this, ever."

Vince Gill, Mel Tillis, and broadcaster Ralph Emery are inducted into the Country Music Hall of Fame at the Medallion Ceremony on October 28.

As a volunteer, I escort Mel Tillis on the media red carpet. Mel and Kris are friends and in between interviews, Mel tells me stories about Kris. I remember one in particular about the day that Kris's old army outfit had a layover at Fort Campbell. After hours of drinking together, Kris asked Mel to go with him to visit his army buddies. Before they could leave, Mel dropped a bottle of whiskey on his front porch and Mel's wife put the kibosh on Mel going anywhere. Kris took Mel's car, too drunk to drive, and rolled the car over at the army base. Kris managed to talk his way onto the plane, determined to go to Vietnam with his old unit. An officer in charge ordered Kris off the plane and Kris slept it off in a guard shack. Mel has me laughing so hard, we miss some of the interview opportunities. Mel doesn't care and neither do I.

After I get Mel safely inside the Hall of Fame lobby, I follow Guy Clark out to the back porch so he can smoke a cigarette. I ask Guy about Susanna. "She is still having this chronic back pain and won't see another doctor. All she does is pop pain pills and watch TV. I guess I can't blame her. They're pretty good pills." Guy laughs. He looks healthy and robust, and I'm happy to see that he has bounced back so well from his lymphoma treatments.

I sit with Raul Malo as we wait for the show to start. We talk about the old days and also toast Frank Callari, our mutual friend and former Mavericks manager, who died suddenly of a heart attack two days prior. He was fifty-five. I met Frank fifteen years ago during the early heyday of the Mavericks, and Frank was always kind and helpful to me. Raul and I reminisce about my Milwaukee radio days and Raul encouraging me to move to Nashville. I never dreamed I'd be part of a community like this one. What a wonderful gift I've been given, to live and work in this community surrounded and loved by people with enormous talent, compassion, and zest for life. "We are the Land of Misfit Toys," Raul says. "It's a beautiful thing."

Everyone who knows me knows that I claim to be Vince Gill's biggest fan. The musical tribute to Vince opens with Rodney Crowell and Emmylou Harris singing "Some Things Never Get Old." Then Michael McDonald, of Doobie Brothers and Steely Dan fame, joins Vince's band members Tom Britt, Dawn Sears, Billy Thomas, Pete Wasner, and Jeff White to sing Vince's "Go Rest High on That Mountain." NRBQ's Big Al Anderson, often a cowriter with Vince, leads the band through one of the songs he and Vince wrote together, "The Next Big Thing." Then Guy performs "Randall Knife." Vince has been an emotional puddle throughout the performances and weeps openly as Guy sings. Opry great Bill Anderson inducts Vince into the hallowed hall. "What can you say about a man whose talent has already said it all? Not just his talent, but his character, his integrity, his generosity, his sense of humor, his humility, and humanity. They've all spoken volumes." Now we are all crying.

In his acceptance speech, Vince jokes that his friends were taking bets on how many times he'd cry during the ceremony. In acknowledging the other Hall of Famers and fellow inductees, Vince says, "I've always tried to be a great student. I've always felt like a sponge. I took this music in, and it kept growing and growing and growing. Thank you from the bottom of my heart for inspiring me with the records you made, the songs you wrote."

A few days later, on November 1, Patty Griffin cleans up at the Americana Honors and Awards show as she takes home the top prizes for Artist of the Year and Album of the Year for *Children Running Through*. The Avett Brothers are right behind her with wins for New/Emerging Artist of the Year and Duo/Group of the Year. Lifetime Achievement Awards are presented to Lyle Lovett, Joe Ely, Ry Cooder, and Willie Nelson. The First Amendment Center presents the Spirit of Americana Free Speech Award to Mavis Staples. This year, I pass the torch to my friend Claire Armbruster to produce the show while I enjoy most of it from the front row with my date Raul Malo.

Many of us start the day at Frank Callari's funeral. Our hearts are heavy, but at least we are all together tonight at the Ryman Auditorium.

I am still the president of the Americana Music Association and present the President's Award. Host Jim Lauderdale introduces me. "It is now my pleasure to introduce a woman of few words, the president of the Americana Music Association, Tamara Saviano, along with her friends Joe Ely and Rodney Crowell."

"Thanks, Jim," I say. "Each year the AMA gives out the President's Award, which recognizes outstanding achievement by an artist or industry contributor who is no longer with us. It is given at the sole discretion of the AMA president. Previous recipients are Doug Sahm, Gram Parsons, the Carter Family, and John Hartford. Last year I gave this award to Mickey Newbury. I grew up in Wisconsin, but there's no bigger fan of Texas singer-songwriters than me. This year I'd like to ask a few of my favorite Texans, Joe Ely, Rodney Crowell, and Guy Clark, to help us celebrate the music and life of their friend Townes Van Zandt."

"Back in Lubbock, we all looked up to Townes," Joe says. "He is one of the reasons we had the courage to write what we wrote, sing what we sang, and do what we do. And even though he's been gone a good while now, I still look up to my old friend. We brought another old friend along to sing one of Townes's songs. Please make welcome Mr. Guy Clark." Guy performs "To Live Is to Fly." Then he and I present the award to Townes's children Will and Katie Belle.

It is Lyle Lovett's fiftieth birthday. We end the night with champagne toasts and birthday cake in Lyle's dressing room. Six years of Americana Music Awards and everything just gets better.

On November 7, the Nashville Songwriters Association International celebrates as Bluebird Café owner Amy Kurland transfers ownership of the storied venue to them. As a founding member of the association in 1967, Kris and his old bandmates—Stephen Bruton, Billy Swan, Donnie Fritts, and Chris Gantry—play together for the first time in decades to celebrate a new era at the Bluebird.

The top capacity at the club is one hundred people. The room is filled with songwriters, music business bigwigs, and press. Denise Quan from CNN; Brian Mansfield from *USA Today*; John Jerome from Associated Press; Beverly Keel, Peter Cooper, and Craig Havighurst from the *Tennessean*; Lydia Hutchinson from *Performing Songwriter*; David Ross from *Music Row* magazine; Bret Wolcott from Great American Country—all there to see Kris perform with his old band. I set up tables in front for Kris's songwriter friends Rodney Crowell, Guy Clark, and Shawn Camp. Lisa and I sit one table over with John Carter Cash.

"Rodney, I can't play with you sitting right in front of me," Kris says. Then he spots the other songwriters and says, "Tamara, did you have to put all of these great artists in front of me?"

"It will keep you on your game," I say.

"Or make me choke," Kris says.

It is fun to watch Kris with his old band. Kris dissolves into laughter easily onstage with just a look from one of his friends. These guys have been through a lot together and know each other well. Kris is more at ease surrounded by his friends than he is as a solo performer.

It is Stephen Bruton's fifty-ninth birthday. On the bus after the show, we bring out a cake covered with flaming candles. Stephen had been diagnosed with throat cancer the year before and he is frail from treatments. He cries openly as we gather around him and sing "Happy Birthday." "I am so happy to be here with all of you tonight," Stephen says. "It's just what I needed. I love you."

We end the night with a group photo in front of the famous Bluebird awning. I stand in front of Kris and he props his chin on top of my head. Our giggling is clearly noticeable in the picture. "We don't like to have fun at all, do we, Tamara?" Kris jokes.

CHAPTER SIXTEEN

CLOSER TO THE BONE

My intention to "be the fisherman" is a remarkable change. My goals for 2008 are to see more live music, work on my book, and give back to my community. Kris spends a good chunk of the year touring through Europe, which gives me a break from the day-to-day with him and time to focus on other things.

It's a year of great concerts. Nick Lowe and Ron Sexsmith at the Belcourt Theater are exquisite. Beautiful and haunting poetry by two master songwriters. I am mesmerized.

There is a Cuban vibe at 3rd and Lindsley as Raul Malo, with his large band and horn section, sings mostly in Spanish. Everyone dances salsa, rumba, and tango throughout the show.

Led Zeppelin rock god Robert Plant and bluegrass prodigy Alison Krauss play together at the Bridgestone Arena to celebrate their duet album *Raising Sand*. I am the guest of my friend Kira Florita. Kira is on producer T Bone Burnett's guest list and we have fantastic seats. It is clear Plant is energized by the band, T Bone, Buddy Miller, and Stuart Duncan. Plant tells the audience that T Bone introduced him to Townes Van Zandt and turned him on to Americana music. The discovery of our music community has inspired Plant. The pairing with Alison is surprising and brilliant. The show is spectacular. There is a big after-party backstage and many colleagues and friends are there to celebrate. It is a room filled with familiar smiles, hugs, and kisses. We are high on music and love for one another.

Levon Helm and Friends at the Ryman Auditorium are like a second coming of *The Last Waltz*, a magnetic three hours of amazing songs, musicianship, and reverence. I sit in the balcony's first row with my dad and Gary Hartman, director of the Center for Texas Music History. On the stage are Levon, Larry Campbell, Buddy Miller, Sam Bush, Delbert McClinton, John Hiatt, Billy Bob Thornton, Sheryl Crow, Alison Krauss, Robert Plant, Amy Helm, Steve Earle, and Allison Moorer. Plus a great blues harmonica player, an awesome horn section, a soulful keyboardist, steel guitar, and Levon on those drums. There is another fantastic backstage after-party.

The concert highlight of the year for me is Harley Davidson's 105th anniversary party at Veteran's Park in Milwaukee. More than one hundred thousand people from all over the world gather at the lakefront to see the Foo Fighters one night and Alejandro Escovedo and Bruce Springsteen the following night. There is a rumble of motorcycles everywhere in town. My husband, Paul, is the video engineer-in-charge, so I have the best seat in the house behind his monitors. It is my first and only Foo Fighters show and I fall in love with Dave Grohl on the spot.

When Bruce and the band arrive, I am standing at the front of stage left by the fence looking out over the audience. Bruce gets out of the limo and the crowd calls his name. He comes over to shake hands and say hello to his fans. Here I am, accidentally standing right next to the Boss as he talks with his fans. Bruce smiles at me and says hello. Then he goes off and performs for three and a half hours, at one point allowing himself to fall back into the arms of a bunch of women and crowd-surf. Bruce calls out songs requested on signs held by audience members. In addition to his own songs, Bruce plays "Born to Be Wild," "Wooly Bully," and "Mountain of Love." As Dave Marsh and I watch from the side of the stage, it dawns on me that I first saw Bruce in concert thirty years ago this summer on the *Darkness on the Edge of Town* tour. I was seventeen. The *Milwaukee Journal* review of Springsteen's Harley Davidson show is above the fold on page 1 with a blaring headline: "Boss Rocks Hog Heaven."

For the first time, I have no clients coming to Austin for SXSW. Kay Clary and I drive to Texas together, taking our time to stop at thrift shops along the way. I work on my book each morning and spend the rest of the day seeing glorious music.

Al Moss turns me on to Belleville Outfit, a young jazz and swing band playing at a coffee shop on Barton Springs Road. I see Mike Farris at the BMI party, James McMurtry at Mother Egan's, Van Morrison at La Zona Rosa, and the Walter Hyatt tribute, featuring David Ball and Jimmie Dale Gilmore, at Austin Music Hall. We go to Antone's for Ray Benson's annual birthday party. Carolyn Wonderland is a wonder. Johnny Rivers sings "High on a Mountain of Love" at the New West party with Buddy Miller's band. The Americana Music Association hosts an event with Joe Ely. As Joe rocks out onstage, we devour Sharon Ely's famous posole and tamales.

My weekly Nashville breakfast club meets at Las Manitas during SXSW. Conan O'Brien talent booker Jim Pitt, *No Depression* editor Grant Alden, Old Crow Medicine show manager Norm Parenteau, publicist and artist manager Traci Thomas, Thirty Tigers executive Nancy Quinn, and radio promoter Al Moss. I'm back at Las Manitas for lunch later in the week with Val Denn and Dave Marsh. Helen Chetwynd from BBC Radio Two is in from London. Helen is producing a documentary-length radio feature on Kristofferson and interviews me for the piece. Helen and I hit it off and run around town seeing music together.

A bittersweet gathering at Pangaea is the official goodbye party for *No Depression*. Grant Alden, Peter Blackstock, and Kyla Fairchild did everything they could to keep *No Depression* viable, but music magazines are vanishing. Readers and advertisers are shifting to the World Wide Web and the new social media platform Facebook. Artists are building relationships directly with fans. Great for artists and fans. Not so great for conventional media channels. This is *No Depression*'s last SXSW, and they will publish the final issue in June. Tonight is filled with music—Bruce Robison, Bonnie Bramlett, and Daniel Lanois—the love of old friends, and many tears.

Gary Hartman, the director for the Center for Texas Music History at Texas State University, and his wife Francine take me to the Texas Chili Parlor for the first time. The Chili Parlor sits next to the state capitol, a meeting place for government workers and locals until Guy Clark exalted the joint in song. My iPhone ringtone plays "Dublin Blues" to identify Guy when he calls. As we wait for our chili, my phone sings,

"I wish I was in Austin, at the Chili Parlor bar drinking mad dog margaritas and not caring where you are." We laugh. "That's Guy calling me," I say as I answer the call on speaker. "Hey Guy, guess what? I'm at the Chili Parlor bar." Long pause. "Tamara, don't drink the mad dog margaritas. They taste like petroleum and sea water." After the call, Gary asks me if I would consider writing a biography on Guy for the Center for Texas Music History's music book series. "Guy would never cooperate with me on a biography and I wouldn't do it without him," I say. "Just ask him," Gary says. "Maybe he'll surprise you."

It is gratifying to give back to my community as a volunteer. Booking agent Val Denn, songwriter Gretchen Peters, and I host a panel discussion about building a team at the Folk Alliance conference. Gary Hartman, Casey Monahan from the Texas Music Office, and I moderate a Texas music panel on Americana, with musical guests Radney Foster, Rosie Flores, Cody Canada, and Bruce Robison. At the BMI dinner I escort my old friend Hal Ketchum on the red carpet.

I serve on the Leadership Music Closing Retreat committee for the class of 2008. Our big surprise to the class is our keynote speaker, the delightful Steve Wozniak, inventor of the Apple computer. Woz and I are friends from his days on the American Roots Publishing board of directors. Steve Fishell and I pick Woz up at the airport. He has an issue with his laptop, so we take him to the Apple Store at the Green Hills Mall. Bringing Woz to an Apple Store is like taking the Beatles to a record store in Piccadilly Circus. Pandemonium. Putting my PR skills to good use, I swoop in and line the kids up for autographs and pictures with Woz.

Closing retreat is a great success. Woz is sweet and engaging and everyone in Leadership Music falls in love with him. His speech is fantastic. Woz talks about the beginnings of Apple, and how all he wanted to do was keep his job at Hewlett-Packard and get married and have kids. When he finally agreed to go ahead with Apple and Steve Jobs, he made an agreement with Jobs that he would remain an engineer and not have anything to do with the business side. Once things took off and Woz made money, he left Apple to do the things he wanted to do, build schools and teach and give back to the community. It is inspiring to hear him talk about following his own bliss and not caring about Wall Street.

Kris comes to town to record a track for a Shel Silverstein tribute album and to tape a PBS special, *Legends and Lyrics*, as a favor to Roger Miller's son Dean. After recording the Shel track at Gary Paczosa's studio, we head down to the historic Mason Lodge on Lower Broadway. *Legends and Lyrics* is broadcast from a beautiful one-thousand-seat theater in the lodge. Instead of taking advantage of the stunning ambiance of the room, the production crew treats it like a boring black box studio. No one here got the "less is more" memo. When you book fantastic songwriters Kris Kristofferson, Patty Griffin, and Alabama's Randy Owen for an intimate acoustic set in the round, in a gorgeous historic venue, why in the world would you choose to cover it up with superfluous gear, flashing lights, boom cameras, and over-the-top production? It's like Vegas in here.

There is a lot of downtime between rehearsal and the show. Kris says he has been listening to *The Pilgrim* on repeat. "I still haven't written you a thank-you note for making that album," Kris says. "It's the best birthday present I've ever gotten." I tell Kris there is no need for a thank-you note. It's heartwarming just to know that he likes it. I can't imagine any better satisfaction.

Radney Foster hires me to help with public relations and marketing on his next record, *Revival*. Radney and I met back in my radio days at WMIL. Cyndi Hoelzle, Radney's wife, wrote for me at *Country Music* magazine. We've all known each other a long time. Paul and I spend several hours at Sound Emporium studio filming Rad's first recording sessions. My goal is twofold: to use footage for marketing the album and to give my friend Steve Fishell footage to market his new Music Producers Institute. Steve offers a chance for fans and prospective producers to sit in on recording sessions. The tuition subsidizes the recording costs for the artist, and students learn in a real-world environment with a Grammy-winning producer.

After months of prodding from Gary Hartman, I email Guy Clark's manager, Keith Case, about the possibility of writing Guy's biography. Within a few hours, Keith calls me to tell me that Guy is "enthusiastically in."

"What? I don't believe it," I say.

"I'm a bit surprised, too," Keith admits. "But he seems excited about the idea."

I need confirmation from Guy, so I drive over to his house in West Nashville. I sit in my usual spot in front of Guy's workbench as Guy rolls a joint. "Guy, are you sure you're up for this?" I ask. "I want you to spend hours and hours with me and let me interview you about your life. I want you to introduce me to your family and friends and cowriters and colleagues and anyone who is important to your story and tell them to speak honestly with me. Then I'm going to write the book. And you can't read it until it is published."

Guy takes a long toke off his joint, holds the smoke, and exhales—unfazed. "Sounds fair to me, Tamara."

I'm skeptical. At this point, we've known each other for a decade. Guy is enigmatic and vague about the buried treasures of his life. By and large, his songs speak louder than he does. Guy wrote the song "Exposé," with lyrics that spell out his coolness:

> Now when you write your exposé
> I wish you'd leave me out
> I'd just as soon you didn't use my name
> I'm not crazy about the way
> Your book might make me look
> I might have been there but
> You can't hold me to blame

When I ask about it, Guy downplays the "Exposé" lyrics. I propose that we meet for our first interview and cut our losses if he is not forthcoming. We agree to start working on his biography after I wrap up album projects for Radney Foster, Gretchen Peters, Ashley Cleveland, and the various-artists compilation *Undone: A Musicfest Tribute to Robert Earl Keen*, recorded in Steamboat Springs, Colorado. I finish my memoir *The Most Beautiful Girl: A True Story of a Dad, a Daughter, and the Healing Power of Music*, and turn it in to my agent. Now I can turn my attention to Guy.

Guy captivates me from the moment I turn on my tape recorder and ask about the striking turquoise ring he wears. Without hesitation, Guy dives in and talks about Bunny Talley, Susanna's sister. Bunny killed herself in 1970 during the time when she and Guy were lovers. Guy and Susanna fell in love in the aftermath of Bunny's suicide.

Holy moly. I know from this first moment that Guy is serious about the biography. From then on, I am at Guy's house several days a week. Guy is a pack rat—this researcher's dream subject. At Guy's urging, I rummage through his file cabinets, comb through every drawer, crawl under the bed, haul boxes out of closets, and examine every corner of his life. Over seven years, I interview Guy relentlessly. I speak with hundreds of his friends, family members, and colleagues.

Writing a biography for an academic press about a folk singer is not going to make me any money. I take on Radney Foster as a management client in time for the 2009 release of his *Revival* album and to spearhead Radney's fiftieth-birthday celebration concerts in Austin and Nashville.

I continue to work with Kris and Guy. I oversee public relations campaigns for Guy's September 22 Dualtone Records offering, *Somedays the Song Writes You*. The following week, New West Records issues Kris's album *Closer to the Bone* on September 29.

Kris and I go to Austin to shoot the music video for the single "Closer to the Bone." Danny Clinch, known for his work with Bruce Springsteen, directs. We film at Hill's Café, in an old motel room, at the outdoor music venue on the back patio, and in the restaurant. Before we finish shooting, a New West employee hands Kris the keys to a vintage truck and asks Kris to drive it down South Congress Avenue so Danny can film it. Kris has not driven a car in many years and is hesitant. "Kris doesn't drive," I say to rescue him. Instead of graciously backing off, the New West guy continues to push and puts Kris on the spot. "Okay, I'll do it," Kris says. He struggles to drive the old truck and I hold my breath in the chase car behind him. Kris is pissed when we finally return to Hill's. "I never should have done that," Kris whispers to me. "Let's wrap this up and get the hell out of here." Kris wants to use studio footage from the recording sessions as the official video but he is overruled by the label. The studio footage is more meaningful to Kris because Stephen Bruton is present. It was the last time Kris and Stephen worked together before Stephen's death.

168 • Chapter 16

Paul and I fly to LA for a week of media appearances with Kris. Paul and I stay at our usual and favorite hotel, the Malibu Beach Inn. Every morning we pick Kris up from his house in Las Flores Canyon. We rent an SUV to haul him around. Paul drives, Kris rides shotgun, and I'm in the back seat behind Paul as we battle traffic driving all over Los Angeles. Kris pops *The Pilgrim* into the CD player. He says he has questions about the recordings as we travel around. "The more I listen to this record, the more I love it," Kris says. His favorite track is Marta Gomez singing "The Circle." But he also loves Rosanne Cash's version of "Loving Him Was Easier," and Emmylou Harris singing "The Pilgrim (Chapter 33)." We discuss the album and the decisions I made on song selection and artists. I am deeply moved by Kris's affection for the album. We made this record three years ago, and he still listens to it.

We drive to Burbank for the *Tavis Smiley Show* on public broadcasting station KCET, where we run into director Tim Burton and country star Tim McGraw at the studio. Kris worked with Burton on the *Planet of the Apes* remake. Then back to Hollywood for interviews with Sirius Satellite Radio, Daytrotter, and *Aquarium Drunkard*.

Our last stop for the day is actor Billy Bob Thornton's house on North Roxbury Drive in Beverly Hills. Billy Bob is making a Willie Nelson documentary. The crew is setting up in Billy Bob's basement studio, so Billy Bob leads us to the control room to wait. I'm sandwiched between Kris and Paul on a loveseat and Billy Bob pulls up an office chair until he is knee-to-knee with all of us. He says, "This is the closest I'll get to landing a helicopter on your lawn. Do you mind if I play you some songs?"

Kris, gracious as ever, agrees. Billy Bob hands him three pages of lyrics, puts a CD in the player, cranks it up, and leaves the room. After three songs, he returns and bends down next to Kris to take the CD out of the player. Kris points to the lyric sheet and deadpans: "You forgot a *y* here." It's all I can do to suppress my giggles. Billy Bob says, "Oh, yeah, well, that's just a draft." Then he places another CD in the player and hands Kris three more pages of lyrics. Again, he turns the music up loud and leaves the control room. After the second song, Kris gets up to find a restroom. Billy Bob intercepts Kris before he can escape the control room, turns him around, and makes him listen to the third song. The third song is about

Willie Nelson's sidekick and stage manager Poodie Locke, who died earlier this year. Billy Bob recues the song. Kris whispers in my ear that he has to pee. The minute the song is over, Kris jumps up to find a bathroom. "What did you think?" Billy Bob asks as Kris walks toward the door. "Oh, yeah, that's so sweet that you wrote a song about Poodie."

On November 1, our last night in Los Angeles, Kris performs a show at the Walt Disney Concert Hall, the fourth hall of the Los Angeles Music Center, designed by innovative architect Frank Gehry. Because we are in LA, backstage is crowded with Kris's family and friends; the Kristofferson kids; Cameron Strang from New West Records and his wife, Tori; Kris's agents Steve Levine and Rick Ferrell; and many of Kris's lifelong friends.

Los Angeles Times reporter Randy Lewis writes, "'Closer to the Bone,' the title track from Kris Kristofferson's latest album, made an ideal choice as the opening number at the esteemed singer and songwriter's solo show Sunday night at Walt Disney Concert Hall. It addresses the tendency as the years go by to home in on those things that truly matter most and dispense with anything else that can sap precious time and attention."

Coming from the heartbeat
Nothing but the truth now
Everything is sweeter
Closer to the bone

It's a metaphor for the raw tenderness I feel for Kris these days, under the skin and closer to the bone.

CHAPTER SEVENTEEN

A MOMENT OF FOREVER

"Everything Kris writes is a standard, and we've just got to live with that," Willie Nelson says from the stage at the Fifty-Seventh Annual BMI Country Awards on November 10, 2009.

Tonight, Kris is the BMI Icon Award honoree. For the occasion, I wear vintage formal wear and a 1960s beehive hairdo. Kris barely recognizes me when I meet him and Lisa in the lobby of the Loews Vanderbilt Hotel. "Wow, Tamara, you look beautiful." "Don't look so surprised," I say. "Jimmy Smits should see you now," Kris says. We belly laugh our way to the tricked-out Cadillac sent to pick up me, Kris, Lisa, Jessi Colter, and her date, Nick Lowery. The BMI lobby is transformed into an ethereal ballroom with a larger-than-life photo of Kris draped in silver satin and festooned with flowers. "Jesus baldheaded Christ, I feel like I'm at my own funeral!" Kris says. More belly laughs. Before the show, we stand in a circle of poets and dreamers. Vince Gill, Chet Flippo, Jack Ingram, Keith Urban, Taylor Swift, and Kris's old friends Bob Beckham, Donnie Fritts, and Billy Swan.

This is a private event, but a fan with no manners sneaks in and hands her camera to Vince. She asks him to take a picture of her with Kris. "Sorry about that," I say after security escorts her out. I'm horrified at her bad behavior. "That's okay," Vince says. "I cut Kris's head off in the picture." The belly laughs continue.

At our table, songwriters flock to Kris to thank him for decades of inspiration. Kris spends much of the night whispering in my ear, "Who was that?"

Enraptured, Kris watches Vince, Patty Griffin, and Willie sing some of his most popular songs, "Why Me," "Help Me Make It through the Night," "Loving Her Was Easier (Than Anything I'll Ever Do Again)," and "Me and Bobby McGee." Rosanne Cash shows up on a massive video screen and says, "Kris, you just get better and sweeter every year. I love you like a brother, a father, and a friend."

I am happy I stood my ground with BMI and did not let them push us into having young mainstream country artists pay tribute to Kris. It would've been completely meaningless. "I want to thank Vince and Patty and Willie for making me cry at my table," Kris says during his short acceptance speech.

After the ceremony and dinner, we return to the lobby for dancing and dessert. Country Music Hall of Fame members Harold Bradley and Charlie McCoy swing with the classic country band onstage. Jack Ingram and I drink, dance, laugh, and stare at the bigwigs in the room—songwriters, country stars, and music business moguls. We are "total dorks together," as Jack says.

After spending many months with Guy Clark working on his biography, I long to produce a tribute to him. Gary Hartman introduces me to an oilman who dabbles in music and owns a small label in Houston. The label owner is a Guy fan and agrees to finance and distribute the album. I call on Shawn Camp as bandleader and coproducer, Verlon Thompson to play lead guitar, and one of my best friends, Jen Gunderman, to play piano and accordion.

We gather in the studio for the first time on January 27, 2010. The wonderful John McBride, owner of Blackbird Studio in Nashville, gives us a super sweet deal because he loves Guy. Blackbird's marketing copy says it is "a haven for artists of all genres to make music without limits. Here you will find refuge, inspiration, and a dedicated space packed with the world's finest gear." It is delicious to record in such luxury. Our engineer Niko Bolas is known for his work with Neil Young, Warren Zevon, Don Henley, Steve Perry, and many other greats. We round out the band with Kenny Malone on drums and Mike Bubb on upright bass.

We kick off the morning with Rodney Crowell. He brings in Steuart Smith, who most notably plays guitar with the Eagles, to sweeten the track with more piano and guitar. "Let's give it a go and make ol' Guy proud of us," Rodney says, setting the tone for the entire album. Rodney sings "That Old Time Feeling" and we capture the magic in one take.

After Rodney, the band lays down the music bed for "Desperados Waiting for a Train" with Shawn's scratch vocal. We'll send the track to Willie Nelson to record his vocal from Hawaii this week. We break for lunch. Paul and I dash out the door to pick up Kris and Lisa. Kris has an interview at RFD-TV. After the interview, we bring Kris back to Blackbird to record "Hemingway's Whiskey."

Steve Fishell and his Music Producers Institute observers clap and cheer when Kris walks into the studio. The band and crew are just as excited to be with Kris. As we set up the mics, Kris says, "I saw Hemingway once at a bullfight in Spain. Hemingway drove up in this little Volkswagen and we locked eyes and he turned around and jumped in the car and drove off. I think I scared him. Maybe he just thought I was a fan."

We get several keeper takes from Kris and then we are off to the Ryman for soundcheck for Kris's show tonight. Kris's Ryman shows are always fundraisers for the Country Music Hall of Fame. My phone rings nonstop from artist managers and artists looking for complimentary tickets. I finally record a voicemail greeting that says, "Kris's show tonight is a benefit for the Hall of Fame. There are no comp tickets available."

Tonight is one of the best Kris shows I've had the pleasure to witness. He is relaxed and has great rapport with the audience, which is filled with songwriters and music business luminaries. I witness songwriters in the audience weep as they listen to Kris. After the show, he is so high on the night that he stands outside and signs autographs for an hour. After that, Kris, Lisa, Paul, and I sit on the bus until 2:00 a.m., sandwiched in the alley between the Ryman and the clubs on Lower Broadway. We raise our glasses of red wine and toast the exquisite night.

The next morning we are back in the studio for the Guy Clark tribute sessions. Radney Foster records "L.A. Freeway." I'm irked that Radney brings his electric guitar. I am dead set on the album being 100 percent acoustic. "Trust me," Radney says. I do, and I'm not sorry. The electric guitar adds something without taking away from the vibe. Jack Ingram records "Stuff That Works" with heart and sensitivity. Verlon lays down

"Good Love after Bad," which remains one of my favorite tracks on the album.

By the time we burn rough mixes and get everything loaded on hard drives, it's too late for me to drop mixes off at Guy's house. I want him to hear the work we've done the last couple of days, but it will have to wait.

We wake up the following morning to several inches of snow and a city shut down by weather. Guy is scheduled to have sinus surgery, and I am scared he isn't going to make it through the surgery. I want Guy to hear this music. Paul is game and we venture out in the snow. The car makes it halfway up the hill on Stoneway Trail. Paul parks and I hike the rest of the way up the hill and down into the Stoneway Close dead-end street where Guy lives. He is surprised to see me. "Tamara, how did you get here?" Guy asks as he stares out at the snow, which is unblemished with the exception of my boot tracks. I hand Guy the CD. "Paul is parked halfway down Stoneway Trail. I wanted you to hear the tribute recordings before you go into surgery," I say. My expression says it all. Guy understands that I'm worried. He grabs me into a bear hug. We hold each other for several minutes in his doorway, snow falling silently around us.

Twelve inches of snow are expected in Chicago as Kris and Merle Haggard play the Rosemont Theater on February 21. Lisa and I sit on a road case on the side of the stage twelve feet from Kris and Merle as they duet on the classics. "Tonight the Bottle Let Me Down," "Help Me Make It through the Night," "I'll Just Sit Here and Drink," "Why Me." Kris solos on "Sunday Morning Comin' Down," "The Pilgrim (Chapter 33)," and "Me and Bobby McGee." Lisa has tears in her eyes as Kris turns to sing to her, "Loving you is easier than anything I'll ever do again."

We retreat to Merle's bus after the show for a celebratory toast. "Nice to see you, young lady," Merle says, kissing my cheek. Not many people can get away with calling me young lady, but Merle Haggard is certainly one of them. It's late when Kris, Lisa, and I walk to Kris's bus. I stay for a few minutes but the bus is pulling out soon. On to the next show. Kris and Lisa watch me walk through the snow across the deserted parking lot to get to my hotel. I turn to wave goodbye and we blow kisses to each other.

Kris and Lisa come back to Nashville in June for Bonnaroo, a four-day music festival in the middle of nowhere on a seven-hundred-acre farm in Manchester, Tennessee. Bonnaroo is one of the top music festivals in the country, but we all hope we never have to do this again. Kris, Lisa, Paul, and I are at Bonnaroo in the best possible way, with all-access passes and a shuttle escort to and from the stage. It is one hundred degrees with 75 percent humidity out in this godforsaken farm field filled with tens of thousands of young people drinking and drugging.

Lisa and Paul deal with Kris's guitars and gear in the air-conditioned dressing room trailer as Kris and I stand outside backstage talking with Austin-based journalist Andy Langer. Jamey Johnson and his entourage spill out of a van and saunter over to us. Jamey has two or three towering, ripped, brickhouse sturdy dudes with him. Kris cranes his neck as he looks up at Jamey's bodyguards. "This is my muscle," Jamey says. Kris pauses, then nods and points his thumb toward me. "This is mine." We all bust up laughing while Kris keeps a straight face. Kris is hilarious. One time we pull into the parking lot at Blackbird Studios where Kris is about to record with Patty Griffin. I get out of the driver's side and Kris crosses in front of the car to meet me. He is talking to and looking at me without paying attention to where he is walking. He smacks his knee on the trailer hitch of the truck parked in front of us. Kris hits that hitch so hard that I hear the loud crack. Kris hops up and down holding his knee and screams every cuss word imaginable, and some unimaginable because he is a creative cusser. "Kris, are you okay?" I ask. "Do we need to go to the emergency room? Do you think you broke it?" After a few more hops and screams, Kris settles down and shakes it off. He throws his arm around me and says with a straight face, "That would have hurt a lesser man." Maybe you had to be there but it still make me laugh out loud to think about it.

On August 29, Kris, Willie Nelson, and Fred Foster are honored at the Seventh Annual Leadership Music Dale Franklin Awards. We start the day at Sound Emporium Studios, where Kris and Willie record a song with Randy Travis. After the session, we all go home to change and get ready for soundcheck and rehearsals at the Renaissance Hotel ballroom.

We arrive in time to hear Dolly Parton rehearsing "Dumb Blonde," which she will perform in honor of Fred Foster tonight. Lyle and April Lovett show up and Lyle rehearses for his tribute to Kris. Vince Gill is here to host. Guy comes early just to say hello. No one is expecting to see him. Guy has been in and out of the hospital all year. Guy is skeletal, his hair is thin, his skin is gray, and he needs a cane to walk.

Vince tells me that his wife, Amy Grant, is not going to make it to the show, so I escort Guy to our table. Vince leans over and whispers to me, "I can't believe I'm sitting at a table with Kris Kristofferson, Guy Clark, and Lyle Lovett." He is so sincere about it. I whisper back, "I can't believe I am sitting at a table with Vince Gill, Guy Clark, Lyle Lovett, and Kris Kristofferson." We laugh.

To Vince's right, Guy smokes a cigarette and asks me how the tribute is coming along. I take that opportunity to invite Vince to sing "Randall Knife" for the album. "Man, I don't know if I can get through that," Vince says. "No pressure, but I'd love for you to do that song. If not, you can choose another," I say. I want Vince to record "Randall Knife" because he pays tribute to it in "The Key to Life," Vince's song about his father, with the lyric, "The pain of losin' him cuts like a Randall Knife."

Six hundred Leadership Music alumni show up to honor Kris, Willie, and Fred. The show is a warm and loving tribute to the three friends. It's Shawn Camp's forty-fourth birthday and he is here to lead the house band: Charlie McCoy, Guthrie Trapp, and Dennis Crouch join Shawn in the band.

"It seemed like the pinnacle of my life that night," Shawn says. "I was a little overwhelmed to have Charlie McCoy in the band. Charlie has been the bandleader on so many of my favorite records. Charlie was so gracious and cool and just happy to be a part of it."

The first segment honors Fred Foster, the founder of Monument Records. A groundbreaking record man and producer, Fred signed Roy Orbison, Dolly Parton, Willie Nelson, and Kristofferson in the 1960s. Rodney Crowell sings "Dream Baby," capturing the rockabilly swing of Roy Orbison's original Monument recording. Billy Swan follows with "I Can Help," and Dolly brings the house down with "Dumb Blonde," her debut 1967 single produced by Fred. Dolly sticks around to present the award to

Fred with a sweet speech. "I would not have a career without Fred Foster," Dolly says. "Everything started with him." Kris catches my attention and whispers, "I wouldn't have a career without Fred, either."

Lyle and I are escorted backstage as the Kristofferson segment kicks off with a video message from Combine Music founder Bob Beckham. Lyle and I stand next to each other going over our notes. "I'm nervous," I say to Lyle. "Me, too," he says.

Shawn Camp takes the mic to sing "Sunday Morning Comin' Down." "When I sang 'Sunday Morning Comin' Down,' I sang the lyrics the way that Kris does instead of like Cash recorded it," Shawn says. "There were a few little tweaks I made to make sure it was like Kris's version, and it was a real honor to be able to do that."

As Shawn finishes singing, the crowd stands up and roars. "Today is my birthday and this is the best gift ever," Shawn says. Lyle hugs me, walks onstage, talks about Kris's legacy, and sings an absolutely stunning version of "Me and Bobby McGee." Lee Ann Womack follows Lyle and performs the tender "Loving Her Was Easier."

An announcer calls me to the stage. "Ladies and gentlemen, please welcome Tamara Saviano." I walk up onstage, my knees weak, to present Kris with the award. There's a spotlight on our table. I see Kris, but the rest of the room is black. Perfect.

"Good evening. I'm Tamara Saviano, Leadership Music class of 2007. I am honored to be here tonight to say a few words about my friend and colleague, Kris Kristofferson. As you know, this award was created to recognize music industry leaders who exemplify the highest quality in leadership, and leading by example. The selection committee has chosen well. I've learned that some leaders lead from the head of the parade. Some from behind, pushing and prodding. And some, like Kris, choose the hardest leadership style, leading from within the group as part of a team. I've been with Kris and Lisa for many honors, including his induction into the Country Music Hall of Fame, Songwriter Hall of Fame, the Texas Film Hall of Fame, and the BMI Icon Award. The Kris I know is a reluctant icon. He is unassuming and rather shy. Although he is always kind and gracious when celebrated and praised by admirers, I've seen Kris wince when he hears the word *legendary*. He is genuinely perplexed by the recognition.

Kris is modest. Kris once told me that when he moved to Nashville to be a songwriter he was not looking to change anything, he just wanted to fit in. And write songs. Kris did not set out to be a trailblazer and he certainly could not have imagined that he would inspire the next generation of songwriters. But we all know it now. Kris's songs did redefine the art of songwriting, and whether he wanted to or not, Kris became a leader by example. Fitting in but leading all the while. Fred and Willie met Kris early in his journey, when he was a lonely, struggling songwriter. I work with the older and wiser Kris, the devoted husband, father, and grandfather, who clearly loves to write and perform, but is happiest when surrounded by his family. The trappings of stardom have no part in Kris's day-to-day life. He has no entourage when he tours or makes appearances. His wife, Lisa, is his tour partner. Sometimes a couple of the kids are with them, sometimes not. Kris doesn't need to be in front of a parade to lead. When Kris comes to Nashville, he spends a good deal of his time helping younger artists and songwriters. He has made guest appearances on many recordings, music videos, and documentaries. He has come to town to pay tribute to his contemporaries and heroes. He gives his time and money to causes that sustain all of us. Kris fits it all in because he remembers what it was like to be the upstart, and he remembers when guys like Fred and Willie helped him. Kris leads others to find their voice, not by prodding and pushing, but by participation. Each of us in this room has benefited in one way or another from Kris's gifts. I say with confidence that all of us would be better leaders by following Kris's example. Kris, on a personal note, you have enriched my life beyond measure. I'll use your words here: I'm so glad I was close to you for a moment of forever. I love you. Friends and colleagues, I'm happy to present the Leadership Music Dale Franklin Award to Kris Kristofferson."

Kris walks up to accept the award and we both cry. "I'm kind of speechless," Kris says. "I'm so honored to be up here with Fred Foster and Willie Nelson. I can't tell you what it means to me." Kris and I leave the stage holding hands. Vince says, "Thank you, Kris, thank you, Tamara, that was sweet."

Back at our table, I relax and enjoy the rest of the show. The Willie segment, introduced by Stephen Colbert via video, flies by with performances by Jamey Johnson ("Angel Flying Too Close to the Ground"), Lorrie Morgan ("Crazy"), and Randy Travis ("Funny How Time Slips Away"). Brenda Lee presents the award to Willie. "Listening to people say all of these nice things, I almost gave myself a standing ovation," Willie jokes. "Thank y'all."

Shawn and Willie call all of the artists up to the stage to sing a rousing version of "On the Road Again" to conclude the show.

After the show, we stick around the ballroom and Kris takes pictures with everyone who wants to say hello. We are the last to leave. I ask Kris what he wants to do now. "Take me to Willie's bus," he says. A security guard escorts Kris, Lisa, Paul, and me through back hallways and out to the loading dock.

Willie and Annie Nelson, Kris and Lisa, and Paul and I sit on Willie's bus for about thirty minutes. Kris and Willie sit across from each other at the table in the front lounge. Willie has a newfangled self-lighting marijuana pipe. He tries to show Kris how to use it but Kris isn't getting it. I giggle watching these two old men with their heads together studying the pipe.

After Willie hits the road, we walk to the Bridge Bar to buy Shawn a birthday drink.

"That was one of the highlights of my evening," Shawn says. "Ronnie Hawkins was there and I got to hang out with him. He's a hero of mine. Ronnie is from Arkansas, so I had a little bit of common ground with him. All that stuff he did with Levon Helm and the Band meant a lot to me, a big influence on me."

We sit with Shawn, Chris Stapleton, and Mike Sistad from ASCAP. Kris gets up to sing "Happy Birthday" and Shawn beams. Stapleton complains that people have been mistaking him for Jamey Johnson all night. From my 2025 vantage point, I wish I could tell him that it will not be a problem a few years from now.

MerleFest, founded in 1988 in memory of Eddy Merle Watson, is a premiere Americana music festival. Longtime Americana supporters pictured here (*left to right*) at the 2006 festival: Sugar Hill Records staffer Tasha Thomas, MerleFest director Claire Armbruster, radio promoter Al Moss, artist manager Traci Thomas, and Sugar Hill Records staffer Molly Nagel. Photo courtesy of Tasha Thomas.

AMERICANA HONORS & AWARDS
HISTORY BY CATEGORY

Jack Emerson Lifetime Achievement Award for Executive
2006 – Barry Poss
2005 – The Rounder Founders: Ken Irwin, Marian Leighton, Bill Nowlin
2004 – Jack Emerson
2003 – Sam Phillips
2002 – T Bone Burnett

Lifetime Achievement Award for Instrumentalist
2006 – Kenny Vaughan

Lifetime Achievement Award for Performing
2006 – Alejandro Escovedo
2005 – Marty Stuart
2004 – Chris Hillman
2003 – Levon Helm
2002 – Emmylou Harris

Lifetime Achievement Award for Producer/Engineer
2006 – Allen Toussaint

Lifetime Achievement Award for Songwriting
2006 – Rodney Crowell
2005 – Guy Clark
2004 – Cowboy Jack Clement
2003 – John Prine
2002 – Billy Joe Shaver

President's Award
2006 – Mickey Newbury
2005 – John Hartford
2004 – Carter Family
2003 – Gram Parsons
2002 – Doug Sahm

First Amendment Center/Americana Music Association "Spirit of Americana" Free Speech Award
2006 – Charlie Daniels
2005 – Judy Collins
2004 – Steve Earle
2003 – Kris Kristofferson
2002 – Johnny Cash

Album Of The Year
2005 – *Universal United House Of Prayer* by **Buddy Miller** (New West)
2004 – *Van Lear Rose* by **Loretta Lynn** (Interscope)
2003 – *American IV: The Man Comes Around* by **Johnny Cash** (Lost Highway)
2002 – *Buddy & Julie Miller* by **Buddy & Julie Miller** (Hightone)

Artist Of The Year
2005 – John Prine
2004 – Loretta Lynn
2003 – Johnny Cash
2002 – Jim Lauderdale

Instrumentalist Of The Year
2005 – Sonny Landreth
2004 – Will Kimbrough
2003 – Jerry Douglas
2002 – Jerry Douglas

New/Emerging Artist Of The Year
2005 – Mary Gauthier
2004 – Mindy Smith (first year)

Song Of The Year
2005 – "Worry Too Much" by **Mark Heard**; appears on *Universal United House Of Prayer* by **Buddy Miller**
2004 – "Fate's Right Hand" by **Rodney Crowell**; appears on *Fate's Right Hand* by **Rodney Crowell** (DMZ/Epic)
2003 – "Hurt" by **Trent Reznor**; appears on *American IV: The Man Comes Around* by **Johnny Cash** (Lost Highway)
2002 – "She's Looking At Me" by **Jim Lauderdale**; appears on *Lost In The Lonesome Pines* by **Jim Lauderdale, Ralph Stanley & The Clinch Mountain Boys** (Dualtone)

The first five years of Americana Honors and Awards winners. Courtesy of Tamara Saviano archives.

Sugar Hill Records founder Barry Poss in 2006. Barry was honored with the Jack Emerson Lifetime Achievement Award for executive at the 2006 Americana Honors and Awards. Photo courtesy of Barry Poss.

No *Depression* founders Grant Alden (*left*) and Peter Blackstock (*right*) with noted Muscle Shoals musician David Hood (*center*) at the 2006 Americana Honors and Awards. Photo courtesy of Tamara Saviano archives.

Author Tamara Saviano with her clients and friends Guy Clark (*left*) and Kris Kristofferson (*right*) at Kristofferson's Country Music Hall of Fame Artist-in-Residence program, August 2007. Guy Clark was the Hall of Fame's artist in residence in 2006. Photo courtesy of Tamara Saviano archives.

Left to right: Tamara Saviano, Will Van Zandt, Guy Clark, and Katie Belle Van Zandt. As president of the Americana Music Association, Saviano presented the President's Award posthumously to Townes Van Zandt in 2007. Guy Clark was on hand to sing a Townes song, and Townes's children Will and Katie Belle accepted the award. Photo courtesy of Tamara Saviano archives.

Kris Kristofferson (*center*) reunites with his old band to celebrate the Nashville Songwriters Association International's purchase of the Bluebird Café in Nashville, November 2007. *Left to right:* Chris Gantry, Stephen Bruton, Kristofferson, Billy Swan, and Donnie Fritts. Photo courtesy of Tamara Saviano archives.

Left to right: Radney Foster, Gary Hartman, Rosie Flores, Bruce Robison, Tamara Saviano, and Cody Canada at the American Music Association conference in September 2008. Hartman, director of the Center for Texas Music History, moderated a panel on the role of Texas music in Americana. Foster, Flores, Robison, and Canada performed. Photo by Lynne Margolis.

Don Was with Kris and Lisa Kristofferson at the 2009 BMI awards. Kristofferson was honored with the BMI Icon Award. He gives a thumbs-up to the performers Willie Nelson, Vince Gill, and Patty Griffin. Photo courtesy of Tamara Saviano archives.

Left to right: Vince Gill, Guy Clark, Tamara Saviano, Kris Kristofferson, Fred Foster, Willie Nelson, and Lyle Lovett at the Leadership Music Dale Franklin Awards honoring Kristofferson, Nelson, and Foster, August 2010. Photo courtesy of Tamara Saviano archives.

Kris Kristofferson and Tamara Saviano at the Leadership Music Dale Franklin Awards in August 2010. Saviano presented Kristofferson with his leadership award. Photo courtesy of Tamara Saviano archives.

Shawn Camp and Kris Kristofferson drink red wine in red Solo cups on Kristofferson's bus parked in the alley behind the Ryman Auditorium in November 2010. Photo courtesy of Tamara Saviano archives.

The author's fiftieth birthday celebration with besties in Nashville at Jim McGuire's studio, March 2011. *First row, left to right:* Jim McGuire, Kathi Whitley (holding Maude), and Sonata Stanton. *Second row, left to right:* Taylor Holliday, Jen Gunderman, Tamara Saviano, and Kay Clary. Photo courtesy of Tamara Saviano archives.

Left to right: Verlon Thompson, Lyle Lovett, Jessie Scott, Terry Allen, Joe Ely, Rodney Crowell, Rosie Flores, Terri Hendrix, Liz Foster, Kelly Mickwee, and Shawn Camp sing "Happy Birthday" to Guy Clark at the Center for Texas Music History's seventieth birthday tribute to Guy at the Long Center, Austin, Texas, November 2011. Photo by Lynne Margolis.

CHAPTER EIGHTEEN

HEAVEN

The Sheraton Grand Hotel in downtown Nashville is the host hotel for the Americana conference for the first time in 2010. It's a more intimate venue than the convention center. Raul Malo performs in the Skye Lounge, the twenty-eighth-floor crown of the hotel with panoramic views of Music City. John Kunz, owner of Austin's Waterloo Records, is my dance partner for the night. We are not alone on the dance floor. The club is filled with our friends, and we drink champagne and dance until 2:00 a.m. as the night lights sparkle for miles in the distance.

Holly Lowman and Courtney Gregg produce the Americana Honors and Awards at the Ryman. I am like a proud mama. Holly and Courtney started as interns and production assistants the first year I produced the show. It is wonderful to see them take charge and create a world-class show. Passing the torch to the next generation is an important part of the Americana community and vital to keep things fresh. As in any large group, there are a few folks who keep a death grip on roles, but for the most part this community does an excellent job of mentoring new leaders. It's my favorite part of being here.

Rosanne Cash wins Album of the Year for *The List*, her album of cover songs inspired by the list her father gave her to expand her knowledge of country music. "Most of all, I want to thank my dad for making this list for an eighteen-year-old girl who had a dream to be a songwriter," Rosanne says in her acceptance speech. I call Kris and put him on the phone with Rosanne to congratulate her.

Ryan Bingham, whose "The Weary Kind" won an Academy Award as part of the *Crazy Heart* movie soundtrack, takes home the Artist of the Year award. The film *Crazy Heart*, based on the 1987 novel, follows an alcoholic country singer, played by Jeff Bridges, who tries to turn his life around after meeting a young journalist. The film is dedicated to Stephen Bruton. Stephen cowrote most of the original songs performed by Jeff Bridges and Ryan Bingham.

Hayes Carll wins the Emerging Artist award and the Avett Brothers take home the duo/group trophy. Jack White from the White Stripes brings Rock and Roll Hall of Famer Wanda Jackson to the stage to accept the Lifetime Achievement Award for Performer, calling her a founding mother of rock 'n' roll. Robert Plant presents band leader Buddy Miller, the coproducer of Plant's new *Band of Joy* album, with the Instrumentalist of the Year award.

Plant caps the show with a half-hour set with his Band of Joy, which includes Patty Griffin, Buddy Miller, Darrell Scott, Byron House, and Marco Giovino.

The highlight of Americana week for me is Guy Clark, accompanied by Shawn Camp, at the Station Inn. Shawn is filling in for Verlon Thompson, who is home recovering from broken wrists. The Station Inn is packed, with a line around the block of people hoping to get in to see Guy. For more than two hours, Guy and Shawn pull out song after song and the crowd sings along to all of them. Guy's voice sounds strong and he seems to be feeding off the adoration of the crowd. With his failing health, we never know if this is the last time he'll be on the stage. By the end of the night, Guy is exhausted. It is a struggle to get him out the back door and into his jeep. People try to get him to sign autographs, take photos, and talk to them. Guy is just too weak. Shawn and I get Guy into his jeep. As he drives off, Shawn and I share a moment, a look, where I know we are both thinking the same thing: Guy is not going to be here forever, and time seems to be growing short.

Kris and I are back in LA in late September.

My room at the Malibu Beach Inn now doubles as a documentary studio. Director Jim Shea interviews Kris for a John Prine documentary. Two cameras and enough lights and audio that it feels like a soundstage. I sit cross-legged on the bed, the only empty space in the room.

I remain in my position as Sophie Huber and her documentary crew take over my room and set up to interview Kris and Harry Dean Stanton together for Sophie's film *Harry Dean Stanton: Partly Fiction*. Harry Dean walks into the room, lights a cigarette, and requests red wine and a Manhattan. Harry knows there's no smoking inside anywhere in California but he doesn't care. "Look at you, Harry," Kris says. "You're eighty-four, healthy, and a walking advertisement for bad living."

I hand Harry a glass of wine.

"Hi, I'm Harry," he says. "What's your name?"

"I'm Tamara. Nice to meet you."

Harry asks me to spell my name. I do.

"What does your name mean?"

Kris has prepared me for this question, so I am ready. "The most widely accepted meaning of Tamara is 'date palm.' In ancient times the date palm was a symbol of beauty and strength."

Harry turns to look at Kris. "You gave me up, didn't you?" Kris and I bust out laughing.

"What nationality are you?" Harry asks.

I wonder if he is trying to trip me up. I tell him that my family comes from many places but my father, Mike Saviano, is Italian and Irish.

"What is the origin of Saviano?"

I tell him that Saviano is a town at the base of Mount Vesuvius near Napoli.

"Where did it come from before that?" Harry asks.

"I don't know," I say.

"Well, find that out," Harry instructs.

Harry wears a pin on his jacket lapel. I ask about it. "It's a pin from the restaurant Dan Tana. Have you been there?" When I tell Harry I have not been to Dan Tana's, he looks at Kris and says, "You're falling down on the job. Take Tamara to Dan Tana's. Every Italian needs to go to Dan Tana's."

Sophie and crew are ready. Kris and Harry sit next to each other on the couch. Room service brings a Manhattan up for Harry and he lights another cigarette. The room service guy is about to say something. Harry gives him a look and he turns to leave without saying a word.

Kris strums his guitar and Harry blows on a harmonica, with the cigarette between his fingers. "Do you have A?" Kris asks. "I'll be playing in A."

Harry tests another harmonica.

"That's E," Kris says.

Harry points to the harmonica. "This says A."

They go back and forth for a bit trying to find the sound. Kris tunes his guitar. After a few minutes, Kris jumps right in and sings "The Pilgrim (Chapter 33)." Harry changes harmonicas every few seconds trying to find the right one. He sips the Manhattan and puffs his cigarette in between. Kris finishes the song. "Your harmonica is so loud!"

"Well, I wasn't drowning out the vocal," Harry says.

"Yeah, well, it's easy to drown out mine," Kris says.

On September 23, Kris joins Vince Gill, Emmylou Harris, R&B star Lionel Richie, and Taylor Swift at the Nokia Theater for the Country Music Hall of Fame's "All for the Hall" benefit concert.

We share a dressing room with Vince. Vince and I talk about the Nashville music business. He tells me about his early days on RCA Records when Barry Beckett broke the news to Vince that RCA didn't want him to cut any of his own songs. They passed on "When I Call Your Name." It is painful to hear that story even all these years later. Luckily, Vince got out of the RCA deal and MCA recognized his talent. We discuss the power that radio programmers have and that between the major labels and corporate radio, it's a wonder real talent ever rises to the top. Things are much easier in Americana, where the art comes before the commerce. Often, there isn't much commerce at all in Americana, especially in the age of streaming and people expecting music to be free.

Vince and Kris meet the other artists for media interviews. Taylor's publicist, Paula Erickson, asks me if Kris is willing to have his picture taken with Taylor. "I'm sure he would love that. Let me ask him." "I'd love to have my picture taken with Taylor," Kris says. "But why does she want to be with an old man like me?"

From my vantage point in 2025, Taylor Swift is the biggest pop star on the planet. In 2010, she has three phenomenal albums under her belt, and we see the future. "That girl has it all. Taylor's going to be bigger than any of us," Vince predicts that day.

Taylor, wearing a sunny yellow dress that contrasts with Kris's old black shirt, takes control of the shoot. She commandeers the *Los Angeles Times* photographer, leads us to a private cabana, and pulls Kris down on the vinyl bench beside her. In one shot, Taylor and Kris hold up their fingers to form the shape of a heart between them. Taylor is a delight and Kris is smitten with her. In truth, we are all enamored with Taylor.

The show is exceptional. The artists swap songs. Taylor, Vince, Emmylou, and Kris on acoustic guitars and Lionel on piano. Taylor not only holds her own onstage with that group of veterans, she shines. Her fans scream from the balcony seats. Unusual for a guitar pull and lots of fun.

Randy Lewis writes about the show in the *Los Angeles Times* with the headline "Taylor Swift Gets a Seat at Adults Table."

"After selling more than ten million albums in the last four years, the last thing Taylor Swift needs is a raise. But Thursday night, the young country pop hitmaker got a major promotion in terms of her status as a singer and songwriter. There she sat on stage at Club Nokia for the annual All For the Hall concert benefiting Nashville's Country Music Hall of Fame and Museum, according an equal place alongside such esteemed country music figures as Kris Kristofferson, Emmylou Harris, and Vince Gill, as well as 70s and 80s Pop R&B king Lionel Richie. 'These are the best role models I could have,' Swift, twenty, told the crowd of about 2000 who had paid up to $1000 a seat to witness the guitar pull.... The addition of Swift on this year's show translated into a large vocal contingent of teen and preteen girls who erupted in a chorus of squeals when the master of ceremonies brought Taylor on stage."

I return to Nashville in time for Shawn Camp's 1994 album release party at Warner Brothers. I'm leading the public relations campaign for the album, titled 1994 for the year it was made.

The album had been buried in the Warner vault for sixteen years after Warner declined to release it unless Shawn removed the fiddles and dobros. Shawn refused. Fast-forward sixteen years, and Shawn is in Leadership Music with Warner president John Esposito.

"We were at closing retreat at Montgomery State Park," Shawn says. "By now I've been sitting next to Espo at Leadership Music events for eight months. He heard me play and sing at the guitar pull and came up to me and said, 'I'd like to put a record out on you. How would I go about doing that?' I said, 'Well, if I were you, I'd just walk over to the vault at your record label and pull out my album that's been sitting there for sixteen years and release it.'"

"Shawn is beloved in this community," Espo says. "The record is fantastic. The right thing to do is to put this album out into the world."

At the release party, Shawn and his band play a rocking forty-five-minute set in front of a packed Music Row crowd. Guy sits in front with me. Cowboy Jack Clement dances. Mark Wright, who produced Shawn's first record, is here. Pat Higdon, the publisher of Shawn's early songs, beams from the audience. The entire Nashville press corps shows up. Many of us shed tears of joy to see Shawn in the spotlight, where he belongs. Shawn, the Warner staff, and I gather in Espo's office after the party to drink champagne and toast our friend Shawn. It took sixteen years to release his album, but it's worth the wait.

Gretchen Peters is one of the most beloved and respected songwriters in Nashville. Gretchen wrote "The Chill of an Early Fall," a hit song for George Strait in 1991. Pam Tillis took Gretchen's song "Let That Pony Run" to the top ten in 1993. In 1995, Gretchen's "Independence Day" was a monster hit for Martina McBride and earned Gretchen her first Grammy nomination. The following year, Patty Loveless released Gretchen's "You Don't Even Know Who I Am," and the Grammys recognized her with another Song of the Year nomination. As a writer and vocalist, Gretchen is pure Americana, and she started recording her own albums in 1996. I work with Gretchen on her 2007 album *Burnt Toast and Offerings*, a brutally honest, achingly sincere, autobiographical work that explores the messiness of love.

Gretchen and her love Barry Walsh get married on October 2, 2010. The night before, we celebrate with a prewedding party and concert at Green's Grocery out in charming Leipers Fork. Gretchen and Barry, Rodney Crowell, Tom Russell, Suzy Bogguss, Matraca Berg, Jeff Hanna, and Marshall Chapman play separately and together in jam sessions onstage. We all sing along, dance, talk, and howl.

We are handed flutes of champagne as we gather the next day in the Assumption churchyard in Germantown. Rodney officiates the intimate ceremony under a tree. After he pronounces Gretchen and Barry married for life, the party starts. Gretchen's cowriter and friend, rock star Bryan Adams, sings his hit "Heaven" for Gretchen and Barry's first dance. Those who belong on a stage take turns singing together and the rest of us stand under the tent and sing along. Rodney leads everyone on "Voila, an American Dream." Suzy and friends sing "Outbound Plane." The group performs "Elvira," "Mystery Train," and other fun sing-alongs. For much of the night, a bluegrass trio performs so the bride, groom, and guests aren't required to entertain.

A week later, Radney Foster and I fly to Chicago together. He has a show at Shank Hall in Milwaukee and is opening for Patty Loveless at Chicago's Old Town School of Folk Music the following night. It's fun to take Rad to my hometown. We stay at the Wyndham hotel by the airport. In my twenties, the Wyndham was the Red Carpet Hotel, home of El Robbo's Disco. I danced the night away many times at El Robbo's and also worked as a cocktail waitress there. Rad wants to take a picture of me in the old disco space but the doors are locked.

My nephew Jake and his friend Nate meet us at Shank Hall to sell merch for Radney. The audience at Shank Hall is small but enthusiastic. After the show, we meet friends from my radio days over at Elsa's on the Square for burgers and drinks. We have a day off before Chicago so I give Rad a tour of my hometown. The At Random Cocktail Lounge is a time capsule of the 1960s with retro cocktails and ice cream drinks. When I lived in Milwaukee, it was *the* late-night place to be. Rad and I slide into a green vinyl banquette as Sinatra croons on the hi-fi. "I have never seen anything like this," Rad says. He drinks a love punch bowl. The drink is meant for two people to share, but Rad manages to polish the whole thing off.

Radney is a bit hungover on our drive to Chicago the next day. We drop our bags at a hotel near Lincoln Square before soundcheck at the Old Town School. Patty has two shows tonight and Rad is performing a thirty-minute set before each show. Patty is fantastic. It is a thrill to see her perform again after all these years. She includes "You Don't Even

Know Who I Am," written by my pal Gretchen Peters, in her set. Her poignant delivery of "Nothin' but the Wheel" crushes me. Patty ends her show with Stephen Bruton's "Too Many Memories" and talks about Stephen's heartbreaking death last year. It is an emotional, bittersweet, magnificent night with Patty.

At the end of October, we are back in Austin to record songs for the Guy Clark tribute album. For our first session, Terry Allen records "Old Friends." Terry plays piano as Jen Gunderman takes accordion duties. Shawn and Verlon play acoustic guitar and Glenn Fukunaga joins on upright bass. Our guru, the legendary Lloyd Maines, plays dobro and mandolin and warms the room with his being.

Guy is in town to play the Paramount Theater the next day. For dinner, we meet him on the patio at Polvo's, his favorite Mexican restaurant in Austin. It is a wonder to witness Guy, Terry, and Lloyd together, old Texas friends reminiscing about shared adventures.

We return to the studio after dinner and Joe Ely records a pristine "Dublin Blues." The next morning, Robert Earl Keen records "Texas 1947." Robert wants to slow the song down a bit. It is a tough lyric. "Screaming straight through Texas like a mad dog cyclone" is particularly tongue twisting and it takes a while to find the groove. We get three or four great takes. Hayes Carll comes in to lay down "Worry B Gone." Shawn and Verlon sing backup vocals. The song has a bluesy, groovy vibe and we're all thrilled with it. Hayes tells a story about getting really stoned with Guy in his basement. Hayes walked upstairs to the kitchen and startled Susanna, who was in her bathrobe and pulling a tray of taquitos out of the oven. Susanna screamed. The taquitos flew up in the air, and Hayes says he almost had a marijuana-induced heart attack.

We cut the session at four o'clock. Shawn and Verlon have to meet Guy at soundcheck, and we are all going to the show tonight. Guy's Paramount show is fantastic. The Paramount is packed, yet the room is silent while Guy sings, accompanied by Shawn and Verlon. The crowd claps enthusiastically after each song. The only time they erupt during a song is when Guy starts "Dublin Blues." "Well, I wish I was in Austin"—everyone stands and cheers—"in the Chili Parlor Bar drinking mad dog margaritas and not caring where you are." Guy stands out in the alley and greets fans after the show. We end up at the Chili Parlor. Although I repeated Guy's admonishment about the petroleum and sea water taste, everyone except me drinks mad dog margaritas until closing time.

I meet Kris back in Nashville for the Tootsie's fiftieth anniversary celebration on November 7. Kris is on the redeye and is exhausted when I pick him up. We are ambushed by two guys wanting him to sign guitars. How do they know when Kris is arriving? It's a mystery to all of us. We arrive at the Loews Vanderbilt Hotel to find that the Tootsie's people booked the room for the wrong day. They won't have a room for Kris until that night. I take him home to nap in my guest room.

After he sleeps, I make him a turkey sandwich. Kris blows on a cup of coffee and says he is flying to DC after the Tootsie's show. Professor Weissmiller, Kris's college English teacher, died earlier this summer and his memorial service is this week at Arlington National Cemetery. "Professor Weissmiller changed my life more than anyone else," Kris says. "It's interesting how one person can affect another so deeply, and it becomes a chain reaction. If our hearts are right, we remember it and use our power to help others."

"Just like you did for me," I say. "When I was fired from GAC, you hired me to show your support. My name was mud in this town and because of you I've been able to stay in this business and do amazing things."

"Oh, no, Tamara, I am the lucky one in this relationship," Kris says. "I couldn't do any of this without you."

"Well, thank you for hiring me and allowing me to have a big mouth," I say.

Kris snorts. "You have a big mouth? Mine has been getting me in trouble for many years!"

"We make a good team," I say.

"Yes, we do," Kris says.

After Professor Weissmiller's funeral, Kris is heading back to Tampa to continue filming *Dolphin Tale* with Morgan Freeman, Harry Connick Junior, and Ashley Judd. Kris says the director, Charles Martin Smith, played a small role in *Pat Garrett and Billy the Kid* when he was a young actor. He asked Kris to be in the film because he felt like Kris really helped him in that early role. Another instance of Kris influencing someone.

Chapter 18

Kris asks about Guy and I tell him that today is Guy's sixty-ninth birthday and he is in the hospital having a toe amputated. I detail Guy's health issues. "And Guy is so young," I add. "Tamara, I hate to break it to you, but sixty-nine is not young."

I am determined to finish the Guy tribute album and biography while Guy is still here to see them. Bob Edwards from Sirius XM is in town doing interviews for a series about Nashville. I invite him to Guy's. Susanna sits at the kitchen table in her nightgown, drinking coffee and smoking a cigarette. She looks like hell after her recent surgery to remove part of her lung. Guy stands with a cup of coffee and a cigarette, one knee in a brace and a medical boot on the other foot. He has just come from the doctor and has to go back to the hospital after the interview to get the infection scraped off his toe. The surgeon delayed Guy's knee surgery because they can't operate if he has any infection in him. Guy struggles to get down the stairs to his workshop. His knee buckles and he almost falls. He is frustrated and in pain.

The day of the Tootsie's show, the City of Nashville gives Kris a star on the Music City Walk of Fame. We start our marathon day when I pick Kris and his son Johnny up at the hotel at noon. Before the ceremony, Bill Cody interviews Kris for his GAC *Master Series* show. We love Bill Cody so it's a piece of cake. I enlist Rodney Crowell to present Kris's star. When Rodney arrives, we hang out in the greenroom until the ceremony. I fill Rodney in on Guy's situation. Rodney is trying to find a delicate way to reinsert himself into Guy's life. Earlier this year, Susanna asked Rodney to pick up a prescription for Guy. When he arrived at the Clarks', Rodney found Guy near death and called 911. He ended up being persona non grata around Guy's house for a while. Susanna called it "meddling." It's a difficult position to be in with Guy and Susanna. They are proud, private people and want to be left alone to take care of themselves. Shawn meets us in the greenroom. He had been to the hospital to visit Guy and says he is in good spirits.

Shawn stays with Kris, Johnny, and me for the day. We sit on Kris's bus, parked in the alley behind the Ryman. It's great to have a private place to escape the backstage madness of the Tootsies fiftieth anniversary celebration. As road manager, Johnny has to deal with all of the bullshit.

Shawn and I get the easy job of hanging out with Kris. After soundcheck, Kris takes a nap. Shawn and I meet songwriters Billy Burnette and Dennis Morgan at the Palm for dinner. After Kris plays his three songs, we crack open a bottle of red wine on the bus and high-five each other for making it through this fiasco.

"I remember Kris got up to throw the empty wine bottle in the trash and I stopped him," Shawn says. "I said, 'I don't want to be a fan girl, man, but is there any way I could get you to sign that wine bottle to me?' Kris wrote on the label, 'Enjoyed killing this bottle with you. See you down the road.' I'm so glad I did that because it was the only time I ever killed a bottle of wine with Kris Kristofferson, you know? It was real cool."

A few days later, Jim Lauderdale is honored with the Inspiration Award at the SESAC dinner. Buddy Miller and Byron House sing "King of Broken Hearts" and Jim is near tears with the rest of us. Our Jim Lauderdale, King of Americana and all-around amazing human being. The first show I saw on my first full night in Nashville was Jim Lauderdale at Ace of Clubs. Buddy was in his band that night. Full-circle moments with poets and dreamers. Individually and collectively, we have grown beyond our wildest imaginations.

CHAPTER NINETEEN

THIS ONE'S FOR HIM

Emmylou Harris and John Prine record a gorgeous version of "Magnolia Wind" for the Guy Clark tribute. Emmylou and John got together the night before our session to rehearse. They come in and nail it in one take. We do a few more passes. All of them are keepers.

We go back to Cedar Creek Studios in Austin to record Lyle Lovett, Patty Griffin, Rosie Flores, Kevin Welch, Terri Hendrix, and Ray Wylie Hubbard. The band lays down a track for "The Guitar," for Ramblin' Jack Elliott to put a vocal on.

Kevin Welch's version of "Magdalene" gives me chills. During playback, some of the band comment on Kevin's outstanding performance. Kevin points at me and says, "It was all Tamara. That's the first song she sent me and told me she wanted me to do it." It is sweet of Kevin to say that and a big confidence booster. Sometimes I feel like an imposter as a producer because I am not a musician. But then I remember my conversations with the great Jerry Wexler. Before his death, Jerry and I talked on the phone often. I voiced my misgivings to him. "It's your job to get the right people in the room and then get out of the way," Jerry advised. "You keep your eye on your vision and let the musicians and singers do what they do." Jerry's voice rings in my head and keeps me moving forward.

Terri Hendrix makes "The Dark" her own. It is Guy's favorite track on the tribute. He says he can never sing it again after hearing Terri's version.

Patty Griffin's ethereal voice is ideal for "The Cape." Lyle Lovett kills "Anyhow I Love You." Lyle can hear stuff deep in the layers, like a ringing guitar string on one of Shawn's solos. No one else can hear it until Lyle points it out. We work for a long time to get "Anyhow I Love You" just right for Lyle. I'm in awe of his process and keen sensibilities. In contrast, Ray Wylie Hubbard comes in to record "Homegrown Tomatoes." He does two takes and says, "Yeah, we got it." And we did, rough and raw and marvelous.

We bring a cake for Verlon Thompson on his birthday. When we finish in the studio, Shawn, Verlon, Jen Gunderman, and I go to dinner at Enoteca for Verlon's birthday. The four of us pitch quarters outside Enoteca as we wait for our table and talk about everything. I confide in them that I am struggling with the record label. When Ray Wylie is in the studio, the label president whispers in my ear that I should tell Ray to phrase "pinto and navy" the way Guy does in "Homegrown Tomatoes." I say we should let Ray do the song the way he wants to do it. The label president also insists we have no percussion on the record. John Silva plays cajon on "Magdalene" at Kevin's request. It is so beautiful we add it to more tracks. I'm not going to take it off, but this is the first time I've had a record label guy up my ass and I'm over it. Verlon, Shawn, and Jen are shocked that I've been dealing with this alone. Verlon says, "We Guyotes have your back, Tamara." The Guyotes. It sticks. We are the Guyotes. Poets and dreamers.

We finish tracking the Guy tribute in Nashville with Suzy Bogguss singing "Instant Coffee Blues," and Shawn records "Homeless." We lay down the tracks for "Better Days" and "All She Wants Is You" for Rosanne Cash and Shawn Colvin to put vocals on.

On the last day of recording, I get word that Ron Sexsmith is in town writing with Big Al Anderson. I burn up the phone lines to track down Ron. I want him on my Guy tribute. He will be the only artist Guy doesn't know, but I love Ron as a songwriter as much as I love Guy. To me, it is no coincidence that Ron is here from Toronto at the exact moment I need him. His manager, the late Cathy Hendrix, is a Guy Clark fan and she gets Ron on the phone with me within an hour. Ron asks to hear a couple of songs. I want him to sing "Broken Hearted People." I drop a disc off for Cathy and tell her that "Broken Hearted People" is my first choice—my only choice, really—but if Ron doesn't like it we can figure something else out. A few hours later, Ron is in the studio recording "Broken Hearted People." After Ron, Jerry Jeff Walker comes in to record a song Guy just finished writing. "My Favorite Picture of You" has not been recorded yet. Jerry Jeff is a character, but he is easy to work with and we have a lot of fun. Jerry Jeff says he is going to make T-shirts for all of us that say YOU DON'T HAVE TO BE NICE IF YOU'RE GOOD. We get Jerry Jeff out the door and Shawn and Verlon add harmonies on Ron's and Suzy's tracks. There's still a lot of work to be done with the mixing and mastering, but we are getting close to having a finished record.

I pick up Vince's track from his studio and Steve Earle's track from his producer Ray Kennedy. I fly back to Austin to meet Shawn Colvin at Cedar Creek to get her vocal. I bring Lloyd Maines in to produce the Trishas' vocals. I'm way out of my league with a four-part harmony but Lloyd is a genius. He works with Jamie, Kelley, Liz, and Savannah and they make magic together.

My friend Val Denn is in town from Nova Scotia. We meet in Wimberley for a Kevin Welch concert. I drop my bags at Kevin's and meet Val at the Cypress Café for dinner, and then we go to the Wimberley United Methodist Church. Kevin plays as part of the Susanna's Kitchen songwriter series. In recent years, I've seen Kevin perform as part of the Kane, Welch, Kaplan trio, but this is the first solo show I've attended in many years. It's a magical musical night with Kevin. After the show, a bunch of us go back to Kevin's house for an after-show party. Everyone leaves around 1:00 a.m., but Kevin and I drink red wine and talk until 5:00 a.m.

Back in Nashville, Susanna Clark is in the ICU at Saint Thomas Hospital. Doctors amputate another of Guy's toes. Both of the Clarks are frail. Guy and I are two years into the biography, stopping and starting as his health spirals. I'm grateful and honored for the privilege of documenting Guy's life, yet it is bittersweet at this point in Guy and Susanna's lives.

Maria Drummond, a Belmont University senior, starts work at my office as an intern. Maria is smart, ambitious, and eager to learn. I throw her in the deep end from day one. We start with building a strategic plan for the new Foster and Lloyd record. After a twenty-year break, Radney Foster reunites with his duo partner Bill Lloyd for *It's Already Tomorrow*. As Radney's manager, I oversee the launch. Maria assists me with the album photo shoot. Independent records rarely have the budget for location fees, so Bill, Radney, photographer Ed Rode, Maria, and I sneak into the Melrose Pool Hall for the first setup. Then we run over to the historic Hermitage Hotel and covertly hijack the vintage art deco men's room to finish the shoot.

Red Beet Records hires me as publicist for the tribute album I Love: Tom T. Hall's "Songs of Fox Hollow," produced by Eric Brace and Peter Cooper. For the Songs of Fox Hollow press day, Maria and I join the Red Beet team at Tom T. Hall's farm, and later for Tom's seventy-fifth birthday celebration at the Country Music Hall of Fame.

SXSW 2011 is filled with music, friendship, and fun. Joe and Sharon Ely host an Italian dinner prepared by friends visiting from Milan. Foster and Lloyd play Ray Benson's sixtieth birthday party, a showcase at the Saxon Pub, and a short set at Threadgill's for Music Fog.

I am captivated by artist Brian Wright's set at Threadgill's. Brian plays his song "Maria Sugarcane" and it feels like the second coming of Townes Van Zandt. I ask around about Brian and find out Gary Paczosa signed him to Sugar Hill Records. I want to know more, but it will have to wait, as I'm late for dinner with Dave Marsh and Val Denn. Dave and I see Alejandro Escovedo together the next day, followed by a late dinner at Guero's. We run around together the rest of SXSW week. We see Hayes Carll in the Waterloo Records parking lot, Joe Ely and his Italian friends at Maria's Taco Xpress, and Kevin Welch at Zax, and we finish the week at Dave's annual SXSW Sunday party.

Kris is on location in Montreal shooting a film, but he takes a break to fly to Nashville for the Nashville Film Festival's screening of his film Bloodworth. The Sony Pictures publicist, Staci Griesbach, is from Hortonville, Wisconsin. We hit it off immediately.

A car picks Kris, his son Johnny, and me up at the Loews Vanderbilt Hotel and takes us to the Green Hills Theater. A thunderstorm rages, and sheets of rain pound the car as lightning flashes around us. The dark sky is menacing, the temperature has dropped, and tree limbs block the main road. Tornadoes are touching down just south of us. Beautiful night for a film premiere. The car drops us at the Gibson bus, Kris's dressing room for the event. We crack open a bottle of wine and Emmylou shows up to say hello. She is presenting Kris with a career achievement award before the screening. Kris and Emmy walk the red carpet together, which is too long and exhausting, but Staci handles all of the press so I can just escort Kris. Emmy gives Kris the award, we watch the film, then the filmmakers and actors answer questions from the audience. As we leave the theater, Kris is mobbed. "Mickey Mouse in fucking Disneyland," Kris whispers to me as I try to get him out the door.

We spend the next afternoon in the Loews ballroom with Kris doing press interviews for *Bloodworth*. Again, Staci is on top of it and all I have to do is be there for Kris. After the press day, Paul drops us off at Jack White's Third Man Records. Jerry Lee Lewis is in town to do a show for Record Store Day. The show is supposed to be outside but it is postponed because of weather. Instead, the Killer performs inside Jack's tiny studio in front of about seventy-five people. I stand ten feet from Jerry Lee Lewis, watching his hands fly across the piano keys, as Kris and I dance and sing along with "A Whole Lotta Shakin' Going On" and "Great Balls of Fire." Steve Cropper plays guitar, Jim Keltner is on drums, Jack Lawrence is on bass, and Jerry Lee's longtime bandleader Ken Loveless rounds out the stage. It is one of those magical Nashville moments.

Brian Wright is in town from LA to play 3rd and Lindsley. The show is fantastic. Gary Paczosa introduces me to Brian and we meet for coffee. I think Brian is special. I'm interested in working with him, but I'm torn about committing myself to a young artist. I don't know if I can give him what he needs. I decide to follow Brian back to LA to see his full band show at Hotel Café and meet with his managers Jim Hustead and Lauren Sheftell.

Stephanie Hopson from Sugar Hill, Amanda Hale from New West, and my Wisconsin pals Chris Richards and Staci Griesbach meet me for Brian's show. I want to see how they respond to Brian. Do they see what I see? Is Brian as good as I think he is? I'm half hoping I won't be impressed by Brian so I can walk away and forget about him. His performance blows all of us away. Brian is a fantastic band leader and musician, a great songwriter, an incredible live performer. I'm in. He's just so good, and he's got that special something, a magnetism onstage. He is a star, but no one knows it yet.

The following night, I have dinner with Jim and Brian. Jim is larger than life and towers over us. With his long blond hair and Nordic features, Jim's nickname is "the Norwegian." I fall in love with both Jim and Lauren immediately. I feel like I've known all of them forever. I offer to be an adviser and help them with whatever Brian needs. He is not making any money yet, so there's no percentage to be had, but I want to be part of this. Brian has a label deal with Sugar Hill, but now we need to find him a booking agent and get him a showcase at the Americana conference. All of that is much more difficult than it sounds.

On June 9, 2011, I'm stretched out in the back seat of a brand-new Cadillac with Verlon Thompson behind the wheel. Guy Clark rides shotgun and smokes a freshly rolled cigarette, indifferent to the red No Smoking symbols sprinkled across the dashboard of the rental car. We've been on the road for nearly seven hours, driving from Baton Rouge on our way to Guy's hometown of Rockport, Texas. We are almost there. Guy takes a deep breath. "My blood pressure drops a bit when I get back home to Texas," he says.

As the car turns onto Fulton Beach Road, soybean and cotton fields give way to palm trees and sand, quaint beach-side inns, and shrimp boats in the harbor. A hot wind blows from the Gulf of Mexico. Guy rolls down the car window and points out the dramatic sculpted live oak trees, permanently bent from the wind off the Gulf. "People come from all over the world to see these trees. Japanese artists like to paint them because they resemble bonsai."

Guy nods toward the water. "Down the road a bit is a ski basin. Four or five of us guys would get up early in the morning and go water skiing before school. We'd be dressed for school and just stand on the sandy slope. The boat comes around and leaves a big slack in the line and just hits it. As the line tightens up you just step onto the ski. We'd never even get wet."

Rockport, named for the rock ledge foundation of its shore, spans the Live Oak Peninsula thirty miles northeast of Corpus Christi on Texas Highway 35. The town is anchored by barrier islands, which sustain the Aransas National Wildlife Refuge, and is surrounded by the waters of Aransas and Copano Bays. Whooping cranes, pelicans, egrets, and herons make their home on the coastal hideaway. Since the 1800s they've shared the land with fishermen, townspeople, and well-heeled snowbirds. A city sign reads "Rockport-Fulton: Charm of the Texas Coast."

It's been more than a decade since Guy has been back here. The town has grown since Key Allegro Isle was built on Frandolig Island out in Aransas Bay, a mud flat once used by fishermen and duck hunters. Now it is populated by million-dollar homes and affluent tourists, and even country star George Strait escapes to Key Allegro when he needs a break.

Guy is here this weekend to play the Rockport Music Festival on Fulton Beach, which is just a mile down the road from the former site of the Shack, Peg Leg Furlong's thatch-roofed, beach-themed, indoor-outdoor joint where Guy, his high school friend Carl Snyder, and Ellis Clark's law partner Lola Bonner played acoustic guitars and sang for the customers.

Guy is glad to be back but hates these kinds of gigs on an outdoor stage, during the day, sunlight in his eyes, with kids and dogs running around. Guy and Jerry Jeff sit at a picnic table backstage and grouse to each other. Every time I walk past them, Guy rolls his eyes at me. I have no idea why. Guy's nephew Jonathan and Townes's son JT are here backstage. It is uncanny how much they resemble a young Guy and Townes. I want to take a picture of them together, but I don't ask. I still regret it.

Later in the month, Shawn and I spend a week at Cedar Creek with our mixing and mastering engineer, Fred Remmert, to finish *This One's for Him: A Tribute to Guy Clark*. The label is not willing to spend money on decent artwork and packaging for the Guy tribute. Fred talks to his boss, Kelcy Warren at Music Road Records, and Kelcy offers to buy the album and put it out on his Music Road label so we can do it right. I lobby the label to sell to Kelcy, but they won't budge. Kelcy gives us the money for packaging anyhow. He says it is his gift to us. What an angel.

Radney and Bill arrive in Austin to promote *It's Already Tomorrow*. We fortify ourselves with a delicious dinner at Botticelli to prepare for several days of running around Austin. We start at KUT with an interview with the great Jody Denberg. Over at the Gibson showroom, Rad and Bill tape an episode of *Texas Music Scene* with host Ray Benson. We load into Waterloo Records for an in-store performance and record signing.

Gary Hartman, Brian Atkinson, Alejandro Escovedo, Rosie Flores, Phil Madeira, Brian Owings, and Will Kimbrough are in the audience. Phil, Brian, and Will are in town with Emmylou for a show tonight. Glenn Fukunaga shows up with his adorable, four-year-old twin grandsons. We end the long day with a late-night hang at Guero's.

My research assistant Brian Atkinson and I drive through the godforsaken desert for six hours to get to Guy Clark's birthplace, Monahans. It's crystal clear to me why Guy's dad moved the family to the pretty little beach town of Rockport. I think Guy was lucky to get out of Monahans at a young age even if it did provide him with a few outstanding songs about West Texas. This is not my kind of place, brown dirt and dust and desert in every direction. The only bit of green is the scrub brush blowing past the oil wells.

We arrive in Monahans and check into the Best Western. The parking lot is full of Halliburton employees in red jumpsuits. We ask the desk clerk to recommend a restaurant with a good wine list. He laughs. There is no wine in this dry county. We opt for the Bar Eight Steakhouse, a brightly lit shed with mediocre food.

The next morning, we head to the Monahans Cemetery to find the graves of Guy's grandmother Rossie and her boyfriend Jack Prigg. We find Jack's headstone, but not Rossie's. I call city hall and learn that Rossie is buried next to Jack, but there is no headstone. Next, we drive to the sites of the old Clark Hotel and Green Frog Café. We stop at the Million Barrel Museum and get a history lesson on the oil business in Monahans and the importance of the train. Everyone we speak to recalls the excitement of the first passenger trains. Just like in Guy's song "Texas 1947," the entire town shows up at the depot to watch the streamline train blow through town.

Paula Bard, editor of the *Monahans News*, takes us to lunch. She introduces us to Joy Fletcher at the Tejas Bank. As children, Joy and Guy played together on the steps of the Clark Hotel.

One of my favorite moments is interviewing one-hundred-year-old Glenn Ratliff, who was in a supper club with Guy's parents. Mr. Ratliff says that Guy's mom, Frances, introduced all of them to caviar. "None of us liked it," Mr. Ratliff says. "But Frances was a caviar woman."

After Monahans, we drive to Abilene to meet Guy and Verlon. They are playing the West Texas Book and Music Fest. Guy is distraught. Wendy, a woman who has worked with Guy and Susanna for many years, embezzled several hundred thousand dollars from Guy, which is most of his money. Between Guy's illness and Susanna's bad health, Guy says he just wasn't paying close attention. Verlon points out that Wendy must have been in cahoots with the accountant because the accountant never questioned outrageous charges. In the end, Wendy dies before Guy recovers any of his money.

From Texas, I fly to San Francisco. Kris and Guy are both playing the Hardly Strictly Bluegrass Festival. Kris and Merle Haggard share the Star Stage and play solo and together. Kris's oldest son, Kris Jr., and his family are on the bus with us, and Kris is happy to be surrounded by grandchildren. Security escorts us to the stage in a golf cart. It's only one hundred yards to the stage, but fans surround us and yell and grab and poke at Kris the entire distance. After the set, Steve Earle is trying to talk to Kris as fans gather around the golf cart. I order Steve to get on the cart and come with us to the bus. When Steve leaves, Kris turns to me and asks, "Who was that?"

"Steve Earle," I reply.

"Man, I can't remember anyone," Kris says. "I love Steve Earle. Why didn't I recognize him?"

"Maybe it has something to do with Steve's long beard. That's new," I say gently.

"Tamara, you're sweet to let me off the hook, but we both know my memory is fading."

I leave Kris and go to the Rooster stage for Guy. Steve is in Guy's dressing room when I get there. "Kris didn't know who I was, did he?" Steve asks. I smile. "He remembered you when I reminded him." I slip Steve a finished copy of the Guy tribute and tell him to keep it to himself for now. I tell Guy we are going to use the Polaroid picture of him and Susanna in front of the Volkswagen bus on the tribute album cover. I also break the news on the label situation but reassure Guy that Kelcy Warren is stepping in to cover the art and packaging costs. "Wow, that's really nice of Kelcy to do that," Guy says. Yes, it is.

On November 2, Gary Hartman and the Center for Texas Music History present "Wish I Was in Austin, a 70th Birthday Tribute to Guy Clark" at the Long Center in Austin. What a night. Every moment is extraordinary. The show is a fundraiser for the center and a chance to launch *This One's for Him: A Tribute to Guy Clark*. The house band for the show is our tribute band, Shawn Camp, Verlon Thompson, Jen Gunderman, Lloyd Maines, Glenn Fukunaga, and John Ross Silva.

I watch Guy's old friends Joe Ely, Terry Allen, Lyle Lovett, and Rodney Crowell cut up together backstage. Minor Wilson, Guy's friend from his Houston and San Francisco days, is here to film the show. Travis Rivers, who introduced Guy to photographer Jim McGuire forty years ago in Nashville, is here. Guy's dearest collaborators and friends mill around backstage: McGuire, Tim Dubois from ASCAP, Guy's former publicist Liz Thiels, and Guy's longtime manager, agent, and friend Keith Case. Most of the artists from the tribute album perform. Terry Allen, Joe Ely, Lyle Lovett, Jerry Jeff Walker, Jack Ingram, Rodney, Shawn Colvin, Rosie Flores, Kevin Welch, the Trishas, Terri Hendrix, Ray Wylie Hubbard, James McMurtry, J. T. Van Zandt, Shawn, and Verlon. Rodney grabs me backstage with tears in his eyes. "This is an important night, a great gift to Guy. You should be proud." This moment makes the whole thing worthwhile. Jody Denberg finds me a glass of wine before I take the stage to introduce Guy. I'm nervous.

"I was fourteen years old in 1975 when I heard Guy's first LP, *Old No. 1*. Those ten perfect songs changed everything for me. Story song after story song, from 'Rita Ballou' to 'Desperados Waiting for a Train' to 'Texas 1947,' took me to wild and wonderful places I never imagined. I was a teenager in Wisconsin, but somehow related to all these colorful Texans, who danced the Slow Uvalde and played Moon and Forty-Two. 'She Ain't Going Nowhere' became the theme song for my teen angst. All of you know what a glorious experience it is to be moved by Guy Clark songs. Guy is a poet whose words invite us into his stories. His melodies awaken our emotions. We taste and touch and feel all the heartache and hope that he delivers like no one else. He teaches lessons. When I was a young girl with feelings that needed some repairing, Guy taught me that it's all right to lay it down and live it like I please. Talk about a gift. Guy has given all of us so many gifts. His songs continually enrich our lives. I hope this tribute album and my forthcoming biography will play a small part in celebrating and preserving Guy's unparalleled musical legacy for future generations. I'm proud to be here tonight to introduce the finest songwriter from the great state of Texas, Guy Clark."

Guy takes the stage to end the show with a nine-song set. "This is the first time I wrote a set list in about thirty years," Guy says. "Everybody else sang all my songs tonight." We interrupt Guy in the middle of his set to surprise him with a lavish birthday cake. The band, artists, and crew gather onstage to sing "Happy Birthday." The packed house sings along. Thousands of voices rise in honor of our sweet Guy Clark, who chokes back tears as the chorus surrounds him.

I am exhausted after the week of events surrounding Guy's birthday and just want to go home and rest. But I need to be in New York with Kris for his show with Joan Baez at the Beacon Theater, an appearance on *The Late Show with David Letterman*, and the film premiere for *The Greening of Whitney Brown*.

"I don't want to go to New York," I whine to Paul. "Tamara, this great thing you have going with Guy Clark and Kris Kristofferson is not going to last forever," Paul says. "Enjoy every minute of it now, because it is going to be over before you know it." My husband is wise. I fly from Austin to New York and meet Kris and his bus at the Sheraton in Weehawken, New Jersey. The next morning a car picks us up to take us to Letterman.

The Letterman taping is a disaster. Kris and Joan had agreed beforehand to sing John Prine's "Hello in There." At the last minute, they decide to do "Me and Bobby McGee." They practice in Joan's dressing room for a long time, but it is not coming together. The show rehearsal goes a bit better and I think maybe they'll muddle through it. At the show taping, it is clear they are not in sync with each other. They stand next to each other and sing the lyrics at different times in different keys. Kris's agent Steve Levine and I watch the train wreck on a monitor in Kris's dressing room. As Kris and Joan finish the song, we race down six flights of stairs. I pray that the producers will let them perform it again. When we get to stage level, Kris and Joan are in the greenroom. Sheryl Zelikson and Sheila Rogers from Letterman are asking Joan's manager if they'll run through the song again. Joan's manager is against it; he does not want them to sing it again. I jump in and say, "I think Kris will want to do it again." I corner Kris in the greenroom. "Kris, they are offering the chance for you and Joan to redo the song. I think you should." Kris says, "Was it that bad?" "Yes, it was that bad," I say. I keep my eyes on Kris and don't look at Joan so as not to piss off her manager. "You do not want millions of people to see that performance," I add. I can see out of the corner of my eye that Joan looks mortified. She says, "Well, if everyone thinks it sucked, I guess we need to do it again." I don't want to disappoint the legendary Joan Baez. I love her. But my concern is for Kris. The Letterman people insist that they do it again, and Steve Levine agrees. At least I'm not alone. Frankly, the second take is not much better than the first one (you can watch it on YouTube), but it does have some charm and the Letterman folks are satisfied.

CHAPTER TWENTY

FOR THE SAKE OF THE SONG

On January 2, 2012, I sit at a small table at the Bluebird Café with *Performing Songwriter* editor Lydia Hutchinson and singer Amy Grant. We are here to see legendary songwriter Carole King in the round with Nashville songwriters Georgia Middleman, Gary Burr, and Jim Photoglo. We are breathless, close enough to Carole to reach out and touch her as she sings hit after hit: "I Feel the Earth Move," "You've Got a Friend," "You're So Far Away," "Chains," "Pleasant Valley Sunday." Carole and I share a February 9 birthday. Although she is two decades older than me, I feel an Aquarian connection to Carole and her music. The year is off to a fantastic start.

I'm back in Austin for the Texas Heritage Songwriters Hall of Fame show in March. Townes Van Zandt, Robert Earl Keen, and Lyle Lovett are inducted into the Hall of Fame. It's unusual for the honorees to perform rather than have other artists pay tribute, but Lyle and Robert are different cats. They met in 1976 as students at Texas A&M University. The old friends trade songs and swap stories. The authentic vibe between them is arresting.

"One of the greatest things about my friendship with Lyle is, being an English major in college, you read all these different histories of all these writers—of people actually sitting around talking about writing," Robert told *Garden and Gun* magazine. "I am always disappointed in the world about that. I meet other songwriters, and they never want to talk about writing.

But Lyle wants to talk about writing. He wants to talk about how this particular bridge turns into this chorus. And I always think it's thrilling."

Steve Earle is on hand to honor his friend Townes Van Zandt. A few years earlier, Steve put out *Townes*, an entire album of Van Zandt songs. Townes, a doomed romantic figure to his cult following, died in 1997 at age fifty-two after a lifetime of alcohol and drug abuse.

Townes recorded his first record in Nashville in 1968. *For the Sake of the Song*, produced by Cowboy Jack Clement, mixed funny barroom songs with tales of desperation. "Being around Townes made you laugh one minute, and cry the next," Kris Kristofferson says. That first album, along with the ones that followed, established Townes as an Americana trailblazer. He was never famous by today's standards, but his powerfully written songs and haunting voice made him a beacon to a generation of songwriters, including the illustrious artists onstage here tonight.

To close the night, Steve, Robert, and Lyle raise their collective voices and sing a stunning "Snowing on Raton." I like to think Townes is watching from somewhere.

A few days later, the Radney Foster crew meets at Austin's Cedar Creek Studios. Radney is recording *Del Rio, TX Revisited: Unplugged and Lonesome*, a revamp of his 1992 debut solo album, *Del Rio, TX 1959*. Twenty years later, Rad records the same songs with an all-acoustic arrangement. It's more than nostalgia. This is the record that put Rad on the map. It is beloved by fans and young Americana artists often cite it as an influence. Steve Fishell produced the original *Del Rio* and he is back in the studio today to play on the record and interview Radney in front of seventeen fans who paid to be here. Fantasy camp in the studio. Radney's take of the fees is more than $8,000, and that will pay for most of the recording costs. The crackerjack band surrounding Radney includes Dixie Chick Martie Maguire on fiddle, Jon Randall Stewart on guitar, Glenn Fukunaga on doghouse bass, Michael Ramos on Wurlitzer and accordion, and Fishell on resonator guitars. We spend a couple of days working and eating and drinking at our favorite Austin restaurants.

"I wore out my cassette of the original *Del Rio*," Maguire says. "It feels good to be here, back in Cedar Creek, for this. This is such a Texas-sounding record. I feel right at home here."

Chapter 20

Brian Atkinson and I drive to Dallas for two nights with Guy at Poor David's Pub. Walt Wilkins opens for Guy on the first night. The club is packed. Every chair is taken, every corner at the bar, every inch of space in the hallway, in front of the bar, between the tables. It's impossible to find a place to stand. The club holds about three hundred, but I wouldn't be surprised if there are more people here. The room is filled with cowboy hats and baseball hats and men and women of all ages. I lean against the wall between the bar and the men's room with a good view of the stage. I hope it remains that way when Guy takes the stage. He walks to the stage to a standing ovation—lots of warm applause and catcalls. I hope it lasts once he starts his set. Guy is struggling mightily with many health issues. Susanna is in bad shape at home, and worry is etched on Guy's face.

Several fans wipe tears from their eyes as Guy sings "L.A. Freeway." "Tell the grapefruit tree story," someone yells out. "Sometimes I tell it and sometimes I don't. It depends on my memory," Guy says. "Tonight my memory is for shit. My wife says I can hide my own Easter eggs."

Brennen Leigh and Noel McKay open for Guy on the second night. Hanging out at the hotel earlier in the day, Guy asks me if I plan to be at the club early enough to see Brennen and Noel. I have dinner plans with Brian Ongaro, my boss from my Sundance Broadcasting days. I tell Guy I'll get there as soon as I can after dinner. "Tamara, if you can't make it to see Brennen and Noel, don't come at all," Guy says. Minnesota native Brennen Leigh and Texan Noel McKay have no bigger champion than Guy Clark. Guy says Brennen "plays guitar like a motherfucker and sings like an angel." Guy and Noel recently cowrote the song "El Coyote." After a few false starts, Guy manages to sing "El Coyote" tonight. "Guy pitched me the idea for 'El Coyote,'" Noel says. "He showed me some lyrics and we knocked ideas around. Guy told me to take it with me to see what I could do with it." Noel drove from Nashville to Austin thinking about the song and pulling over to write lyrics. It took a couple of years for Guy and Noel to edit the song to Guy's satisfaction. "The only way I knew that Guy thought the song was finished was when I heard him perform it. He played it over the phone. It was amazing to hear him sing this song we had worked on for so long."

I fly back to Nashville to meet Kris and Lisa Kristofferson for the honors gala benefiting the T. J. Martell Foundation, a music industry group that funds innovative medical research focused on finding treatments and cures for cancer. The gala is honoring Kris with the Frances Williams Preston Music Industry Award at a $1,000-a-plate dinner. All the money goes to cancer research. Vince Gill is the host. Vince's nickname in Nashville is "Benefit." He and his wife, Amy, contribute to every good cause in town with time and money.

We sit with the folks from BMI, including eighty-three-year-old Frances Preston. At a time when women were encouraged to stay home and raise babies, Frances worked her way up from the WSM mailroom to the chief executive position at BMI. Although Frances retired eight years ago, she remains one of the most influential women in the music business. Frances and Kris are old friends. "I can't believe they are giving me an award with your name on it," Kris says as he kisses Frances's cheek. "We're still fooling all of them, aren't we, Kris?" Frances says.

I somehow end up seated between Kris and Frances. She looks elegant but frail. I introduce myself. "I remember you, we met with Kay," Frances says. She's right. Kay Clary introduced me to Frances at a Country Music Hall of Fame Medallion Ceremony a while ago. I'm surprised she remembers. I thank Frances for being a pioneer and paving the way for women like me in the music business. "I just cracked the door open," Frances says. "The rest of you blew the door off the hinges and raised the ceiling." It's nice of her to say, although Nashville is still way behind the curve.

Ronnie Dunn, half of the country duo Brooks and Dunn, bids on a Kristofferson Gibson acoustic guitar during the auction. The final price is $20,000. Ronnie sits at the table behind us. "Well, for that kind of money, I better ask him if he wants me to sign it. Although that will certainly bring the value down." Kris laughs. For a $25,000 donation, Steve Moore from the CMA wins the auction for a private concert with Kris.

People come up to the table every few minutes to see Kris. We stand up to say hi, sit back down, take a bite of food, stand up again, sit back down again. On and on through dinner. Lisa is most gracious about it. She is the kindest, most generous and grounded woman I know. Kris and Lisa met when she was in law school at Pepperdine University in Malibu,

California. They worked out at the same gym, and one day Lisa asked Kris if he wanted to go for a run. He said he wasn't looking for a relationship. Lisa said, "I asked you to go for a run, not to get married." It didn't take Kris long to realize Lisa is the best damn thing that ever happened to him. They married in 1983, Kris's third marriage, and have five children together: Jesse, Jody, Johnny, Kelly, and Blake. I would think raising five kids and being stepmother to Tracy, Kris Jr., and Casey might be chaotic, but Lisa makes it look easy. She also runs the family business, coordinating every aspect of Kris's tours and acting as liaison between the agent, accountants, lawyers, me, and whoever else is on hand to help with Kris's career. I've never witnessed Lisa lose her cool, no matter the circumstances. I want to be more like Lisa.

Kris and I have our frustrated moments. Tonight is one of them. Every time we sit down, Kris looks at me, sighs, roll his eyes, and pours more wine in each of our glasses. Kris's memory is not good and I think that's part of it for him. He remembers Frances because they have a long history, but he does not remember most of the people who come over to greet him. I think it's tough on him that he can't recall those acquaintances. As Lisa says, Kris is befuddled during events like this. He isn't sure why he's here, why he's being honored, and why people care about him so much. He is not just humble but really stumped by all of it. I think the attention makes him uncomfortable.

The next day, I meet the rock band the World Famous Headliners (Shawn Camp, Al Anderson, Pat McLaughlin, and Michael Rhodes) at Jim McGuire's studio for a photo shoot for the new album. The band name is not so ironic when you lump together the prestigious music credits of all the band members. Big Al Anderson is best known for his work with NRBQ. Al, Shawn, and Pat have had their songs cut by an astonishing list of country stars. Michael Rhodes, a member of Rodney Crowell's revamped Notorious Cherry Bomb band, has played on too many chart-topping country and Americana albums to count. Al, Shawn, and Pat write for Big Yellow Dog Music Publishing, the boutique company owned by Kerry O'Neil and Carla Wallace. Big Yellow Dog is dipping into the indie record business with this album and brought me on board as project manager and publicist.

After the success we had with Shawn's 1994 record, Warner hires me to handle public relations for Ashley Monroe's upcoming album *Like a Rose*. Guy Clark introduced me to Ashley, one of his favorite cowriters. Guy and Ashley wrote the title song together. Last year, Ashley teamed up with Miranda Lambert and Angaleena Presley as the Pistol Annies. Miranda's fame helped sell the trio, but Ashley's role landed her a record deal with Warner.

"Hey, I'm working with Ashley Monroe," I announce to Guy one afternoon in June. "That's great, Tamara," Guy says. "But we still have a lot of work to do here. Don't fall down on the job." He winks at me. I spend all day at Guy's collecting files, photos, and slides to take back to my office to scan. Shawn Camp helps me load everything into my car. It takes two trips to bring it all to my office. I spend that evening with a loupe and a light board looking through slides. For the last four years, I've searched for the right cover image for my book. I don't want to use a well-known photograph of Guy. I try to have faith that the right image will show itself at the right time. Now is that time. I stare at the slide with butterflies in my stomach. A young Guy, wearing a blue shirt with pearl snap buttons, sits with his back against an old house. Guy smokes a cigarette, his long fingers and turquoise ring conspicuous. It is a McGuire photo from the mid-1970s but this image is new to me. If it's new to me, I'm confident not many people have seen it.

I separate the slide from everything else and keep it in my pocket as I carry Guy's stuff back into his house. "Guy, I found the cover picture!" I set a box on the dining room table, where Susanna sits in her nightgown chain-smoking Marlboro Reds. I pull the slide out of my pocket, set up a small light board on the table, and hand a loupe to Susanna. She bends her head down over the slide. "I don't remember this picture, Guy, do you?" Guy works his way over to the table using his walker. He sits next to Susanna and pulls the light board over. "Oh yeah," Guy says. "McGuire and I walked around Sylvan Park [neighborhood in Nashville] and found this house, I think it's on Wyoming Avenue. It looked like a good background so we just made ourselves at home in the yard. This might have been for that first album, that was supposed to come out before *Old No. 1*. Or maybe we took these pictures after *Old No. 1* but before *Texas Cookin'*. I can't remember."

"This is the book cover," I say.

"Are you asking me or telling me?" Guy asks.

"I hope you agree with me that it's the right image, but I'm using it whether you like it or not." I smile at Guy.

"I expect nothing less, Tamara. I do like this picture," Guy says. "I'd be pissed if you decided to use a photo other than McGuire's."

"I wouldn't even consider that," I say. "McGuire is a big part of your story. It would be inauthentic to use anyone else's picture."

After I carry in the rest of the boxes, I ask Guy if I should put them back where I found them. The house is strangely quiet today. Susanna's caregiver is not here, and Guy and Susanna are spending the day at home like an old married couple. "Let's put those boxes of pictures on the table," Guy says. "Maybe Susanna will want to look through them and we can take a trip down memory lane." For the next several hours, Guy, Susanna, and I sort photos. I did not expect to interview either of them today, but I turn on my tape recorder. Susanna is more animated than I have seen her in years. She tells story after story about her family. She talks about her parents, her siblings, and her first husband. Susanna recalls the early years with Guy and Townes, and Rodney and Emmylou, and the large circle of friends she and Guy have cultivated in their forty-year marriage. As she talks, Guy and I share glances across the table. He is as surprised as I am at how lucid and engaging Susanna is today.

The house phone rings and Guy makes his way to the kitchen to answer it. Susanna asks me to help her to bed. In our last few minutes together, Susanna says, "Tamara, you've got a big job on your hands to write this book."

"Yes, I know, but it's fun."

Susanna laughs and raises her eyebrows at me. "Fun?!" She chuckles to herself. She asks me to lift her legs up onto the bed and under the covers. I tuck her in the way I tucked in my daughter when she was small.

I return to the dining room, intending to clean up the boxes and leave Guy and Susanna alone. Guy says, "You might want to stick around. Robert Shivers, a friend from high school, is on his way over in case you want to get a look at him."

When Robert shows up, Guy tells him I was recently in Rockport and had lunch with a group of the ne'er-do-wells from their high school days and then asks me to list off their names. Guy refers to them as ne'er-do-wells about ten times. It makes me laugh because those ne'er-do-wells called Guy a goody-two-shoes about as many times when I was with them.

Susanna gets out of bed briefly to say hello to Robert. Then Guy escorts her back to bed. As he comes out of the bedroom he calls back to her, "You just sleep, baby. I'll take care of everything here." It is an endearing moment and a sweet afternoon. It's the last time I see Susanna Clark alive.

Susanna dies on June 27, 2012. The next day, I go over to Guy's to check on him. He's holding up. "I've been grieving Susanna's demise for years," Guy says. "There's nothing to do but get on with it." Guy has piled three boxes by the door. "Take those with you when you go, Tamara," he says.

"What's in them?" I ask.

"Those are Susanna's diaries."

I am surprised. "Have you read them?"

"No, Tamara, but whatever is in there is Susanna's truth and you're welcome to it."

A few days later, McGuire, Claire Armbruster from Keith Case's office, and I take Guy to lunch at the Southern. Guy eats shrimp and grits with gusto and smiles and laughs throughout. The only thing concerning Guy at this moment is his upcoming knee replacement surgery. He says he'll be ready to dance by September. Guy's sister Jan, a nurse, is coming up from San Antonio to stay with Guy for a few months and to help him clean out the house. We decide to take the summer off and not work on the book again until fall. Guy has his surgery scheduled and I've got a couple of other projects. Plus, Paul is on the road with Springsteen and if I want to see my husband, I'll have to travel to do it.

Stacy Dean Campbell calls and asks me to meet him in Fredericksburg, Texas, to talk about the possibility of producing his new record. He's got a bunch of songs and wants to play them for me. Stacy has a full-time gig as a television host and personality. He works for London Broadcasting as the talent on *Bronco Roads*, a Texas travel show where Stacy drives an old Ford Bronco around Texas and reports interesting stories from small towns. He's also part of a music show called *Troubadour*

Texas. London Broadcasting founder Terry London was one of the founders of the Nashville Network back in the heyday. A few years ago he invested in television stations in Texas. London also produces programming to sell to cable networks. According to Stacy, London has 70 percent coverage across Texas and the budgets to match. London encourages Stacy to record an album. They believe they can capitalize on his television following. Stacy is super talented. With or without the television shows, I'd love to work on an album with him.

I meet Stacy and the London Broadcasting crew at Tonkawaya Ranch just outside Fredericksburg. Joe and Becky Howard own the ranch and rent small cabins out as part of a bed-and-breakfast business. "We named it Tonkawaya because one of the original Native American tribes from this area were the Tonkawa Indians," Becky says. "During the time the United States was being developed, they were a remnant tribe of many different native people from all over the States that came together. US soldiers started a war that tore apart Native American tribes and their home places that they had lived for centuries. As they were driven south and into Texas following the buffalo for their food and supplies, many of these bands of fleeing Native Americans were captured or killed by our government. The remnants of many of the tribes were accepted by the Tonkawa Indians, who had been a very fierce people. Tonkawaya is an Americanized way to speak their name, which means 'the people that stay together.' They recognized that their well-being was based on taking care of each other. Joe and I always felt that was a very special place, and we found many artifacts on the property that showed us centuries of their history here. They made it home long before us. I always feel their spirit and presence when I take the time to sit and be thankful for the opportunity to be the caretaker of this land for a short time. Joe and I are both well aware that we don't own any land, we are all here for a journey, and our opportunity to be good stewards of this place is a gift. I've never felt more connected to any place I've lived. The right thing to do is to share our ranch with travelers and newfound friends."

Stacy and his crew shoot the first show of season 2 of *Bronco Roads* at Luckenbach. I feel an instant connection to Stacy's producer Deborah

Mash, a badass woman from Oklahoma with envious news credentials. Audio engineer Jeff Mack tells me he is a big fan of our Kristofferson tribute album, which is nice to hear. We are all on the same page with our musical tastes. Sweet Waylon Payne is here to hang out. It's always fun to be at Luckenbach, and especially fun for me today because I don't have a job to do. I just soak it all in and watch the *Bronco Roads* crew work. I meet Abbey Road, Luckenbach's event director, for the first time. Everyone in the know credits Abbey for Luckenbach's recent renaissance. Abbey is the one who tells me that Guy Clark inspired the song "Luckenbach, Texas (Back to the Basics of Love)." She knows the whole story, how Guy and Susanna were with Chips Moman the night before they flew to Texas to watch Jerry Jeff Walker record *Viva Terlingua!* at Luckenbach. After drinking a bunch of whiskey, Guy tries to convince Chips to come to Luckenbach with them: "Come on, Chips, let's go, let's go to Luckenbach, Texas." The next day Bobby Emmons shows up to write with Chips and Chips suggests they write a song called "Let's Go to Luckenbach, Texas." Chips and Bobby never stepped foot on Luckenbach soil, but that didn't stop them from writing a song about it. "I never heard this story," I say to Abbey, grateful that she filled me in. "Guy must be holding out on me."

I step away to call Guy, appalled that I have to hear this nugget from someone other than him.

"Yeah, it's true, Tamara," Guy admits. "I don't know why I didn't mention it. It just hasn't come up yet. We can talk about it more when you get home."

"Were you pissed off that they wrote that song and it became a hit?" I ask.

"Well, I don't think I'm offended by it," Guy says. "Maybe I am. I damn sure should have written a Luckenbach song long before that. I think I'm more mad at myself that I didn't."

Joe and Becky Howard, the *Bronco Roads* crew, Stacy, Waylon, and I meet for dinner at the Navajo Grill in Fredericksburg. It's a jovial feast and we are all old friends by the end of it. After dinner, we watch the sunset from the top of the hill where Joe and Becky's house sits. After dark, Joe builds a fire down by our cabins and we sit together singing songs, telling stories, and drinking wine late into the night.

The next morning, I take a walk around the ranch and then Waylon and I drive into town. We talk about Kris and Lisa, and Kris's long friendship with Waylon's mom, country music torch singer Sammi Smith. Sammi had a big hit and won a Grammy for her recording of Kris's song "Help Me Make It through the Night." Waylon's father, Jody Payne, played with Merle Haggard and Ray Price in the early days and was a mainstay in Willie Nelson's band from the 1970s until Jody retired in 2002. Named after his godfather, Waylon Jennings, Waylon Payne is no slouch. Waylon's 2003 debut album, *The Drifter*, got rave reviews. Charlie Robison, Lee Ann Womack, Keith Gattis, and more have recorded his songs. Waylon transformed into Jerry Lee Lewis in the 2005 film *Walk the Line* and portrayed musician Hank Garland in the movie *Crazy* in 2008. Waylon is a bright light in every room he walks into and I adore him.

Waylon and I duck into Walmart so he can buy blank CDs. On our way out we find a huge bin of five-dollar CDs. We dig through the bin for about twenty minutes and find a few treasures. On the way back to the ranch, we listen to Kristofferson's *The Austin Sessions* and sing along to "Help Me Make It through the Night."

Back at Tonkawaya, Stacy and I spend several hours listening to spartan vocal demos of his new songs and discuss the direction of his album. We are on the same page. I'm flattered that Stacy considers me good enough to produce his record. On the way back to Austin, we swing by Blue Rock Artist Ranch and Studio in Wimberley to check it out. Blue Rock is an artist retreat, recording studio, and concert and workshop venue built in an enchanting setting by Billy and Dodee Crockett. It's a place where artists and crew can hole up away from the outside world and create. Stacy and I want to record here.

With a rough plan in place, I write a budget and proposal for the London Broadcasting team. After some back-and-forth, in the end, they decide not to invest in a Stacy Dean Campbell record. The biggest argument against it is that they don't believe Americana records sell.

I try one last Hail Mary to get them to reconsider with an email to the team: "To further our discussions about Americana music, I just took a glance at the *Billboard* Top 200 this week. For what it's worth, the country music establishment, like Americana, has but one entry in the top twenty,

Kenny Chesney at number eight. The Lumineers, Americana, sit at number seventeen with a bullet. The Lumineers sold 28,900 CDs this week. 125,846 total so far. They are number six on the Alternative Album Chart. They've sold 37,379 single downloads and are at number fifty on the digital song chart. At least these are the numbers according to SoundScan. I don't know if they turn in the road sale numbers to SoundScan. Americana on the Billboard Top 200 finds Bonnie Raitt still sitting in the top forty. The top sixty includes Mumford & Sons and Alabama Shakes. Having said all of that, I hate chart comparisons, because they do not accurately tell the story of Americana.

"I don't believe the majority of our artists report their CD road sales to SoundScan. Why? They simply don't care. To them SoundScan is just another part of the establishment and major label system. It is meaningless in our world. For example, Kristofferson sold more than 40,000 CDs on the road in 2011 and we did not report one of them to SoundScan. Kris's SoundScan sales on the last album are at 78,000. We are not reporting one third of Kris's album sales. Let's contrast that with artists who are not as well-known as Kris. Many of them a couple hundred days on the road touring the United States and Europe each year. I just took a look at my Radney Foster statement history and he sold 10,000 CDs at the merch table over the last 130 concert dates. We did not report those to SoundScan. What you have in Americana is a bona fide grassroots artist development genre. Overall, Americana artists do not care about garnering top ten singles radio. Americana artists are making music to tell a story and they have fans who are listening. Many of these artists are making middle class income without name recognition. In my opinion that's what has legs for the long term."

My email does not help at all. London is not going to fund a Stacy Dean Campbell album. Stacy and I had fun dreaming about it, though, and that's worth a lot.

CHAPTER TWENTY-ONE

THESE DAYS

This One's For Him: A Tribute to Guy Clark wins Album of the Year at the 2012 Americana Honors and Awards. After all the time, love, effort, and drama that went into making our record, I am gratified that the Americana community likes the record enough to vote for it.

Guy, Verlon, and Shawn are backstage as Jen Gunderman and I take our seats. Guy's sister Jan sits with us and we are surrounded by friends. Booker T. Jones sits in with the house band to open the show with "Green Onions," followed by the Instrumentalist of the Year award for Dave Rawlings. Host Jim Lauderdale introduces Guy. Guy, Verlon, and Shawn walk to the stage as the crowd roars. Guy says, "I wrote this song for my wife, Susanna, who died a couple of months ago. I wish she was here to hear me sing it." Emotional, Guy stumbles a bit on the lyrics of "My Favorite Picture of You," but his delivery is charming and the crowd responds with a long and loud standing ovation.

Guy, Verlon, and Shawn leave the stage. Lauderdale returns to the podium and says, "Here to announce the winner of Album of the Year are Rodney Crowell and Brandi Carlile."

A video guy is standing next to my row with a camera on me and Rodney Crowell is onstage. I know before they announce it that we've won. My heart is pounding and Jen and I hold hands. Rodney's voice shakes as he says, "Here are the nominees for Album of the Year in alphabetical order: Steve Earle, Jason Isbell, *This One's For Him: A Tribute to Guy Clark*, and Gillian Welch." Brandi Carlile opens the envelope, looks at Rodney, and says, "Do you want to read this?" Rodney's voice cracks. "The award goes to *This One's For Him*." Jen and I scream, hug each other, hold hands, and run to the stage. Guy, Verlon, and Shawn return to the stage to greet us. Everyone hugs. Our emotion is palpable. My heart pounds. I feel like a total dork.

"I produced this award show the first few years, so it is extremely weird to be here at the Ryman tonight as a nominee and now to be honored with this award," I say. "Especially in the company of magnificent artists Gillian Welch, Steve Earle, and Jason Isbell. This is my friend and coproducer Shawn Camp. Shawn and I have known each other for nearly twenty years and have been on many adventures together. I'd say this project is the highlight. It took a village to make this record. Shawn, Verlon Thompson, Jen Gunderman, and I named ourselves the Guyotes. The four of us worked together through the entire two-year recording process. We worked with thirty-three artists, countless musicians, several engineers, a video guy, photographer, writer, radio promoter, and record label. We'd be here all night if we tried to thank everyone so we will celebrate with our compadres later and thank them in person. All of this is happening because of our brilliant friend Guy Clark. On the first day of recording the first track, Rodney Crowell kicked things off by saying, 'Let's give her a go and make old Guy proud of us.' I hope we did. Guy, this one's for you."

After a champagne celebration backstage and many rounds with the event photographer, we put Jan and Guy in a car and the rest of us walk to the Sheraton Grand Hotel bar to celebrate. Jen, Verlon, Shawn, and I stand at the bar surrounded by our friends and colleagues. Jim Hustead, Lauren Sheftell, and Brian Wright are here from LA. My girlfriends Lisa Jenkins, Kay Clary, Wendy Stamberger, Molly Secours, and Jeannie Naujeck are here. Taylor Holliday and Craig Havighurst walk in the door, faces lit up and Taylor with tears in her eyes. There is no greater happiness than going through life with old friends who know the backstory, recognize the behind-the-scenes complexity and minutiae of making art, prop us up during the difficult moments, and celebrate the wins.

We frolic again the next day with beer and gumbo at Gary Paczosa's house for his annual Americana party. Gary hugs me and seems genuinely excited about our win. "I felt like a big dork up there onstage," I say.

"You did great," Gary says. "Your speech was sweet and sincere and everyone in the audience was excited." A big compliment coming from a primo producer like Gary.

Kelcy Warren, the guy who saved our bacon by paying for great artwork and packaging on the Guy tribute, brings me onboard to coproduce a Jackson Browne tribute album with Kelcy and folk singer Jimmy LaFave. Jimmy is signed to Kelcy's Music Road Records. Fred Remmert, who engineered our Guy Clark tribute, is the engineer for the project. Fred runs the label with help from Ashley Warren and Jimmy.

Don Henley is the first artist to sign on to the project. Don's manager returns my call within an hour to tell me Don has dibs on "These Days." "It is astounding to me that Jackson wrote this song at sixteen," Don says. "He was way ahead of his time, and always a step ahead of the rest of us."

"I was completely immersed in the songs of the Beatles and Bob Dylan and wrote a lot of songs in those days," Jackson says. "I didn't think of 'These Days' as particularly revelatory, I was just writing the truth of my life at the time."

Henley and Browne hung out together in the early 1970s in LA when Henley's Eagles bandmate Glenn Frey and his songwriter roommate J. D. Souther lived above Browne in the same apartment building. Browne cowrote the Eagles' "Take It Easy" with Frey, and Browne's song "Nightingale" also landed on the Eagles' debut album. From then on, Browne and the Eagles enjoyed a fruitful creative collaboration and close friendship.

Don and I exchange emails and phone calls for several weeks regarding the arrangement for "These Days." First, he asks Bruce Hornsby to join him and we put together a band around Don and Bruce as the core. A week before our scheduled session, Don changes his mind and wants to do a simple cello and violin accompaniment. I cancel Bruce. I don't care that Don changes his mind. I like that he is giving the track this much attention. I book a cellist and violin player. Then Don calls to tell me he has to go to New York to do something with the Eagles and we need to reschedule the session. While we are on the phone Don says, "Do you know this band Blind Pilot?" I don't. Don sends me YouTube links and I understand what he is hearing in his head. Blind Pilot is a crazy talented West Coast indie rock band and I dig their sound as much as Don does. I call Blind Pilot's manager and ask him if they would be willing to accompany Don on "These Days" for a Jackson Browne tribute album. The band turns us down. I can't believe it. Who says no to Don Henley? Of course, as they are a young band, Don Henley and the Eagles might not be as important to them as they are to my generation. "What do we have to do to make this happen?" I ask the manager. I want to make this happen for Don. I call Kelcy. We have a great budget for this record and now I ask him to consider putting out extra dough for one track. Kelcy says, "Give Don whatever he needs." When Blind Pilot's manager calls back with a number, I'm prepared. "We'll pay it," I say. "And Don will come to Portland and record in the studio of their choice." I had done my homework. Blind Pilot works at Tucker Martine's Flora Recording and Playback studio in Portland, Oregon. Tucker is a Grammy-winning engineer and producer and has worked with My Morning Jacket, the Decemberists, Neko Case, and many other cool artists. I think it will be good for Don to go to Portland and work on their turf.

Don and Blind Pilot are not the only great artists on *Looking into You: A Tribute to Jackson Browne*. We have an embarrassment of riches: Bonnie Raitt, the Indigo Girls, Lyle Lovett, Ben Harper, Keb Mo, Lucinda Williams, Shawn Colvin, Bruce Springsteen, Joan Osborne, Karla Bonoff, Marc Cohn, Sara and Sean Watkins, Bruce Hornsby, Kevin Welch, and Paul Thorn record their own tracks and ship them to us. We record Jimmy LaFave, Griffin House, and Bob Schneider at Cedar Creek. I recruit Gary Paczosa to record J. D. Souther in Nashville. I prefer to work with one house band instead of collecting tracks scattershot, but it is a joy to work with Kelcy Warren and I'm happy to be part of the team. Kelcy has a big heart and discerning tastes. It's a welcome change to work with him after the pain and difficulty of working on the Guy Clark tribute.

Jon Randall Stewart introduces me to actor, musician, and singer John Corbett. Corbett hires me as project manager and publicist for his new record *Leaving Nothin' Behind*, produced by Randall and Gary Paczosa. Corbett is best known for his roles as disc jockey Chris Stevens in the television series *Northern Exposure* and Carrie Bradshaw's boyfriend Aidan in *Sex and the City*. He also played Lars Hammond in the film *Serendipity* and Ian Miller in the *My Big Fat Greek Wedding* trilogy. Corbett grew up in West Virginia and his uncle owned a country night club. He saw Buck Owens and Merle Haggard play there when he was a kid. He knows about country music and we are the same age. John stays in our guest suite for a week to work on the record.

I bring Kelsey Waldon, my new intern from Belmont, into the fold to teach her how to launch an indie record and throw her in the deep end with Corbett. Between running Kristofferson's KK Records label and Radney Foster's Devil's River Records and releasing my own projects on American Roots Publishing, I've become an expert at independent distribution. I work with Think Indie Distribution, a music distributor founded by the Coalition of Independent Music Stores. Think Indie's mission is to connect great artists and great record shops with great releases. Think Indie's Scott Register (Reg) is a passionate and enthusiastic advocate for my artists.

Running around town with Corbett reminds me of escorting Kris. There is no safe place for celebrities. He is accosted at restaurants by waiters and diners. Customers swarm him at Walgreens and the grocery store. At dinner we talk about fame and its consequences. Corbett feels like Aiden is a cartoon character come to life and he, John, is violated because of it every day. I observe women attempt to grope and kiss John. They constantly interrupt him for autographs and photos. I've seen it all with Kris and it breaks my heart to witness it with Corbett. Why do fans feel like they are owed someone else's autonomy? It's not enough that an individual makes art loved by many; the artist is expected to give up personal freedom for the pleasure of others. It's sadistic.

By the end of our week together, Corbett and I are old friends. It's eerie how much we have in common. Our mothers are both named Sandy. His mother and my stepdad have May 7 birthdays. All of them have Lithuanian ancestry. He grew up with a single mom and I was a single mom. We listen to the same music and share pop culture references from our youth. We were born exactly three months apart, me on February 9, John on May 9. We're both animal lovers. John is kind of a silly dork and so am I.

I take John to Jen Gunderman and Audley Freed's Halloween party (a place where people treat him with respect). We see Guy Clark play at 3rd and Lindsley, John's first time at a Guy Clark concert. He is blown away by the show, especially by Shawn and Verlon. "Are they the best musicians in town?" John asks. "They might be," I say. "I'd put Vince Gill right up there with them, too."

John takes me as his date to the ASCAP awards. Lyle Lovett is an honoree tonight. We sit with Jon Randall and Jessi Alexander. Guy is at the next table. Jon, Jessi, Guy, and Robert Earl Keen perform tribute songs to Lyle. Guy plays Lyle's "Waltzing Fool," accompanied by Jon Randall on guitar and Mike Bubb on upright bass. Guy tells me he is going to put it on his new record instead of a Townes Van Zandt song. Guy has put a Townes song on every album since Townes's death. "This will be my last album and I want to record Lyle's song for it," Guy says.

It's fitting that Guy pays tribute to Lyle. He's loved Lyle from the moment he heard Lyle's demo tape. Lyle may be the most well-known beneficiary of Guy's generosity with songwriters. On Lyle's first trip to Nashville in 1984, he left a cassette tape of his songs with Sam Ramage at CBS Songs. Sam shared the songs with Guy. "After that first trip, I'd go to Nashville every four or six weeks just to make the rounds and see if I could stir up any interest in my songs," Lyle says. "I'd meet somebody and they'd say, 'Oh yeah, Guy Clark told me about you.'"

"I listened to Lyle's tape every day for weeks," Guy says. "It was the best thing I'd heard in years. I thought everyone should hear it." Guy slipped the tape to MCA Records VP Tony Brown one day at lunch. Brown signed Lyle and produced his first album. "I really feel like it is because of Guy Clark that I have a career," Lyle says.

After the ASCAP awards, Corbett and I stop for a night cap at Sunset Grill. We sit at the bar trading stories until closing time. The following night, as the CMA Awards show is in progress down the street, Corbett and I meet Gary Paczosa, Jon and Jessi, and Will Hoge and his wife for drinks and dinner. After dinner, we hit the Capitol Records CMA party at Sambuca. We spot Keith Urban across the room. "C'mon, I want to introduce you to Keith," John says, and he takes my hand and pulls me in Keith's direction. I haven't seen Keith in many years, so maybe he doesn't remember me. We get to Keith's side. As Corbett begins to speak, Keith spots me and pulls me into a big hug. "You know each other?" John asks. Keith and I laugh. "We have some secrets," Keith says.

A few weeks later, I'm driving home late at night from the Music City Roots show at the Loveless Café Barn. My cell phone buzzes with Peter Cooper's name on the display. It's too late for Peter to call me. I think it must be bad news.

"Peter, what's going on? I'm on my way home from Music City Roots."

"Pull the car over," Peter says. Oh no. I'm afraid he is going to tell me someone died.

"Oh, no, just tell me, Peter. What's going on?"

"This is all off the record, okay?" Peter confides that he is working late at the *Tennessean* tonight because the Grammy nominees will be announced in the morning. "I could get in a lot of trouble for telling you this, but I can't wait," Peter says. "Your Guy tribute is nominated for a Grammy for Best Folk Album."

Now I pull the car over as tears sting my eyes. This album has been an embarrassment of riches and I'm beginning to feel like I'm standing out in public in my underwear. I'm proud of *This One's For Him*, but it's a bit unreal to me that I am not a musician or a songwriter or a singer and I have won a Grammy and Americana award. Now I'm nominated for a second Grammy award. I can't wait to tell Guy.

The year 2013 dawns with three important record releases for my media company: Ashley Monroe's *Like a Rose*, John Corbett's *Leaving Nothin' Behind*, and Kris Kristofferson's first album on his own indie label, *Feeling Mortal*.

Around the same time, Rodney Crowell and Emmylou Harris release their duet record *Old Yellow Moon*, which features the Kristofferson song "Chase the Feeling." The song debuted on Kris's 2006 album *This Old Road*. It's been a long time since someone covered a "new" Kris song, and it thrills Kris that Rodney and Emmy recorded it.

We launched KK Records the previous year in preparation for *Feeling Mortal*. For years, Lisa and I have been after Kris to release his record independently.

"You'll have more creative control, and make money," I tell him.

"Tamara, in my day only losers put out their own records," Kris says.

"Well, now it's a smart business move, especially for someone in your position," I say.

Produced by Don Was, who also helmed Kris's 2006 record *This Old Road* and his 2009 *Closer to the Bone*, *Feeling Mortal* reflects on a life fully lived. Kris is seventy-six years old and faces his mortality head on in the title track:

Wide awake and feeling mortal
At this moment in the dream
That old man there in the mirror
And my shaky self-esteem
Here today and gone tomorrow
That's the way it's got to be
With an empty blue horizon
For as far as I can see

In addition to his age, Kris is well aware of his cognitive decline. His short-term memory is growing shorter. "I can't remember what I had for breakfast," he often jokes.

Kris and Lisa come to Nashville for media interviews, a Cowboy Jack Clement tribute concert, and a Nashville Songwriters Association International (NSAI) event at the Bluebird Café where Willie Nelson receives the inaugural Kris Kristofferson Lifetime Achievement Award. Paul and I pick Lisa and Kris up at the hotel and meet Willie's bus in the parking lot behind the Bluebird. I don't get high intentionally, but I always feel a little buzz after twenty minutes on Willie's bus.

Willie, Kris, Lisa, Guy, and I sit at a table in front as Bart Herbison from NSAI talks about the new Kris Kristofferson award for songwriting. He says it is fitting that the award is named for Kris, as Kris is one of the founding members of the association. The Kristofferson award will be given in recognition of a lifetime of achievement to music creators whose songs have inspired generations and touched listeners worldwide.

Kris and Willie get up in front of a room filled with songwriters, friends, and press. Kris cradles a heavy glass rectangle in his hands. "If I had seen what's happening right now before right now, I would have thought I was dreaming," Kris says. "When I came to Nashville, it was the most exciting place for creative artists to be. The people I hung around with were serious songwriters who were totally unselfish and their hero, and my hero, was a guy that nobody else knew. It was Willie Nelson. He's unlike anybody else. He is one of the best songwriters who ever wrote in any language. He's absolutely a unique singer, who doesn't sound like anybody else. He doesn't phrase like anybody else. He's probably the funniest human being I've ever known. Sometimes I try to envision who God might be and he always comes out looking like Willie Nelson." The audience roars.

"You're digging a hole there, you know," Willie chimes in. Kris and Willie bend over and howl.

After they compose themselves, Kris continues. "Anyway, I'm really proud to be giving you this. I'm embarrassed that my face and my name is on it," Kris says.

"We can take that right off," Willie jokes. The crowd roars again. Kris hands Willie the award. "Honestly, I thought I was coming here tonight to give you an award," Willie says. "So I have a great speech all lined up."

"Do it," Kris says.

"Nah," Willie says. "It couldn't match what you just said. Thank you, Kris."

Kris and Willie trade a couple of songs and end the night singing "Sunday Morning Comin' Down" together. We go back to Willie's bus and toast the night and each other.

Standing backstage at the tribute to Cowboy Jack Clement the following night, Kris introduces me to Charley Pride.

"Saviano?" Pride says. "Well, my name is Charley Priderelli and I think we should get married."

"Well, let's go then," I say. "My car is outside."

Kris sings "Big River" with Shawn Camp and bass player Dave Roe backing him up. During the show, we sit at a table with Rodney Crowell and Claudia Church, John and Fiona Prine, Del McCoury and his wife, and Vince Gill. I look around the table at all the couples and say to Vince, "Looks like you're my date." He responds, "Oh hell, Tamara, you can do a lot better than me but I'll do my best." With the exception of my husband, I don't think I can do any better than Vince Gill, unless it's Charley Pride.

Sirius XM disc jockey Mojo Nixon hosts a town hall with Kris to commemorate the release of *Feeling Mortal*. The special airs on the Outlaw Country and Willie Nelson channels. "Nashville didn't change Kris Kristofferson, he changed Nashville," Nixon says in his introduction. Kris answers questions and sings songs from *Feeling Mortal* to a small crowd in the Sirius XM studio in Nashville. Shawn Camp, Bruce Robison, Kelly Willis, Rod Picott, Josh Turner, Jon Randall, Earl Brown, Billy Swann, Donnie Fritts, and Chris Gantry join Kris onstage for a finale of "Why Me." At the event, my current intern, Kelsey Waldon, meets my former intern Maria Drummond Ivey. Maria now runs her own successful public relations company. That day sparks a friendship between them that leads to Maria becoming Kelsey's publicist when Kelsey kicks off her own songwriting career. Kelsey eventually signs to John Prine's Oh Boy Records label. Another full-circle moment in this exceptional community.

Paul and I are back in LA for the Grammys in February. A few weeks earlier, in a closet filled with elegant formal wear at Frances Preston's estate sale, I find a vintage Bob Mackie gown. It's a gorgeous black velvet off-the-shoulder number. With a few alterations, it fits perfectly. And it's got Frances Preston mojo all over it.

Guy is too sick to come to LA, but a number of our team make it for the party: Shawn Camp, Jen Gunderman, Jack Ingram, engineer Fred Remmert, radio promoter Jenni Finlay, and liner note author Brian Atkinson. Jen breaks the happy news that she landed a job as pianist in Sheryl Crow's touring band. Jim Hustead hooks us up with a great deal at the Farmer's Daughter Hotel on Fairfax.

My fifty-second birthday is the day before the Grammys. Our crew meets at the Beverly Hills Hotel for lunch. Rodney Crowell and Emmylou Harris play the Troubadour that night. A perfect birthday celebration.

On Grammy day, a limo van picks us up and takes us to the Nokia Theater for the Grammy pre-telecast. Most of the Grammy awards are handed out during the preshow: Gospel, Jazz, Americana, Bluegrass, Folk, Reggae, Contemporary Christian, Latin, World Music, Spoken Word, Comedy. Hosted by LL Cool J, the glitzy live televised portion of the Fifty-Fifth Annual Grammy Awards at the Staples Center is reserved for the rich and famous celebrities in bigger categories.

The preshow is three hours long. The nominees in the Folk Album category are *The Goat Rodeo Sessions* (Yo-Yo Ma, Stuart Duncan, Edgar Meyer, and Chris Thile); *Leaving Eden* (Carolina Chocolate Drops); *Election Special* (Ry Cooder); *Hambone's Meditations* (Luther Dickinson); and *This One's For Him: A Tribute to Guy Clark*.

The Goat Rodeo Sessions wins the Best Folk Album Grammy. Of course, we are disappointed but I'm also a bit relieved. Winning the award would mean stretching out our relationship with the record label, and I want to be finished with them. We started recording the album more than three years ago. It is time for it to take its place in history so we can all move on.

The televised Grammy broadcast is four hours long. We stay for almost three hours until we can't take it anymore. Jim Hustead and Lauren Sheftell host an after-party at the Foundry on Melrose. We drink champagne with our Americana friends who are in town from all over the country. The soiree with our friends is my favorite part of the Grammys. Awards are the icing, but this is the cake.

CHAPTER TWENTY-TWO

OLD FRIENDS

After the Grammys, I spend the next few months wrapping up the Kristofferson, Ashley Monroe, and John Corbett music projects. Rod Picott and I finalize our book project *From Art to Commerce: A Workbook for Independent Musicians* and host a workshop at Folk Alliance.

Kris, Guy, and Radney all perform at the Mack, Jack & McConaughey benefit concert in Austin. Mack, Jack & McConaughey is a joint fundraising effort created by University of Texas coach Mack Brown, Americana artist Jack Ingram, and actor Matthew McConaughey to benefit children's charities.

Kris comes back to Nashville for Keith Urban and Vince Gill's All for the Hall charity event to benefit the Country Music Hall of Fame and Museum. Then it's off to Dallas. Kris tapes interview segments and performance pieces for the *Troubadour Texas* series. London Broadcasting films Kris for a concert special at their 41 Production Studio with a small audience, about forty people. I invite my Jackson Browne tribute coproducer Kelcy Warren and his wife, Amy. My old Sundance Broadcasting boss Brian Ongaro and his wife, Barb, also come to the intimate show. Brian remains my favorite mentor. I could not possibly know when I met Brian all those years ago that my life would be such a beautiful journey, much of it because of his leadership and encouragement.

Guy is not well. He is in and out of the hospital as his health issues keep piling up. When he is at home, Guy insists we work on the book as much as possible. Dualtone releases Guy's final album, *My Favorite Picture of You*, in July. For the remainder of 2013, I focus on the book and spend almost every day at Guy's house. As time goes on, our conversations are more and more intimate. Where do I draw the line between journalist and friend? What stories belong in the book, and how do I distinguish those conversations from the personal?

My memoir *The Most Beautiful Girl: A True Story of a Dad, a Daughter, and the Healing Power of Music* is released in February 2014, the same month Guy wins his first Grammy award for *My Favorite Picture of You*. Guy is too sick to tour, too sick to record, and struggles to write songs. "It's ironic that I win a Grammy after all these years and I can't work anymore," Guy says.

Shawn Camp works up some music from my memoir and joins me to play at a book release event at Grimey's in Nashville. Guy shows up in a wheelchair. He is frail and it likely took every bit of his energy to get here. "Guy, I can't believe you are here." I kiss his cheek. "I wasn't about to miss this, Tamara," he says. I take a few days to work on promotion for my book, but then I'm back at Guy's full time. I am determined to finish this biography. Every week, I make a pot of soup for Guy. All he wants to eat is soup, bread, and sweets.

In April, a documentary filmmaker calls Keith Case and pitches him on making a film about Guy. Guy breaks the news to me as we sit at the kitchen table eating chicken and vegetable soup.

"Wow, Guy, that sounds great," I say.

"I'm not going to do it," Guy says. "I've spent all these years with you and I don't want to start over with someone new."

I get the impression that Guy is dumping this job in my lap. "Guy, I'm not a filmmaker. I've got my hands full with this book and I'm scared I'm not going to finish it."

"I don't care if there is a documentary about me or not," Guy says. "I'm just saying that I'm not starting over with anyone new. I've told you everything about my life. We've gone through every scrap of paper in this house. I'm not doing that again."

In an act of divine intervention, Lari White calls me that week to make a lunch date. Lari is a true artist: songwriter, producer, author, actor of stage and screen. Lari is best known for her hit country songs in the 1990s "That's My Baby," "Now I Know," and "That's How You Know

(When You're in Love)." Lari is the green-eyed woman who wows Tom Hanks at the end of the film *Cast Away*. But more importantly, for all of the Nashville music community, Lari is a kind and loving soul sister.

Lari and I have known each other casually since meeting when I worked at Sundance Broadcasting. We always have interesting conversations and I enjoy being around her. As the years fly by, Lari sends me encouraging emails about my work. I am a fan of her work, too, and love the discussions we have about music and art.

I'm vulnerable with Lari at our lunch. She can sense something is off and asks me if I'm okay. I break down and cry as Lari holds my hand and I reveal my fears. Guy is dying and I'll never finish this biography in time for him to see it. I think there *should* be a documentary about Guy but I'm not strong enough to do it.

"As women, we expect so much of ourselves," Lari says. "We feel like we have to solve all the problems for everyone. You don't have to take on a Guy Clark documentary if you don't want to do that. But if you *do* want to do it, you can just take it one baby step at a time. Maybe things will fall in place, maybe they won't. Don't think about the whole big project, just think about the next baby step."

Sage advice. My husband, Paul, is a respected and admired video engineer. He works for the Boss, Bruce Springsteen, one of the biggest rock stars on the planet. I ask Paul to make the documentary with me. We agree that because of Guy's bad health, we will get him on camera as much as possible and worry about making the film later. We film Guy and I ask him as many questions as he can handle in a session. Guy is in terrible health and it shows. I have no idea what our documentary storyline will be, but it's clear Guy is not going to be around to see it.

In a twist of fate, documentary filmmakers Ken Burns and Dayton Duncan and their Florentine Films team hire me (along with several of my fellow country music historians) as an adviser on the eight-part PBS series *Country Music*. One of my first orders of business is getting both Kris and Guy on camera with the Burns team. As a group, we make sure Florentine lands interviews with the old-time greats before we lose them. Working with Florentine is a crash course in documentary filmmaking. They come into my life at the exact moment I need them.

Kris needs to be in Austin on a Sunday night in June 2014 for the Texas Heritage Songwriters' Association Hall of Fame event honoring Waylon Jennings. The following Thursday, Kris is participating in the *Austin City Limits* fortieth anniversary special. Lisa asks me if I want to take him into the studio to record on the days in between. Sony Music owns all of Kris's masters and they aren't going to give them up. Kris wants to rerecord as many of those songs as possible to take control of his own catalog. I jump at the chance to produce a Kris record. I call Shawn Camp and ask him to come to Austin to coproduce and lead the band.

We spend three days in the studio with Kris the week of his seventy-eighth birthday. Shawn plays guitar and we hire Michael Ramos on keyboards, Mike Meadows on drums, and Kevin Smith on bass to round out the band. Lloyd Maines sweetens some of the tracks with mandolin.

Kris's memory is spotty but he still knows all of the songs. The band is together live in the studio and we put Kris in the vocal booth with Lisa and a teleprompter to help him remember lyrics. "Whatever happens, just keep playing as long as Kris wants to sing," I tell the band. Once Kris loosens up, he grooves to the music and channels 1970s-era Kris, with an extra dose of gravel in his voice. Kris calls out classic song after classic song: "For the Good Times," "Help Me Make It through the Night," "Me and Bobby McGee," "Jody and the Kid," "To Beat the Devil." The band follows Kris's lead and keeps playing for hours without breaks. If this were a union session, we'd be in deep trouble. On the second day, we record seven songs from the album *Easter Island*. On our last night of recording, Sheryl Crow comes in and sings with Kris on "The Loving Gift," a song he's never recorded before. We record twenty-five songs with Kris in three days. Fred Remmert mixes and masters the double-CD set, dubbed *The Cedar Creek Sessions*.

Sheryl Crow and actor Jeff Bridges host the *Austin City Limits* anniversary show. Backstage buzzes with artists, musicians, and entourages. Lloyd Maines leads the ace house band. Bonnie Raitt, Alabama Shakes, Jimmy Vaughan, Gary Clark Jr., Robert Earl Keen, Joe Ely, Doyle Bramhall II, and Latin funk rockers Grupo Fantasma mill around the catering room. Jeff Bridges comes to Kris's dressing room to say hello. Kris and Jeff met on the set of the 1980 film *Heaven's Gate* and share a decades-long friendship.

"How are you doing, Kris?" Jeff asks.

"Well, I can't remember what I ate for breakfast, but other than that I think I'm doing okay."

Jeff looks at me and I hold out my hand to shake his.

"Hi, I'm Tamara. I work with Kris."

"You do?" Kris says.

"Yes, what do you think I'm doing here?" I laugh.

"You're my best friend," Kris says. Jeff and I exchange glances. This might be Jeff's first experience with Kris's fading memory.

Joe and Sharon Ely, Connie Nelson, and Mary Bruton hang out backstage with Kris, Lisa, and me. I ask Connie what she thinks about the possibility of making a Guy Clark documentary. "You've got to do it," Connie says. "And I'll help you." Frankly, that makes the decision easy for me. With Connie Nelson onboard, we can do anything.

Connie is a member of my fascinating core group of Austin friends, along with talent manager Denise McLemore and Lubbock-bred artists Joe and Sharon Ely and Terry and Jo Harvey Allen.

Kris introduced me to Connie many years ago. She is Willie Nelson's ex-wife and the mother of artists Paula and Amy Nelson. Her role as Willie's ex is but a tiny sliver of her meaningful life. Connie is a connector. You know that game Six Degrees of Kevin Bacon? Well, in our circles, the apt game is One Degree of Connie Nelson. Connie is a beacon of light and love to all of us—and one of my most important teachers.

"That feeling of light and hope and positivity is what draws me to certain people," Connie says. "I just try to give back what I get from everybody else. And it seems to work. I know that sounds cheesy, but it's just the truth."

Connie Koepke met Willie at the 21 Club in Conroe, Texas. She took the night off from her job at a glass factory to see Willie sing "I Never Cared for You" live. The bass player from Willie's band brought Connie and her girlfriend to a front table. After the show, the band member invited Connie and her friend to meet the band at the Conroe Hotel. After a night of partying and swapping stories in the hotel room, Willie asked Connie for her number. Willie was not yet famous when he and Connie got together in the 1960s. It was Connie who encouraged Willie to record "Red Headed Stranger," a song he sang to his kids, and build an album around it. It was Connie's idea for Willie to record with Julio Iglesias. Willie and Connie stayed together for twenty years until Connie was no longer willing to put up with Willie running around with other women.

Compassion, justice, and community inspire Connie. She sits on the board of the International Leonard Peltier Defense Committee and has worked tirelessly to get Peltier released from prison. After Connie's brother Mike died from AIDS contracted from a blood transfusion in 1990, Connie produced benefit concerts to raise awareness and funding to fight AIDS. Connie also sits on the board of the Texas Heritage Songwriters' Association and is a connector between the organization and artists.

Americana radio promotion guru Al Moss introduced me to Denise McLemore at a Music Fog session at Threadgills during SXSW in 2011. Founded by Jessie Scott, Music Fog is a production company that travels all over America filming and recording Americana artists at festivals and in private studio sessions. Music Fog created abundant content and built a popular music channel on YouTube long before anyone else was doing it. Before joining the Music Fog staff, Denise co-owned a renowned talent agency in Austin. She lived in Brussels for six years, where she and her husband introduced their European friends to Americana music. When the marriage broke down, Patty Griffin's album *Children Running Through* got Denise through her divorce.

"I came back to the States and decided I wanted to work on Patty Griffin's management team," Denise says. Through the grapevine, as she tried to connect with Patty's manager, Denise met Jessie Scott. Jessie hired Denise as business manager at Music Fog.

"How lucky can I be?" Denise says. "I took an inaugural trip with them to see if I was a good fit with the culture. They were renegades. Celebrity Coaches sponsored us, so we had these tricked-out touring buses. And I mean, it was the Wild West in video back then. It was the early days of uploading videos to YouTube. I loved it. It was Americana band camp, hanging out with everyone in studios, festivals, on the bus. I had the time of my life."

Terry and Jo Harvey Allen and Joe and Sharon Ely are members of a long line of Lubbock natives who ended up in Austin. Artists are heroes in Austin. The city's tagline, "Keep Austin weird," celebrates the laid-back cosmic cowboys and cultural creatives. Yet, long before Austin became the Live Music Capital, Lubbock artists, perhaps the most progressive in all of country music, put Texas on the map. Terry, Jo Harvey, Joe, Sharon, Buddy Holly, Waylon Jennings, Mac Davis, Lloyd Maines, Butch Hancock, Jimmie Dale Gilmore, Delbert McClinton, Ponty Bone, Sonny West, Bob Livingston, Kimmie Rhodes, and scores of other musical mavericks come from the Hub City, a place too barren and conservative to hold them for long.

In high school, the ethereal Sharon Ely acted in plays and worked on costumes and makeup in the theater department. She took art classes in college before dropping out to attend Jesse Lee's Hair Design Institute of Technology. "I did really well in cosmetology school," Sharon says. "So I immediately got a job working in the beauty business and then ended up going in on a barbershop on Main Street in Lubbock." A building came up for sale next to the barbershop. Sharon, Joe, and friends opened the Shriek Boutique. Named by Joe and Butch Hancock, it was part vintage clothing store, part performance art venue. "It was absurd," Sharon says. "We had drag shows and art shows there. It had a big window in the front and I put my friend in the front window ironing clothes with a sign that said: 'I do ironing.' Performance art. Stevie Ray Vaughan was in town playing at Stubb's and we opened the store that night so he could pick out a bunch of stage clothes for the show."

During a lonely time, and inspired by Greek mythology's nine muses, Sharon made life-size muse dolls to keep her company. "I made the dolls out of satin, velvet, and lace and I embroidered their faces," Sharon says. "I started making them because I wanted to have a cocktail party because I didn't have any friends around at the time. But then, I started selling the dolls and they attracted so much attention and people were coming around and we started having all these parties, fashion shows, photo shoots, and dances. It was fantastic. And I didn't have time to make dolls anymore."

When Buddy Holly fans started showing up in Lubbock, Sharon bought a Cadillac convertible with bullhorns on the front and took people on tours around Lubbock. She staged cabarets before Joe's annual New Year's Eve shows. "I got to be a chorus girl, which I always wanted to be," Sharon says. Sharon made clothes out of black velvet and asked her friends to paint them. "Terry and Jo Harvey were staging a show in San Antonio and Terry made a suggestion that Joe and I could join them. Joe did a performance art piece, Jo Harvey did a one-woman show, and I did a painted black velvet fashion show. Jo Harvey modeled a cape that Terry painted with a giant rat on the back. I modeled a black velvet wedding dress. Many of our friends modeled these painted black velvet pieces."

Sharon worked in wardrobe, hair, and makeup for films including *There Will Be Blood*, Willie Nelson's *Red Headed Stranger*, *Angels Sing*, and *Everybody Wants Some!!* She created her own line of Holy Posole soup from a hundred-year-old recipe. At first, Sharon made the soup for parties and sold it in farmers' markets. Eventually, the grocery chain HEB was buying Holy Posole by the truckload, until Sharon decided that working in food distribution with grocery chains and trucking companies was not how she wanted to spend her time. A generous bon vivant, Sharon is happiest with her own kind: artists and writers, philosophers, and free spirits.

As recorded earlier in this book, Sharon's husband, Joe, released twenty-one solo albums between 1977 and 2022, and six with the Flatlanders. Over the years, Joe toured with English band the Clash, opened for Linda Ronstadt, performed with Bruce Springsteen, and played with the Joe Ely band around the world. In 2007, he toured in a songwriter circle with Guy Clark, Lyle Lovett, and John Hiatt. Joe won a Grammy as part of the Tex-Mex supergroup Los Super Seven. He wrote a novel, *Reverb: An Odyssey*, and a memoir, *Bonfire of Roadmaps*, and was inducted into the Texas Institute of Letters in 2017.

Terry Allen is the most nonconformist of all the Lubbock rebels, and his body of work crosses all boundaries. He's created a singular and psychedelic mixture of music, sculpture, paintings, lithographs, drawings, longform audio and video, plays, multimedia installations, and more. It's impossible to keep up with Terry's limitless flow of avant-garde art. The only way to experience it is to dig in deep and get your mind blown over and over.

Terry and Jo Harvey Allen married at eighteen and left Lubbock for California, where Terry enrolled in the Chouinard Art Institute in Los Angeles. "Chouinard was the first place that I encountered like-minded people that, for whatever reason, felt like outcasts from their own culture," Terry says. "It was the first time I met people who were serious about making art. It was fortuitous to be in LA at that time because the sixties busted wide open and we were out there the entire time. It was a great time to be there."

The couple started a radio show in the late 1960s on KPPC, an underground, freeform radio station broadcast from the basement of the Pasadena Presbyterian Church.

"My main goal in life was to have kids," Jo Harvey says. "One day Terry asked me if there is anything else I wanted to do. And I said, 'Yeah, I'm going to radio school.' Well, I'd never heard of radio school. I just made it up on the spot. Then the next day, Terry said, 'Are you still going to radio school? Because I got you a radio show.'"

"Our show was called *Rawhide and Roses*," Jo Harvey says. "Terry and I coproduced the show. We worked on it every Saturday. Terry programmed the music and we did research at the UCLA archives. I told stories on the air and played rock and country music. We were playing Willie Nelson for the first time in LA. I was actually the first woman country music DJ in the country. It was a novelty at the time to have a woman on the air."

Rawhide and Roses was followed by the *Bernie Pearl Blues* show and then *Fireside Theater*.

"Bernie Pearl's brother owned the Ashgrove. Some of the people that played at the Ashgrove on Saturday night would come and be on his show," Terry says. "And then we had access to them as guests. We'd all hang out all day at the church."

"Then on Sunday night, we'd hang out and go someplace together," Jo Harvey says. "A lot of times people came over to our house and I always made beans and cornbread, or spaghetti, and peach cobbler. That show was really my first opportunity to ever interview other people. Once, on a trip to New Orleans, I went to Maybelle Carter's hotel room and interviewed her. I sat on the bed with her and she just was so wonderful. It was really the beginning for me of doing documentary stuff."

Terry's 1970s-era mesmerizing albums *Juarez* and *Lubbock (on Everything)* are more provocative than any other outsider Americana music. Terry returned to his hometown to record *Lubbock (on Everything)*.

"I ended up getting a grant from the NEA [National Endowment for the Arts] on my artwork and used part of that money to record," Terry says. "Lloyd Maines was working at Caldwell Studio and I called him up and told him I had like twenty or so songs I wanted to record. Lloyd ended up really putting the thing together. He brought in Jesse Taylor on guitar, Lloyd's brother Kenny played bass, and Richard Bowden on fiddle. That was the first time I met Lloyd. It was the first time I met Joe Ely. I knew Jimmie and Butch from high school, but they were younger than me and we never spent time together. And Stubbs [Barbecue master Christopher Stubblefield] was pivotal too. He showed up in the studio around three o'clock with piles of meat to give to all the musicians. It was my first encounter with him."

Terry and Jo Harvey lived in Fresno for seventeen years, raising their sons Bukka and Bale. Experimental artist Yvonne Rainer taught at a college in town. Jo Harvey studied with Yvonne and began to stage one-woman shows. Terry wrote a play, *The Embrace…Advance to Fury*, and Jo Harvey acted in it.

Throughout the years, Jo Harvey has written and performed in a long list of plays, including *A Moment's Hesitation*, *Hally Lou*, *Homerun*, *As It Is in Texas*, and *Duckblind*. She collaborated with Terry, Bukka, and Bale on *Do You Know Where Your Children Are Tonight?* As a screen actor, Jo Harvey has appeared in films including *True Stories* with David Byrne, *Fried Green Tomatoes*, *The Client*, and *The Wendell Baker Story*. Terry and Jo Harvey both appear in Martin Scorsese's acclaimed *Killers of the Flower Moon*.

My favorite Jo Harvey project, *The Beautiful Waitress*, is a book of photographs and interviews with waitresses around the country. Jo Harvey transformed the work into *Counter Angel*, a play directed by Joan Tewkesbury, writer of Robert Altman's cult film *Nashville*. Jo Harvey performed *Counter Angel* in truck stops, cafés, galleries, and theaters. In the 1990s, Terry and Jo Harvey collaborated with their Lubbock pals Butch Hancock, Jo Carol Pierce, and Joe and Sharon Ely on the play *Chippy: Diary of a West Texas Hooker*.

Terry and Jo Harvey continue to create larger-than-life art, and a life larger than art. Being with them is a gas. Their matchless sense of humor keeps the rest of us laughing so hard our guts hurt.

As Paul and I struggle to piece together a documentary on Guy, Connie, Sharon, Joe, and Terry come to Nashville for Guy's seventy-third birthday.

We shoot the centerpiece for our film, the *Old Friends Reunion*, on November 6. Guy, Rodney Crowell, Steve Earle, Ramblin' Jack Elliott, Terry Allen, Joe Ely, Robert Earl Keen, and Jerry Jeff Walker gather at Jim McGuire's studio. We set up a three-camera, three-hour, multitracked audio, over-the-top film production of the old friends swapping songs and stories. The only problem is, Guy is so sick he can't get through one song or finish one story. It's lucky he made it to the studio at all. We come away with a ton of footage, but the footage of Guy is completely unusable. It's an expensive misstep. If your subject is dying, it's not a good idea to put this much pressure on a production. We have to rethink the documentary. Guy is not going to be able to participate in the ways we'd hoped. Guy and I discuss the reality. "Well, Tamara," he says, "I'll follow your lead. You and Paul can come over here and interview me on camera as much as you want. Maybe you'll end up with something worthwhile." We do.

CHAPTER TWENTY-THREE

DESPERADO WAITING FOR A TRAIN

Things are grim with Guy. On top of everything else, he has a bad ear infection and had a severe allergic reaction to a new cancer drug. There are many enemies in his body trying to take him down, but Guy is not giving up yet. We soldier on together to finish the book and work on the documentary.

The most important piece in the documentary is the music. Without it, the story loses its meaning. Unfortunately for us, Guy's publishing is owned by two major corporations, Sony Music Publishing and Warner Chappell Music. Five different record companies own Guy's master recordings. Music licensing is an expensive proposition for our film. Guy and I discuss it and he calls one of his contacts at Sony, who is wholly uncooperative. It pisses Guy off, but Guy has no power here.

My Leadership Music brother Stacy Widelitz, cowriter of "She's Like the Wind" from the film *Dirty Dancing*, introduces me to Andrea von Foerster, a music supervisor in Los Angeles. Andrea helps me figure out a ballpark budget for the songs I want to license for the film. It will be a minimum of $100,000 to license the songs for theatrical, broadcast, and streaming worldwide, in perpetuity. If we want to press DVDs, it's going to cost us more.

Writing a book about Guy Clark is one thing. I can put my own sweat equity into that without the burden of hiring others. A film, on the other hand, is a massive undertaking. On top of the music supervisor, we will need a production crew to shoot the film, postproduction video and audio editors, graphic designers, an archivist to find and license historical photographs and footage, lawyers to keep it all legal, an accountant to handle the money, and so forth.

As much as I love Guy, I'm not sure there is enough of an audience for a documentary to make it worth the time and money to do it. Crowdfunding is an option to test the waters. If we create a compelling crowdfunding campaign, we may raise enough money to get started and find a core fan base of Guy fans.

I know nothing about crowdfunding and spend the first few months of 2015 studying campaigns on Kickstarter. We decide on Kickstarter because there is an easy out. We must meet our stated financial goal within thirty days. If we miss the goal, all the money raised goes back to the donors. If that happens, I can back out of making the film entirely. Even this early on, I am a reluctant filmmaker.

Our goal is $75,000. If we raise three-quarters of the music licensing, perhaps we'll find investors to help with the rest. I have no idea what I'm doing, but it seems plausible. We blow past the $75,000 goal in three days. By the end of the four-week campaign, 1,879 backers pledge $182,294. This is great. After Kickstarter fees, we take in $168,000. Enough for the music and to start putting together the film.

I'm not sure where we go after the Kickstarter campaign closes, but a glimmer of our destiny shows up in my email inbox a few days later:

Tamara,
Due to biblical flood conditions in Austin, I wandered around the internet a bit this morning. I stumbled and settled in to learn about the Guy Clark Documentary project. Serendipity doo dah a day or too late.

I grew up on Guy, have seen him play a bunch, even invoked my status to have him booked into ACL [Austin City Limits] Music Festival which my partners and I started in 2002. I did all the underwriting and sponsorship for the TV show and the festival for years, partly for the business, partly b/c I knew how vital that show, and this city, and this kind of music had been to me, and to so many others. My kids know the lyrics, my littlest one laughs still at "Homegrown Tomatoes." I cannot overstate how influential and welcome his words have been in my life.

Anyway, if you need help—money, fundraising, anything down here—I am raising my hand.

And, I should have said first, thank you for doing what you are doing, and I hope you are able to produce the film that you intend to. There has to be a deeper, even richer story buried inside that man that I, and the whole world, will appreciate.

You got more help here if you need it.

Best,
Bart Knaggs
Austin, TX

Wow. Who is this guy? I write back to Bart with more information about the film and we agree to meet for lunch when I get to Austin in a few weeks. I have to be in Texas for a Kristofferson event and to speak at the Kerrville Folk Festival. I build a production schedule around my trip and we plan to film in Luckenbach and Rockport.

The History Channel hosts the "Texas Honors" event at the Alamo in San Antonio on May 18 to celebrate the epic new five-part miniseries *Texas Rising*. The series dramatizes the Texas Revolution against Mexico. Kris, from Brownsville, Texas, plays President Andrew Jackson in the series. Fort Worth native Bill Paxton stars as Texas hero Sam Houston. Jeffrey Dean Morgan, Ray Liota, Brendan Fraser, Olivier Martinez, Cynthia Addai-Robinson, and Rob Morrow round out the cast.

The event also launches a fundraising campaign to raise money for the preservation and improvement of the Alamo. Rock star Phil Collins is on hand to donate his collection of Alamo artifacts back to the Texas mission. A media red carpet welcomes the actors and dignitaries, followed by a speech from the San Antonio mayor. I take Kris to a media tent for interviews as everyone mingles with champagne and eats chili rellenos. Chuck Mead leads the house band rocking on an outdoor stage.

Kris sings a couple of songs with the band backing him. He recorded a cover of Tom Petty's "Won't Back Down" for the series trailer.

We've been to hundreds of events together. As always, everyone wants to say hi to Kris, but this is a cool crowd filled with actors who know what it's like to have personal space invaded. Everyone is respectful and sweet as they approach our table. Here, for a change, Kris is not Mickey Mouse in Fucking Disneyland. It's a long day and night but also fun and pleasurable. Back in the hotel lobby later, Kris, Lisa, and I marvel at the ease of the event. No car chase back to the hotel. No clumps of fans thrusting items to be signed. No women smacking into us for selfies. As we say goodnight, Kris grabs me in a bear hug with childlike enthusiasm and says, "Tamara, you're my best friend." Lisa and I look at each other. Tears form in both of our eyes. His memory is fading, but Kris Kristofferson is still the sweetest man I know.

After I speak at the Kerrville Folk Festival in late May, Paul and I meet our film crew in Fredericksburg: associate producer Connie Nelson, camera operator Glen Danles, production assistant Mike Saviano (my dad), and still photographer Wendy Brundage Thessen (my Austin-based cousin).

Wendy and Connie pick up Dad and Glen at the Austin airport. By the time we meet at the Airbnb in Fredericksburg, Dad, Connie, Wendy, and Glen have sampled half of the wineries in town. The four of them did not know each other before today, but they are happy old friends now. Working on a creative project together is a bonding experience like no other. Even eight years later, it warms my heart to think about the six of us traipsing around Luckenbach, soaking in its rich history. The tagline "Everybody's Somebody in Luckenbach" is no joke. Congenial folks ramble around and drink long necks, eat barbecue, and listen to songwriters pick around a fire pit. We film and photograph every inch of the property. We interview Hal Ketchum under a canopied oak tree and shoot Rosie Flores and her band playing in the dance hall.

Luckenbach remains one of my favorite places in Texas. The tiny village started as a trading post in the 1800s, housing a post office, general store, and beer joint. A blacksmith shop, cotton gin, school, and dance hall came later. In 1970, the postmaster retired and placed an ad in the local paper: TOWN FOR SALE. Colorful Texans Hondo Crouch, Guich Koock, and Kathy Morgan took over. Hondo dubbed himself mayor and "imagineer." Musicians, artists, and misfits flocked to Luckenbach. In 1973, Jerry Jeff Walker and the Lost Gonzo Band recorded the seminal album *Viva Terlingua!* at Luckenbach. The town's fate was sealed after Guy Clark passed the story of Luckenbach to Chips Moman. Chips and Bobby Emmons wrote "Luckenbach, Texas (Back to the Basics of Love)" and Waylon Jennings made it a hit. Hondo didn't live long enough to hear his holy place memorialized in song, but his spirit lives on and continues to attract believers.

Wendy, Connie, Glen, and Dad drive from Fredericksburg to Rockport, a four-hour drive to the south coast of Texas, in Wendy's SUV. The four of them are tight now, and I can't even convince my own father to ride with Paul and me in the minivan. Paul and I joke to each other that we feel like the boring parents and the four of them can't wait to escape us to have some fun. They stop at the Alamo and other sites along the way. Paul and I make a beeline for Rockport. We've got preproduction work to do. I suppose directing and producing a film using other people's money requires some responsibility.

I met many of the townspeople the first time I came to Rockport with Guy in 2011. I've been back several times since then, rifling through family archives and falling in love with Rockport and its people. Craig Griffin owns Charlotte Plummer restaurant and the Inn at Fulton Harbor, which is home base for our production crew. Guy's sisters Caro and Jan throw a shrimp boil party at the Clark home and most of the town comes to welcome us. Captain Tommy Moore takes our crew out on his boat in Aransas Bay to film from that perspective. On our last night in Rockport, Craig hosts Caro and Jan, Steve and Sherol Russell, our film crew, and a few other friends for a full-moon party at his house on Water Street. By the end of our trip, Rockport feels like home.

Back in Austin in mid-June, Paul, Connie, and I meet Bart Knaggs for lunch at La Condesa, which is one of the restaurants owned by Bart and his partners at New Waterloo. We learn that Bart, an Austin native, is one of the founders of Capitol Sports and Entertainment, the Austin City

Limits Music Festival (ACL), and Mellow Johnny's Bike Shop. He's got an MBA from the University of Texas at Austin. He's married to Barbara and has three daughters. Bart wins me over just talking about his family. One can learn a lot about a person's character by the language they use to describe those closest to them. Bart's devotion to Barb and his girls is absolute. His business acumen is clear. He is a hell of a nice guy.

After saying our goodbyes to Bart, Paul, Connie, and I walk a couple of blocks from La Condesa to the Moody Theater. Guy is an honoree tonight at the second annual Austin City Limits Hall of Fame celebration, along with Loretta Lynn, Flaco Jimenez, Asleep at the Wheel, and Townes Van Zandt. I ask: "Well, what do you think about Bart?" It's unanimous. All three of us love Bart. He is in the club. We don't know yet what role he will play, but boy, we are about to find out.

Backstage at ACL is chaotic and fun. Guy's sisters are here along with Sharon and Joe Ely, Connie Nelson, Lyle Lovett, Vince Gill, Gillian Welch, David Rawlings, and Jason Isbell. Caro offers Guy an edible. Instead of taking one square of the THC chocolate, Guy swallows three.

Host Dwight Yoakam is ready to take the stage, along with Lloyd Maines and his house band. Patty Loveless waits in the wings. She is first up to sing Loretta's "Don't Come Home a Drinkin'" and "Coal Miner's Daughter." Meanwhile, all of us with Guy are gathered at a table in catering, eating, laughing, and enjoying ourselves. Paul and I sit across from Guy. Paul leans over and says, "I think something is wrong with Guy." Guy is slumped over. All of us jump up and gather around Guy to try to rouse him but he is out cold. Someone from ACL calls an ambulance as Connie dials Dr. Donald Counts, Guy's longtime friend and Austin physician. "Tell the ambulance to take him to St. David's," Dr. Counts says. "I'll meet him there."

Vince is called to the stage to duet with Patty on "After the Fire Is Gone" and Lyle follows to sing for Guy. The original plan called for Guy to accept the award, but that's not happening now. Lyle, always graceful and calm, accepts the award on Guy's behalf and sings "Step Inside This House" and "Anyhow I Love You." Jason Isbell performs "Desperados Waiting for a Train," followed by Gillian Welch and Dave Rawlings playing "Black Diamond Strings." All of this to honor Guy and he's missing it, we are all missing it, thanks to an overdose of edibles. Caro, Jan, and Connie follow Guy to the hospital. I stay to deal with the ACL business. Of course, the word gets out on social media that something happened to Guy backstage at ACL. Rumors are flying around. He's dead. He OD'd. He had a stroke, or a heart attack. Paul and I walk out of ACL with Sharon and Joe Ely long before the show is over. Sharon carries Guy's award. We'll get it to him later. Dr. Counts calls to tell me Guy is going to be okay but they're keeping him overnight for observation. Paul and I go back to the hotel to pack. I'm flying to Phoenix in the morning; my mom has been diagnosed with advanced lung cancer. Terry Allen's number comes up on my phone. "Is he dead?" Terry asks. "Not this time," I reply.

I spend the rest of the summer going back and forth between Phoenix and Nashville, spending time with my mom as she goes through chemo and working with Guy to finish the biography. Guy is angry that he missed the Austin City Limits event. He tries to pin it on his sister Caro.

"It's your own damn fault," I say. "Caro offered you the edible, but you could have said no. Or taken just one instead of three."

"You don't let me off the hook for anything, do you, Tamara?" Guy says. He's clearly miffed.

"Not this time, Guy Charles," I say, using his middle name for emphasis.

Much to my surprise, I finish the Guy manuscript in September. The final line of the book is a fitting quote from Terry Allen. I read over the pages one last time and let it go. There's a saying among writers that the work is never finished, it is abandoned. And that's how this feels. I could tinker with this book for the rest of my life, but it is time to abandon it. It is a relief to email the Word document over to Texas A&M University Press. There is only one thing to do now. I get in the car and drive to Guy's house.

Guy sits in his sunporch rolling a cigarette. I take the chair across from him, the way I have for the last eight years. It feels different today. This is the end of our book journey. I stare at his hands for a moment and take it all in. "Hey Guy, I turned in the manuscript about thirty minutes ago," I say. Guy leans back and lights his cigarette. "Tamara, I haven't seen you look this relaxed in ten years," he says. We both laugh.

Americana artists Kevin Welch and Terri Hendrix at Guy Clark's seventieth birthday celebration, the Long Center, Austin, Texas, November 2011. Photo by Lynne Margolis.

Left to right: Shawn Camp, Jim Lauderdale, Guy Clark, Tamara Saviano, and Buddy Miller in Buddy's backyard after recording the *Buddy and Jim Radio Show* for Sirius Satellite Radio's outlaw country channel in 2012. Photo courtesy of Tamara Saviano archives.

Kris Kristofferson, Joe Ely, and Terry Allen at the Newport Folk Festival, July 2016. Photo courtesy of Tamara Saviano archives.

Left to right: Verlon Thompson, Tamara Saviano, Chuck Mead, and Shawn Camp celebrate the release of *Without Getting Killed or Caught*, Saviano's Guy Clark biography, with a program at the Country Music Hall of Fame in January 2017. Photo courtesy of Tamara Saviano archives.

Shawn Camp and Tamara Saviano at a Grammy nomination party, Nashville, 2017. Camp and Saviano produced Kris Kristofferson's Grammy-nominated *Cedar Creek Sessions*. Photo courtesy of Tamara Saviano archives.

Without Getting Killed or Caught wrap dinner at Botticelli's in Austin, Texas, January 2018. *Left side of table, front to back:* Sharon Ely, Barry Poss, Tamara Saviano, and Paul Whitfield. *Right side of table, front to back:* Joe Ely, Verlon Thompson, Jo Harvey Allen, and Terry Allen. Photo courtesy of Tamara Saviano archives.

Leadership Music class of 2007 pals at Randy Wachtler's house in 2018. *Left to right:* Hit songwriter Bob DiPiero (who wishes he was in the class of 2007); Fred Vail, who worked with the Beach Boys in the early 1960s; Randy Wachtler, founder of 615 Music; Ellen Lehman, founder of the Community Foundation of Middle Tennessee; Leslie DiPiero, president of Jonas Group Publishing; music attorney Bruce Phillips; Tamara Saviano; composer Stacy Widelitz, cowriter with Patrick Swayze of "She's Like the Wind" from *Dirty Dancing*; and Jessie Scott, program director at Americana WMOT radio and longtime Americana radio personality. Photo courtesy of Tamara Saviano archives.

Left to right: Garry Talent, Bruce Springsteen, Mike Delevante, and Bob Delevante at Stone Pony, Asbury Park, New Jersey, July 2019. Photo by Julie Delevante.

Left to right: Terry Allen, Joe Ely, Jo Harvey Allen, Tamara Saviano, Connie Nelson, Rodney Crowell, Sharon Ely, and Steve Earle backstage at Austin City Limits before Steve's show, July 2019. Photo courtesy of Sharon Ely.

Left to right: Kay Clary, Tamara Saviano, and Denise McLemore at the Austin Music Awards, where Saviano received the Margaret Moser Award honoring women in the music business, March 11, 2020, at the ACL Moody Theater. Photo courtesy of Tamara Saviano archives.

Left to right: Without Getting Killed or Caught editor Sandra Adair; executive producer and writer Bart Knaggs; writer, producer, and director Tamara Saviano; and producer and director Paul Whitfield at an Austin Film Society special outdoor screening at Laguna Gloria sculpture garden, Austin, Texas, May 2021. Photo courtesy of Tamara Saviano archives.

Robert Earl Keen stands on his ranch outside Kerrville, Texas, in September 2022 as photographer Dan Winters prepares the shot. Robert made the cover story of the December 2022 issue of *Texas Monthly*. Photo courtesy of Tamara Saviano archives.

Tamara Saviano and Americana legend Rodney Crowell speak at the 2024 Antlers and Acorns Boone Songwriters Festival at the Appalachian Theater, Boone, North Carolina. Photo courtesy of Tamara Saviano archives.

I know it's true. I never thought I'd finish this book. I owe it all to Guy. He pushed me, insisting every week that I come to his house to talk with him, look through his archives, and work on this book together. I know now that Guy is feeling mortal. I realize that he knew all along this would be his last chance to get his life down on paper. To tell his story. To leave a legacy in paragraphs and pages, not just songs. To be able to talk about Susanna and their monumental love. I'm grateful for Guy's trust. I'm proud that we did this work together. And, oh God, I hope Guy lives long enough to see the book published. Guy has said all along that he didn't believe he would still be here when the book comes out. I can't bear the thought of doing this without him. I want to celebrate with him, watch other people celebrate him, and witness Guy bask in all of it. At the tribute concert on Guy's seventieth birthday, it was clear that he felt loved. What a wonderful thing it was for him to experience that unconditional love. For all of us to experience it. I want Guy to have that again before it's too late.

"You're not through with me yet," Guy says, as though reading my thoughts.

"I know. Paul and I will be back next week with our camera gear."

Paul and I continue to film and photograph Guy and everything in his house. I fly back and forth between Phoenix and Nashville, sitting with my mother, sitting with Guy. When I look back on it now, the memories feel sacred.

Mom and I deeply explore our lives together. We apologize for the wrongs, revel in the good memories. We sit on her bed together and look through photographs and family archives. I record hours of our conversations, a little trick I picked up from Susanna Clark.

Although the book is finished, I still spend many mornings at Guy's kitchen table or across from him in the sunroom. He doesn't even bother to put on pants anymore, just sits there in boxer shorts and a shirt, drinking coffee and smoking. Guy can no longer get to his basement workshop. Even with a chair lift, he is too weak to travel downstairs. I don't record our intimate conversations, but I am present as Guy withers.

On his seventy-fourth birthday, Guy is too sick for the usual party at McGuire's. I bring him a small chocolate cake from Whole Foods and sing "Happy Birthday" in the middle of the kitchen. It's not much, but I can't let the day go unrecognized. And we love chocolate cake.

I still have no idea how to piece together a documentary about Guy. I wrestle with my book copy. I listen to Guy tell stories. How do I fit Guy's remarkable life into a compelling ninety-minute film? I am so close to this project, I need a pair of objective eyes. I'd rather those eyes belong to someone I don't know well, yet someone who has had some experience with Guy and knows his music and story. My gut tells me this person is Bart Knaggs. The conversations between Bart and me over the last months make it clear that he knows Guy's musical history as well as anyone. I also believe Bart will push me to places I can't get to on my own. I feel a sense of kinship with Bart due to our mutual love for Guy.

My arguments persuade Bart. We trade emails and discuss the storyline.

"I really want to understand what is in your head and heart on this one," Bart writes. "I hadn't considered the relationship among Susanna, Guy and Townes to be that relevant earlier. Now, I don't know how to separate them. They are three parts of a whole—conjoined in love, pain and purpose."

"In my opinion, that relationship is the most important part of the Guy Clark story as it colored all of his adult life," I respond. "How to take that love, pain and purpose and translate it to film is the challenge. I think the three main themes for the film are that relationship, Guy's struggle with the recording industry, and his influence as a songwriter. Culling all of that down to a 90–100 minute film, well, that's our job now, isn't it? Thanks for coming along on this journey with me."

I run down to Austin in February 2016 to work with Bart. Within a week, bad news comes from Nashville. The chemo isn't working on Guy anymore and his condition is serious. The doctors put him on an experimental drug, which may buy him a year. If Guy doesn't respond well to the new medication, doctors say he will be gone within a few months.

I'm not surprised by this news, but my heart is in denial. A week ago, Guy and I talked about him joining me in Austin for the Texas Book Festival in November. I spend the afternoon bawling and writing an obituary for Guy. I'm a journalist. I know that we will need it. And no one is going to be in any shape to write it after Guy's death. Guy, I'm not ready to say goodbye.

    I cut my Austin trip short and go back to Nashville. Guy has been at the Richland Place nursing home since Valentine's Day. He can't walk and has many other issues. He is in so much pain and anguish, and it is heartbreaking to witness. I spend a few days with Guy, and then it's back to Phoenix with Mom. My brothers and I take turns spending a week or two at a time in Phoenix.

    March and April are a blur of Nashville and Phoenix. Phoenix and Nashville.

    May 6 is a beautiful day in Nashville. An orderly pushes Guy in his wheelchair outside to the front portico at Richland Place. I sit on a bench next to Guy as we breathe in the sunshine and fresh air. Guy and I are quiet, just taking in the day, when my phone rings. It's Mom. She tells me that the spots in her brain are growing; the radiation is no longer working. Mom is dying. Guy is dying. They came into the world three months apart, Mom in August 1941 and Guy in November. Now they are dying at the same time.

    I tell Mom I'll be on a plane to Phoenix tomorrow. She convinces me to wait a few days. Two of my brothers are there but have to leave soon. "I'd like to be with my only daughter, the two of us alone for a little while," Mom says.

    We hang up. I turn to look at Guy. He's heard the conversation. "Bad news?" I fill him in as best I can while also trying to be sensitive to him. Guy grabs my hand. We sit together holding hands for a long time. I have never held hands with Guy before this. It is comforting to me, and I can tell he needs the comfort, too. "Tamara, I'm so sorry that your mom and I are dying at the same time," Guy says. I say, "I'm sorry, too, but we are together right now and I'm happy about that." Guy cries. I never thought I'd see Guy Clark cry. I cry with him and say a silent prayer. I do not want to lose Guy, but I do not want to see him suffer. It has been too much. Just too much suffering for him. "I love you, Guy," I say. "I love you, Tamara," he replies.

    Guy goes home the next day, hospice care in place. He says he wants to be home, in his own bed, surrounded by his books and music and art and

Susanna's memory. The last time I see Guy alive is May 10. I stop at the house before getting on a plane to Phoenix to be with my mom. He's conscious but can't talk. I kiss his cheek, tell him I love him, and walk out the door as tears stream down my face.

Rodney, Verlon, and Shawn keep me posted on Guy's condition while I'm in Phoenix tending to Mom. On the evening of May 16, Rodney calls and tells me to get on the next plane home. He says Guy will be gone within a few days. I book a 6:00 a.m. flight to Nashville on May 17. Three hours before my flight, Verlon texts me. Guy is dead.

I postpone my flight until later that night. I need to send out a press release and deal with the media. I mess up the first release. My Leadership Music brother Derek Simon calls to give his condolences and gently point out the error. Damn. I send the second release out. My phone rings constantly and emails pour in. I sit in front of my computer and cry. Mom gets out of bed to make me breakfast. "No, Mom, I'm okay. Go back to bed." She hugs me. "I'm so sorry about your friend," she says. Ten days ago Guy comforted me about my mom. Now Mom is comforting me about Guy. It's all too surreal. I take a break to drive to McDonald's for iced tea. As soon as the car starts, I hear Elizabeth Cook announce Guy's death on her radio show on Sirius Outlaw Country. "L.A. Freeway" bounces around the car speakers and I stare at Superstition Mountains in the distance. I need to hear a voice from home. I call Kathi Whitley, who is also one of Guy's good friends. Crying with Kathi gives me the strength to get through the rest of the day.

I fly back to Nashville. A small group of us go to the funeral home to see Guy's body before he's cremated. Rodney has rolled two cigarettes and a joint and places them in the breast pocket of Guy's old blue shirt. He is laid out in a box that can't contain the length of his torso and long jean-clad legs. Guy is so tall they took his boots off to make him fit. Still, the top of his head is scrunched against one end of the box and his feet are square against the other end. Guy Clark does not fit in a box.

Jim McGuire hosts a wake—a typical Guy Clark picking party, one of many that took place at McGuire's studio over the years. Guy's family and Nashville friends gather around an altar on which we've placed his ashes, his old boots, and our favorite picture of Guy. We take turns playing Guy Clark songs. At the end of the night, Verlon leads a chorus of "Old Friends" that knocks the wind out of the room.

At midnight, a small group of us board a tour bus to take us—and Guy—to Santa Fe and Terry Allen. Guy's last wishes are clear. He is to be cremated and his ashes sent to Terry Allen to be placed in a sculpture. It's Guy's final road trip. We sleep little during the eighteen-hour drive; we have too many Guy stories to tell. Grief shared is grief diminished.

We arrive in Santa Fe by dinnertime on May 25. Guy instigated this party. His son Travis and closest friends are here: Rodney Crowell, Verlon Thompson, Vince Gill, Emmylou Harris, Shawn Camp, Jim McGuire, Terry, Jo Harvey and Bukka Allen, Joe, Sharon and Marie Ely, Robert Earl and Kathleen Keen, Lyle and April Lovett, Steve Earle, Jack Ingram, and Paul Milosevich.

We set up another altar, gather around, and tell more Guy stories. After a feast of green chili enchiladas, tamales, guacamole, and homemade salsa, we huddle around a fire pit on the stone and adobe patio. Hanging wisteria perfumes the air as old friends toast Guy, clinking glasses of wine against bottles of Topo Chico and cans of Robert Earl Keen beer. Under a night sky blanketed with stars, a guitar comes out. This time there is a rule, and it is simple. "Play a song Guy would have made you play," Steve says. Three among this group have written songs about Guy. Shawn sings "This Guy, Guy," written with Gary Nicholson. Verlon plays his ode, "Sideman's Dream." Then Vince shares the song he wrote on his way to Santa Fe, "There's Nothing Like a Guy Clark Song," a perfect benediction to the master songwriter's life. Through this song—and many more of his own—there's no doubt Guy Clark will live forever.

CHAPTER TWENTY-FOUR

A SEASON OF GRIEF

I fly from New Mexico to Austin for Memorial Day weekend. I rushed around in the weeks after Guy's death helping with memorial services, renting a tour bus and handling the logistics for the road trip, and spending time with Guy's family and friends. I'm exhausted and need time to myself. I spend three days alone. I walk miles and miles on the Lady Bird Lake trail, spend hours in the bookstore, eat my fill of tacos and Italian food, and sleep a restorative nine hours a night.

I'm due in Memphis the following week. Steve Dunavant and Bryan Hayes from the Memphis Americana Music Society hired me last summer to produce *Red Hot: A Memphis Celebration of Sun Records*, a fundraiser for St. Jude Children's Research Hospital. Many consider Sun Records the birthplace of rock and roll. Sun Records owner and producer Sam Phillips launched the careers of icons Elvis Presley, Johnny Cash, Jerry Lee Lewis, Charlie Rich, and Carl Perkins.

Because it is a Memphis-centric project, I suggest Luther Dickinson as a coproducer. I don't know much about the Memphis music landscape. Although I have produced a handful of tribute albums, it feels inauthentic for me to take this on without the Memphis music inner circle.

Luther and his brother Cody, sons of famous Memphis producer Jim Dickinson, play together in the North Mississippi All Stars. Their 2000 debut album, *Shake Hands with Shorty*, earned them a Grammy nomination for Best Contemporary Blues Album. More than that, there is enthusiastic buzz about the band, and word of Luther's prowess as a musician has spread. By the time I track him down, he's played with the Black Crowes and John Hiatt. He founded the supergroup the South Memphis String Band with Jimbo Mathus and Alvin Youngblood Hart, and the Wandering with Valerie June, Amy LaVere, Shardé Thomas, and Shannon McNally.

Luther is a clear leader in the Memphis music scene and my gut tells me he is the right person for the job. One big problem. I don't know Luther and no one on his management team responds to my inquiries. I show up at Luther's showcase during the Americana Music Festival in Nashville. I write my pitch and phone number on a napkin, and ask a security guard to take it to Luther. I hope like hell the note reaches him. I don't have to wait long to find out. Luther texts me the next day to tell me he is in.

For many months before the June recording sessions, Luther and I work together via text and email on song selection and a wish list for artists. It's important to both of us that all of the musicians and artists have a connection to Memphis or Sun Records.

Luther leads the house band, which includes his brother on drums, John Paul Keith on guitar, Amy LaVere on bass, and Lucero's Rick Steff on keyboards. We choose a stellar list of songs, written and recorded at the original Sun Records on Union Avenue and Sam Phillips Recording Service studios on Madison Avenue back in the 1950s. For the modern tribute, we go back to these historic Memphis studios to record. Matt Ross-Spang records and mixes our Phillips sessions, and Kevin Houston is our Sun engineer. We stay in a giant rental house near the studios and settle in for a week of recording. I invite my close friend Alanna Nash to join me and to write the liner notes for the album. Among other books, Alanna is the author of *Elvis Aaron Presley: Revelations from the Memphis Mafia*, *Baby Let's Play House: Elvis Presley and the Women Who Loved Him*, and *The Colonel: The Extraordinary Story of Colonel Tom Parker and Elvis Presley*. Yes, Alanna knows a thing or two about Memphis music history. On top of that, I'm numb with grief and need my sister with me this week.

Every moment in the studio is joyous and it's just what I need. I dance and sing along in the control room as John Paul Keith lays down "Red Cadillac and a Black Moustache," a rockabilly number recorded by Warren Smith back in the Sun Records heyday. Bob Dylan and Brian Setzer have covered this song, but John Paul breathes new, dynamic life into the tune.

I stand inches from Valerie June in Sam Phillips's old control room at Sun Records as she sings "Sure to Fall (in Love with You)." Carl Perkins wrote and recorded the song and the Beatles covered it later. Valerie's exquisite voice gives me goosebumps.

Shawn Camp channels Charlie Rich with his take on "Lonely Weekends." Chuck Mead leads the cast of the CMT television series *Sun Records* (Drake Milligan, Kevin Fonteyne, Christian Lees, and Jonah Lees) on "Red Hot," the 1957 Billy Lee Riley hit. The call-and-response of "my gal is red hot," "your gal ain't doodley squat" is a classic moment in rock and roll. Virtuoso upright bass player Amy LaVere leads a swinging version of the 1956 Miller Sisters tune "Ten Cats Down." Luther unveils his inner Howlin' Wolf on a soulful reading of "Moanin' at Midnight." Jimbo Mathus, Brian Hayes, Alvin Youngblood Hart, and Bobby Rush round out the album.

From Memphis, it's off to Los Angeles for a photo shoot with Kris. We're releasing the *Cedar Creek Sessions* this month for Kris's eightieth birthday. I'm only on the ground a couple of days in California before I fly back to Phoenix to be with Mom. My brothers pack up Mom's house and move her back to Wisconsin to live with my brother Rick for the remainder of her life.

We all go to Wisconsin as Kris opens for Willie Nelson on an unofficial double bill at Summerfest on June 29. It's nourishment for my soul to be back here on a perfect summer day on the Lake Michigan shore. For the first time, I have rock star parking at Summerfest, my beloved hometown festival, behind the stage next to Kris's tour bus with a gorgeous view. I drink a famous Summerfest wine cooler for nostalgia and guide Lisa and my dad around my old stomping grounds while Kris naps. I am home and it feels good to be here.

The fans in my hometown do not disappoint. An overflow crowd hustles for seats at the BMO Harris Pavilion to see two legendary artists on the other side of eighty. Kris is backed up by Merle Haggard's band the Strangers, led by Merle's sons Noel and Ben. The Strangers have backed Kris regularly since Merle's death a few months ago. Kris keeps them working, and they all have each other to lean on. A woman in the audience holds up a sign reading, "Take the ribbon from my hair," and the crowd goes crazy and sings along with every note on "Help Me Make It through the Night." Kris and the Strangers rollick through an hour-long set of hits by Kris and Merle.

We have the best seats in the house for the impressive opening-night fireworks over Lake Michigan before Willie takes the stage. Kris, Lisa, Dad, my dear friend Rick Hagopian, and I watch Willie and the band from stage left. At the end of Willie's set, Dad and I join Kris and Lisa on the bus. Lisa goes to settle up and scrounges a couple of beers for Kris and Dad from backstage. We stay late into the night, until after the festival grounds are cleared. Long after midnight, the tour buses rumble to life and the smell of diesel mixes with Lake Michigan's earthy scent. We wave goodbye in the dark Wisconsin night. I hear waves lapping peacefully behind us as Dad and I climb into my minivan. *Cherish this day*, I think to myself. *Cherish every moment of all of these days. They won't last.*

A few weeks later, I meet Kris and Lisa at the Newport Folk Festival. Forty-seven years ago Kris debuted at the 1969 Newport Folk Festival when Johnny Cash and June Carter brought him out to sing a few songs. This is Kris's first return to Newport and no one expects him. Terry Allen and Joe Ely are here to play, too, and I'm happy to see them in the green-room tent. Word gets around about Kris's surprise show. I hold Kris's hand as we struggle through a packed, cheering mob at the two-hundred-capacity indoor Museum stage. Kris rips through a twenty-song set and plays all his classics. The warmed-up crowd roars as Terry and Joe take the stage after Kris.

Later, we move to an outdoor stage where Kris joins the Texas Gentlemen, a sextet of ace Dallas session musicians, to play a few songs. The band and Kris run through "Sunday Morning Comin' Down" and "Help Me Make It through the Night." Margo Price, a rising Americana artist, is the buzz of Newport. Her album *Midwest Farmer's Daughter* is a breakout this year. Margo joins Kris and the Gentlemen on "Me and Bobby McGee." Surrounded by young artists, two or three generations removed from him, Kris steps back and nods his head encouragingly. The band rocks as Margo channels Janis Joplin's bluesy growl.

Emotion overwhelms me as I witness this passing of the torch. Decades melt behind me, and even more years vanish in Kris's wake. It doesn't seem that long ago that I was the invincible newcomer. Standing stage right today, in the middle of my fifties, it's a privilege to watch a new era of poets and dreamers stake their claim.

Hardly Strictly Bluegrass festival producers Dawn Holliday and Sheri Sternberg offer to sponsor a memorial concert for Guy Clark. Rodney Crowell brings his son-in-law, producer Dan Knobler, into the circle with Dawn, Sheri, Kathi Whitley, and me to put the show together. Frankly, I'm worthless as a coproducer right now. I muster up the energy to help with a few things, but the rest of the team does the heavy lifting on this one. The show is August 16 at the Ryman Auditorium and almost everyone who loves Guy shows up to perform: Verlon Thompson, Vince Gill, Rodney Crowell, Emmylou Harris, Jerry Jeff Walker, Terry Allen, Bobby Bare, Shawn Camp, Robert Earl Keen, Joe Ely, Lyle Lovett, Gillian Welch, Dave Rawlings, Steve Earle, Ramblin' Jack Elliott, Chris and Morgane Stapleton, Delbert McClinton, Jedd Hughes, Radney Foster, Bill Lloyd, Sam Bush, Angaleena Presley, Jack Ingram, Lee Roy Parnell, Mickey Raphael, Gary Nicholson. There are notices plastered backstage that read, "Guy's songs are more interesting than your stories," a reminder to keep the music flowing. Of course, everyone tells stories anyhow. How can we not? Being in the presence of Guy Clark demands storytelling. I am physically present for the three-hour show and the two-hour after-party. Mentally, I'm not there at all. My mom is dying at my brother's house in Milwaukee and I just want to get back there. The best recall I have of the memorial concert is standing next to Steve Earle stage right watching the performances as Steve checks on me periodically. "Are you okay?" Steve asks as he drapes his arm around my shoulders. I lean in and let Steve hold me up.

I grab a couple hours' sleep and am on the road to Milwaukee by 5:00 a.m. Mom dies on August 21, 2016, just two days shy of her seventy-fifth birthday. She was born three months before Guy Clark and died three months after him. I hope Guy is waiting to greet her on the other side.

My grief over my mom and Guy is complicated enough. Yet, after Mom's funeral, things get more troublesome. My daughter is an addict.

It is clear to all of us she is at rock bottom, although she can't see that yet. It is her story to tell, but the drama around my daughter's addiction adds to my anguish.

I want to kidnap my daughter and force her into compliance. My brother and husband remind me that I can't save her. They both insist I go out on my planned book tour for *Without Getting Killed or Caught: The Life and Music of Guy Clark*. I'm not sure how I will make it through this tour, but we spent eight years working on this book and I owe it to Guy to get out there and promote it.

Our first event is at the Bluebird Café during Americana week. Carlene Carter and Kelsey Waldon join me in a night to celebrate the songs of Susanna Clark. Carlene and Susanna cowrote "Easy from Now On." Carlene has great stories about Susanna and Guy and, hell, she's Carlene Carter. I'm thrilled to be onstage with her and my former intern Kelsey Waldon, now an Americana star in her own right.

I drive from Nashville to Tulsa on October 17. I cry the entire nine-hour drive. For my mom, my daughter, Guy...there is plenty of heartbreak to go around. I meet Kris and Lisa Kristofferson the next day for an event at Cain's Ballroom. Kris, fresh from his induction into the Austin City Limits Hall of Fame last week, receives the Woody Guthrie Prize. Rodney is there to honor Kris, and I'm relieved to have a fellow mourner at my side. Being with Kris and Lisa Kristofferson is always a salve, and now is no different. Our promoter friend Johnny Buschardt takes tender care of all of us.

I stay in Tulsa for a few days and Deana McCloud at the Woody Guthrie Center hosts me for a book event. After Tulsa, I meet Radney Foster in Oklahoma City, Susanna Clark's hometown, and open for him at Greg Johnson's club the Blue Door. It is my first time on a club stage opening for a musical artist. It's weird, but fun. Rad plays a couple of Guy songs. I talk about Susanna's connection to Oklahoma City, and how she and Guy got together. The story is not well known and it drops some jaws.

Radney and I drive to Dallas together the next day, stopping along the way for some delicious Oklahoma fried pies. I drop Radney at Dallas Love Field and check into the Belmont Hotel. Jeff Burns, owner of the Belmont and all-around music people connector, hosts a weekend celebration of

Guy. Friday night, Shelly Colvin invites us to the Billy Reid store. Jack Ingram and Dan Dyer sing a few songs and I read from my book. Brunch at the Belmont the next day includes music by Jon Randall, Jessi Alexander, Jamie Lin Wilson, and Kelly Mickwee. Jack, Jon, Jessi, Leon Bridges, Ryan Beaver, the Trishas, the Texas Gentlemen, Carl Anderson, Dan Dyer, Shelly Colvin, Wesley Geiger, Van Darien, Tennessee Jet, and Brandon Pickard play Saturday night out by the Belmont pool. With a gorgeous backdrop of the Dallas skyline, a cadre of Americana artists with the same moxie and spirit as Guy sing his songs together.

I drive 180 miles from Dallas to College Station on Sunday. Between crying jags, I check in with my brother Rick to see if he's heard from my daughter. Nothing. I send prayers to my mom into the cosmos, asking her to watch over her first grandchild.

The next day I sit in the Texas A&M University Press conference room and sign six hundred books. I love the people here and it softens my sadness to share time and meals with them. The next day I drive to Rockport for a book event. I check in at the Inn at Fulton Harbor, spend a couple of days with Guy's sisters Caro and Jan, and walk along the water for hours. It brings me solace to be here in this sacred place on the south coast of Texas. The Aransas County Historical Society hosts a book event at the Paws and Taws convention center and 150 people show up. Many of them knew Guy and it is comforting to be with all of them.

I drive from Rockport to Houston for an event at Cactus Records. Guy's Houston gang is here. Richard Dobson, Chris Borreca, Elise Moore, and Guy's former roommate Francie show up and tell stories of 1960s Houston. Richard, John Egan, and Sergio Trevino perform. It feels like Guy might be looking out for me. I swing through San Antonio, where Brennen Leigh and Noel McKay join me at the Twig Book Shop at the Pearl.

Paul and my dad fly into Austin in time for Sharon and Joe Ely's Halloween party. Friends gather to eat Sharon's famous posole under the five-hundred-year-old oak tree strung with colorful lights. It's a lovely respite from the road.

Joe Ely and Terry Allen join me for the Texas Book Festival to play some songs and talk about Guy. *Texas Monthly* reporter Michael Hall interviews us onstage at the Paramount Theater. After the program, my editor, Thom Lemmons, leads me out to the book tent to sell and sign books. There is a long line of people and Thom puts on his publicist hat to guide everyone through the line. Although I am happy to meet fellow Guy Clark fans and sign books, it is uncomfortable. I'm an introvert and accustomed to being the publicist, not the artist. Guy would get a kick out of this.

A few weeks later, Sugar Hill Records founder Barry Poss emcees a book event at the Regulator Book Shop in Durham, North Carolina. Sugar Hill alumni Bev Paul, Tasha Thomas, Lynn Lancaster, and Holly Lowman are there. Tom Rankin, the director of documentary studies at Duke University, interviews me. Tom's wife is the novelist Jill McCorkle, and we have mutual friends in Marshall Chapman and Matraca Berg. Susanna Clark's niece Suzie and nephew Chris also show up.

After the event, Barry takes us across the street to Asian restaurant JuJu to celebrate. Again, being with folks who knew and loved Guy is a salve on my heart. Especially my sweet friend Barry. He started Sugar Hill Records in 1978, and Sugar Hill became synonymous with American roots music. Thanks to Barry, there are great records out in the world by Terry Allen, Guy Clark, Townes Van Zandt, Robert Earl Keen, Peter Rowan, Dolly Parton, Nickel Creek, and many more. "There were two guiding principles for me when I started, and they haven't changed since day one," Barry says. "I never intended Sugar Hill to be all things to all people. I wanted to make a statement, to stand for something. And I wanted to have a select roster of prestige artists. At the beginning, I never thought that would carry the label through for thirty years, but it has. We were clearly a niche market, but that niche has gotten stronger. We grew more successful, but we didn't do it by moving towards the mainstream."

On December 6, we get word that Kris's album *The Cedar Creek Sessions* is nominated for a Grammy award for Best Americana Album. I had no designs on a Grammy when we took Kris into the studio in Austin to record. So much so that I did not submit the album for a Grammy nomination. I call my coproducer Shawn Camp to tell him the news. "How did that happen?" Shawn asks. To this day, I have no idea who put the album forward on our behalf. The other nominees in the category are the Avett

Brothers' *True Sadness*, Lori McKenna's *The Bird and the Rifle*, the Time Jumpers' *Kid Sister*, and the album that ultimately wins the Grammy, William Bell's *This Is Where I Live*.

Later in December, Paul and I meet our friends back in Austin for the unveiling of Terry Allen's sculpture *Road Angel*, a bronze 1953 Chevy inspired by Terry's memories of driving the dark backroads of the Texas Panhandle. "A dozen carloads of friends headed out to the cotton fields, loaded down with beer and whiskey," Terry says. "We'd park in a circle with the headlights aimed in, tune our car radios to the same station, and dance in the dirt until the Wolfman came on border radio XERF, and then we'd raise drinks and dust to the Wolfman."

Road Angel rests hidden in the lush vista of the Contemporary Austin's Laguna Gloria sculpture park. As we walk the tangled paths to *Road Angel*'s spot next to the Colorado River, a looped soundtrack blares hauntingly from behind the trees—a collage of stories and songs recorded by Terry's friends. I contributed a spoken word piece about my first car, and it's eerie to hear my own voice echo from a dark chamber somewhere inside *Road Angel*.

Laguna Gloria throws a party to celebrate. We join Terry and Jo Harvey's family—sons Bukka and Bale and their children—and our friends Connie Nelson, Steve Earle, Joe and Sharon Ely, and other Austin artists and hippies to toast Terry and his latest stunning creation. Terry, Jo Harvey, Connie, Steve, Joe, Sharon, Paul, and I have dinner at South Congress Hotel after the unveiling, with a plan for a bonfire at Sharon and Joe's after we eat. The temperature drops thirty degrees while we are in the restaurant. No bonfire tonight. But it is a sweet and healing gathering of friends, capping the year that we lost our friend Guy.

The year 2017 breaks cold in Nashville. Paul leaves for Australia and New Zealand with Springsteen. I escape to Austin for the winter. Joe Ely and I share a February 9 birthday and we often spend our birthdays together. This year is Joe's seventieth and my fifty-sixth birthday. Sharon, Joe, Terry, Jo Harvey, and I have an intimate dinner together at Vespaio on the ninth. The big blow-out party is Joe's birthday concert at the Paramount the following night. Lloyd Maines, Glenn Fukunaga, David Grissom, and Davis McLarty back Joe up as he sings hit after hit after hit.

Terry Allen, Jimmie Dale Gilmore, and Butch Hancock join in. It is a rock show with three or four electric guitars going at the same time.

I run down to New Braunfels to see Rodney Crowell play a Valentine's show at the Brauntex Theater. A week later, Kris comes to Austin for the Texas Medal of Arts Awards gala. The Texas Cultural Trust celebrates the state's most influential artists and art supporters. The gala, hosted by Debbie Allen, awards Kris in the multimedia category. Other honorees include Jaclyn Smith for television, Janine Turner for film, singer Yolanda Adams, artist Leo Villareal, architect Frank Welch, writer John Phillip Santos, journalist Scott Pelley, and Kenny Rogers for Lifetime Achievement. Kris, Lisa, and I are plagued by the annual Austin cedar fever allergies. We stay for the necessary allotted time and call it a night. At this point, I've been with Kris at so many honors and awards celebrations, they all seem the same.

Bart Knaggs and I take a five-week screenplay fundamentals workshop from Jill Chamberlain, author of *The Nutshell Technique*. I read Jill's book on the recommendation of the *Straight Outta Compton* screenwriter, whom I met at the Nashville Film Festival. It is providence that Jill lives in and teaches workshops in Austin. Over five Mondays in Jill's classes, our beat sheet comes together and the script evolves into something cohesive thanks to Jill's technique. Now we have a roadmap for Paul to follow as he pulls our visual and audio elements together in the editing process.

Paul is back in the States in time for the SXSW Film Festival. We drop into a panel discussion about documentary editing. Panelist Sandra Adair yanks me to attention with her undeniable filmmaking prowess and sparkling smile. Sandra is editor on almost all of director Richard Linklater's films, including cult classic *Dazed and Confused*, the *Before Sunset* trilogy, *A Scanner Darkly*, *Fast Food Nation*, *School of Rock*, and *Bernie*. Sandra landed an Oscar nomination for the 2014 film *Boyhood*, an epic coming-of-age story Linklater filmed from 2002 to 2013. Sandra's directorial debut, the documentary *The Secret Life of Lance Letscher*, premieres at the festival.

After watching Sandra on the panel and screening her documentary, I want her as our editor for the Guy documentary. I know in my gut she is perfect for the job. I want to learn from Sandra and I want her guidance.

I ask around to see if we know any of the same people. A longtime Americana friend, Erika "Pinktips" Schultz, is my key. Erika introduces Sandra and me via email. Sandra graciously agrees to a meeting and is interested in our project, but there is a problem. Linklater has her sewn up as editor on Where'd You Go, Bernadette, starring Cate Blanchett. Sandra is tied up for the next couple of years. I'm not sure about our film timeline yet and we agree to keep in touch.

In April, the Texas Heritage Songwriters' Association honors me with the Darrell K. Royal Texas Music Legend Award for my work with Texas songwriters. We convene at the Paramount Theater in Austin. The vintage marquee reads, "Texas Heritage Songwriters DKR Homecoming Honoring Guy Clark/Awarding Tamara Saviano." It's a kick to see my name on the marquee next to Guy's.

Paul and I sit in the front row next to Bart and Barbara Knaggs. The night kicks off with an eight-minute video. Radney Foster's recording of "Texas in 1880" plays as a huge photo of me lights up the video screen. My face gets hot and I can feel hives start to bubble up on my chest. The video plays a short interview with me talking about my history with Texas songwriters, conducted a few weeks earlier at the Saxon Pub. Kris's voice pops up next singing, "Freedom's just another word for nothing left to lose," as I talk about my history in the music business. Rodney Crowell, Joe Ely, Terry Allen, Jack Ingram, Radney Foster, and Robert Earl Keen show up on-screen and say nice things about me. I feel like I'm on the old television show *This Is Your Life*. My friends congratulate me from the video screen and I try to hold it together. I weep openly when Kris pops up and says, "Tamara, I love you for all the help you've given me for all these years and you deserve this honor."

Jody Williams from BMI, last year's DKR Award recipient, introduces me and brings me to the stage. Rodney presents me with a shadowboxed award and a state flag flown over the Texas Capitol in my honor. I'm crying so hard I can barely make it through my speech:

"There's been a well-worn path between Texas and Tennessee for many generations. To me, Austin and Nashville are sister cities, united in our collective quest to write great songs and discover great songwriters. Texans Kris Kristofferson, Guy Clark, Rodney Crowell, Steve Earle, Lee

Roy Parnell, Gary Nicholson, Radney Foster, and many others have made their way from Texas to Nashville in search of publishing and recording deals. Yet these Lone Star natives never lose the Texas in them. Even before I visited Texas, the independent spirit, beautiful hearts, and mind-blowing lyrics that live inside these Texas cowboy poets captivated my imagination. The first time I came to Texas more than twenty years ago I saw Jack Ingram play at Stubb's and went to a Flatlanders gathering at Joe Ely's house. From that moment my biggest dream was to work with Texas songwriters, and spend as much time as possible in Austin. And then I met you, the people of Texas, who have welcomed me like one of your own. I fell in love with all of you along the way. A few years back in a sweet little ceremony Terry Booth made me an honorary Texan. I'll take it if you'll have me. Guy would be so proud tonight. I still can't believe he's gone and miss him every day. Many of his friends and family are here tonight, onstage and off, and we haven't been together under one roof since Guy's memorial. Grief shared is grief diminished and tonight I feel only joy and gratitude. Coach Royal once said: 'I want to be remembered as a winning coach, but I also want to be remembered as an honest and ethical coach.' I love that quote. It's how I want to be remembered, too, as an honest and ethical woman, and a friend and advocate of my dear Texas songwriters."

My legs continue to tremble, but I manage to make it back to my seat without falling. Rodney is the producer and emcee of the show, joined by the amazing house band, guitarist Scrappy Jud Newcomb, pianist Johnny Nicholas, bassist Bruce Hughes, drummer John Chipman, and fiddler Brian Beken. The band backs Rodney, Verlon Thompson, Shawn Camp, Terry Allen, Joe Ely, Jack Ingram, Bruce Robison, Lee Roy Parnell, Brennen Leigh, Noel McKay, the Trishas, and Terry McBride as they play Guy Clark songs. I wish Guy were here.

CHAPTER TWENTY-FIVE

SERENDIPITY

Without Getting Killed or Caught: The Life and Music of Guy Clark wins the prestigious Belmont Award from the International Country Music Conference for the best writing on country music for 2016. I'm in a celebratory mood as I follow Joe and Sharon Ely out to Marfa in early July 2017 for Terry and Jo Harvey Allen's fiftieth wedding anniversary party.

We stop at the Auslander in Fredericksburg for lunch. As we get in our cars for the four-hundred-mile drive to Marfa, Joe says, "Let's try to stay together but if we lose each other, make sure you stop and fill up your gas tank every time you see a station." We stop in the only towns along the way on Interstate 10: Sonora, Ozona, and Fort Stockton. At Fort Stockton, we turn south toward Alpine on US Route 67. Tumbleweeds float across the austere and isolated highway. Gorgeous rock formations and mountains rise up to greet us on the road to Alpine under an infinite sky.

Marfa is in the high Chihuahuan Desert in far West Texas between the Davis Mountains and Big Bend National Park. Once known mostly for cowboys and ranching, Marfa lured artist Donald Judd from New York City in the early 1970s. He established the Chinati Foundation, an art center that catapulted Marfa into the national spotlight as an artist mecca.

Giant, the classic Texas magnum opus starring Rock Hudson and Elizabeth Taylor, was filmed in Marfa in 1956. Fifty years later, the Marfa landscape was the setting for critically acclaimed films *There Will Be Blood* and *No Country for Old Men*.

I rent a small house a block from the classic town square, behind the Presidio County Courthouse where attorney Dick DeGuerin recites the Declaration of Independence on the morning of July 4. The historic Hotel Paisano is down the street, and the new Hotel Saint George a few blocks farther. The main street is lined with vintage stores and small bohemian shops selling crystals and handmade jewelry. The Hotel Saint George and its pool house are the rendezvous points for Terry and Jo Harvey's weeklong celebration. Sharon and Joe rent a beautiful old house with a wraparound porch, also a daily gathering point for partygoers.

Sugar Hill Records founder Barry Poss comes in from North Carolina and we wander around together and see the El Cosmico bohemian campground dotted with teepees, yurts, and trailers; Chinati; Marfa Public Radio; the farmers' market; Hotel Paisano; and other sites. Back at the Saint George, there is music every night in the pool house. Verlon Thompson, David Byrne, Charlie Sexton, and many more of Terry and Jo Harvey's musician friends share the stage each night as the rowdy crowd kiss and hug and sing and dance. Dick and Janie DeGuerin host a barbecue and Verlon leads a singalong of Guy Clark songs. This is the first Terry and Jo Harvey anniversary party without Guy, but he is here in spirit. We carry grief and joy together.

Back in Austin, Bart Knaggs suggests we have lunch with Keller Williams real estate mogul Gary Keller to pitch him on investing in the Guy documentary. I walk into Café No Se a few minutes before the appointed time. Gary is early and Bart is late. Gary and I sit awkwardly together as we wait for Bart. We make small talk. I ask him about his family. We talk about the weather. Gary asks me about the music business in Nashville. He says that in Austin, the music businesses are silos and no one makes a real effort to work together. I tell Gary about Leadership Music and he is fascinated. He pulls out pen and paper to take notes. By the time Bart shows up, it's clear we will not be discussing the documentary, but we are on to something bigger for Austin. Gary asks me to write up a proposal to launch a leadership program to build a stronger and more connected creative industry in Austin and Texas as a whole.

Leadership Music is a successful model, but Austin needs a program specific to its unique Texas spirit. I write a proposal, using the bones of the Leadership Music model, to create a dynamic eight-month educational program. ALL ATX Leadership will explore how all segments of the creative industry operate; facilitate collaboration, fellowship, and discussion among industry leaders; expose participants to different points of view and philosophies; and assist established leaders in their roles as decision makers.

Gary hires me as director of the new ALL ATX Leadership program. Our inaugural class of 2018 includes Austin mayor Steve Adler and government stakeholders Brendon Anthony, Frank Rodriguez, Gavin Garcia, and Erica Shamaly; music venue owners Will Bridges and Joe Ables; concert promoters Emmett Beliveau, Amy Corbin, and Kevin Hayden; artists Bruce Robison, Bukka Allen, and David Grissom; Tom Gimbel from Austin City Limits; Lisa Fletcher from Arlyn Studios; John Kunz from Waterloo Records; James Minor from SXSW; Robert Sanchez from Yeti; agent Chad Kudelka; publicist Elaine Garza; Rebecca Reynolds from the Music Venue Trust; and other business allies.

I rent a small apartment at Riverwalk Condos on South Riverside Drive. Built in 1971, the property is known affectionately as "Groover's Paradise." Two- and three-story buildings dot the parklike setting next to Lady Bird Lake. I have a view of the lake from my back patio in an oak tree–canopied courtyard. Downtown Austin is just across the lake, which is looped with ten miles of walking trails.

My first week in Austin, I fall on a slippery metal sidewalk cover and break my right wrist. I can't drive, wash my hair, or write a sentence. With great assistance from my comrade Miranda Bolton, we pull off the first ALL ATX Leadership opening retreat.

A few days later, I fly back to Nashville and pack winter clothes to spend the last week of October in Walpole, New Hampshire, with the Ken Burns and Florentine Films *Country Music* crew and advisers.

Museum curator and historian Brenda Colladay and music industry professor Don Cusic and I travel together from Nashville. Brenda is my guardian angel, helps with my luggage, gets me through security unscathed, and generally takes care of me and my broken wrist. Brenda and I have rooms across from each other on the third floor of a historic inn in Walpole, and she escorts me up and down those stairs more times than I can count. In addition to Brenda and Don, country music historians Mike Streissguth, Alice Randall, Bob Oermann, Bill and Bobbie Malone, Bill Ivey, Del and Carolyn Bryant, Kathy Mattea, Jon Vezner, Paul Kingsbury, and Erin Morris join us as advisers on the film.

Walpole, an idyllic New England town with fewer than four thousand residents, resembles a classic Currier and Ives lithograph of 1800s New England. It's a picture-perfect village of colonial architecture and a landscape dense with sugar maple, balsam, aspen, birch, and elm trees.

Ken built a four-story barn next to his 1820s farmhouse in Walpole. The barn serves as a production headquarters and is our home for the week as we watch and discuss sixteen and a half hours of the *Country Music* rough cut in the large, open screening room.

The first day, Ken tells us he is eager for our notes and wants to make sure every bit of the documentary series is factually correct. However, Ken is clear that he is *not* interested in our feedback on his storytelling method or creative choices. It's a revelation for me as a filmmaker. I intend to be like Ken on the Guy documentary. I will not solicit creative feedback, and I will ignore anyone who throws out those suggestions. This is my film to make the way I want to make it.

Country Music is lovingly written by Dayton Duncan, directed by Ken Burns, and produced by Burns, Duncan, and Julie Dunfey. John Prine's recording of "My Old Kentucky Home," from *Beautiful Dreamer: The Songs of Stephen Foster*, shows up in the first episode. In the second, Mavis Staples sings "Hard Times Come Again No More" from the same album. Episode 6 tells the Kristofferson story and episode 7 features Guy Clark.

My life's work is validated right in front of me on the screen. Watching the series unlocks enormous grief in me. Guy's death. Kris's cognitive decline. My own aging. Looking back on my thirty-year career in music and knowing the road ahead is shorter. It's a lot to untangle. The glory days with Guy and Kris are gone. Songwriting giants. I've worked with the best. I feel enormous gratitude for the honor of living this life among these poets and dreamers.

We watch an episode each morning, break for a catered lunch in Ken's barn, and watch another episode in the afternoon. Each evening, the Florentine crew takes us to a different restaurant and we spend joyous nights in each other's company. On our final night in Walpole, a few of the Florentine crew join us, the advisers, at the Inn. We take over a long communal table in the bar. Fourteen of us sing country songs, loudly, as Bill Ivey strums an acoustic guitar. The customers in the bar don't know what to make of us, a rowdy group of old country music nerds singing "Folsom Prison Blues," "Ring of Fire," and "Coward of the County." Del Bryant leads us singing "Rocky Top," "Times a Wastin'," and "Bye Bye Love," all written by his parents, Boudleaux and Felice Bryant. If I am forced to pick one favorite moment in my thirty-year career, this is it.

The next two years fly by. I live in Austin from September through May and direct the ALL ATX Leadership program. Kris tours nonstop with the Strangers throughout 2018 and 2019.

Most importantly, Paul and I work to finish the Guy Clark documentary. We take Verlon Thompson in the studio to record guitar instrumentals of Guy's songs to use in the film soundtrack. We find a vintage Volkswagen bus and spend two days shooting on the Natchez Trace for the opening scene in the film. We work with archivist Chris Skinker to find historical footage and photographs. And I spend many, many hours with contracts and lawyers to license everything. I learn the hard way that the film producer role is just as much administrative as creative.

The week after Christmas in 2018, Paul and I talk about Stephen King over pancakes and eggs at our favorite diner in Hillsboro Village. I'm a fan of King's book *On Writing*, and it comes up a lot. Talking about King makes me think of the film *Carrie*. Sissy Spacek's face pops into my head and I yell out loud, "Oh my God, Sissy Spacek is Susanna!" My intuition is powerful. I know in my bones that Sissy is the perfect Susanna for our film narration.

Sissy won an Oscar for her impeccable portrayal of Loretta Lynn in *Coal Miner's Daughter*. Before that, Sissy scared the hell out of us as teenage killer Holly in Terrence Malick's *Badlands*. And again as Stephen King's unstable Carrie, a girl with telekinetic powers and a ruthlessly religious dictator mother. She delved deep into her roles in *In the Bedroom*, *The Help*, and the recent film *Old Man and a Gun*, where she plays Robert Redford's love interest. Sissy is matriarch Sally Rayburn in the popular Netflix series *Bloodline* and a lobbyist in the HBO series *Big Love*.

I pick up Sissy's autobiography and read it in one sitting. The connections are magical. Sissy and Susanna grew up one hundred miles apart in East Texas: Sissy in Quitman, Susanna in Atlanta. After Sissy won an Oscar for her portrayal of Loretta Lynn in *Coal Miner's Daughter*, Sissy recorded the album *Hangin' Up My Heart*, produced by our own Rodney Crowell.

Rodney and I meet for breakfast. "You know, there's a Susanna Clark song on Sissy's album," he says. "There's a good chance Sissy and Susanna met while we were recording." Rodney texts Sissy while we are together. Sissy hits Rodney back right away. She is interested but wants to see the film first. We promise to send a rough cut to her manager as soon as its ready. We've got miles to go before we have a rough cut to show Sissy, but I am convinced she is our Susanna and I won't entertain other options.

In January 2019 more than twenty artists and 180,000 fans gather together at Nashville's Bridgestone Arena for a four-hour, star-studded concert dubbed "Willie: Life and Songs of an American Outlaw." Big names in Americana share the stage to play their favorite Willie Nelson songs. Backstage is a noisy family reunion of old friends: artists, managers, agents, publicists, journalists, and hangers-on.

For many of us working the show, the mood at the all-day rehearsal is magnetic. We dash in and out of each other's dressing rooms sharing stories and laughs and meals. Kris shares a room with Chris Stapleton. Lyle Lovett, Vince Gill, Rodney Crowell, Sheryl Crow, and Emmylou Harris are on either side of us. Small circles gather in the hallway and people wander from group to group to greet old friends.

We wander in and out of the hall as the house band, led by music director Don Was, warms up and practices with the artists slated for the show. Kris, Lisa, and I sit in the front row as George Strait and Willie Nelson take the stage together for rehearsal. We are here to witness the king of modern country sing with the icon for the first time ever. The song is the amusing "Sing One with Willie," where George bemoans,

> Now I've heard him with Merle, Waylon and Cash
> Jones and Toby, that man is totally gracious
> But I'm thinking: damn, why not me?

We could even sing it on TV
Just like him and old Julio Iglesias

One after another, artists take the stage, speak of their love for Willie, and channel that love into song.

Chris Stapleton belts out a soulful "Whiskey River." Vince Gill's heavenly voice shines on "Blue Eyes Crying in the Rain." Modern outlaw Margo Price, with a Best New Artist Grammy nomination under her belt, duets with Bobby Bare on "Mammas Don't Let Your Babies Grow Up to Be Cowboys" and joins Steve Earle on "Sister's Comin' Home." Lyle Lovett croons "My Heroes Have Always Been Cowboys." Everyone falls into stillness as Alison Krauss's gorgeous "Angel Flying Too Close to the Ground" echoes through the empty arena.

A few artists sing with Willie. Emmylou Harris and Willie sing Townes Van Zandt's "Pancho & Lefty." Willie grins as he and Sheryl Crow duet on "After the Fire Is Gone." Chris Stapleton and Derek Trucks join Willie for "Always on My Mind." Emotions run high as lifelong friends Kris and Willie join together in "Me and Bobby McGee."

Norah Jones, Asleep at the Wheel, the Avett Brothers, Sturgill Simpson, Jason Isbell, and Jamey Johnson round out the show. Willie and George Strait close the show with "Good Hearted Woman." And every artist in the house joins the rowdy finale of "On the Road Again," "Will the Circle Be Unbroken/I'll Fly Away," and "Roll Me Up and Smoke Me When I Die."

The after-party runs late and by the time we are ready to leave, the production shuttle drivers are long gone. Jamey Johnson graciously offers us a ride. Kris, Lisa, and I pack into his pickup truck. I am exhausted and exhilarated. What a day. What a night. Music and friendship. Friendship and music. This is my life.

Three years after Guy's death, Terry Allen is ready to unveil the sculpture containing Guy's remains. Guy was obsessed with crows in the last few years of his life. Every time a new person came to the house, Guy pulled out photos of Dust Bowl–era crows' nests on display at the Windmill Museum in Lubbock. He loved the beauty of the objects themselves and the ingenuity of the crows that built them. Crows constructed the nests with barbed wire and baling wire and installed them in the nooks and crannies of windmills. Guy tackled the job of turning his fascination into a song. With help from Rodney Crowell, the two songwriters wrote "Caw Caw Blues."

"I think at some point it stopped being about the crows," Terry Allen says. "Guy was facing his own mortality. That registered with me and the image of the crow became poignant. So I decided to make a sculpture of a large crow, about the size of a raven, and incorporate his ashes into the bronze. I opened the sculpture up, too, and put the bulk of the ashes inside the crow. On one hand, it works as an urn, yet you can see Guy's ashes as these gold flecks throughout the sculpture."

Paul and I fly to Santa Fe to film the *Caw Caw Blues* sculpture for the closing of our documentary. The crow is spectacular. Paul sets up a time-lapse shot that makes a perfect ending to the story.

Meanwhile, Sandra Adair emails me and says she is free until September to help us with editing if we need it. Paul has a rough cut, but we need fresh eyes to take us home with a final edit. The SXSW Film Festival submission date is October. Sandra's timing is perfect. Paul and I spend a week in Sandra's cutting room at Detour Films on the Austin Studios lot. We painstakingly go through every inch of the film, writing each scene on colored index cards and posting them up on two bulletin boards. Sandra's eye and intuition on story arc are impeccable.

We need to fill in some blanks. Vince Gill obliges and we get him on camera to talk about the outlaw scene in country music, Nashville as a creative center, and Guy and Susanna as a power couple. Paul jokes that he finally understands we made a film about Susanna that has a lot of Guy in it. Paul, Sandra, and Bart all agree the Luckenbach story is superfluous and want to cut it, but I won't let them.

Sandra turns in a beautiful cut by mid-September. We will make minor changes and it still needs sound editing, color correction, and narration, but the story has a beginning, a middle, and an ending. I love every inch of the film. When we started this project five years ago, I did not know what it would become. Now that it's finished, I know I made the exact film I wanted to make.

Before we send the film to Sissy Spacek, we hire actor Katherine Willis to lay down temporary—or maybe permanent—narration. Best known for her role as Joanne Street in the television series *Friday Night Lights*, Kat is a true pro and does a great job. She knows she is here as Sissy's understudy, but we are thrilled with her work and it gives me confidence to know that if Sissy doesn't come through, we have a great narrator in Kat.

As it turns out, Sissy loves the film. I'm betting Kat's narration is a big part of that. In another twist of fate, Sissy owns a house in my Travis Heights neighborhood in Austin. I walk over to Sissy's on a Friday afternoon in December to go through the script with her. We are scheduled to be in the studio the following two days, and Sissy wants to understand Susanna's character before we record. Sissy is just what one would expect. Her long reddish-gray hair floats around her shoulders. Her face lights up with smiles. Sissy radiates warmth and kindness. We talk about our mutual friends Rodney Crowell and Kris Kristofferson. Sissy says she loves the film but can't remember if she met Guy and Susanna. "They are so colorful. I can't imagine I'd forget either of them." We spend several hours combing through the script as Sissy peppers me with questions about Susanna's motivations and her relationship with Guy and Townes. As we say our goodbyes, I remind Sissy that I have Soundcrafter studio and sound editor Tom Hammond locked in for two days. "That's great," Sissy says. "But I bet we can do it in one day."

I'm nervous about directing an Oscar-winning actor and I invite Alanna Nash to join us in the studio to assist. Back in 1985, Alanna spent time at Sissy's Virginia farm and interviewed her for a major *Esquire* magazine feature titled "Sissy Spacek Grows Up."

Sissy, Alanna, and I huddle together in the Dolby studio while Tom, Paul, and Bart take over the control room. Sissy tells us she started out her career wanting to be a folk singer. Sissy was fifteen when her best friend's cousin came through Quitman and taught Sissy to Travis pick an acoustic guitar. "This girl was a few years older than us," Sissy says. "She spent the weekend in Quitman and played for our church group. I was enamored with her, this beautiful girl and her guitar."

Sissy is right. We finish the narration in one day. Sissy morphs into Susanna Clark and nails it. We take a short break for tacos in the middle of the day and wrap by 6:00 p.m. Now that we have Sissy in the can, I announce our good fortune on Facebook. In the comment thread that follows, Guy Clark's first wife, Susan Spaw, chimes in: "I met Sissy when she was fifteen. My cousin was her best friend. I taught Sissy how to Travis pick on her acoustic guitar."

It's unbelievable (but true) that Guy's first wife taught teenage Sissy Spacek to Travis pick her acoustic guitar. This entire project is nothing less than serendipity.

CHAPTER TWENTY-SIX

DARKNESS AND LIGHT

My fifty-five-year-old brother Steve dies suddenly on January 7, 2020. It is the first hint of the darkness to come. I sit in Steve's hospital room with my family. As we wait for someone to collect my little brother's body, my email blings with the message that *Without Getting Killed or Caught* has been accepted for the SXSW Film Festival in March. In this moment, I just don't care.

A few weeks later, Paul and I are back in Austin at Soundcrafter with Tom Hammond working on the final audio mix for the film. Bart Knaggs texts me from his fishing trip in New Zealand. He fell in a remote river, fractured his femur, and almost bled to death in the backcountry. A helicopter medic saved his life and Bart spent four days in a hospital in New Zealand. But he is alive and on his way home.

Ominous news circulates about a novel respiratory virus outbreak in Wuhan, China. Anecdotally, we hear reports throughout the music community about people getting sick at events. Paul believes a pandemic is on its way and will shut down our film debut at SXSW. I don't believe it.

Joe Ely and I celebrate our birthday together. Our small group decides to stay in at Joe and Sharon's house to watch the Academy Awards. Sharon makes posole and we snuggle in front of the television. A couple of weeks later, the news of the virus is louder and stronger as we gather for the Texas Heritage Songwriters' Homecoming. Blues artist T-Bone Walker, Jerry Jeff Walker, Susanna Clark, and songwriters Jim Collins and Larry Henley are inducted into the Hall of Fame the weekend of February 21. I accept Susanna's award on behalf of her family. Guy and

Susanna's families are in Austin to celebrate Susanna and we take them to Soundcrafter studio to show them the documentary.

Without Getting Killed or Caught is scheduled to premiere at SXSW on March 13. We realize things are serious when, in response to the COVID-19 threat, the City of Austin announces on March 6 that the festival is canceled for the first time in its thirty-four-year history. More than four hundred thousand people attended it in 2019. The decision to pull the plug on an event of this magnitude is alarming. Paul is in Nashville, scheduled to fly to Austin in a few days. We change our plans. I will drive home to Nashville. I waver about my commitment to be at the Austin Music Awards. They are honoring me with the Margaret Moser Award. It feels wrong to ditch the show.

The *Austin Chronicle* writes, "The Margaret Moser Award—recognizing women with impactful roles on Austin Music—goes to Tamara Saviano, who embedded with songwriting legend Guy Clark for years and wrote his definitive history, *Without Getting Killed or Caught*. Saviano remains a lynchpin of the Americana genre, having produced multiple award-winning tribute LPs as well as co-producing Kris Kristofferson's Grammy-nominated *Cedar Creek Sessions* album. She also now serves as director for the All ATX Leadership program, aimed at connecting and cultivating Austin's music industry. Previously, the Moser Award—named for the late *Chronicle* journalist—recognized Rose Reyes, Dianne Scott, [and] Liz Lambert."

I'm anxious about spending a night at the Moody Theater with thousands of people. We don't yet know that wearing masks can help prevent the spread of COVID-19. Hell, at this point, we don't know much. Denise McLemore and Kay Clary accompany me to the awards. We sit nervously at a four-top table in the balcony until it's time for me to meet Jack Ingram backstage. Jack gives a sweet speech and, in a moment of silliness, presents me with the award down on one knee. After Jack's performance, we stand together for a few trade photos and then I grab Denise and Kay and we get the hell out of there. We walk down the street to La Condesa, wondering out loud if it's even a good idea to go inside a quiet restaurant.

The following night is the Texas Film Awards at the Austin Studios. There is no good reason for me to be here, but I kicked in a significant chunk of cash to share a table and it doesn't feel right to bail out. Everyone is skittish throughout the night. After washing our hands at portable sinks at the entrance, we stand awkwardly in small groups during the cocktail party, bumping elbows to greet each other. Huge ceiling fans swirl above us, either clearing the virus out of the room or spreading it around. We have no way of knowing. Janet Pierson, director of film at SXSW, gets up from her seat during dinner to acknowledge those of us in the room who were set to premiere films at the festival. There is no precedent for this. It's clear that all of us are doing the best we can to act normal but it's not working. I can't wait to get out of here.

Bart and I have lunch on the patio at Polvo's the next day, looking over our shoulders for an invisible virus that might kill us. We have no idea what is about to hit us, but the foreshadowing is apocalyptic enough. I'm packed and ready to drive back to Nashville, relieved to not have to fly but anxious about being on the road alone without having a clear understanding of the risks.

By the time I get home, the US government has declared a national state of emergency. The world goes on lockdown as scientists race to create a vaccine. The entire music business is shuttered. Paul and I hunker down at home, grateful that we have a little savings to tide us over. Who knows when we'll be able to work again?

One by one, several friends who attended the Austin Film Awards call to tell me they are sick with COVID-19. Country star Joe Diffie, Fountains of Wayne front man Adam Schlesinger, and folk icon John Prine die from COVID-19 within ten days of each other. Thousands of people are dying each day. In my daily walks around the Vanderbilt University campus, I see bodies loaded into refrigerated trucks.

Between the spring of 2020 and spring of 2021 until we are vaccinated, Sharon and Joe Ely, Terry and Jo Harvey Allen, Connie Nelson, Denise McLemore, and I meet every Sunday night on Zoom. It's the one thing we have to look forward to each week. Seeing their faces and talking to my friends for a couple of hours brings me comfort.

"Those Zoom meetings kept me hopeful," Connie says. "Everything looked so dark. I was thinking, Is this going to be how our life ends? I think we gave each other strength and purpose in those weekly meetings. By God, we were going to make it through this together and laugh while doing it."

Kris decides to retire in 2020. He's eighty-four and in cognitive decline. It's time. The end of an era. Two decades of adventures with Kris and Lisa. Kris's son Johnny takes over the family business. I have no doubt Johnny and his team will do great things. But my heart is with the old guard and it's time to leave the party. I know with every fiber of my being that I do not want to do this without Kris and Lisa. It's been a wild ride and I loved every single moment of it. Now I move on with clear eyes and a full heart into whatever is next. Kris, Lisa, and I will remain friends for the rest of our lives, so I may be losing the work but not the love.

I have no idea what to do with the Guy documentary and it's not a priority. Throughout 2020, the only things that matter are my husband, my family, and my friends.

The first blush of 2021 is hopeful. The FDA authorizes vaccines for COVID-19. By spring, everyone who wants a vaccine will have one. My sixtieth birthday is in February, and SXSW invites us to premiere *Without Getting Killed or Caught* at their virtual festival in March. We accept.

Meanwhile, Bart Knaggs and I have several disappointing conversations with film distributors. There is limited access to distribution channels. Distributors take the majority share of the revenue and charge enormous fees, which makes it impossible to recoup our investment. Traditional film distribution has been disrupted by streaming services, and those services aren't willing to shell out for niche independent films. The model is broken. But we have what many filmmakers do not—a direct relationship with our target audience, Guy Clark fans. We decide to release the film ourselves.

Lyle Lovett introduces me to Brian Whitman. Brian and his team at Seer developed a digital distribution system, which allows us to sell tickets and show the film from our website. First, we set up six virtual event screenings in April. Fans buy a ticket and log in at the designated time to see artist interviews and special content followed by a screening of the documentary. In May, we partner with the Austin Film Society for special outdoor screenings at the Contemporary Austin's Laguna Gloria sculpture garden.

We hire an independent theater booker, Michael Tuckman, and he books the film into independent theater and art houses around the country. Michelle Conceison and Molly Nagel at Mmgt help with marketing and project management. I bring in my former intern Maria Drummond Ivey to handle public relations for music media and film publicist Staci Griesbach to pitch film media outlets.

Our theatrical run opens at the Austin Film Society's AFS Cinema the weekend of July 23. It's a rousing success and they hold the film over for another week. The Angelika Theater in Dallas and Plano screen at the end of July. We open in Nashville on August 6 at our neighborhood theater, the Belcourt, where we have been seeing great films for two decades. The delta and omicron virus variants dampen the rest of our theatrical screenings, but we end up slightly in the black and the great press drives demand to see the film. With our partners at Seer, we launch the film on demand worldwide on November 6 for Guy's eightieth birthday.

The music business is far from back to normal when Robert Earl Keen and his colleague Cindy Howell call me in January 2022 to ask me to help with his final tour. Robert announced the tour with a video message on his website: "You've heard people say 'time flies.' It's a cliché. Funny thing about clichés and what makes them ubiquitous, is they ring true.... Fortunately, I have been blessed with a lifetime of brilliant, talented, colorful, electric and magical folks throughout my life. This chorus of joy, this parade of passion, this bulrush of creativity, this colony of kindness and generosity are foremost in my thoughts today.... It's with a mysterious concoction of joy and sadness that I want to tell you as of September 4, 2022, I will no longer tour.... I'm not sick or experiencing any existential crisis. I feel that making a decision and quitting the road while I still love it, is the way I want to leave it."

Since the pandemic, I also feel a call to do something new. Young people thrive in the music business. At my age, it feels like a lot of "been there and done that." What was exciting twenty years ago is now blasé. I accept Robert's invitation to work his final concert tour. Secretly, I think of it as my last hurrah in the music business, too. It's a chance to revisit old haunts one last time, clear out what does not serve me anymore, and make room for new creative ideas and adventures.

Robert and his band (Bill Whitbeck on bass, Brian Beken on fiddle and guitar, and Tom Van Schaik on drums) play more than ninety shows in six months for the epic final journey. Tour manager Brett Brock, a godsend to all of us, keeps it all together despite Murphy's law cropping up again and again: "Anything that can go wrong will go wrong, and at the worst possible time."

Robert's back goes out right before he tapes Austin City Limits in April, forcing him to perform sitting in a chair for most of the tour. Tom Van Schaik breaks his elbow, resets his drum kit, and plays through the pain. In July, set to play a two-night stand at Irving Plaza in New York City, Robert wakes up to find half his face paralyzed by Bell's palsy. The bus driver's mother dies. Brian Beken suffers a herniated disc. In August, after a gig at the House of Blues in New Orleans, the band bus catches fire on the way back to Texas.

It's enough to make anyone throw in the towel, but Robert is in high spirits for the final stretch of his I'm Coming Home tour at John T. Floore's Country Store over Labor Day weekend. Floore's, one of Robert's favorite venues, is located in Helotes about fifteen miles outside San Antonio. Hand-painted signs outside the café advertise "world's best homemade tamales sausage and bread," "Willie Nelson every Sat. nite," and "80 years in Helotes, there must be a reason." Inside, seafoam-green painted cinder-block walls surround a cement floor dotted with picnic tables and worn wooden four-tops and chairs. Strings of tiny white lights crisscross the ceiling, where cowboy hats and boots dangle from the beams.

Out in the backyard, bartenders tap thousands of draft beers at makeshift bars. On the stage, Lloyd Maines joins the band on pedal steel. Several thousand giddy fans spread across the concrete plaza and bop and dance and sing along to their favorite Robert Earl Keen songs. Throughout the weekend, special musical guests, including Kevin Galloway, James McMurtry, Eric Church, David Beck's Tejano Weekend, and Cody Canada and the Departed, join Robert in his farewell party.

Champion rodeo cowboy Phil Lyne inspired Robert's path to retirement, an example of someone going out on top. "He is here tonight to stand by my side, so you wonderful people could see this amazing man and know that heroes are real," Robert says as he introduces Lyne to a roaring crowd.

The final adieu: Robert Earl Keen lands on the December cover of *Texas Monthly*. We spend a gorgeous day at Robert's ranch with the *Texas Monthly* crew and photographer Dan Winter. Winter sets up multiple shots of Robert at the Snake Barn studio, in his Scriptorium writing cabin, and on a hillside with a breathtaking view of the Hill Country.

The end of 2022 brings me the kind of music business closure I hoped for. I spent the year saying goodbye to old friends and old haunts. Maybe I will continue in the business and maybe I won't, but if I leave the party now there are no regrets. I've lived every dream.

I take a six-month sabbatical in 2023 and rattle around Europe for six weeks. My favorite moment is the Elton John concert in Manchester, England, part of Elton's Farewell Yellow Brick Road tour. Being an Elton fanatic, I've been to many Elton shows over the years. But this is different. Elton has been with me for more than fifty years. My love affair with his music started the first time I heard "Your Song" in 1970. My junior high best friend Julie and I shared our Elton obsession.

Tonight is goodbye. The minute Elton comes out and takes a seat at his piano, I burst into tears. The emotion surprises me. I cannot stop crying. Tears of joy, yes, but also grief for my own youth and how quickly the time has passed. I was nine when I discovered Elton. His music and personality have been a mainstay for most of my life. Now I'm sixty-two. Elton is seventy-six. He deserves a beautiful retirement. And I'll always have his music. But it is difficult to say goodbye. Being here, in Elton's home country, with the beautiful people of Manchester, is a memory I will cherish forever. The people around me ask if I am okay, this old American woman bawling at an Elton John concert. The woman sitting in front of us turns around and gives Paul the side-eye. "Are you okay?" I reassure her that my husband is not the one making me cry. "I'm just so happy to be here," I say. The young man next to me pats my shoulder throughout the show. "I hope I'm not making you uncomfortable," I say. "No, just the opposite," he replies kindly. "Your emotion and love for Elton makes tonight even more special."

I take a Beatles tour in Liverpool, attend a folk music show at Whelen's Irish Pub in Dublin, listen to a symphony at the Jardin du Luxembourg in Paris, and sit for an hour hearing a lonely fiddle in London's Hyde Park. For the first time in thirty years, I wander at a leisurely pace and listen to music that has nothing to do with my work. Back in the States, I meet my husband at a Springsteen show at Wrigley Park in Chicago, my old stomping grounds. While Paul and the crew run around getting ready for the show, I walk to a pub to meet an old high school classmate. I'm removed from the day-to-day excitement of the music business. And I like it.

Craig Havighurst is my date for the Country Music Hall of Fame Medallion Ceremony on October 22. The class of 2023, Tanya Tucker, Patty Loveless, and songwriter Bob McDill, are formally inducted into the hallowed Country Music Hall of Fame today. The Medallion Ceremony is an annual family reunion. We stand in line to get in the theater and chat with Bonnie Garner and Joanne Gardner. Chuck Mead and Brenda Colladay sit in front of us. Barry Mazor and Nina Melechen are to my left. Jim Lauderdale is in the front row with Patty Loveless. Many friends are scattered throughout the audience. Lisa Kristofferson and I stand in the aisle and hug for the longest time before the Hall of Fame members, wearing their medallions, march in together and take their seats right before the ceremony starts. Vince Gill and Ricky Skaggs hold hands with Kris. My heart swells.

Patty's longtime bandmate Deanie Richardson performs with her bluegrass trio Sister Sadie to sing Patty's "Sounds of Loneliness." Rock star Bob Seger surprises Patty—and all of us—when he takes the stage to sing Patty's 1996 hit "She Drew a Broken Heart." Patty's good friend and fellow Hall of Famer Vince Gill sings "Lonely Too Long" and then brings Patty into the Hall of Fame fold, describing her as "the little sister I'd always wanted to sing with."

It's a full-circle moment as Brandi Carlile honors Tanya Tucker. Brandi and Shooter Jennings coproduced Tanya's last two records, the 2019 Grammy-winning *While I'm Livin'* and *Sweet Western Sound*, released in June 2023. As part of the show, original outlaw Jessi Colter teams up with modern outlaw Margo Price to sing Tanya's hit "It's a Little Too Late."

The four women onstage in front of me symbolize different pieces of my life in Americana music.

Tanya, the madcap escort of many great adventures during my 1990s music journalism days.

Brandi, the upstart who presented us with the Americana Album of the Year award in 2012 for *This One's For Him: A Tribute to Guy Clark*.

Jessi, who mesmerized me with "Storms Never Last" in the 1970s and shares a friendship with the Kristoffersons.

Margo, who sang the hell out of "Me and Bobby McGee" with Kris at the Newport Folk Festival seven years ago.

I feel it deeply, this passing of the torch. Tanya to Brandi. Jessi to Margo. The transformation to a new generation of Americana disciples melting into an unbroken circle of poets and dreamers.

Margo produced Jessi's new record, *Edge of Forever*. Although I love all of Jessi's album, my favorite song is "Angel in the Fire," written for and dedicated to our mutual friend Lisa Kristofferson.

"Lisa's been a gift in my life from the first day I met her," Jessi says. "Kris brought her to where we were recording for *The Johnny Cash Show* near the Alps. We were all in the hotel, Johnny and June, me and Waylon, Connie and Willie, and Kris walks in with Lisa. When I looked over and saw her face and saw her eyes, I witnessed what she was feeling and felt connected to her immediately. Years later, when Kris and Lisa made the decision to spend more time in Maui, I said to Lisa, 'Gosh, that is so far away.' And Lisa said, 'You know, Jessi, there's no distance in friendship.' We have stayed very close, even though we're miles and miles apart. Lisa makes the effort to keep our friendship alive. And if she's anywhere in the area, she calls me to get together. As you know, and all of Lisa's friends know, she's got such a wonderful way about her. No matter the hardship or heartbreak, Lisa keeps her feet on the ground. She rolls with the punches. And she has a generous, generous heart."

In the music video for "Angel in the Fire," Jessi sits at a grand piano and plays the opening notes as the message, "For all my girlfriends near and far...," pops up on the screen. Pictures of Lisa Kristofferson and Jessi's other friends, including Connie Nelson, fade in and out around her. Jessi and I share a friendship with Lisa and Connie. And I think of my close girlfriends. I have a deep, creative tribe of badass women who surround me with love every day. Poets and dreamers, all of us.

"Jessi's been a good friend to me," Margo Price says. "She gives me advice and prays for me, and acts as a mother figure in a lot of ways, too. I was at her house one day and she showed me all these recent songs she'd written. They were so good. I said, 'These songs are incredible. You've got to make a record. Me and my band would love to back you up and I would love to produce it.' I don't even know what possessed me to even suggest that, but I wanted to make sure that the album got made. The title song, 'Standing on the Edge of Forever,' is so wise and smartly written and that's what we named the album. Jessi has this style of playing piano that is so uniquely her own. Jessi sounds best when she's singing and playing at the same time. She's done that her whole life, singing live and playing live. So pretty much everything you hear on the record is Jessi on piano, her live vocal, and the band playing with her. It absolutely was a joy to work with Jessi."

I ask Margo how she feels about being part of the Americana community.

"I feel at home here," Margo says. "The people and music aren't contrived and the focus is the song. There is an authenticity to the lyrics and stories. This genre grew from open-minded artists being kicked to the outskirts and I love what has sprung out of that. Yeah, I feel very much at home here."

EPILOGUE

Kris Kristofferson died on September 28, 2024.
I spent the better part of twenty years with Kris. You know when you're in the moment and you just don't think about the significance of your day-to-day life? That's how I felt most of the time. I bounced back and forth between Kris and Guy Clark while also handling other clients.

Honestly, Kris was my anchor and I worked everything else in around him. Guy didn't mind. My other clients knew the score. Sometimes, when I couldn't be with Guy somewhere because it conflicted with Kris's schedule, Guy joked about it: "Tell Kris I'm still waiting for him to come over and write with me." Kris sometimes introduced me to people by saying, "This is Tamara. Guy Clark is her favorite songwriter." I'd just roll my eyes at each of them and laugh.

People have asked me how I lasted with these two for so many years. It's simple. They trusted me because I always did the right thing. I was honest with them. Sometimes I had to tell them things they did not want to hear. I did it with love, but I did it. I never bullshitted either one of them. There are a lot of bullshitters in the music business. Probably in every business. But artists are around a lot of people who fall all over them and stroke their egos. The last thing either of these men wanted was an entourage or people telling them how great they were.

I pride myself on being a professional and in the beginning did not intend to be personal friends with either of them. But when you work that closely together, and spend weeks and months on the road in close quarters, it just happens organically. I loved them. If I had met either Kris or Guy under other circumstances, we still would have been friends. Sometimes there's just a spiritual connection where you know in your soul these are your people.

Guy's physical health started failing around the same time Kris's memory began to go. Guy was sharp but his body was frail. Kris's body was strong, but he was cognitively challenged. I leaned in with both of them. I cleared my roster so I could focus on the two of them.

Guy died in May 2016. A month later, Kris forgot my name for the first time. But he still lit up when he saw me. And always said, "I love you." When the pandemic hit, Kris retired. It was time. His memory had been failing for years, and being locked up at home during a worldwide pandemic stole his chances to live life in the moment on the road and onstage.

Kris's wife, Lisa, and son Jody brought Kris to our home for a "goodbye" visit in October 2023. I knew it was the last time I'd see him. I sat with Kris, caressed his hand, and whispered my gratitude and love. Kris was largely nonverbal by then. We took pictures before they left. I asked Kris if I could hug him goodbye. He put his hands on my cheeks, kissed me on the lips, pulled back, and said one word: "Love."

Lisa burst into tears. I quickly followed. Paul and Jody helped Kris to the car while Lisa and I stood on my front porch hugging each other and crying. The day was both agonizing and beautiful.

And now I go forward with a full heart into whatever is next. Kris will always be with me. As my friends in Luckenbach, Texas, displayed on their sign after Kris's death, "Kris Kristofferson 1936–2024. He was somebody to everybody." Godspeed, my sweet friend.

SOURCES

Author's Note

Poets and Dreamers is a work of nonfiction featuring real people and real events. While it is a memoir, it is the work of a seasoned reporter, me, and involved substantial research and interviews. I talked to dozens of friends and colleagues and collected hundreds of historical documents related to the rise of Americana music. I reviewed my own journals, and the bulk of the stories from my point of view came directly from those diaries.

I have made every effort to verify the sequence of events in this book. While it is impossible to tell the whole story of Americana music, I tried to touch on as many stories as possible that were important to me during thirty years in the business. I cross-referenced my diaries and personal archives with other available data and stories from my friends and colleagues. If accounts of events deviated significantly from person to person, I either chose to leave them out or presented those conflicts within the text.

The dialogue and conversations are verbatim from my journals or personal interviews, or used with credit from other journalism sources. I worked to represent the tone of the conversation and personalities of the people involved using my prior knowledge and research from others who were there. Personal history is tricky for a researcher and memoirist. Memories of all parties are distorted by personality, experiences, and emotions. I collected many perspectives, yet there will undoubtedly be disagreements about what I've written. Walking the line between a personal story and journalistic work can be difficult, but I spent many hours researching and reporting for due diligence while also telling my own personal history of living and working in the Americana music community.

INTERVIEWS AND PERSONAL CONVERSATIONS

Ables, Joe
Adair, Sandra
Alden, Grant
Allen, Jo Harvey
Allen, Terry
Barnes, Deborah
Batcha, Jean
Beckham, Bob
Black, Louis
Blackstock, Peter
Bleetstein, Rob
Bridges, Jeff
Burns, Jeff
Camp, Shawn
Campbell, Stacy Dean
Carter, Carlene
Carter Cash, June
Case, Keith
Cash, Johnny
Cash, Rosanne
Clark, Guy
Clark, Susanna
Clary, Kay
Colladay, Brenda
Colter, Jessi
Conner, Kevin
Cooper, Peter
Corbett, John
Cowan, John

Crow, Sheryl
Crowe, Russell
Crowell, Rodney
Delevante, Bob
Delevante, Mike
Dickinson, Luther
Duncan, Dayton
Earle, Steve
Ely, Joe
Ely, Sharon
Fishell, Steve
Flores, Rosie
Foster, Fred
Foster, Radney
Garner, Bonnie
Gill, Vince
Grady, John
Grimson, Jon
Gunderman, Jen
Haggard, Merle
Hanna, Jeff
Havighurst, Craig
Henley, Don
Hoelzle, Cyndi
Holliday, Taylor
Howard, Rebecca
Ingram, Jack
Jenkins, Lisa
Keen, Robert Earl
Knaggs, Bart
Kristofferson, Kris
Kristofferson, Lisa
Leigh, Brennen
Lewis, Luke
Lomax, John, III

Lord, Dennis
Lovett, Lyle
Macias, David
Maines, Lloyd
Malo, Raul
Marsh, Dave
May, J. D.
McCall, Michael
McConaughey, Matthew
McGuire, Jim
McKay, Noel
McLemore, Denise
Mead, Chuck
Monroe, Ashley
Morrow, Shilah
Mosher, Annie
Moss, Al
Nash, Alanna
Nelson, Connie
Nelson, Willie
Ongaro, Brian
Parnell, Lee Roy
Paul, Brad
Payne, Waylon
Peters, Gretchen
Poss, Barry
Price, Margo
Road, Abbey
Robison, Bruce
Ruditys, Sandra
Scott, Jessie
Secours, Molly
Spacek, Sissy
Stamberger, Wendy
Stanton, Harry Dean

Stewart, Jon Randall
Stiff, Denise
Strong, Danna
Stuart, Marty
Tepper, Jeremy
Thompson, Verlon
Thornton, Billy Bob
Tillis, Mel
Urban, Keith
Walker, Jerry Jeff
Welch, Kevin
White, Jill
White, Lari
Whitfield, Paul
Williams, Jody

ARCHIVES

AllMusic
Americana Music Association (AMA)
American Society of Composers, Authors, and Publishers (ASCAP)
Austin City Limits (ACL)
Broadcast Music, Inc. (BMI)
Cedar Creek Studios
Center for Creative Leadership
Center for Texas Music History
Country Music Hall of Fame
Country Music Television (CMT)
Country Radio Seminar—Nashville Incorrect panel
Florentine Films Country Music series
Folk Alliance
Grand Ole Opry
Great American Country (GAC)
History Channel
Internet Movie Database (IMDb)
Kickstarter

The Late Show with David Letterman
Leadership Music
Luckenbach, Texas
Music Road Records
Nashville Songwriters Association International
Nashville Songwriters Hall of Fame
National Public Radio (NPR)
New West Records
Public Broadcasting System (PBS)
Red Beet Records
Sirius XM Satellite Radio
Society of European Stage Authors and Composers (SESAC)
South by Southwest (SXSW)
Spotify
Sugar Hill Records
Sundance Broadcasting
Tamara Saviano journals
Texas Heritage Songwriters' Association
The Tonight Show with Jay Leno
Wittliff Collections
YouTube

PERIODICALS

Austin American Statesman
Austin Chronicle
Billboard
Country Music
Country Weekly
Gavin Report
Los Angeles Times
Milwaukee Journal
Nashville Scene
New York Times
No Depression
Pollstar

Tennessean
Texas Monthly
Wall Street Journal

Books

Emerson, Ken. *Doo-Dah! Stephen Foster and the Rise of American Popular Culture.* New York: Simon & Schuster, 1997.

Kingsbury, Paul, and Alanna Nash. *Will the Circle Be Unbroken: Country Music in America.* New York: DK, 2004.

Malone, Bill. *Country Music, U.S.A.* Austin: University of Texas Press, 1968.

Price, Margo. *Maybe We'll Make It: A Memoir.* Austin: University of Texas Press, 2022.

Ray, Paul H., and Anderson, Sherry Ruth. *The Cultural Creatives: How 50 Million People Are Changing the World.* New York: Crown, 2001.

Saviano, Tamara. *The Most Beautiful Girl: A True Story of a Dad, a Daughter, and the Healing Power of Music.* Nashville: American Roots, 2014.

———. *Without Getting Killed or Caught: The Life and Music of Guy Clark.* College Station: Texas A&M University Press, 2016.

Streissguth, Michael. *Outlaw: Waylon, Willie, Kris, and the Renegades of Nashville.* New York: HarperCollins/IT Books, 2013.

Whitburn, Joel. *Joel Whitburn's Top Country Singles, 1944–2017.* Menomonee Falls, WI: Record Research, 2018.

INDEX

Ables, Joe, 144–45, 262
Academy of Country Music Awards, 79
Adair, Sandra, 257–58, 267
Ahern, Brian, 12, 13, 66
Alden, Grant, 54, 56, 57, 69, 73, 163
Alexander, Jessi, 122, 219, 223, 254
ALL ATX Leadership program, 164, 261–62, 264, 271
Allen, Bukka, 247, 262
Allen, Jo Harvey: career, 231, 234; family, 233, 234, 256; fiftieth wedding anniversary party, 260–61; friends of, 229; at Guy Clark's funeral, 247; personality of, 233; shows, 232, 233; writings, 234–35; Zoom meetings, 272
Allen, Terry: artistic output, 232–33; education, 233; family, 233, 234; fiftieth wedding anniversary party, 260–61; friends, 229, 242; at Guy Clark's funeral, 247; *Old Friends Reunion* film, 235; sculptures by, 247, 256, 266–67; show and events, 251–52, 254–55, 256–57, 258, 259; songs and albums, 94, 186, 234; tribute to Guy Clark, 186, 199; Zoom meetings, 272
alternative country, 37, 43, 54, 213

AMD Live! Soundtrack Award, 145
Americana Honors and Awards, 8, 12, 16, 122, 133–35, 147–49, 158–59, 179–80, 214–16
Americana music: *Billboard* chart, 212–13; filmography, 65–66, 75–77; *Gavin Report*'s chart, 10, 11, 41, 42, 43, 69, 71, 73, 74; genre, 43–44, 74, 148; icons, 11, 12–19, 28–29, 42, 140; radio broadcasts, 35–38, 40–43, 67–68, 73–74
Americana Music Association (AMA), 10, 11, 71, 73–74, 114, 118, 122, 140, 163
American Roots Publishing: board of directors, 89, 115, 164; closing of, 154; establishment of, 17, 110, 126, 127; publishing projects, 124, 137, 141, 152, 218
American Society of Composers, Authors, and Publishers (ASCAP), 69, 140, 178, 199, 219
Anderson, Al, 158, 191, 206
Anderson, Bill, 22, 84
Arista Records, 51, 52
Armbruster, Claire, 159, 209
Asleep at the Wheel (musical group), 241, 266
Atkins, Chet, 1, 84
Atkinson, Brian, 197, 204, 223

Atlantic Records, 16, 45
Austin, TX: Film Society, 145, 272, 274; music culture in, 2, 231, 271
Austin City Limits Music Festival (ACL), 228, 240-42, 262, 275
Austin Studios, 145, 271
Avett Brothers (folk rock band), 158, 180, 255-56, 266

Baez, Joan, 40, 200-201
Bakersfield Sound, 2, 6, 7, 32
Ball, David, 32, 50, 124, 126, 163
Bare, Bobby, 12, 252, 266
Barnes, Deborah, 68-69, 84
Barr, Cliff, 61, 63-64, 65
Beatles (rock band), 57, 164, 216, 250, 277
Beautiful Dreamer: The Songs of Stephen Foster (tribute album), 124, 126, 127-28, 129, 130, 149, 263
Beck, David, 7, 275
Beckham, Bob, 170, 176
Beecher, Lavonne, 26, 46, 47
Beken, Brian, 259, 275
Benson, Ray, 163, 193, 196
Berg, Matraca, 65, 184, 255
Billboard (magazine), 10, 30, 58, 61
Black, Clint, 6, 27, 84
Blackbird Studio, 171-72, 174
Black Eyed Peas (hip hop trio), 128
Blackstock, Peter, 54, 55, 56-57, 163
Blake, Norman, 76, 127
Blake, William, 3, 156
Bleetstein, Rob, 38, 41-43, 57, 64, 73, 114
Block, Billy, 42, 49, 50, 73
bluegrass music: artists, 4, 12, 40, 75-76, 133, 152, 161, 185, 277; awards, 79; bands, 28, 120; festivals, 198, 252; Nashville's club, 118, 150; records labels, 44
BMI Awards, 140, 150, 170-71, 176, 205, 258
Bogguss, Suzy, 32, 59, 114, 184-85, 191

Bottle Rockets (rock band), 45, 54, 114
Bowles, Woody, 46, 57
BR549 (rock band), 50, 51, 52, 86, 124
Bridges, Jeff, 180, 228-29
Bronco Roads show, 209, 210-11
Brooks, Garth, 6, 27, 28, 59, 62-63, 73, 121, 205
Brown, Tony, 29, 65, 219
Browne, Jackson, 23, 216, 217
Bruton, Stephen, 54, 144, 145, 159, 160, 167, 186
Bryant, Boudleaux, 5, 104, 264
Bryant, Felice, 5, 264
Bunetta, Al, 17, 84-85, 98-99, 112, 124
Burnett, Joseph Henry "T Bone," 15-16, 75-76, 80, 161
Burnette, Billy, 152, 154
Burns, Ken, 128, 227, 262, 263
Burton, James, 13, 121
Bush, Sam, 28, 162, 252

Cakewalk, Charanga, 130
Callari, Frank, 48, 157-58, 159
Camp, Shawn: albums, 118, 120-21, 141, 152, 183-84, 207; concerts and events, 120-22, 134, 150, 160, 176, 178, 180, 186, 214-15, 222, 223, 252, 255, 259; friends, 37, 189, 191; at Guy Clark's funeral, 247; songs, 36, 39, 250; television and radio interviews, 122; tribute to Guy Clark, 171, 172, 175, 196, 199; World Famous Headliners photo shoot, 206
Campbell, Glen, 1, 67
Campbell, Stacy Dean, 54, 118, 131, 141, 144, 209-11, 212-13
Campbell, Tim, 61, 62
Canada, Cody, 164, 275
Capitol Records Nashville, 28, 32, 57, 58-60, 70, 86, 128, 219
Carlile, Brandi, 214-15, 277-78
Carll, Hayes, 180, 186, 193

Carpenter, Mary Chapin, 6, 27, 69
Carter, Deana, 59, 69
Carter Cash, June, 7, 16–17, 69
Carter Family (folk music group), 21, 76, 159
Case, Keith, 165, 199, 209, 226
Cash, Johnny: albums, 10, 29, 150; awards, 8, 9–10, 112; career of, 42, 248; concerts and events, 8–10, 16–17, 116; death and funeral of, 7, 17, 110–11; iconic photos of, 86; Kris Kristofferson and, 3, 102, 103, 105–6, 107, 251; museum dedicated to, 17; publicity of, 54, 69, 74; social activism of, 3; songs of, 4, 7, 10, 17, 38; tributes to, 156
Cash, Rosanne: albums, 130, 179; concerts and events, 29, 149, 171; honors and awards, 179; Johnny Cash and, 111–12; personality, 154–55; publicity, 69; songs, 5–6, 7, 12, 36, 65, 74, 143
Cashman, Jean, 30, 31
Catino, Bill, 57, 58, 59, 60
CBS (Columbia Broadcasting System), 77, 120, 219
Cedar Creek Sessions, The (album), 228, 250, 255, 271, 291
Cedar Creek Studios, 93, 203
Chapman, Beth Nielsen, 39, 91, 131, 152
Chapman, Marshall, 130, 184, 255
Charles, Ray, 77, 129
Cherry Bombs (band), 29, 65
Clark, Guy: albums, 18, 29, 140–41, 146, 150–51, 225; biography of, 164, 165–66, 171, 207–9, 242–43, 253–55, 270, 271, 273; concerts and events, 15, 88, 133–34, 150, 157, 158, 159, 160, 204, 214–15, 218, 252; death and funeral of, 245–47, 248, 261; documentary about, 226, 227, 229, 235, 236–37,

244, 263; friends and collaborators of, 5–6, 14, 68, 120, 136, 163, 207, 219, 221, 247, 255, 280; habits of, 18–19, 83; health issues, 173, 175, 188, 192, 198, 209, 223, 225–26, 236, 241–42, 243–44, 245, 281; honors and awards, 123, 133, 146–47, 226; house of, 82–83, 167; iconic photos of, 86; influence of, 211, 244; interviews with, 166–67; life in Nashville, 5; manager of, 165; marriage of, 267, 268–69; music style of, 12, 27; *Old Friends Reunion* film, 235; Paramount show, 186–87; personality of, 83; public relations campaigns for, 167; publishing rights, 236, 244; radio shows, 42; songs of, 6, 44, 65, 166, 258, 259, 267; tributes to, 171, 172–76, 190–92, 196–201, 216, 220, 224, 253–54, 266–67, 278; trip to Rockport, 195–96
Clark, Susanna: death of, 209; friends of, 14, 186, 255; honors and awards, 270–71; marriage of, 5, 267, 268; relationships with Guy, 192, 207–9, 214, 243, 244; songs of, 253, 265
Clark, Terri, 46, 57
Clary, Kay, 12, 48, 162, 205, 215, 271
Clement, Jack "Cowboy," 102, 103, 120, 146, 156, 184, 203, 221, 222
Cody, Bill, 85, 188
Coen, Ethan, 75, 77, 78
Coen, Joel, 75, 77, 78
Colladay, Brenda, 262–63, 277
Colter, Jessi, 2, 23, 25, 38, 130, 170, 277–79
Columbia Records, 2, 3, 10, 13, 86, 99, 103, 150
Colvin, Shawn, 40, 56, 192, 199, 217
Cooder, Ry, 158, 224
Cooper, Peter, 136, 148, 193, 220
Corbett, John, 217–19, 220, 225

cosmic cowboy music, 37, 38
Costello, Elvis, 75, 149
country music: festivals, 33, 146; genre of, 6–7, 27, 67, 74; icons of, 1–3; politics and, 90–91, 96–97; radio shows, 27–28, 30, 32–33, 41–43
Country Music (magazine), 18, 69–70, 84, 85, 165
Country Music (TV documentary), 262, 263–64
Country Music Association Awards, 4, 79, 115, 137, 219
Country Music Hall of Fame: artist in residence program, 146, 156; events at, 71, 140, 146–47, 171, 172, 183, 205; inductees, 120, 123, 132, 157
Country Music Television (CMT), 28, 79, 88, 120, 123, 154, 155, 250
country rock, 29, 37, 42, 134
Country Weekly (magazine), 60–61, 62, 63, 65, 69, 82, 83–84
Cowan, John, 28
Craven, Jay, 131–32
Crow, Sheryl, 22, 94, 162, 228, 265
Crowe, Russell, 108, 130
Crowell, Rodney: albums, 34–35, 36, 220, 265; awards, 149, 159, 214; band of, 29, 65, 206; career of, 13–15, 74; concerts and events, 88, 130, 150, 184–85, 188, 222, 252, 253, 257, 258, 259; friends of, 14–15, 29, 91, 112, 160, 207, 223, 247, 268; at Guy Clark's funeral, 247; at Johnny Cash funeral, 111; music style of, 12; *Old Friends Reunion* film, 235; prison time, 35; songs of, 5, 6, 13, 14, 15, 35–36, 267; tribute to Guy Clark, 171–72, 175, 199; tribute to Vince Gill, 158
Cyrus, Billy Ray, 77, 84, 88

Daniels, Charlie, 90–91, 96, 98
Danles, Glen, 239, 240
Davis, Mac, 22, 231
Dead Reckoning Records, 44, 71–72, 73
Dean, Billy, 33, 58–59
DeGuerin, Dick, 260, 261
Delevante, Bob, 52, 53
Delevante, Mike, 52, 54
Delevantes (band), 29, 51, 52, 53–54
Dement, Iris, 27, 29, 39, 42, 43
Denberg, Jody, 196, 199
Denn, Val, 163, 192, 193
Derailers (band), 44, 70, 86
DeVito, Hank, 13, 29
Dickinson, Cody, 248, 249
Dickinson, Luther, 224, 248–49
disco music, 22, 24, 185
Dixie Chicks (band), 69, 92–97, 115, 148, 203
Dobson, Richard, 13, 254
Douglas, Jerry, 12, 40
Drummond, Maria, 192–93, 223
Dualtone Music Group, 8, 140–41
DuBois, Tim, 52, 199
Ducas, George, 32, 59
Duncan, Dayton, 227, 263
Duncan, Stuart, 161, 224
Dunn, Ronnie, 121, 205
Dylan, Bob: albums, 3, 4, 16, 22, 57; career of, 40, 76, 107, 129; on Johnny Cash, 156; *Philosophy of Modern Song*, 128; songs, 2, 3, 249

Eagles (rock band), 23, 67, 171, 216, 217
Eakes, Bobbie, 88, 89
Earle, Steve: albums, 11, 54, 203; awards, 127; concerts and events, 51, 88, 133, 162, 198, 215, 252, 258, 266; friends, 14, 15, 65–66, 247; at Guy Clark's funeral, 247; move to Nashville, 5; music style, 27; *Old Friends Reunion* film, 235; publicity, 69–70; songs, 43, 53, 57
Elliott, Jack, 107, 235
Elliott, Ramblin' Jack, 235, 252
Ellis, Rob, 31, 37

Ely, Joe: albums, 17, 43, 57; awards, 158, 159, 232; band, 15; birthday celebrations, 256–57, 270–71; books, 18, 89, 110, 232; career, 231, 232; concerts and events, 38, 55, 68, 114, 163, 228, 241, 251, 252, 254, 258, 259; friends, 193, 199, 272; *Old Friends Reunion* film, 235; publicity, 42, 54; songs, 186; tribute to Guy Clark, 199, 256; trip to Marfa, TX, 260
Ely, Sharon, 193, 231, 232, 247, 256, 272
Emergent Music record label, 110, 115, 126
Emerson, Jack, 11, 12, 13, 73
Emmons, Bobby, 211, 240
Escovedo, Alejandro, 44, 55, 149, 162, 193, 197
Esposito, John, 183, 184

Fey, Liz Allen, 71, 118
First Amendment Center, 8, 9, 91, 133
Fishell, Steve, 65, 89, 114, 123, 126, 131, 164, 165, 172, 203
Flatlanders (country band), 12, 15, 17, 39, 86, 232, 259
Fleck, Bela, 12, 27, 28, 39, 40, 66
Flippo, Chet, 2, 16, 68, 170
Florentine Films, 227, 262, 264
Flores, Rosie: albums, 29, 43, 65; concerts and events, 51, 64, 114, 164; life in Nashville, 49; music style, 12; tribute to Guy Clark, 190, 197, 199
Folk Alliance, 64, 140, 164
folk music, 20–21, 67, 76, 107, 277
Foo Fighters (rock band), 22, 162
Forbert, Steve, 12, 53
Foster, Fletcher, 86, 87
Foster, Fred, 1, 3, 4, 104, 174, 175–76, 177
Foster, Radney: albums, 65, 94, 141, 165, 166, 167, 192–93, 196, 203; career, 27; concerts and events, 164, 185–86,

252, 253, 258, 259; Devil's River Records, 218; friends, 91; publicity, 70; record sales, 213; tribute to Guy Clark, 172
Foster, Stephen: death of, 126; songs, 20, 124, 125–26; tribute album to, 115, 124, 126, 127–28, 149, 263
Franklin, Aretha, 129, 135
Frey, Glenn, 7, 216
Fritts, Donnie, 159, 170, 223
Frouge, Tom, 17, 18, 89, 126, 127, 129, 130
Fukunaga, Glenn, 197, 199, 203, 256

Gantry, Chris, 159, 223
Garcia, Jesse, 25, 26
Garvan, Stephen Bond, 89, 114
Germino, Mark, 38, 57
Gill, Vince: career, 6, 27–29, 32, 65; concerts and events, 146, 182, 205, 225, 241, 252, 265, 266, 277; friends, 183, 222, 247; at Guy Clark's funeral, 247; honors and awards, 149, 157; musical tribute to, 158; publicity, 84; tribute to Guy Clark, 170, 171, 175
Gilmore, Jimmie Dale: career, 17, 65, 75, 231; concerts and events, 15, 38, 55, 56, 257; songs, 42, 94, 163
Glaser, Tompall, 2, 23, 38
Gordy, Emory, Jr., 13, 29, 65, 120
Grady, John, 78, 80
Grammy Awards: Album of the Year, 65, 80; Best Americana Album, 255–56; Best Contemporary Blues Album, 248; Best Contemporary Folk Album, 65; Best Country Album, 92; Best Folk Album, 220, 224; Best New Artist, 266; Best Traditional Folk Album, 127, 128, 129–30; Song of the Year nomination, 184, 212; televised show, 223–24
Grant, Amy, 175, 202

Great American Country (GAC), 84, 85, 87–89, 91, 98, 99, 124, 133, 188
Griesbach, Staci, 193, 194, 274
Griffin, Patty, 88, 94, 130, 158, 165, 171, 174, 180, 190, 230
Griffith, Nanci, 12, 27, 40, 55, 65, 88
Grimson, Jon, 38, 39–40, 41, 42, 43, 64, 73
Grissom, David, 256, 262
Grohl, Dave, 22, 162
Gunderman, Jen, 171, 186, 191, 199, 214, 215, 218, 223
Guthrie, Woody, 4, 21

Haggard, Merle: albums, 4, 43; concerts and events, 173, 198, 212, 218; country music award, 106; death of, 250; music style, 2; publicity, 54, 69, 84
Hall, Tom T., 84, 193
Hammond, Tom, 268
Hancock, Butch, 15, 17, 38, 55, 94, 231, 235, 257
Hanna, Jeff, 4, 184
Hardly Strictly Bluegrass Festival, 198, 252
Harris, Emmylou: albums, 5, 29, 57, 220; American Roots Publishing and, 89; awards, 88; band, 12, 65; concerts and events, 15, 64, 94, 130, 134, 182, 183, 252, 265, 266; deal with Warner Brothers Records, 13; friends and collaborators, 14–15, 29, 35, 208, 223, 247; at Guy Clark's funeral, 247; movies soundtrack, 66, 77; on music, 148; music style, 27; publicity, 54, 63, 69, 70, 84; radio shows, 42; tribute to Guy Clark, 190, 193–94, 197; tribute to Vince Gill, 158
Hart, Alvin Youngblood, 128, 249, 250
Hartford, John, 77, 78, 134, 159

Hartman, Gary, 162, 163, 164, 165, 171, 197, 199
Havighurst, Craig, 67, 68, 69, 215, 277
Hayes, Brian, 248, 250
Helm, Levon, 161–62, 178
Henderson, Mike, 44, 72
Hendrix, Terri, 94, 190, 199
Henley, Don, 7, 171, 216–17
Henley, Larry, 117, 270
Hiatt, John, 12, 162, 249
Hill, Faith, 52, 95, 123
Hillman, Chris, 4, 5, 12
Hinojosa, Tish, 39, 44
Hinton, Bruce, 31, 77
Hoelzle, Cyndi, 69, 165
Holliday, Taylor, 215
Holly, Buddy, 231, 232
Hopson, Stephanie, 194
Hornsby, Bruce, 216, 217
Horse Thief Canyon festival, 28
Hot Band, 5, 13, 29, 65
House, Byron, 180, 189
Howard, Becky, 210, 211
Howard, Joe, 210, 211
Hubbard, Ray Wylie, 94, 190–91, 199
Hustead, Jim, 194, 195, 215, 223
Hyatt, Walter, 50, 163

Ingram, Jack: concerts and events, 86, 114, 225, 252, 254, 258, 259; friends, 223, 247; at Guy Clark's funeral, 247; interviews, 65; publicity, 70; tribute to Guy Clark, 170, 171, 172, 199
Isbell, Jason, 214, 215, 241, 266
Ivey, Bill, 263, 264

Jackson, Alan, 6, 27, 32, 62, 84
Jackson, Michael, 24, 79
Jarvis, Duane, 42, 49, 50
Jayhawks (country rock band), 27, 57
Jenkins, Lisa, 48, 215

Jennings, Shooter, 130, 277
Jennings, Waylon: albums, 2, 23–24, 38, 212; career, 15, 68; connection to Austin, 231; friends, 107, 117, 144, 212; life in Nashville, 51; publicity, 84; songs, 2, 35, 240
Jimenez, Flaco, 16, 65, 241
John, Elton, 21, 276
Johnson, Jamey, 174, 177, 266
Jones, George, 52, 84, 86
Jones Radio Network, 84, 85
Joplin, Janis, 4, 138, 251
June, Valerie, 249, 250

Kane, Kieran, 44, 49, 72
Keen, Robert Earl: *Austin City Limits* anniversary show, 228; career, 41, 43, 44, 68; concerts and events, 133, 219, 252, 258, 274–76; at Guy Clark's funeral, 247; honors and awards, 202; interviews, 202–3; *Old Friends Reunion* film, 235; records, 53, 54, 94, 186, 255
Keith, John Paul, 249–50
Keith, Toby, 96, 155
Keller, Gary, 261, 262
Keller Williams Realty, 261
Kennedy, Ray, 65, 192
Ketchum, Hal, 32, 62, 69, 239
King, Carole, 23, 202
Knaggs, Bart, 238, 240, 244, 257, 258, 261, 273
Krauss, Alison, 29, 40, 75, 76, 77, 161, 162, 266
Kris Kristofferson Lifetime Achievement Award, 221
Kristofferson, Kris: artist in residence at the Country Music Hall of Fame, 156; *The Austin Sessions* album, 212; "Best of All Possible Worlds" song, 104, 106; *Broken Freedom Song* album, 108, 109; career, 4, 99–103, 106, 107, 112, 156, 161, 251; *The Cedar Creek Sessions* album, 228, 250, 255, 271, 291; children, 133, 137, 146, 188, 193, 198, 206, 273, 281; *Closer to the Bone* album, 167, 169, 221, 223; concerts and events, 51, 113, 115, 119, 132–33, 137, 145, 149–50, 156–57, 159–60, 169, 187–88, 193–94, 198, 200, 205, 225, 228–29, 238–39, 250–52, 258, 265, 277; "Darby's Castle" song, 106; dearth, 280, 281; on Dixie Chicks, 110; "Duvalier's Dream" song, 104; education, 100; family, 103, 104, 111–12, 169, 205–6; *Feeling Mortal* album, 220; film production, 22, 107, 120, 131–32, 135–36, 143, 145–46, 193–94; friends and collaborators, 3, 15, 68, 110, 159, 160, 183, 203, 268; health issues, 227, 281; honors and awards, 112, 120, 123, 132, 145, 154–56, 170–72, 174, 176–78, 188, 194, 205, 253, 257; iconic photos of, 86; "Jody and the Kid" song, 104; at Johnny Cash funeral, 110–11; KK Records label, 218; life in Hawaii, 154; "Me and Bobby McGee" song, 106, 107, 123; media attention to, 160, 168; military service, 101; on Nashville, 5, 220–21; Newport Folk Festival, 106; opinion of the United States, 109; outlaw mix, 38; parents of, 99, 100–101; personality of, 108, 116; photo shoot, 116; political songs, 109; popularity, 119; publicity, 181, 263; radio broadcasts, 25, 74, 113, 122–23, 137–39, 143–44, 163, 180–82, 221–22; record sales, 213; relationships with Lisa, 178, 206, 266, 273, 281; retirement, 273, 278; Shel Silverstein tribute album, 165;

Kristofferson, Kris (cont.)
Song of America project, 152; *Spooky Lady's Sideshow* album, 109; "Sunday Morning Comin' Down" song, 105–6; "The Pilgrim (Chapter 33)" song, 111, 130, 173, 182; *This Old Road* album, 138, 141–43, 144, 220–21; "To Beat the Devil" song, 103, 104; tribute in honor of, 129; tribute to Guy Clark, 172, 173–75, 198, 200–201; TV appearances, 108–9, 120, 137–39, 143–44, 180–82, 221–22, 225; "Vietnam Blues" song, 104; "Why Me" song, 133

Kristofferson, Lisa: at Bruce Springsteen concert, 137; CMA week, 123; friends, 109, 278; at Johnny Cash's funeral, 111; at Kris's concerts and events, 146, 156, 170, 172, 173, 174, 205, 221, 239, 251, 253, 265, 277; at Medallion Ceremony, 132–33; relationships with Kris, 178, 206, 266, 273, 281; at screening of *Walk the Line* film, 136; "This Old Road" single video shoot, 141, 142; TV appearances, 108

Kristofferson, Tracy, 103, 104, 206
Kunz, John, 44, 179, 262

LaFave, Jimmy, 216, 217
Landreth, Sonny, 12, 134
Lauderdale, Jim: awards, 15, 189; career, 51; concerts and events, 51, 214, 277; friends, 19, 49, 159; publicity, 54; records, 12, 38, 39, 42, 44–45
LaVere, Amy, 249, 250
Leadership Music: Dale Franklin Awards, 174–77; events, 184
Leigh, Brennen, 204, 254, 259
Levine, Steve, 120, 169
Lewis, Jerry Lee, 13, 135, 194, 212, 248

Lewis, Luke, 76, 77, 78, 79, 81
Linde, Dennis, 28, 93
Linklater, Richard, 145, 257, 258
Lloyd, Bill, 27, 192–93, 196, 252
London, Terry, 210, 213
London Broadcasting, 209, 210, 212
Looking into You: A Tribute to Jackson Browne (album), 217, 291
Lord, Dennis, 73–74, 114
Los Lobos (rock band), 41, 42, 75
Loveless, Patty, 65, 84, 120–21, 184, 185–86, 277
Lovett, Lyle: career, 12; concerts and events, 22, 27, 241, 252, 265, 266; fiftieth birthday, 159; friends, 199, 273; at Guy Clark's funeral, 247; honors and awards, 145, 158, 202, 219; interviews, 202–3; *Music Town* album, 50; publicity, 84; tribute album for Guy Clark, 175, 190–91, 199; tribute album for Jackson Browne, 217
Lowe, Nick, 7, 161
Lowman, Holly, 179, 255
Lubbock artists, 231–32, 235
Lynn, Loretta, 1, 2, 51, 63, 84, 241, 264, 265

Macias, David, 110, 115, 123, 126, 152
Mack, Ronnie, 49, 50
McBride, Martina, 155, 171, 184
McClinton, Delbert, 49, 65, 68, 86, 149, 162, 231, 252
McConaughey, Matthew, 145, 225
McCoury, Del, 40, 70, 222
McCoy, Charlie, 171, 175
McEntire, Reba, 6, 32–33, 85
McGraw, Tim, 52, 95, 118, 122
McGuinn, Roger, 4, 124, 126
McGuire, Jim, 86, 199, 206, 207, 209, 235, 246, 247
McKay, Noel, 204, 254, 259
McLemore, Denise, 229, 230, 271, 272
McMurtry, James, 149, 163, 199, 275

Madeira, Phil, 131, 197
Maguire, Martie, 91, 94, 96, 203
Maines, Lloyd: concerts and events, 96, 199, 228, 241, 256, 275; connection to Austin, 231; music style, 93–94; records, 192, 234; tribute album for Guy Clark, 199
Maines, Natalie, 91, 93, 94, 96
Malo, Raul, 36–37, 45, 122, 124, 126, 148, 157–59, 161, 179
Marsh, Dave, 89, 129, 130, 137, 162, 163, 193
Marshall, Jim, 10, 143
Mathus, Jimbo, 249, 250
Mavericks (band), 29, 31, 36, 37, 42, 65
May, J. D., 8, 71–72
MCA Records, 17, 31, 36, 37, 48, 50, 65, 77, 182, 219
Mead, Chuck, 51, 52, 124, 238, 250, 277
Mercury Records, 31, 48, 65, 76–77
Miller, Buddy: albums, 12, 45, 57; awards, 15, 148; band, 161, 180; concerts and events, 49, 51, 88, 124, 162, 189
Miller, Julie, 12, 15, 64, 88
Miller, Roger, 51, 106
Moman, Lincoln Wayne "Chips," 240, 249
Monroe, Ashley, 207, 220, 225
Montreux Jazz Festival, 38–39
Monument Records, 1, 3, 104, 175
Moorer, Allison, 50, 65, 70, 162
Morgan, Jeffrey Dean, 238
Morgan, Mitch, 29, 33, 36
Morris, Erin, 48, 263
Mosher, Annie, 131, 132, 141, 152
Moss, Al, 73, 114, 126, 163, 230

Nash, Alanna, 69, 121, 249, 268
Nashville, TN: 328 Performance Hall, 51; Bluebird Café, 51, 159, 202, 221, 253; Film Festival, 257; music culture, 5, 48, 49, 50, 77, 78, 84–85; Palomino night club, 44, 49; Robert's Western World, 51, 124
Nashville Music Festival, 1–2, 6, 249
Nashville Songwriters Association International (NSAI), 221
Nashville Songwriters Hall of Fame, 123–24, 140
Nelson, Connie, 229–30, 239, 241, 256, 272–73, 275, 278
Nelson, Tim Blake, 75, 76
Nelson, Willie: albums, 2, 23, 38, 84, 95, 230, 232; band, 212; career, 3, 68; concerts and events, 83, 115, 137, 233, 250, 265, 266, 275; documentary about, 168; ex-wife of, 229–30; friends, 51, 107; honors and awards, 158, 174, 175, 221; influence, 15; interviews, 83, 146, 221, 222; publicity, 84; radio shows, 45, 74, 223; records, 2, 121, 123, 175; tribute to Guy Clark, 171, 172; tribute to Kris Kristofferson, 130, 177, 178
Newbury, Mickey, 149, 159
new grass music, 28, 29, 37, 43, 44
New Grass Revival (band), 28, 29, 44
Newport Folk Festival, 3, 106, 251
New West Records, 126, 142, 194
Nichols, Joe, 115, 116
Nicholson, Gary, 94, 247, 252, 259
Nine Inch Nails (NIN) (rock band), 7, 17
Nitty Gritty Dirt Band, 4, 7, 65, 77, 91, 116
No Depression (magazine), 12, 54–55, 56–57, 69, 127, 163

O Brother, Where Art Thou? (film): soundtrack, 75–81
O'Connell, Maura, 39, 56
Oermann, Bob, 69, 263

Oh Boy Records, 17, 73, 84, 87, 98, 118, 121, 223
O'Neil, Kerry, 118, 206
Ongaro, Brian, 26, 27, 45–46, 204, 225
Orbison, Roy, 68, 175
Osborne, Joan, 54, 57, 217
Outlaw Country (radio channel), 45, 223
outlaw country music, 37, 69, 114, 246, 265–66, 267
Owens, Buck, 1, 2, 5, 70, 218

Pabst International Folk Festival Stage, 21
Paczosa, Gary, 193, 194, 215–16, 217, 219
Parnell, Lee Roy, 18, 82, 258–59
Parsons, Gram, 4, 5, 12, 13, 44, 159
Parton, Dolly, 1, 2, 5, 51, 69, 70, 84, 175–76, 255
Paul, Bev, 73, 255, 256
Paul, Brad, 38, 40–41, 43, 44, 64, 73
Perkins, Carl, 248, 250
Peters, Gretchen, 136, 152, 164, 166, 184–85
Phillips, Sam, 248, 250
Picott, Rod, 223, 225
Pilgrim: A Celebration of Kris Kristofferson (tribute album), 130–31, 136, 141, 142–43, 146, 168
Plant, Robert, 161, 162, 180
Poss, Barry, 44, 149, 255, 261
Praxis International label, 11, 12, 73
Presley, Angaleena, 207, 252
Presley, Elvis, 13, 121–22, 248, 249
Preston, Frances, 205, 206, 223
Price, Margo, 251, 266, 277–78, 279
Price, Ray, 4, 106, 133, 212
Pride, Charley, 1, 21, 222
Prine, John: albums, 29; concerts, 88; death, 272; friends and collaborators, 17, 120, 180, 222; honors and awards, 112, 134; Oh Boy Records, 84–85, 223; songs, 65, 124, 128, 200, 263; tribute album for Guy Clark, 190
progressive country music, 2, 16, 37, 38, 43, 67
Pryor, Ellen, 48, 136

radio: music programs, 35–38, 40–43, 135; record labels and, 34; stations and networks, 2, 24, 25, 29–30, 40, 43, 46, 67, 69, 84–85, 140
Radio and Records (magazine), 30, 58
Raitt, Bonnie, 213, 217, 228
Ramos, Michael, 203, 228
Ranch (country music trio), 51, 70
Randall, Jon, 70, 122, 131, 219, 223, 254
Rawlings, Dave, 15, 214, 252
RCA Records, 24, 73, 103, 182
Red Hot: A Memphis Celebration of Sun Records (album), 248, 291
Reed, Jerry, 14, 15
Remmert, Fred, 196, 223, 228
Reno, Janet, 127, 128
Reznor, Trent, 7, 17
Rich, Charlie, 248, 250
Richey, Kim, 29, 54, 149
Richie, Lionel, 182, 183
Ringenberg, Jason, 11, 12
Rising Tide Records, 64–65
Robinson, Scott, 8, 73
Robison, Bruce, 70, 86, 94, 95, 130, 164, 223, 259, 262
Robison, Charlie, 70, 86, 95, 212
Rockport, TX, 195–97, 209, 238, 240, 254, 292
Rodgers, Jimmie, 2, 14, 76
Rogers, Kenny, 13, 27, 38, 257
Rogers, Tammy, 44, 72
Rolling Stones (magazine), 2, 65, 68
Ronstadt, Linda, 23, 70, 232
Rounder Records, 40, 54, 134
Rowan, Peter, 42, 44, 255

Rubin, Rick, 7, 10
Ryman Auditorium: Americana Honors and Awards, 122, 140, 148, 159, 179, 215; concerts and events, 29, 77–78, 106, 133–34, 146–47, 150, 161–62, 172, 252

Sahm, Doug, 16, 64, 159
San Quentin Prison, 2, 10
Saviano, Mike, 239, 240
Saviano, Tamara: Americana Music Association, 118, 140, 147–48, 159; at Annual Leadership Music Dale Franklin Awards, 176–77; background, 20–22, 24–25, 29; birthday celebrations, 223, 256–57, 270–71, 273; books, 225, 226, 242–43, 253–55, 260, 270, 271, 273–74; Capitol Records Nashville and, 58–60; clients of, 108, 154; community engagement, 152, 161, 164, 258–59; *Country Music* and, 69–70; *Country Weekly* and, 60–64, 65; crowdfunding campaign, 237–38; Great American Country and, 84, 85, 87–89, 91, 98, 99, 124, 187; honors and awards, 153, 271–72; losses and griefs, 27, 245, 252–53; move in Nashville, 46–47; neighbors, 117–18; personality of, 154; professional achievements, 108, 140–41, 150–51, 291; public relations, 164; Sundance Broadcasting, internship at, 24–27, 29–32, 36
Sayles, John, 120, 145
Scott, Darrell, 94, 180
Scott, Jessie, 67–68, 73, 230
Scruggs, Earl, 4, 84, 146
Scruggs, Randy, 4, 130, 131
Seger, Bob, 35–36, 277
SESAC (performing rights organization), 73–74, 140
Sexsmith, Ron, 161, 191–92

Shaver, Billy Joe, 12, 15, 38, 43, 66, 123, 133
Sheftell, Lauren, 194, 215
Shivers, Robert, 208–9
Silva, John Ross, 191, 199
Sirius Satellite Radio, 45, 121, 140, 168
Sirius XM, 188, 223
Skaggs, Ricky, 27, 28, 64, 69, 84, 277
Smith, Connie, 133, 135
Smith, Sammi, 4, 106, 212
Snider, Todd, 29, 65, 90, 118, 123, 130, 133, 148
Sony Music, 93, 95, 96, 131
South by Southwest (SXSW) Festivals, 55, 71, 118, 144, 146, 162–63, 193, 230, 257, 267, 270–71, 272, 273
Souther, J. D., 216, 217
Spacek, Sissy, 264–65, 267, 268, 269
Spirit of Americana Free Speech Award, 9–10
Springsteen, Bruce, 53, 57, 98, 128, 129, 137, 162, 217
Stamberger, Wendy, 69, 215
Stanley, Ralph, 12, 76, 77, 80, 84
Stanton, Harry Dean, 181–82
Staples, Mavis, 122, 124, 128, 159, 263
Stapleton, Chris, 79, 178, 252, 265, 266
Stewart, Jon Randall, 203, 217
Stiff, Denise, 77, 78, 80
Stinson, Harry, 44, 72, 134
Strait, George, 6, 10, 27, 32, 62, 95, 118, 196, 265–66
Strang, Cameron, 89, 126, 142, 169
Strangers (country band), 250, 251
Strayer, Emily, 91, 93, 95, 96
Streisand, Barbra, 22, 107
Streissguth, Michael, 69, 263
Stuart, Marty, 49, 65, 69, 84, 94, 131, 133, 134–35, 137, 149
Sugar Hill Records, 18, 44, 149, 193, 194, 195, 255, 261
Summerfest music festival, 21–22, 32, 250–52

Sundance Broadcasting, 24–26, 29–30, 36, 45–46, 58, 60, 69, 204, 225, 227
Sun Records, 248, 249
Sussex Publishing, 69, 84
Swan, Billy, 104, 159, 170, 175, 223

Tallent, Garry, 53, 54
Taylor, James, 22, 106
Telecommunications Act of 1996, 60
Tepper, Jeremy, 45, 114
Texas: film industry, 145, 271; music culture in, 15, 68, 199, 238, 257, 259
Texas Gentlemen (musical band), 251, 254
Texas Heritage Songwriters' Association, 144, 145, 202, 258, 270
Texas Tornados (rock band), 16, 38
Thessen, Wendy Brundage, 239, 240
Thiels, Liz, 48, 199
Thile, Chris, 94, 224
This One's for Him: A Tribute to Guy Clark (album), 196, 199–201, 214–15, 220, 224, 278
Thompson, Verlon: concerts and events, 134, 150, 180, 186, 214–15, 252, 259, 261; at Guy Clark's funeral, 247; tribute to Guy Clark, 171, 172–73, 191–92, 195, 198–99, 264
Thornton, Billy Bob, 134, 162, 168
Tillis, Pam, 84, 184
Travis, Randy, 6, 123, 177
Trishas (rock band), 192, 199, 254, 259
Tritt, Travis, 6, 27, 84, 115–16
Troubadour Texas (music show), 209–10, 225
Tucker, Tanya, 32, 61, 67, 277–78
Turner, Dallas, 85, 86
Turturro, John, 75, 76
Tyminski, Dan, 76, 77, 79, 80

Uncle Tupelo (country music group), 27, 29, 39, 54, 55
Urban, Keith, 51, 70, 86–87, 170, 219, 225, 255

Van Zandt, J. T., 196, 199
Van Zandt, Townes: albums and songs, 5, 44, 203, 219, 255, 266; Austin City Limits Hall of Fame celebration, 241; career, 68; concerts, 55; death of, 203; friends, 14, 15, 207, 268; honors and awards, 159, 202; iconic photos, 83, 86; influence, 6, 193

Waldon, Kelsey, 218, 223, 253
Walker, Jerry Jeff: albums and songs, 4, 35, 94, 192, 211, 240; concerts and events, 252; honors and awards, 270; *Old Friends Reunion* film, 235; tribute to Guy Clark, 196, 199
Walpole, NH, 262–63, 264
Warner Brothers Records, 13, 31, 36, 38, 39–40, 48, 64, 183, 207
Warren, Kelcy, 196, 216, 217, 225
Was, Don, 221, 265
Waterloo Records, 179, 193, 196, 262
Welch, Gillian, 12, 15, 66, 76, 77, 214–15, 241, 252
Welch, Kevin: albums, 29, 39, 72; concerts and events, 38–39, 191, 192–93; Dead Reckoning Records, 44, 72; radio shows, 42, 49; songs, 70, 190; tribute album for Guy Clark, 190, 199; tribute album for Jackson Browne, 217
Western Beat, 38–39, 42, 49, 50, 51, 54, 71
Wexler, Jerry, 16, 129–30, 190
White, Joy Lynn, 51, 86

Index • **303**

Whitfield, Paul: at Austin City Limits Hall of Fame celebration, 241, 243; career, 85, 87, 122, 129, 227; documentary on Guy Clark, 235, 267; friends, 128, 256; at Grammys, 223; at Kris Kristofferson Lifetime Achievement Award, 221; personality, 87, 88, 98, 200; travels, 132, 141, 172, 173
Whitley, Kathi, 65, 89, 246, 252
Williams, Hank, 5, 99, 102, 103, 105
Williams, Hank, Jr., 5, 27, 38, 99–100, 115
Williams, Jody, 52, 258
Williams, Lucinda, 42, 43, 45, 49, 65, 66, 217

Willis, Kelly, 69, 130, 223
Wisconsin State Fair, 32, 37
Without Getting Killed or Caught: The Life and Music of Guy Clark (Saviano), 253–55, 260, 270, 271, 273–74
Wolfe, Kerry, 26, 36
Womack, Lee Ann, 36, 69, 84, 146, 176, 212
Wozniak, Steve, 89, 164
Wright, Brian, 193, 194–95, 215
Wright, Mark, 131, 184

Yoakam, Dwight, 27, 31, 32, 39, 41, 43, 66, 69, 241

ABOUT THE AUTHOR

Tamara Saviano is an author, producer, communications expert, marketing strategist, and creative ringleader.

Tamara is a three-time Grammy nominee and took home the statue for producing the 2004 Grammy-winning Best Traditional Folk Album, *Beautiful Dreamer: The Songs of Stephen Foster*. She produced *The Pilgrim: A Celebration of Kris Kristofferson* in 2006. The Grammy-nominated *This One's for Him: A Tribute to Guy Clark* won the Americana Music Association's Album of the Year award in 2012. She collaborated with Austin artist Jimmy LaFave to make the 2014 album *Looking into You: A Tribute to Jackson Browne*. In 2016, Tamara partnered with Memphis artist Luther Dickinson to produce *Red Hot: A Memphis Celebration of Sun Records*.

Tamara produced iconic songwriter Kris Kristofferson's double-CD set *The Cedar Creek Sessions* and the album was nominated for a Grammy for Best Americana Album in 2017. Over two decades, her work with the legendary songwriter morphed into a long-standing friendship. Kristofferson wrote the foreword to Tamara's memoir *The Most Beautiful Girl: A True Story of a Dad, a Daughter, and the Healing Power of Music*. The book was listed as one of the best books of 2014 in the *Chicago Review of Books*.

Without Getting Killed or Caught: The Life and Music of Guy Clark, Tamara's biography of legendary songwriter Guy Clark, was released by Texas A&M University Press in 2016 and won the prestigious Belmont Award from the International Country Music Conference for the best writing on country music that year. Her documentary feature on Clark, *Without Getting Killed or Caught*, is the winner of South by Southwest's 2021 Louis

Black Lone Star Award and the 2021 Rockport Film Festival's Audience Award.

Since 2002, Tamara has specialized in the folk and Americana music genres. She worked with documentary filmmaker Ken Burns and his team as an adviser for the PBS series *Country Music*. She cocreated (with artist Rod Picott) *From Art to Commerce: A Workshop for Independent Musicians*, a comprehensive one-day program that demystifies the perplexing elements of the music business and teaches entrepreneurial skills to independent artists. As a veteran of Leadership Music, a cohort of professionals committed to supporting the industry, Tamara was invited to create ALL ATX Leadership in Austin, which she directed for three years before the pandemic.

Tamara is president and creative director of Guy Clark LLC, Truly Handmade Records, and the Guy Clark Family Foundation. The companies were formed by Guy's grandchildren to cultivate and manage the intellectual property of Guy and Susanna Clark, to amplify and honor the legacy, and to support songwriters who live and work in the spirit of Guy Clark. Guy Clark LLC is managed by a board of directors that includes Tamara, Guy's grandson Dylan Clark, longtime friends Rodney Crowell and Verlon Thompson, and record label executive Scott Robinson.

The Texas Heritage Songwriters' Association honored Tamara in 2017 with the Darrell K. Royal Texas Music Legend Award for her work with Texas songwriters. In 2020, the Austin Music Awards selected Tamara to receive the Margaret Moser Award, which recognizes women in music.